THE
365-DAY
BIBLE
OVERVIEW

A Clear and
Easy Plan for
Understanding
God's Word

GEORGE W. KNIGHT
WITH RAYBURN W. RAY

BARBOUR
PUBLISHING

Previously released as *Welcome to Your Bible*

© 2020 by George W. Knight and Rayburn W. Ray

Editorial assistance by Jessie Fioritto

ISBN 978-1-63609-785-5

Interior design by Greg Jackson, Thinkpen Design

Published by Barbour Publishing, Inc., 1810 Barbour Drive, Uhrichsville, Ohio 44683, www.barbourbooks.com

Our mission is to inspire the world with the life-changing message of the Bible.

ecpa Member of the
Evangelical Christian
Publishers Association

Printed in China.

INTRODUCTION

Christian growth is based on a clear understanding of God's Word, so this book is designed to help you read and understand scripture.

The *365-Day Bible Overview* combines a variety of features that will guide you systematically through the Bible, providing helpful background information on people, places, and things, as well as explanations of confusing words, ideas, or practices.

The content is based on a one-year reading plan that divides the Bible into 365 segments, each taking approximately 15 to 20 minutes to read. These Bible portions are then summarized to enhance your memory of the passages, and dictionary-style entries elaborate on the important characters and other details of the passage you read. When the Bible passage includes an unusual concept or practice, a brief article provides the necessary historical context for understanding.

Based on the King James Version but usable with any translation of scripture, The *365-Day Bible Overview* promises help when you're ready and willing to commit time to God's Word. We hope it will be a powerful aid to your study, whatever your level of biblical experience.

THE PUBLISHERS

ABBREVIATIONS USED
IN *THE 365-DAY BIBLE OVERVIEW*

AD: Ano Domini (Latin for "In the Year of Our Lord,"
used with dates following the birth of Jesus)
BC: Before Christ
CEV: Contemporary English Version
KJV: King James Version
NIV: New International Version
NKJV: New King James Version
NLT: New Living Translation
NRSV: New Revised Standard Version
NT: New Testament
OT: Old Testament

BOOKS OF THE BIBLE

1 Chron.: 1 Chronicles
1 Cor.: 1 Corinthians
1 John: 1 John
1 Kings: 1 Kings
1 Pet.: 1 Peter
1 Sam.: 1 Samuel
1 Thess.: 1 Thessalonians
1 Tim.: 1 Timothy
2 Chron.: 2 Chronicles
2 Cor.: 2 Corinthians
2 John: 2 John
2 Kings: 2 Kings
2 Sam.: 2 Samuel
2 Thess.: 2 Thessalonians
2 Tim.: 2 Timothy
2 Pet.: 2 Peter
3 John: 3 John
Acts: Acts
Amos: Amos
Col.: Colossians
Dan.: Daniel
Deut.: Deuteronomy
Josh.: Joshua
Eccles.: Ecclesiastes
Eph.: Ephesians
Esther: Esther
Exod.: Exodus
Ezek.: Ezekiel
Ezra: Ezra
Gal.: Galatians

Gen.: Genesis
Hab.: Habakkuk
Hag.: Haggai
Heb.: Hebrews
Hosea: Hosea
Isa.: Isaiah
James: James
Jer.: Jeremiah
Job: Job
Joel: Joel
John: John
Jon.: Jonah
Jude: Jude
Judg.: Judges
Lam.: Lamentations
Lev.: Leviticus
Luke: Luke
Mal.: Malachi
Mark: Mark
Matt.: Matthew
Mic.: Micah
Nah.: Nahum
Neh.: Nehemiah
Num.: Numbers
Obad.: Obadiah
Phil.: Philippians
Philem.: Philemon
Prov.: Proverbs
Ps./Pss.: Psalm/Psalms
Rev.: Revelation

Rom.: Romans
Ruth: Ruth
Song: Song of Solomon
Titus: Titus
Zech.: Zechariah
Zeph.: Zephaniah

THE OLD TESTAMENT

The Bible has two grand divisions—the Old Testament and the New Testament. The Old Testament is the larger of these two divisions, containing more than twice as much material as the New Testament. The thirty-nine individual Old Testament books were written under the inspiration of the Lord across a period of many centuries by several different authors. The Old Testament also contains many different types of literature: law, history, poetry, prophecy, and wisdom writings. The word *testament* means "covenant." The Old Testament tells how God called a people, the nation of Israel, to live in covenant with Him.

The five major divisions of the Old Testament are:

1. **Books of the Law**—Genesis, Exodus, Leviticus, Numbers, Deuteronomy
2. **Historical books**—Joshua, Judges, Ruth, 1 and 2 Samuel, 1 and 2 Kings, 1 and 2 Chronicles, Ezra, Nehemiah, Esther
3. **Books of poetry and wisdom**—Job, Psalms, Proverbs, Ecclesiastes, Song of Solomon
4. **Books of the major prophets**—Isaiah, Jeremiah, Lamentations, Ezekiel, Daniel
5. **Books of the minor prophets**—Hosea, Joel, Amos, Obadiah, Jonah, Micah, Nahum, Habakkuk, Zephaniah, Haggai, Zechariah, Malachi

Additional information on each division follows.

KEY

■ Scripture Passage Summary
■ Bible Definitions
■ Local and Biblical Customs

BOOKS OF THE LAW

The first five books of the Old Testament are known as the "Books of the Law." This title is appropriate because the laws and commands of God are the central theme of this section of the Old Testament. God revealed to Moses His expectations of the nation of Israel. Moses recorded these commands as laws in the books of Exodus, Leviticus, Numbers, and Deuteronomy. Genesis contains no specific laws, but it does describe the covenant relationship that God established with His people, the Israelites. This covenant relationship demanded loyalty and obedience from God's chosen people.

These first five books of the Old Testament are also known as the *Pentateuch*, a Greek term meaning "five-volumed." These five books together take us from the creation of the physical world through the formation of the nation of Israel under the leadership of Moses.

JANUARY 1 | Read Genesis 1–3

`1:1–31` God creates the world in six days (Heb. 1:10).

`2:1–25` God creates Adam and Eve, the first man and woman.

`3:1–24` Adam and Eve disobey God by eating the forbidden fruit and are cast out of the Garden of Eden.

. . . .

`Creation` The actions of God through which He brought man and the physical world into existence. God existed before the world, and He produced the universe from nothing (Gen. 1:1–2). As the sovereign, self-existing God, He also rules over His creation (Ps. 47:7–9).

`Adam` The first man. Created in God's image (Gen. 1:26–27), Adam was an upright and intelligent being (Gen. 2:19–20)—the first worker (Gen. 2:8, 15) and the first husband (Gen. 2:18–25). He received God's law (Gen. 2:16–17) and knowingly sinned, along with Eve (Gen. 3:6). Their sin resulted in broken fellowship with the Creator (Gen. 3:8) and brought God's curse (Gen. 3:14–19) and eviction from Eden (Gen. 3:22–24). Adam fathered Cain and Abel (Gen. 4:1–2), Seth (Gen. 4:25), and other children (Gen. 5:3–4). He died at age 930 (Gen. 5:5). As head of the human race, Adam introduced sin into the world. He represents the lost and dying condition of all unrepentant sinners (Rom. 5:12–19; 1 Cor. 15:22). But Christ, referred to in the NT as the "second Adam," offers deliverance from the curse of sin and death (Rom. 5:14–19; 1 Cor. 15:22).

`Eve` The name given by Adam to his wife as the mother of the human race (Gen. 3:20). Fashioned from one of Adam's ribs, she was created to serve as his helpmate and companion (Gen. 2:18–23). Because of her sin and rebellion, Eve was to experience pain and sorrow, especially in connection with the birth of children (Gen. 3:16).

`Fall of Man` A phrase that refers to Adam and Eve's state of sorrow and misery that followed their sin and rebellion against God (Gen. 2–3). Their original sin has afflicted the human race ever since (Rom. 3:23)—a condition cured only by the atoning death of Christ (Rom. 5:6).

JANUARY 2 | Read Genesis 4:1–7:16

`4:1–2` Two sons, Cain and Abel, are born to Adam and Eve.

`4:3–15` Cain murders his brother Abel. God punishes Cain by driving him out of his homeland but protects him by placing a mark on him.

`4:16–24` Cain's descendants are listed.

`4:25–5:32` Adam's descendants are listed.

6:1–8 Wickedness spreads throughout the earth, and God determines to destroy the world. But Noah is looked upon with favor by the Lord because of his righteousness (see Exod. 33:12).

6:9–22 The Lord tells Noah to build a huge ark, or boat, in which he and his family will be safe from the catastrophe that He plans to send on the earth. Noah does exactly as God commands.

7:1–16 Noah and his family enter the ark, along with pairs of different animals. Rain pounds the earth for forty days and forty nights.

Cain The oldest son of Adam and Eve who murdered his brother Abel. Exiled by God, he built a city that he named for his son (Gen. 4:1–17).

Abel Second son of Adam and Eve (Gen. 4:2). Abel's animal sacrifice was pleasing to God (Gen. 4:4). Abel was then killed by his brother Cain in a jealous rage (Gen. 4:5, 8). Jesus regarded "righteous Abel" as the first martyr (Matt. 23:35). Abel's works were called "righteous" (1 John 3:12), and his sacrifices were commended as a testimony of faith (Heb. 11:4).

Noah The person chosen by the Lord to preserve life on earth by building an ark to escape the great flood. Noah was the son of Lamech and the father of Shem, Ham, and Japheth. He "found grace in the eyes of the Lord" (Gen. 6:8) and was described in the NT as a preacher of righteousness (2 Pet. 2:5). After building the ark, he entered with his family and selected animals (Gen. 7:1–24). Upon leaving the ark after the flood ended, he built an altar for worship (Gen. 8:18–22). God covenanted with Noah not to destroy the earth with water again (Gen. 9:1–19). After pronouncing blessings and curses on his sons, he died at the age of 950 (Gen. 9:29). *Noe*: Greek form (Luke 17:26).

JANUARY 3 | Read Genesis 7:17–10:32

7:17–24 The earth is struck with a great flood, which lasts for 150 days. But Noah and his family and the animals are safe in the ark (2 Pet. 2:5).

8:1–22 The floodwaters recede, and Noah and his family leave the ark. Noah builds an altar and offers sacrifices to the Lord.

9:1–19 God makes a covenant with Noah and causes a rainbow to appear in the sky as a token of His promise.

9:20–27 Noah falls into a drunken stupor and pronounces a curse on Canaan, a descendant of Noah's son Ham.

9:28–29 Noah dies after living for 950 years.

10:1–32 Noah's descendants are listed.

Noah's Ark A large wooden ship in which Noah and his family and selected animals were delivered by the Lord. The ark was necessary because God wished to preserve righteous Noah and his family while destroying the rest of humankind because of their wickedness. Noah built the ark according to God's directions (Gen. 6:14–16). Then he and his family entered the ark, along with a pair of all living creatures (Gen. 6:19–20). Rain fell for forty days (Gen. 7:17), and water covered the earth for 150 days (Gen. 7:24). Finally, God sent a wind to restrain the water (Gen. 8:1–3) and the ark rested on a mountain in Ararat (Gen. 8:4). Noah and his passengers were delivered safely to dry land (Gen. 8:18–19). Upon leaving the ark, Noah built an altar and offered sacrifices to God for their deliverance. God promised Noah that the earth would not be destroyed by water again (Gen. 8:20–22).

The ark is symbolic of baptism (1 Pet. 3:20–21) and God's preserving grace (Luke 17:26–27; Heb. 11:7).

Covenant An agreement between two people or groups, particularly the agreement between God and His people that promised His blessings in return for their obedience and devotion (Gen. 15). Through His sacrificial death, Jesus became the mediator of a new covenant, bringing salvation and eternal life to all who trust in Him (Heb. 10:12–17).

Canaan A son of Ham whose descendants founded several tribal peoples in and around Palestine (Gen. 10:1, 6, 15–18).

JANUARY 4 | Read Genesis 11–14

11:1–9 God confuses human languages at the Tower of Babel because of man's pride and arrogance.

11:10–32 Descendants of Noah's son Shem—the ancestors of Abram/Abraham—are listed.

12:1–20 God calls Abram/Abraham to leave his homeland and settle in a new country, Canaan, where He will give him many descendants and make them into a great nation (Heb. 11:8).

13:1–18 Abram/Abraham and his nephew Lot go their separate ways after a disagreement over grazing lands for their livestock.

14:1–24 Abram/Abraham rescues Lot and pays tithes to Melchizedek, a priest and king.

Tower of Babel A tall structure known as a ziggurat built on the plain of Shinar in ancient Babylonia as a show of human pride and vanity. God confused the language of the builders so they could not communicate. After they abandoned the project, they were scattered abroad (Gen. 11:1–9).

Shem The oldest son of Noah who was preserved in the ark (Gen. 5:32). Shem was the father of Elam, Asshur, Arphaxad, Lud, and Aram—ancestors of the Semitic nations known as the Jews, Arameans, Persians, Assyrians, and Arabians (Gen. 10:22).

Abram (Abraham) The father of the nation of Israel (Ps. 105:6, 9). A native of Ur in southern Babylonia, he married Sarah and went to Haran (Gen. 11:26–31). Later he obeyed God's call to leave Haran for a "land that I will shew thee" (Gen. 12:1–5). God made a covenant with Abraham to bless all nations of the world through him (Gen. 12:2–3). The land of Canaan was also promised to Abraham's descendants (Gen. 12:7; 13:14–18). Although Abraham and Sarah were childless at an advanced age, God promised Abraham a son (Gen. 15:1–4; 17:19). At Sarah's urging, Abraham fathered Ishmael by Sarah's servant Hagar (Gen. 16:1–4, 15). God changed the names of Abraham and Sarah from *Abram* and *Sarai* (Gen. 17:5, 15) and established circumcision as a covenant sign (Gen. 17:10–14). The covenant was to be fulfilled through Isaac rather than Ishmael (Gen. 17:20–21; Gal. 4:22–31). Isaac was born in the couple's old age (Gen. 21:1–7).

As a test of faith, God asked Abraham to sacrifice Isaac (Gen. 22:1–13). Then God Himself intervened to save Isaac and again promised to bless Abraham for his unwavering faith (Gen. 22:16–18). Abraham died at 175 years of age and was buried beside Sarah near Hebron (Gen. 25:7–10). He remains a model of righteousness and faith for all believers (Gen. 26:24; Ps. 47:9; Isa. 41:8). An ancestor of Christ, he is viewed as a spiritual father of all who share a like faith in Christ (Matt. 1:1; 3:9; Gal. 3:6–9).

JANUARY 5 | Read Genesis 15–18

15:1–21 God makes a covenant with Abram/Abraham and renews His promise to give him a land and many descendants (Gen. 12:1–2).

16:1–16 Abram/Abraham fathers a son, Ishmael, by the Egyptian servant of his wife, Sarah.

17:1–27 God renews His covenant with Abram, renames him Abraham, and promises that Sarah will bear a son. All males in Abraham's household are circumcised as a sign and seal of the divine covenant.

18:1–33 Abraham pleads with God to spare the wicked cities of Sodom and Gomorrah.

Israelites Descendants of Israel, or Jacob (Gen. 35:9–12), a nation that was designated by God as His special people. The Israelites were regarded as children of the covenant and heirs of the promises that God made to Abraham (Gen. 12:1–3; Rom. 9:4; 11:1).

Ishmael Abraham's son born to Sarah's Egyptian maid Hagar (Gen. 16). After conflicts with Sarah, Hagar fled with Ishmael into the desert, where she was assured by angels that Ishmael would have many descendants (Gen. 21:9–18). Tradition holds that the Arab peoples are descendants of Ishmael.

Sarai (Sarah) A wife of Abraham and the mother of Isaac (Gen. 11:29; Rom. 9:9), originally called *Sarai.* Although barren for many years, she received a new name and God's promise that she would be "a mother of nations" (Gen. 17:15–16), and she bore Isaac past the age of ninety (Gen. 17:17–21; 21:2–3). She is commended in the NT for her faith and obedience (Heb. 11:11; *Sara:* Greek form).

Circumcision The removal of the foreskin of the male sex organ, a ritual performed generally on the eighth day after birth (Lev. 12:3). This practice, probably initiated with Abraham (Gen. 17:9–14), signified the covenant between God and His people, the Israelites. In the NT, the word is often used symbolically for the casting off of sin or worldly desires (Col. 2:11).

JANUARY 6 | Read Genesis 19–21

19:1–29 Lot escapes when Sodom and Gomorrah are destroyed by the Lord (2 Pet. 2:6).

19:30–38 Lot fathers two sons, who become the ancestors of the Moabites and the Ammonites.

20:1–18 Abraham tries to pass off Sarah as his sister in the territory of Abimelech, a Philistine king.

21:1–21 A son, Isaac, is born to Abraham and Sarah; Hagar and Ishmael are banished to the wilderness.

21:22–34 Abraham and Abimelech reach an agreement about a well at Beersheba.

Lot Abraham's nephew. He accompanied Abraham to Canaan and traveled with him to Egypt to escape a famine (Gen. 12:5; 13:1). His uncle gave him first choice of Canaan's land on which to settle. He selected the fertile Jordan Valley (Gen. 13:10–11) and settled with his family near the pagan city of Sodom. Lot escaped the destruction of this city, but his wife looked back on their possessions and was turned into a pillar of salt (Gen. 19:15–26). Lot was an ancestor of the Moabites and the Ammonites, tribes that became bitter enemies of the Israelites in later centuries (Gen. 19:37–38).

Lot's Wife The wife of Abraham's nephew who was turned into a pillar of salt as she looked back on Sodom (Gen. 19:26). Jesus used her experience to warn of the dangers of delay and disobedience (Luke 17:32).

Sodom One of five cities destroyed by God because of its wickedness (Gen. 19:1–28). It is often mentioned in the Bible as a symbol of evil and as a warning to sinners (Isa. 1:9; Rev. 11:8). *Sodoma*: Greek form (Rom. 9:29).

JANUARY 7 | Read Genesis 22–24

22:1–14 God tests Abraham's faithfulness, but Abraham is prevented from sacrificing his son Isaac.

22:15–19 God renews His promise to make Abraham's descendants into a great nation (Gen. 12:1–2).

22:20–24 Abraham's relatives are listed.

23:1–20 Abraham's wife, Sarah, dies; Abraham buys a cave at Machpelah as a burial site.

24:1–67 Abraham's son Isaac is married to Rebekah.

Isaac The son born to Abraham and Sarah in their old age (Gen. 21:1–3) and thus the person through whom God's chosen people, the Israelites, were descended (Gen. 21:9–13). He married Rebekah (Gen. 24:57–67)—a union to which twin sons, Jacob and Esau, were born (Gen. 25:19–26). Isaac was considered a man of faith (Heb. 11:9, 20), a patriarch of Israel (Exod. 32:13), and an ancestor of Christ (Luke 3:34).

Machpelah A field with a cave that Abraham bought as a burial ground (Gen. 23:7–18). Buried here were Abraham and Sarah, Isaac and Rebekah, and Jacob and Leah (Gen. 25:9–10; 49:29–33).

Rebekah The wife of Isaac and the mother of his twin sons, Jacob and Esau. She encouraged her favorite son, Jacob, to obtain Esau's birthright by deceiving the aging Isaac. Then she encouraged Jacob to flee to her relatives in Mesopotamia to escape Esau's wrath (Gen. 27). *Rebecca*: Greek form (Rom. 9:10).

JANUARY 8 | Read Genesis 25–27

25:1–11 Abraham dies and is buried.

25:12–18 Descendants of Ishmael, Abraham's son by Hagar, are listed.

25:19–26 Twin sons, Jacob and Esau, are born to Isaac and Rebekah.

25:27–34 Esau, the older brother, trades his birthright to Jacob for a bowl of stew (1 Chron. 5:1–2).

26:1–35 Isaac digs several wells in the territory of the Philistines; God promises Isaac that the covenant He has made with His father, Abraham, will be continued through him and his descendants.

27:1–46 Jacob tricks his father into blessing him rather than his older son, Esau.

Jacob The son of Isaac and Rebekah and father of several sons who became the ancestors of the twelve tribes of Israel. Jacob was the twin brother of Esau, who was the firstborn son and thus entitled to the birthright of his father, Isaac. But Jacob bought Esau's birthright for a pot of stew (Gen. 25:29–34). With his mother, Rebekah's, help, he deceived his father and received his blessing as well (Gen. 27:6–29).

While fleeing his brother's wrath, Jacob struggled with an angel and was given the name Israel, meaning "prince with God" (Gen. 32:22–30). His descendants were known as Israelites, or descendants of Israel. In his later years, after the birth of many children to his wives, Rachel and Leah, and their handmaids, Jacob mourned his favorite son, Joseph, whom he presumed dead. But his joy was restored when Joseph was discovered alive and well in Egypt. Jacob died in Egypt after moving there at Joseph's initiative to escape a famine in Canaan. He was returned to his homeland for burial.

Esau The oldest son of Isaac who sold his birthright to his twin brother, Jacob, for a bowl of stew (Gen. 25:25–34). Esau was the ancestor of the Edomites. *Edom*: Gen. 36:8.

Birthright The inheritance rights of the firstborn son, who received a double portion of his father's assets (Deut. 21:17) plus the father's blessing and responsibility for family leadership. These inheritance rights could be taken away and conferred on another because of immoral acts or irresponsible behavior by the oldest son (Gen. 25:29–34). Esau sold his birthright to his brother, Jacob, for a bowl of stew (Gen. 25:31; Heb. 12:16).

JANUARY 9 | Read Genesis 28:1–30:24

28:1–22 Jacob travels to Haran in search of a wife; God assures him in a dream that His promise to Abraham will be realized through Jacob's descendants (Gen. 15:1–21).

29:1–30 In Haran, Jacob works seven years for the hand of Leah and seven years for Rachel, daughters of Laban.

29:31–30:24 Jacob fathers many sons by several different wives.

Haran A city of Mesopotamia known as a center of pagan worship (2 Kings 19:12). Abraham lived in Haran for a time before he left at God's command to settle in Canaan (Gen. 12:4–5). *Charran*: Acts 7:2.

Rachel Jacob's favorite wife (Gen. 29:28–30) and the mother of his sons Joseph and Benjamin (Gen. 30:22–24; 35:16–18). She died giving birth to Benjamin and was buried near Bethlehem (Gen. 35:16–20). Jeremiah referred to Rachel weeping for her children carried into the Babylonian Exile (Jer. 31:15; *Rahel*).

Leah Laban's oldest daughter and Jacob's first wife (Gen. 29:16–25). She bore seven children (Gen. 29:32–35; 30:17–21) and remained loyal to Jacob when he had to flee from Laban (Gen. 31:17–20).

Marriage among Relatives *It is better that I [Laban] give her [Rachel] to thee [Jacob], than that I should give her to another man* (Gen. 29:19).

Laban was the brother of Jacob's mother, Rebekah (Gen. 29:10). This relationship would have made Laban's daughter Rachel—the woman whom Jacob wanted to marry—Jacob's first cousin.

Sometimes the term *brother* was used loosely in Bible times to refer to any male relative such as a nephew or an uncle. So Rachel may have been a distant relative of Jacob. Marriage among distant relatives from the same tribe or bloodline was common in OT times. Abraham sought a wife for his son Isaac from among his kinsmen in Mesopotamia (Gen. 24:2–4).

JANUARY 10 | Read Genesis 30:25–32:23

30:25–43 Jacob prospers while raising livestock in the household of his father-in-law, Laban.

31:1–32:23 With Laban's blessing, Jacob returns to Canaan with his family, along with presents for his estranged brother, Esau (Gen. 27:41).

Laban A brother of Jacob's mother, Rebekah, and father of Leah and Rachel, who were given in marriage to Jacob. Jacob visited Laban to escape the wrath of his brother, Esau (Gen. 27:43). He worked seven years for Laban for the privilege of marrying Rachel, only to be tricked into marrying Leah instead. Then Jacob worked another seven years for Rachel (Gen. 29:18–30).

Canaan The region between the Red Sea and the Jordan River where Canaan's descendants settled and the territory that God promised to Abraham and his descendants (Gen. 15:3–7). *Chanaan*: Greek form (Acts 7:11).

JANUARY 11 | Read Genesis 32:24–34:31

32:24–32 Jacob wrestles with an angel; he is renamed Israel and assured of God's blessings.

33:1–20 Jacob is greeted and forgiven by his brother, Esau (Gen. 27:41).

`34:1–31` Jacob and his sons avenge the sexual assault of Jacob's daughter Dinah by Shechem.

`Israel` Another name for Jacob. Jacob was renamed Israel by an angel at Penuel because of his influence with God and man (Gen. 32:28; 35:10). His name was extended to the nation of Israel (Exod. 3:16) and finally narrowed to designate the Northern Kingdom after the nation divided following Solomon's administration.

`Shechem` A tribal prince who was killed by Simeon and Levi for seducing their sister Dinah (Gen. 34).

JANUARY 12 | Read Genesis 35–36

`35:1–15` God renews His covenant with Jacob at Bethel and assures him that his descendants will receive the land promised to Abraham (Gen. 15:1–21).

`35:16–20` Rachel dies while giving birth to Jacob's twelfth son, Benjamin.

`35:21–26` The twelve sons of Jacob by four different wives are listed.

`35:27–29` Jacob's father, Isaac, dies.

`36:1–43` Descendants of Esau, Jacob's brother, are listed.

`Bethel` A city north of Jerusalem where Jacob had a life-changing vision of angels going up and down a staircase (Gen. 28:10–19). Before it was renamed by Jacob, Bethel was known by its Canaanite name, *Luz* (Gen. 28:19).

`Benjamin` The youngest of Jacob's twelve sons and ancestor of the tribe of Benjamin. His mother, Rachel, died at his birth (Gen. 35:16–20). Benjamin was greatly loved by his father, Jacob (Gen. 42:2–4), and by his brother Joseph (Gen. 43:29–34).

JANUARY 13 | Read Genesis 37–39

`37:1–36` Jacob's son Joseph is sold into slavery by his brothers and taken into Egypt.

`38:1–30` Judah, a son of Jacob, fathers twin sons by his daughter-in-law Tamar.

`39:1–23` Joseph is imprisoned in Egypt on a false charge.

`Joseph` The son of Jacob by Rachel who was sold to a band of traders by his jealous brothers. Enslaved and imprisoned in Egypt, Joseph became an important official under the pharaoh. He was eventually reunited with his father and brothers when they came to Egypt to buy grain. A model of faith and forgiveness, Joseph saw God at work in human events (Gen. 37–50; Heb. 11:22). He was called *Zaphnathpaa-neah* by the Egyptian pharaoh (Gen. 41:45).

Judah A son of Jacob and Leah and ancestor of the tribe of Judah (Gen. 29:35). Judah interceded for his brother Joseph to be sold rather than killed (Gen. 37:26–27). He offered himself as a ransom for his brother Benjamin before Joseph in Egypt (Gen. 43:8–9; 44:32–34). His father, Jacob, predicted that Judah's descendants would become the royal line from which the Messiah would emerge (Gen. 49:10). He is listed as an ancestor of Christ (Matt. 1:2–3) and called *Juda* in Luke's ancestry (Luke 3:33). The tribe Judah is spelled *Juda* in the NT (Heb. 7:14).

Potiphar A high Egyptian officer who had Joseph imprisoned because his wife accused Joseph of trying to seduce her (Gen. 39:1–20).

JANUARY 14 | Read Genesis 40–41

40:1–23 Imprisoned with the pharaoh's chief butler and baker, Joseph explains the meaning of their dreams and develops a reputation as an interpreter of dreams.

41:1–43 Joseph is appointed a high official in the Egyptian pharaoh's administration after foretelling a severe famine by interpreting the pharaoh's dream.

41:44–52 Joseph fathers two sons, Manasseh and Ephraim, through his Egyptian wife, Asenath.

41:53–57 The famine that Joseph has foretold strikes Egypt.

Dreams and Visions Mediums of revelation often used by God to make His will known. Joseph distinguished himself in Egypt by interpreting dreams for the pharaoh and his officers (Gen. 40–41). Daniel interpreted King Nebuchadnezzar's dream that he would fall from power (Dan. 4:18–27). Paul's missionary thrust into Europe began with his vision of a man from Macedonia appealing for help (Acts 16:9–10).

Manasseh Joseph's firstborn son whose descendants became one of the tribes of Israel (Gen. 48:4–6) and occupied both sides of the Jordan River (Josh. 16:4–9). *Manasses*: Rev. 7:6.

Ephraim The second son of Joseph who became the founder of one of the twelve tribes of Israel (Gen. 48:8–20). Joshua was a member of this tribe.

JANUARY 15 | Read Genesis 42–43

42:1–6 Because of the famine, ten of Joseph's brothers come to Egypt to buy grain. Benjamin, Joseph's full brother and youngest son of Jacob (Gen. 35:16–20), does not make the trip. The ten brothers appear before Joseph, now one of Egypt's high officials.

42:7–17 Joseph recognizes his brothers, but they do not recognize him. He has them imprisoned for several days after accusing them of being spies.

42:18–38 Joseph holds his brother Simeon as a hostage. He sends the others back to Jacob with the charge to bring their youngest brother, Benjamin, to him in Egypt. This will prove that they are not spies and result in the release of their brother Simeon.

43:1–34 Joseph's brothers, including Benjamin, return to Egypt to buy grain. Joseph releases Simeon and invites all of them to a feast at his house. Again, they do not recognize Joseph.

Famine A time, often an extended period, when food or water is in short supply because of lack of rain and the failure of crops (Gen. 12:10).

Simeon A son of Jacob by Leah (Gen. 29:33) and ancestor of one of the twelve tribes of Israel (Gen. 46:10). He was held hostage by Joseph to assure Benjamin's safe arrival in Egypt (Gen. 42:24, 36).

JANUARY 16 | Read Genesis 44–45

44:1–13 Joseph sends all his brothers back to Jacob with their sacks of grain. But he plants one of his silver cups in Benjamin's sack. Then he sends his soldiers after them to search for stolen merchandise. All the brothers are arrested and returned to Joseph after the soldiers find the silver cup.

44:14–34 Judah pleads with Joseph on behalf of his brother Benjamin. He offers to become a slave of Joseph if he will let Benjamin return to his father.

45:1–28 Overcome with emotion, Joseph finally reveals himself to his brothers. He sends them back to their homeland to tell Jacob that his son Joseph is alive and doing well in Egypt.

JANUARY 17 | Read Genesis 46–48

46:1–47:31 With the help of Joseph, Jacob and his sons and their families move to Egypt to escape the famine (Acts 7:14–15).

48:1–22 Jacob blesses the two sons of Joseph—Ephraim and Manasseh.

Bless To invoke or declare God's goodness and favor upon others, as Jacob did with his twelve sons (Gen. 49:1–28). God also blesses His people by giving life (Gen. 1:22) and forgiving our sins (Rom. 4:7–8).

JANUARY 18 | Read Genesis 49–50

49:1–33 After predicting the future for each of his sons, Jacob dies in Egypt.

50:1–13 Joseph and his brothers return Jacob's body to Canaan for burial.

50:14–21 Joseph assures his brothers of his unconditional forgiveness.

50:22–26 Joseph dies in Egypt.

A Hand of Victory *Judah, thou art he whom thy brethren shall praise: thy hand shall be in the neck of thine enemies* (Gen. 49:8).

Before he died Jacob called his twelve sons together and predicted their future. He foretold the importance of Judah and his descendants—the tribe of Judah—by using the image of Judah's hand on the neck of his enemies. To place one's hand on the neck of another was a symbol of superiority and victory in battle (2 Sam. 22:41; Lam. 5:5). And Judah did become the central tribe in Israel's history. King David was born into this tribe, and it was through David's lineage that the Messiah emerged (Matt. 1:1–17; Judah is spelled *Judas* in the KJV; see Matt. 1:2).

JANUARY 19 | Read Exodus 1–3

1:1–7 The descendants of Jacob/Israel multiply at an astonishing rate in Egypt.

1:8–14 The pharaoh of Egypt enslaves the Israelites.

1:15–22 The pharaoh orders all male Israelite infants killed to control their population growth.

2:1–4 A baby boy named Moses is hidden in a basket on the Nile River to escape the pharaoh's decree (Heb. 11:23).

2:5–10 The pharaoh's daughter discovers Moses and adopts him as her son.

2:11–15 After he reaches adulthood, Moses kills an Egyptian official who is abusing an Israelite slave. Moses flees to Midian to escape the pharaoh's wrath.

2:16–25 Moses becomes a shepherd in the household of a Midianite named Reuel (also known as Jethro) and marries his daughter Zipporah.

3:1–22 God appears to Moses in a burning bush and calls him to deliver His people, the Israelites, from enslavement by the Egyptians (Acts 7:30).

Moses The great lawgiver and prophet of Israel who led the Hebrew people out of Egypt. His life is best understood in three forty-year periods.

Forty years in Egypt. Moses was born into slavery and hidden by his mother to escape the pharaoh's order that all male Hebrew babies should be killed (Exod. 1:22; 2:1–10). Discovered and "adopted" by the pharaoh's daughter, he was raised and schooled as an Egyptian (Exod. 2:10). After killing an Egyptian who was abusing an Israelite slave, he became a fugitive in the desert (Exod. 2:14–15).

Forty years in Midian. Moses became a shepherd (Exod. 3:1) and married Zipporah, the daughter of a priest, and she bore two sons, Gershom and Eliezer (Exod. 18:3–4). Moses reluctantly answered God's call to lead His people out of slavery (Exod. 3:11–4:9) and returned to Egypt, where he enlisted his brother, Aaron, as his helper and spokesman (Exod. 4:27–31). After ten plagues sent by the Lord upon the Egyptians, the pharaoh finally released the Hebrews, who entered the wilderness area in the Sinai Peninsula under Moses' leadership.

Forty years in the wilderness. In the wilderness Moses received the Ten Commandments (Exod. 20:1–24) and other parts of the Mosaic Law, exhorted the people to remain faithful to God, built the tabernacle at God's command (Exod. 36–40), and sent spies to investigate Canaan (Num. 13). He impatiently struck a rock for water at Kadesh (Num. 20:1–13), a sin that led God to deny his entrance into the Promised Land. He died in Moab at Canaan's border at the age of 120 (Deut. 34:1–8).

Miriam The sister of Aaron and Moses (1 Chron. 6:3). Miriam protected her baby brother Moses by arranging for their mother, Jochebed, to care for him (Exod. 2:4–10). She led a triumphant song of praise and thanksgiving to God after the Israelites were delivered from the pursuing Egyptian army at the Red Sea (Exod. 15:2–21). She died and was buried in the wilderness at Kadesh (Num. 20:1).

Midian (1) A son of Abraham by Keturah and founder of the Midianites (Gen. 25:1–4; 1 Chron. 1:32–33). (2) A region in the Arabian desert east of the Jordan River, including Edom and the Sinai Peninsula, that was occupied by the Midianites (Exod. 2:15). *Madian*: Acts 7:29.

Sinai A mountain peak more than one mile high in the wilderness of Sinai where Moses tended sheep and saw the burning bush with God's call to deliver His people (Exod. 3:1–10). *Sina*: Greek form (Acts 7:30). *Horeb*: KJV, NIV, NRSV.

JANUARY 20 | Read Exodus 4–6

4:1–13 God assures Moses through miraculous signs that He will stand with him before the pharaoh.

4:14–31 God deals with Moses' excuses by appointing his brother, Aaron, to serve as Moses' spokesman. Moses returns to Egypt to confront the pharaoh.

5:1–23 The pharaoh responds to Moses' demands by forcing the Israelite slaves to make bricks without straw.

6:1–13 God assures Moses and the Israelites that the covenant He had made with Abraham over 400 years before (Gen. 15:1–21) is still in force; God will bring the Israelites out of slavery into their own land.

6:14–15 The descendants of Jacob's sons Reuben and Simeon are listed (Num. 26:5–14).

6:16–30 The descendants of Jacob's son Levi (Gen. 29:34), who include Moses and Aaron, are listed.

Aaron The first high priest of the Israelites (Exod. 28:1) and Moses' brother (Exod. 4:14). Designated by God as spokesman for Moses (Exod. 4:13–16), Aaron helped Moses lead the Hebrew slaves out of Egypt (Exod. 7:8–12). In the wilderness, he was consecrated by God as Israel's first high priest, and his sons inherited this position from their father (Num. 3:38). Like Moses, Aaron was not allowed to enter the Promised Land because of his act of unfaithfulness in the wilderness (Num. 20:6–12). His earthly priesthood is compared unfavorably to the eternal priesthood of Christ (Heb. 5:4; 7:11).

Egyptian Bricks with Straw *Ye [Egyptian slave supervisors] shall no more give the people [Israelite slaves] straw to make brick, as heretofore: let them go and gather straw for themselves* (Exod. 5:7).

The bricks used in the building projects of ancient Egypt were molded from mud, then placed in the sun to dry. Over time sun-dried bricks would crumble from exposure to the wind and rain. To give these bricks greater strength and stability, chopped straw from wheat or barley stalks was sometimes added. Pharaoh added to the hard labor of the Israelite slaves by forcing them to forage for straw to be used in the manufacturing process. Apparently the Israelites were under a quota system. They were expected to produce so many bricks per day—no excuses accepted (Exod. 5:13–14).

JANUARY 21 | Read Exodus 7–10

7:1–13 Aaron's rod turns into a snake, but this miraculous sign fails to impress the Egyptian pharaoh and his court magicians.

7:14–10:29 God sends nine plagues upon the Egyptians to convince the pharaoh to release the Israelite slaves, but he remains stubborn and unmoved.

Hardness of Heart A symbolic expression for rebellion or a stubborn and unyielding spirit, such as that exemplified by the pharaoh of Egypt in refusing to free the Hebrew slaves (Exod. 9:35).

A Superior God *All the waters that were in the river [the Nile] were turned to blood. And the fish that was in the river died; and the river stank, and the Egyptians could not drink of the water of the river* (Exod. 7:20–21).

The Egyptians viewed the Nile River as sacred because it was essential to their survival as a nation. They worshiped it as a god, referring to it as "the father of life" and "the father of the gods." God's turning the water of this great river into blood was actually a strike at the heart of their pagan religious system. He was showing that He was more powerful than all of their gods and that He was the supreme ruler of the universe.

Deep Darkness *The LORD said unto Moses, Stretch out thine hand toward heaven, that there may be darkness over the land of Egypt, even darkness which may be felt* (Exod. 10:21).

This plague consisted of a thick, heavy darkness that fell across the land of Egypt for three days (Exod. 10:22). This must have been an eerie blackness with no sliver of light, similar to the total darkness a person experiences deep within a cave when all of the lights are turned out. It was so frightening that the Egyptians did not venture outside their houses (Exod. 10:23). Once again, the Lord proved His superiority over the Egyptian gods. The Egyptians worshiped the sun through the sun god Ra. But God was master over the sun and all other forces of nature.

JANUARY 22 | Read Exodus 11–12

11:1–10 God announces through Moses the tenth and final plague—the death of all the Egyptian firstborn.

12:1–30 All the Egyptian firstborn are killed. The Israelites are spared because they obey God's command to mark the doorposts of their houses with the blood of sacrificial lambs (Ezek. 9:6).

12:31–51 Crushed by the widespread death of his people, the pharaoh releases the Israelites, who travel into the desert territory east of Egypt.

· ·

Token A sign or signal. Circumcision was a token of God's covenant with Abraham (Gen. 17:11). The blood on the Israelites' doorposts was a sign for the death angel to "pass over" these houses (Exod. 12:13). *Sign*: NIV, NRSV.

· ·

All the Gods of Egypt *Against all the gods of Egypt I will execute judgment: I am the LORD* (Exod. 12:12).

To be superior to "all the gods of Egypt" was quite a claim, since the Egyptians are known to have worshiped more than thirty pagan deities. These included the bull god Apis, who ensured fertility; Hathor, the goddess of love; and Thoth, the god of wisdom and books. But God proved, through the death of all the Egyptian firstborn (Exod. 12:29), that He held the power of life and death over the Egyptians and their religious system. Months later, after Moses had led the Israelites out of slavery in Egypt, God declared to him, "I am the LORD thy God, which have brought thee. . .out of the house of bondage. Thou shalt have no other gods before me" (Exod. 20:2–3).

JANUARY 23 | Read Exodus 13–15

13:1–20 God directs that the firstborn of both animals and people among the Israelites are to be dedicated to Him.

13:21–22 God leads the Israelites with a cloud by day and a fire by night.

14:1–31 God swallows the pursuing Egyptian army in the Red Sea after the Israelites pass over on dry land (Heb. 11:29).

15:1–22 Through the "Song of Moses," the Israelites celebrate God's miraculous deliverance (Deut. 31:30–32:47).

15:23–27 At Marah, God miraculously turns bad water into good water for the Israelites.

Pillar of Fire and Cloud Supernatural signs that guided the Israelites in the wilderness (Exod. 13:21). Given to protect the Hebrews, the signs represented God's presence with His people (Num. 14:13–14). These signs were repeated in the transfiguration of Christ (Matt. 17:5).

Red Sea The sea between Egypt and Arabia that the Israelites crossed miraculously through God's intervention when fleeing from the Egyptian army (Exod. 14:16; 15:4, 22). This body of water is also called the Sea of Reeds because of its reed-filled marshes at the head of the Gulf of Suez.

Dancing with Joy *Miriam. . .took a timbrel [tambourine, NIV] in her hand; and all the women went out after her with timbrels and with dances* (Exod. 15:20).

Miriam and other women celebrated God's deliverance of the Israelites from the Egyptian army by singing, playing timbrels or tambourines, and dancing. Dancing was a distinctive form of worship and religious expression among the Israelites during OT times. It demonstrated joy and thanksgiving to the Lord. King David danced "with all his might" (2 Sam. 6:14) when the ark was brought home to Jerusalem. The psalmist called on God's people to praise the Lord through dancing (Pss. 149:3; 150:4).

JANUARY 24 | Read Exodus 16–18

16:1–36 God miraculously provides manna, a bread substitute, to feed the complaining Israelites in the wilderness.

17:1–7 The Lord produces water from a rock to sustain His people.

17:8–16 God gives the Israelites a victory over the Amalekites.

18:1–27 Taking the advice of his father-in-law, Jethro, Moses delegates some of his burdensome duties on behalf of the people to other Israelite leaders (Deut. 1:1–18).

Manna Called "bread from heaven" (Exod. 16:4), manna was provided daily except on the Sabbath for forty years. A different substance by this name drops from various trees, particularly the tamarisk, in the valleys near the Sinai wilderness.

Amalekites A tribal enemy of the Israelites. Their animosity against the Hebrews apparently began during the years of wilderness wandering with an unprovoked attack (Exod. 17:8–16). Saul battled this tribe as well (1 Sam. 14:48), and they suffered a major defeat at the hands of David (1 Sam. 30).

Egypt and the Good Old Days *Would to God we [Israelites] had died. . .in the land of Egypt, when we sat by the flesh pots [pots of meat, NIV], and when we did eat bread to the full* (Exod. 16:3).

Soon after leaving Egypt, the Israelites began to whine for the "good old days." They began to think their existence as slaves was preferable to the harsh life of the wilderness. "Flesh pots" or meat pots were three-legged metal containers in which the Egyptians cooked meat over an open fire. But it is likely that meat was a delicacy enjoyed only by the elite of Egyptian society. The Israelites exaggerated when they claimed they had eaten meat regularly from these cooking pots. That's the problem with nostalgia: Looking back, things always seem better than they actually were.

JANUARY 25 | Read Exodus 19–20

19:1–25 God reveals Himself in smoke and fire to Moses and the Israelites at Mount Sinai; He promises to make them "a kingdom of priests, and an holy nation" (v. 6).

20:1–17 God reveals the Ten Commandments to Moses (see also Deut. 5:1–22).

20:18–26 God cautions the Israelites against worshiping false gods.

Priest A religious leader who made sacrificial offerings. The priesthood originated with Aaron, and his descendants were sanctified to the office (Exod. 29:9, 44). Jesus, our faultless high priest, paid for our sins once and for all by sacrificing Himself (Heb. 7:26–28).

Ten Commandments The ethical commands given by God to Moses on Mount Sinai. Also called the Decalogue, the Ten Commandments summarize the basic moral laws of the OT. Four of these commandments enjoin duties to God (Exod. 20:1–11), while six deal with obligations to other people (Exod. 20:12–17). Jesus summed up these commandments in two great principles—loving God above all else and loving our neighbors as ourselves (Matt. 22:37–40).

Idol, Idolatry The worship of false gods or something created rather than the Creator (Rom. 1:25). Idolatry was prohibited by the first two of the Ten Commandments (Exod. 20:3–4). Abraham migrated to Canaan to escape idol worship (Josh. 24:2–3). Prominent idols mentioned in the Bible are the golden calves of Aaron (Exod. 32:4) and King Jeroboam (2 Chron. 11:15) and the grain god of the Philistines known as Dagon (Judg. 16:23).

The prophet Elijah helped overthrow Baal worship in Israel (1 Kings 18:17–40), and the prophet Isaiah described the folly of idolatry (Isa. 44:9–20). In the NT, idolatry is anything that comes between the believer and God (Col. 3:5).

Clean before the Lord *The LORD said unto Moses, Go unto the people, and sanctify [consecrate, NIV] them to day and to morrow, and let them wash their clothes* (Exod. 19:10).

About three months after leaving Egypt, Moses led the Israelites to the base of Mount Sinai in the wilderness (Exod. 19:1–2). Here they would have a dramatic encounter with the living Lord, who had led them out of slavery. In order to prepare the people for this special revelation of Himself, God commanded that the people be both spiritually ("sanctify them") and physically ("wash their clothes") clean. Such cleanliness was essential for those who would stand in the presence of the holy God.

JANUARY 26 | Read Exodus 21–23

21:1–23:33 Various laws governing human relationships, property rights, slavery, and treatment of the poor are listed (Deut. 22:1–25:4).

Three Great Festivals *Three times thou shalt keep a feast unto me [God] in the year* (Exod. 23:14).

God through Moses directed the Israelites to celebrate three great annual festivals, or religious holidays, to commemorate God's leadership in the life of their nation. These three festivals were Passover, or the Feast of Unleavened Bread (Exod. 23:15); the Feast of Harvest, or Weeks (Exod. 23:16); and the Feast of Ingathering, or Tabernacles (Exod. 23:16). These festivals served the same purpose for the Israelites that our holidays serve for us. They gave them rest from their labors, reminded them of important events in their history, and emphasized the values that set them apart as a distinct people.

JANUARY 27 | Read Exodus 24–27

24:1–18 Moses enters the cloud of God's glory and communes with Him for forty days on Mount Sinai.

`25:1–27:21` God tells Moses to rally the Israelites to build the tabernacle as a place of worship; He gives Moses a detailed blueprint of the tent and its furnishings.

`Tabernacle` A tent or portable sanctuary built in the wilderness at God's command as a place of worship for the Israelites (Exod. 40:1–8). It was also called the Tent of Meeting because it was considered a place of encounter between God and His people. The tabernacle foreshadowed Christ's incarnation when "the Word was made flesh, and dwelt among us" (John 1:14).

`Holy of Holies` The sacred innermost sanctuary of the temple and tabernacle, containing the ark of the covenant and the mercy seat, which only the high priest could enter. Even he could go in only one day a year on the Day of Atonement, when he made a special sacrifice for the sins of the people (Heb. 9:2–3, 7). *Holy Place*: NRSV.

`Bread on the Table` *And thou [Israelites] shalt set upon the table shewbread [bread of the Presence, NIV] before me [God] alway* (Exod. 25:30).

A special bread called shewbread or bread of the Presence was to be set on a table in the holiest place in the tabernacle. We know from other Bible passages that this bread consisted of twelve loaves, representing the twelve tribes of Israel (Lev. 24:5–7). The constant presence of these loaves acknowledged that the tribes were guided at all times by the watchful eye of the Lord

JANUARY 28 | Read Exodus 28–29

`28:1–29:46` The Lord instructs Moses to appoint and consecrate his brother, Aaron, and Aaron's descendants as the official priesthood for the Israelites (Num. 3:32).

`Ephod` A sleeveless linen garment, similar to a vest, worn by the high priest while officiating at the sacrificial altar (2 Sam. 6:14).

`Breastplate` The vestment worn by the Jewish high priest. It contained twelve precious stones and was engraved with the names of the tribes of Israel (Exod. 28:15–30). Paul spoke figuratively of the "breastplate of righteousness" for Christians (Eph. 6:14). *Breastpiece*: NIV.

JANUARY 29 | Read Exodus 30–31

`30:1–10` God gives Moses instructions about the altar in the tabernacle on which incense is to be burned as an act of worship.

`30:11–16` The Lord directs Moses to collect a half-shekel tax from every male Israelite to support the tabernacle and its services (Matt. 17:24–27).

30:17–38 God specifies that a special anointing oil is to be used by the priests to consecrate the tabernacle's altar and its vessels and furnishings.

31:1–11 God reveals to Moses that He has selected two craftsmen, Bezaleel and Aholiab, to perform the skilled stonecutting, metalwork, and woodworking required for the tabernacle.

31:12–18 God reminds Moses that the Israelites are to observe the seventh day of the week as the Sabbath; they are not to do any work on this day (Exod. 20:8–11).

Altar A platform, table, or elevated structure on which sacrifices were placed as offerings. Altars were originally made of earth or rocks (Exod. 20:24–25), but they evolved into more sophisticated structures after the construction of the tabernacle (Lev. 9:24). Pagan Canaanite altars were often called "high places" because they were built on hills or high platforms (Num. 33:52).

Shekel A Jewish coin or unit of measure. The silver shekel was worth about sixty cents; the gold shekel about eight dollars (Gen. 23:15; Neh. 10:32; Jer. 32:9).

Sabbath The Jewish day of worship and rest, established when God rested after the six days of creation (Gen. 2:1–3). The fourth of the Ten Commandments calls for the Sabbath to be observed and "kept holy" (Exod. 20:8). The Pharisees placed restrictions on Sabbath observance that prohibited acts of mercy or necessity (Mark 2:23–24). But Jesus declared that "the sabbath was made for man and not man for the sabbath" (Mark 2:27). The OT Sabbath fell on the seventh day of the week, or our Saturday. Most Christian groups observe Sunday as the day of worship because of Christ's resurrection on the first day of the week (1 Cor. 16:2).

JANUARY 30 | Read Exodus 32–33

32:1–35 Aaron and the Israelites sin against God during Moses' absence on Mount Sinai by fashioning a golden calf as an object of worship.

33:1–34:35 Moses pleads for God to forgive the sinful Israelites; the Lord renews His pledge to guide and protect them.

Calf Worship *They [Israelites] have made them a molten calf, and have worshipped it* (Exod. 32:8).
This lapse into idolatry by the Israelites may show how they had been influenced by the pagan worship system of Egypt. The Egyptians worshiped more than thirty pagan gods, including the bull god Apis, who was thought to ensure human fertility. In later years, King Jeroboam of Israel set up pagan golden calves at Dan and Bethel (1 Kings 12:26–33).

JANUARY 31 | Read Exodus 34–35

35:1–35 At the urging of Moses, the Israelites contribute the materials needed for the building of the tabernacle.

Ashtaroth A pagan fertility goddess worshiped by the Philistines and also by the Israelites soon after the death of Joshua (Judg. 2:13). Her symbol was an evergreen tree, a pole, or a pillar near a pagan altar. *Ashtaroth* and *Ashtoreth* are plural forms of her name (1 Sam. 7:4; 1 Kings 11:33). Her name in the singular form was *Asherah.*

FEBRUARY 1 | Read Exodus 36–38

36:1–38:31 The tabernacle is built according to the specifications issued by the Lord (Exod. 25:1–27:21).

Freewill Offering An offering given freely and willingly (Amos 4:5), in contrast to one made to atone for some misdeed (Num. 15:3).

Ark of the Covenant A wooden chest containing two stone tablets on which the Ten Commandments were inscribed. The ark symbolized God's presence to the nation of Israel (Deut. 10:3–4). It was taken into battle by the Israelites (1 Sam. 4:4–5) and captured by the Philistines (1 Sam. 4:10–11). After its return to Israel (1 Sam. 6:1–15), the ark was later placed in the temple in Jerusalem (1 Kings 8:1–9). It was probably carried away by King Nebuchadnezzar of Babylonia along with other treasures after the fall of Jerusalem in 587 BC (2 Chron. 36:7, 18). *Ark of the Testimony*: Exod. 25:22.

Mercy Seat The gold lid that covered the ark of the covenant. It was called the "mercy seat" because God was believed to be present to hear and answer prayers (Exod. 25:21–22). On the Day of Atonement, the high priest sprinkled blood of the sin offerings on the mercy seat as a propitiation for the people's sins (Lev. 16:11–16). *Cover*: NIV.

Laver A container placed near the altar outside the tabernacle where priests could wash their hands and feet before offering animal sacrifices (Exod. 30:17–21). *Basin*: NIV, NRSV.

FEBRUARY 2 | Read Exodus 39–40

39:1–31 The distinctive styles of dress required for Aaron as the high priest and the other priests of Israel are described.

`39:32–43` The features and furnishings of the completed tabernacle are reviewed as they are presented to Moses.

`40:1–38` Moses and the Israelites dedicate the tabernacle as they assemble its furnishings; God shows His pleasure by filling the sacred tent with His glory (Neh. 9:12).

`The Tabernacle` *On the first day of the first month shalt thou set up the tabernacle of the tent of the congregation* (Exod. 40:2).

More than one-third of the forty chapters of Exodus deal with the tabernacle (see Exod. 25–40)—a sacred tent that served as a place of worship for God's people. The tabernacle moved with the Israelites from place to place during their years of wandering in the wilderness. Thus, it served as a constant witness of His guidance.

God gave Moses and Aaron detailed instructions on how to build and equip the tabernacle (Exod. 25–27). The actual building of the structure is recorded in Exodus 35–40. Finally, the book of Exodus comes to a close with a description of how the building was organized and furnished for the purpose of worship (Exod. 40:1–38). The tabernacle was divided into two rooms—the Holy of Holies or "the Holiest of all" (Heb. 9:3) and the Holy Place (Exod. 28:29)—by a lavishly embroidered linen curtain.

It was what the tabernacle represented—the presence of God with His people—that made this structure special.

`The Ark of the Covenant` *Thou [Moses] shalt put therein [in the tabernacle] the ark of the testimony, and cover the ark with the vail [curtain, NIV]* (Exod. 40:3).

This ark of the testimony is better known by its alternate name, "ark of the covenant" (Deut. 31:26). It is also called "the ark of God" (1 Sam. 3:3). It was a sacred portable chest that symbolized God's grace and guidance in the lives of the Israelites. God had already given instructions for the building of the ark (Exod. 25:10–22). In this passage, He directed Moses and Aaron to place it inside the completed tabernacle. It belonged in the most sacred room of the building—the Holy of Holies or Most Holy Place (Exod. 26:34). Inside the ark was a copy of the law, or testimony, that God had revealed to Moses to direct the lives of the Israelites as His covenant people (Exod. 25:21). According to Hebrews 9:4, the ark also contained Aaron's rod and a memorial sample of the manna that God provided for the Israelites in the wilderness.

`Incense Altar` *Thou [Moses] shalt set the altar of gold for the incense before the ark of the testimony* (Exod. 40:5).

Incense was a sweet-smelling substance burned in the tabernacle as an offering to God. It was offered by a priest on this special altar made of gold. The pleasant aroma symbolized the prayers of the Israelites before the Lord. Only incense made by using a formula specified by God (Exod. 30:34–38) was to be burned on the incense altar. Two sons of Aaron were destroyed for burning incense by "strange fire" (Lev. 10:1–3). They may have been offering incense not produced by this divine formula.

FEBRUARY 3 | Read Leviticus 1–4

`1:1–4:35` God prescribes the procedures to be followed by the Israelites and the priests in making various offerings to the Lord (Num. 15:1–31).

`Burnt Offering` A meat sacrifice consisting of an unblemished animal that was totally consumed by fire, except for the hide (Lev. 7:8). Burnt sacrifices were made to atone for sin and to restore the broken relationship between man and God (Num. 6:10–11).

`Sin Offering` An offering of a sacrificial animal presented to God to gain forgiveness for sins, particularly those committed unintentionally or in ignorance (Lev. 4:2–3). A sin offering for all the people was made once a year by the high priest on the Day of Atonement (Lev. 16:6, 15).

`No Yeast or Honey` *Ye [Israelites] shall burn no leaven, nor any honey, in any offering of the Lord made by fire* (Lev. 2:11).

Leaven, or yeast, was mixed with dough to cause bread to rise. Any bread brought to the Lord as an offering was to be baked without leaven. Neither was honey, used as a sweetening agent, to be used in any food items presented to the Lord. The reason for these prohibitions is that both yeast and honey were associated with offerings presented to pagan gods.

FEBRUARY 4 | Read Leviticus 5–7

`5:1–7:38` God prescribes the procedures to be followed by the Israelites and the priests in making various offerings to the Lord (Num. 15:1–31).

`Oblation` An offering sanctified to God, consisting usually of meat, meal, firstfruits of the harvest, or land (Lev. 2). *Grain offering*: NIV, NRSV.

`Trespass Offering` A sacrificial animal offering presented for lesser sins or offenses after full restitution to persons wronged had been made (Lev. 5:6–7, 15–19).

`Three Ways of Baking Bread` *All the meat offering [grain offering, NIV] that is baken in the oven, and all that is dressed in the fryingpan, and in the pan [griddle, NIV], shall be the priest's that offereth it* (Lev. 7:9).

This verse describes three different ways of baking bread in Bible times. The "oven" probably refers to a large stone pitcher with space in the bottom for heating small rocks over a fire. These rocks would radiate heat into the upper part of the pitcher, where bread was placed for baking. The "fryingpan" was a large metal pot placed over an open fire and used mostly for boiling meat. But it could also be used for baking bread. The "pan" was a flat metal plate that could be heated quickly to bake bread over an open fire. This is probably the utensil referred to by the prophet Ezekiel (Ezek. 4:3).

FEBRUARY 5 | Read Leviticus 8–10

8:1–36 Moses consecrates Aaron and his sons as priests in holy service to the Lord and His people.

9:1–24 Aaron and his sons present a sin offering, a burnt offering, and a peace offering on behalf of the people.

10:1–3 Nadab and Abihu, sons of Aaron, are destroyed by fire for using an unauthorized procedure in burning incense at the altar (Num. 16:35).

10:4–20 Moses reminds Aaron and his remaining sons of the responsibility of priests to show reverence and respect toward God and His requirements.

Nadab and Abihu Sons of Aaron who were destroyed for offering "strange fire," or a forbidden sacrifice, to God (Lev. 10:1–7).

Wine The juice of grapes, fermented to produce a strong beverage that was very popular among the Jews (Gen. 40:11). Commonly referred to as *strong drink* (Prov. 31:6), wine was prohibited to Nazarites (Num. 6:3) as well as to priests before they officiated at the altar (Lev. 10:9). Excessive consumption of wine was denounced (Prov. 20:1; Eph. 5:18).

FEBRUARY 6 | Read Leviticus 11–12

11:1–47 God lists the clean animals that may be eaten by the Israelites, but those considered unclean are not to be eaten or even touched (Deut. 14:1–21).

12:1–8 God prescribes the ritual by which a woman may be declared clean after giving birth to a child.

Clean A word used by the Hebrews to describe things that were ceremonially pure (Lev. 11). The word is also used symbolically to signify holiness or righteousness (Ps. 24:4).

Unclean Animals Under Mosaic Law, only animals that chewed the cud and were cloven-footed were considered "clean" and suitable for eating (Lev. 11:2–3). Even touching the flesh of an "unclean" animal made a person unclean (Lev. 11:8).

Purification Ceremonial or spiritual cleansing. The Mosaic Law prescribed purification rites for those ceremonially defiled by touching a corpse, by contact with bodily discharges, by childbirth, and by leprosy (see Lev. 14–15). The mother of

Jesus offered turtledoves and pigeons as a sacrifice in her ceremonial cleansing (Luke 2:21–24).

Unclean Pots *The weasel, the mouse, the tortoise, the ferret, the chameleon, the lizard, the snail, the mole. . .every earthen vessel, whereinto any of them falleth, whatsoever is in it shall be unclean* (Lev. 11:29–30, 33).

These animals were considered unclean and could not be eaten by the Israelites. Their impurity extended even to the things they touched. Thus, if these animals got into a clay jar where water or food was kept, these items had to be thrown away. Even the jar was considered irreversibly contaminated and had to be destroyed.

FEBRUARY 7 | **Read Leviticus 13:1–14:57**

13:1–14:57 God issues regulations for dealing with leprosy—or an infectious skin disease. Even a house or tent that has been exposed to this disease is to be cleansed in accordance with a prescribed ritual.

Leprosy A variety of dreaded skin diseases. The Mosaic Law required a leper to live in isolation from others and to cry, "Unclean," so people could avoid him (Lev. 13:45–46). Jesus healed ten lepers and sent them to the priest for verification and purification (Luke 17:11–14).

Hyssop A plant used in purification ceremonies (Exod. 12:22). It was also symbolic of spiritual cleansing (Ps. 51:7). Hyssop was used to relieve Jesus' thirst on the cross (John 19:29).

Replastering with Morter *They [Israelites] shall take other stones, and put them in the place of those stones; and he shall take other morter [clay, NIV], and shall plaister the house* (Lev. 14:42).

These instructions were intended for the Israelites after they had settled in permanent homes in the land of Canaan. If a plague of mildew or fungus broke out in a house, the owner was to replace the infected stones and replaster the entire dwelling with "morter," or clay. The mortar of Bible times was made by mixing clay with finely chopped straw. Sometimes sand, ashes, or lime was added to give this substance more body and to make it last longer.

If this renovation of the house with new stones and new mortar did not eliminate the plague, the dwelling was to be torn down. The debris was to be carried outside the city to "an unclean place" (Lev. 14:45)—perhaps a garbage dump designated for this purpose.

FEBRUARY 8 | Read Leviticus 15:1–33

15:1–33 Procedures are established by which a person who experiences a bodily discharge may be rendered clean again.

Ablution The ceremonial washing of a person's body or clothing to make him pure. Such washing was commanded in the OT Law (Exod. 40:12–13). True cleansing is found only in the blood of Christ (Rev. 1:5).

FEBRUARY 9 | Read Leviticus 16–17

16:1–34 God specifies how Aaron, the high priest, is to make atonement for himself and all the people on one specific day each year known as the Day of Atonement (Num. 29:7).

17:1–9 God prohibits the Israelites from presenting offerings at any place other than the tabernacle.

17:10–16 God cautions the people not to eat the meat of a slaughtered animal unless the blood has first been drained from the flesh.

Day of Atonement A Jewish holy day (Yom Kippur) on which atonement was made for all Israel (Lev. 16:29–30; 23:27–28). Preceded by special sabbaths (Lev. 23:24) and fasting, this event recognized man's inability to make atonement for himself. On this day the Jewish high priest made atonement first for himself and then for the sins of the people by sprinkling the blood of a sacrificial animal on the altar (Lev. 16:12–15). The scapegoat, representing the sins of the people, was released into the wilderness to symbolize pardon (Lev. 16:21–23).

The writer of Hebrews in the NT declared that this ritual is no longer necessary because Christ laid down His life as a permanent, once-for-all sacrifice to make atonement for our sins (Heb. 10:1–10).

Scapegoat A goat symbolically bearing the sins of the people and sent into the wilderness by the high priest on the Day of Atonement (Lev. 16:8–22). This goat is a symbol of Christ, our sin bearer (see Isa. 53:6). *Azazel*: NRSV.

Laying on of Hands A ritual blessing or ordination for service. This ritual was used by the high priest on the Day of Atonement. By placing his hands on the scapegoat, he ritually transferred the sins of the people to the animal (Lev. 16:21). The patriarchs placed their hands on their descendants to confirm birthright or convey special blessings (Gen. 48:14, 18). The church at Antioch laid hands on Paul and Barnabas to confirm their calling as missionaries and to set them apart for this service (Acts 13:2–3).

FEBRUARY 10 | Read Leviticus 18–20

`18:1–30` God warns the people not to participate in the depraved sexual practices of the surrounding pagan nations.

`19:1–20:27` God calls His people to a high moral standard. They are to honor the Lord with their behavior and to treat other people with fairness and justice.

`Medium` A communicator between humans and the spirit world. The Mosaic Law specified that professing mediums or wizards were to be stoned to death (Lev. 20:27). The prophet Isaiah warned against consulting the dead rather than listening to the Lord (Isa. 8:19–20; 19:3).

`Milcom` The supreme god of the Ammonites (1 Kings 11:5). Solomon built a sanctuary for worship of this pagan god, but it was destroyed during King Josiah's reforms (2 Kings 23:12–13). *Molech*: Lev. 20:2; *Molech*: NIV; *Moloch*: Acts 7:43.

`Sacrifices to Moloch` *Thou [Israelites] shalt not let any of thy seed [children, NIV] pass through the fire to Molech* (Lev. 18:21).

Molech, also referred to as Malcham (Zeph. 1:5) and Moloch (Acts 7:43), was a pagan god of the Ammonites, whose worship involved child sacrifice. Images of this god portray him with a human body and the head of an ox. Some interpreters believe Molech was a hollowed-out metal idol. A fire was kindled within the hollow space, and children were placed by their parents in his outstretched arms, where they were consumed by the flames and heat. It is believed that firstborn children were demanded of parents who worshiped this pagan god as proof of their devotion.

In spite of the Lord's prohibition against child sacrifice, it was practiced on occasion among the Israelites. Both King Ahaz (2 Kings 16:3) and King Manasseh (2 Kings 21:6) of Judah made their sons "pass through the fire." This probably refers to this pagan custom.

FEBRUARY 11 | Read Leviticus 21–23

`21:16–22:16` God establishes strict physical and moral requirements for Aaron and his descendants who serve as priests among the people.

`22:17–33` Animals offered to God as sacrifices are to be healthy and free of physical defects (Mal. 1:8–9).

`23:1–44` God cites the special days and religious holidays or festivals that are to be observed by the Israelites: the weekly Sabbath (v. 3), the yearly Passover and Feast of Unleavened Bread (vv. 5–8), the offering of firstfruits (vv. 9–14), the Feast of Pentecost (vv. 15–21), the Feast of Trumpets (vv. 23–25), the Day of Atonement (vv. 27–30), and the Feast of Tabernacles (vv. 33–36) (Deut. 16:1–17).

Passover and Feast of Unleavened Bread A Jewish festival that commemorated the Exodus from Egypt (Josh. 5:10). The Passover celebrated how God "passed over" the Hebrew houses in Egypt that were sprinkled with blood while killing the firstborn of the Egyptians on the eve of the Exodus (Exod. 12). The seven-day Feast of Unleavened Bread recalled the haste with which the slaves left Egypt (Exod. 12:33–34).

Firstfruits The first or best of crops and livestock. According to Mosaic Law, these were to be presented as sacrifices and offerings to the Lord to express thanks for His provision (Exod. 23:19; Prov. 3:9).

Pentecost An annual Jewish feast or holy period, commemorating the end of the harvest, that fell on the fiftieth day after the Passover. This was the holiday being observed in Jerusalem when the Holy Spirit came in power upon the early Christian believers (Acts 2). This feast was also known as the *Feast of Weeks* and the *Feast of Harvest* (Exod. 34:22).

Feast of Tabernacles A festival, also known as the Feast of Booths and the Feast of Ingathering (Exod. 23:16; Num. 29:12), observed annually during the harvest season to commemorate Israel's wilderness wandering experience. The people lived in tents or booths in remembrance of their days as tent dwellers while waiting to enter Canaan (Lev. 23:39–43).

. . . .

The Drink Offering *They [sacrificial animals] shall be for a burnt offering unto the LORD, with their meat offering, and their drink offerings* (Lev. 23:18).

A drink offering to God was usually given along with other offerings, such as the burnt offering, the sin offering, and the trespass offering. The drink offering was a quantity of wine. It was presented by the worshiper to a priest, who poured it out at the base of the altar of burnt offering.

FEBRUARY 12 | Read Leviticus 24–25

24:1–4 God directs that the oil-burning lamps before the altar in the tabernacle are to be kept burning continuously.

24:5–9 Twelve loaves of fresh-baked bread, representing the twelve tribes of Israel, are to be placed on a table near the altar in the tabernacle each week to replace the old loaves; the old loaves are then to be eaten by the priests (2 Chron. 2:4).

24:10–23 The people stone a man for blasphemy, or disrespect toward God, at Moses' command.

25:1–7 God directs that the farmland of the Israelites, once they possess it, is to be given a Sabbath of its own; after six consecutive years of production, it is to remain idle during the seventh year.

`25:8–55` God decrees that every fiftieth year (following seven "Sabbaths" of seven years each) is to be a liberating year known as the "jubile." During this year, Israelites who were forced to sell themselves into slavery to pay off a debt are to be set free. Tracts of land that were sold because Israelite families fell upon hard times are to be returned to the original owners.

`Blaspheme` To revile, curse, or show contempt toward God. This was considered a capital offense by the Jewish people, punishable by death. Jesus was accused of blasphemy by the Jewish leaders. They considered Him only a man, while He claimed to be God's Son (Matt. 9:3).

`Jubile` A year of celebration devoted to liberty and justice and observed every fifty years by the Israelites. During this year, Israelites serving as indentured servants were released from their debts and set free. All properties that had been given up because of indebtedness since the last Jubilee were returned to the original owners. Cropland was allowed to go unplanted as a conservation measure (Lev. 25:8–55). *Jubilee*: NIV, NRSV.

`A Year of Rest for the Land` *Six years thou shalt sow thy field. . .and gather in the fruit thereof; but in the seventh year shall be a sabbath of rest unto the land, a sabbath for the LORD: thou shalt neither sow thy field, nor prune thy vineyard* (Lev. 25:3–4).

Just as the seventh day of the week, the Sabbath, was a day of rest and worship for God's people, they were to give their land a rest every seventh year. This was known as the sabbatical year. During this year no crops were to be planted. Food for the Israelites would come from meat and from the grain that grew "of its own accord" (Lev. 25:5). These spontaneous crops that grew without cultivation were also intended as provision for the poor (Exod. 23:11; Lev. 25:6).

FEBRUARY 13 | Read Leviticus 26–27

`26:1–46` God declares that His covenant with Israel is conditional. If they obey and worship Him after they possess the land, He will bless and prosper His people. But if they rebel against Him and worship other gods, He will withdraw His presence and visit them with disaster.

`27:1–34` If a person has made a voluntary vow to give himself or his property to God, he is allowed to pay a redemption price to the priest in order to "buy back" himself or the property. God establishes guidelines for determining the redemption price to be paid under various circumstances.

`Redeem` To buy back property that had been forfeited because of indebtedness or to buy back a person who had been sold into slavery (Exod. 6:6). This idea describes perfectly the work of Christ, who "bought us back" from sin and death through His atonement on the cross as our Redeemer (Matt. 20:28).

. . . .

Pagan High Places *[God] will destroy your [pagan worshipers'] high places* (Lev. 26:30).

A "high place" was generally a mountaintop or a hilltop on which pagan worshipers bowed down before images of their false gods. They believed these elevated sites would put them closer to their gods and increase their chance of being heard. God made it clear that He would judge the Israelites if they adopted the worship practices of their pagan neighbors.

FEBRUARY 14 | Read Numbers 1–2

1:1–3 God directs Moses to take a census of all able-bodied Israelite men, twenty years old and above, who are able to go to war (2 Sam. 24:2).

1:4–17 Representatives of each tribe are appointed to assist with the census.

1:18–46 Male descendants of twelve Israelite tribes—Reuben, Simeon, Gad, Judah, Issachar, Zebulun, Ephraim, Manasseh, Benjamin, Dan, Asher, and Naphtali—are counted in the census. The total number of males twenty years old and above is 603,550.

1:47–54 The Levites, descendants of the tribe of Levi, are not included in the census because they do not have a military role in the life of Israel. Their function is to take care of the tabernacle and preside over its religious ceremonies (Num. 3:5–10).

2:1–2 God specifies that the tribes of Israel are to camp at a distance all around the tabernacle.

2:3–9 The tribes of Judah, Issachar, and Zebulun will camp east of the tabernacle.

2:10–17 The tribes of Reuben, Simeon, and Gad will camp south of the tabernacle.

2:18–24 The tribes of Ephraim, Manasseh, and Benjamin will camp west of the tabernacle.

2:25–31 The tribes of Dan, Asher, and Naphtali will camp north of the tabernacle.

2:32–34 The tribal census and the camping order of the tribes around the tabernacle are summarized.

. . . .

Census A count of the population of a country or region (2 Sam. 24:1–9; Luke 2:1–3).

Tribes of Israel The tribes that descended from the sons of Jacob—Asher, Benjamin, Dan, Gad, Issachar, Judah, Levi, Naphtali, Reuben, Simeon, and Zebulon (Gen. 49:1–28)—plus the two sons of Joseph (Ephraim and Manasseh; Gen. 48:5).

After the conquest of Canaan, these tribes were assigned specific territories in the land, with the exception of Levi, the priestly tribe. The Levites were assigned to forty-eight different towns and scattered among all the other tribal territories to perform ceremonial duties.

Standards and Banners *Every man of the children of Israel shall pitch by his own standard, with the ensign [banners, NIV] of their father's house* (Num. 2:2).

God directed the twelve tribes of Israel to camp in three-tribe units on the northern, southern, eastern, and western sides of the tabernacle (Num. 2:3–31). Each of these three-tribe units had a distinct sign on a pole, known as a standard, around which they gathered to make sure they followed the camping arrangement specified by the Lord. These standards may have been similar to those used by the Egyptians as military symbols for different units of their army. Many of these Egyptian standards featured images of their pagan gods. The Bible does not say what symbols were used on the Israelite standards.

The phrase "ensign of their father's house" probably refers to a small flag or banner that was carried by each tribe or even the separate clans that made up each tribe.

FEBRUARY 15 | Read Numbers 3–4

3:1–4 Descendants of Aaron are listed (Exod. 28:41).

3:5–13 The Levites, descendants of the tribe of Levi, are set apart and consecrated for their religious duties on behalf of the other tribes of Israel.

3:14–20 God directs Moses to take a census of the tribe of Levi. All male Levites one month old and above are to be counted. Separate counts are to be made for the three divisions of Levi—Gershonites, Kohathites, and Merarites—that sprang from Levi's three sons.

3:21–26 The Gershonites, 7,500 in number, are assigned specific tabernacle duties from their position west of the tabernacle.

3:27–32 The Kohathites, 8,600 in number, are assigned specific tabernacle duties from their position south of the tabernacle.

3:33–37 The Merarites, 6,200 in number, are assigned specific tabernacle duties from their position north of the tabernacle.

3:38–39 Moses, Aaron, and Aaron's sons are to be positioned to the east and directly in front of the tabernacle for its general oversight and protection.

3:40–51 God directs Moses to take a census of all the firstborn males among the Israelites who are one month old and above. God accepts the Levites as a substitute for these firstborn, who are considered the Lord's own. But the census reveals that the number of firstborn Israelite males exceeds the number of Levites by 273. The redemption price paid by the parents of these 273 sons is to be given to Aaron and his sons, the priests.

4:1–49 God gives a more detailed description of the tabernacle duties required of the three branches of the Levites—Kohathites, Gershonites, and Merarites.

Levites Members of one of the twelve tribes of Israel who were descendants of Levi, third son of Jacob and Leah (Gen. 29:34). Moses and Aaron were Levites of the family of Kohath, Levi's son. When Canaan was divided, the Levites were assigned forty-eight towns in various tribal territories rather than a specific part of the land (Josh. 21:1–8).

Shewbread (Bread of the Presence) Unleavened bread kept in the temple or tabernacle for ceremonial purposes. Its name indicated it was exhibited in the presence of the Lord (Num. 4:7).

Duties of the Levites *Bring the tribe of Levi near, and present them before Aaron the priest, that they may minister unto him* (Num. 3:6).

Since Levi was a son of Jacob (Gen. 29:34), Levi's descendants evolved into one of the twelve tribes of Israel. It was designated as the tribe that would minister on behalf of all the other Israelites. Aaron was a member of the tribe of Levi. Aaron's direct descendants became the priests who officiated at the altar (Num. 3:2–3), offering sacrifices for the people. All the other members of the tribe of Levi were designated as Levites. Their duty was to assist the priests in these sacrificial functions.

The three separate divisions of the Levites were named for Levi's three sons: Gershon, Kohath, and Merari (Num. 3:17). During the days when the Israelites wandered in the wilderness, these three units had specific responsibilities for setting up and taking down the tabernacle, transporting it, and caring for its sacred objects and furnishings (Num. 3:23–37).

The Levites assisted the priests by slaughtering sacrificial animals, baking the showbread for the Most Holy Place in the tabernacle, and serving as doorkeepers and musicians in the tabernacle and temple.

FEBRUARY 16 | Read Numbers 5–6

5:1–4 People with an infectious skin disease and other unclean people are to be banished outside the camp (Lev. 13:45–46).

5:5–10 God makes provision for the atonement of sin through the trespass offering.

5:11–31 A woman accused of adultery is to be proven innocent or guilty through an ordeal known as the water of jealousy, or bitter water.

6:1–21 God establishes regulations and procedures to be observed by any person who vows to be especially consecrated to God as a Nazarite (Judg. 13:5).

6:22–27 God issues a benediction with which the Israelites are to be blessed by the priests.

Water of Jealousy A mixture of water with dust prescribed as a test for a woman accused of adultery by her husband (Num. 5:11–31).

Nazarite A man or woman especially consecrated to God according to the law of the Nazarites (Num. 6:2). Voluntarily or because of a devout parent's promise, a Nazarite assumed strict religious vows, including abstaining from strong drink and not cutting his hair. The vow might be for life or a fixed period. Samson (Judg. 13:4–7), Samuel (1 Sam. 1:11, 28), and John the Baptist (Luke 1:15) were Nazarites. *Nazirite*: NIV, NRSV.

FEBRUARY 17 | Read Numbers 7

7:1–89 At the dedication of the altar of the tabernacle, representatives of the twelve tribes of Israel present offerings to support the Levites and their priestly service.

FEBRUARY 18 | Read Numbers 8–10

8:1–4 The seven-branched candlestick, or menorah, is placed to illuminate the altar of the tabernacle (Exod. 40:25).

8:5–26 The Levites are purified and dedicated to serve at the tabernacle under the direction of Aaron and the priests (Num. 1:47–54).

9:1–14 The Passover is to be observed annually by the Israelites to memorialize their deliverance by the Lord from enslavement by the Egyptians.

9:15–23 God assures Israel of His presence with a cloud over the tabernacle during the daytime and a fire over the tabernacle at night (Exod. 13:21–22). The cloud signals when the people are to camp and when they are to break camp and move on.

10:1–10 Moses makes two silver trumpets to alert the people when to assemble for battle and when it is time to move the camp.

10:11–36 The twelve tribes of Israel move out in orderly fashion when the cloud tells them to leave the wilderness of Sinai and camp in the wilderness of Paran.

Trumpet A wind musical instrument made of animal horn or metal. Trumpets were used in temple ceremonies (1 Chron. 16:6).

Paran A mountainous wilderness region in the Sinai Peninsula, sometimes called *Mount Paran* (Hab. 3:3) or *El-paran* (Gen. 14:6). The Israelites camped here during their years in the wilderness (Num. 10:12; 12:16).

FEBRUARY 19 | Read Numbers 11–12

11:1–35 The Israelites complain about Moses' leadership and the food they are forced to eat. God sustains them with manna and quail meat (Exod. 16:12–15).

12:1–16 Miriam and Aaron complain about the leadership of their brother, Moses. God punishes Miriam by striking her with leprosy, then heals her at Moses' request.

Quails Small game birds provided miraculously by the Lord as food for the Israelites in the wilderness (Exod. 16:12–13).

Full to the Nose *Ye [Israelites] shall not eat one day. . .nor twenty days; but even a whole month, until it come out at your nostrils* (Num. 11:19–20).

The Israelites complained to Moses that they had no meat to eat—only the bread substitute known as manna, which had been miraculously provided by the Lord (Exod. 16:15, 31). This complaining angered God, and He promised to send them so much meat to eat that it would make them sick. Being filled "to the nose" is a common expression for overeating still heard in many cultures today. The Lord kept His promise by sending "quails from the sea" (Num. 11:31) to provide meat for the people, accompanied by a plague to punish the complainers.

FEBRUARY 20 | Read Numbers 13–14

13:1–16 Moses selects one representative from each of the twelve tribes of Israel to go into Canaan on a spying and exploration mission.

13:17–33 The scouts explore Canaan and return with good news and bad news: The land is fertile and productive, but it is inhabited and well defended by several strong tribal groups.

14:1–4 The Israelites moan over this bad news, rebel against God, and declare that they should have stayed in Egypt (Deut. 17:16).

14:5–10 Joshua and Caleb, two of the twelve spies, encourage the people to remain faithful to God. They declare that the Israelites can take the land if they follow His guidance.

14:11–19 God declares that He will wipe out the Israelites because of their lack of faith. Moses pleads for God to show them mercy.

14:20–35 God responds by sentencing the Israelites to forty years of wandering in the wilderness before they will be allowed to enter the Promised Land. During this time the older generation of rebellious Israelites will die in the wilderness.

14:36–45 Some of the Israelites attack the residents of Canaan, but they are turned back in defeat.

Canaan The region between the Red Sea and the Jordan River where Canaan's descendants settled and the territory that God promised to Abraham and his descendants (Gen. 15:3–7). *Chanaan*: Greek form (Acts 7:11).

Joshua Moses' successor who led the Israelites into the Promised Land and rallied the people to victory over the Canaanites. One of two spies who gave Moses a favorable report on Canaan (Num. 13:8), he was the Lord's choice as Moses' successor (Num. 27:18–20). After his conquest of Canaan (Josh. 10–12), Joshua divided the land among the twelve tribes (Josh. 13–19). Before his death, he led the people to renew their covenant with God (Josh. 24:15–27). *Oshea*: Num. 13:8; *Hoshea*: Deut. 32:44; *Jehoshuah*: 1 Chron. 7:27; *Jeshua*: Neh. 8:17.

Caleb One of the twelve spies who scouted Canaan. Along with Joshua, he recommended that Israel attack the Canaanites immediately (Num. 13:30). He lived to enter the land forty years later (Josh. 14:6–14).

Wilderness Wanderings The aimless course taken by the Hebrew people in the Sinai Peninsula for forty years after they left Egypt—God's punishment for their sin of disobedience (Deut. 1:1; Josh. 5:6). God provided food and guidance through Moses until they arrived in Canaan (Exod. 16:35; Neh. 9:24).

FEBRUARY 21 | Read Numbers 15–16

15:1–31 God establishes regulations and procedures for the various offerings to be presented by the Israelites after they enter the Promised Land (Lev. 1:1–7:38).

15:32–36 A man is stoned to death for desecrating the Sabbath by doing work on this sacred day (Exod. 20:8–11).

15:37–41 God directs the Israelites to put tassels on their clothes to remind them to obey His commandments (Deut. 22:12).

16:1–40 God destroys Korah and a group of his followers, including Dathan and Abiram, because they rebelled against the leadership of Moses and Aaron.

16:41–50 God threatens to destroy all the Israelites by sending a plague upon them because they sympathized with Korah. But Aaron turns back the plague by burning incense among the people to atone for their sin.

Land of Promise Canaan, or the land inhabited by the Israelites. This land was promised by God to Abraham's descendants (Gen. 12:1–7). The promise was fulfilled centuries later when Joshua led the Israelites to take the land from the Canaanltes (Josh. 10–12).

Korah A grandson of Kohath who incited a rebellion against Moses and Aaron in the wilderness. Korah and his followers were swallowed by the earth as punishment for their sin (Num. 16:28–33). *Core*: Greek form (Jude 11).

FEBRUARY 22 | Read Numbers 17–19

17:1–13 God causes Aaron's rod to bloom and produce almonds to demonstrate Aaron's spiritual authority over all the tribes of Israel (Heb. 9:4).

18:1–19 Through the offerings of the people, God provides for the material needs of Aaron and his sons and the priests who will come after them.

18:20–32 Through the tithes of the people, God provides for the material needs of the Levites (Deut. 18:1–8).

19:1–22 Moses and Aaron are instructed to use the ashes of a red heifer to make a solution called the water of separation. People who have been made ritually unclean are to be cleansed when sprinkled by a priest with this special solution.

Water of Separation Water mixed with ashes to purify a person after defilement through contact with the dead (Num. 19:13–22). *Water of cleansing*: NIV.

Aaron's Priesthood Confirmed *On the morrow Moses went into the tabernacle of witness; and behold, the rod of Aaron for the house of Levi was budded* (Num. 17:8).

Some Israelites questioned Aaron's right to serve as priest and for his descendants to continue his priestly work among the nation (Num. 16:1–3). So Moses conducted a test to determine who should serve in this leadership position. Moses placed twelve staffs or sticks, representing the twelve tribes of Israel, in the tabernacle overnight. The next morning Aaron's staff had budded and produced almonds. This was undeniable proof that Aaron of the tribe of Levi and his descendants had been selected by the Lord for this ministry.

FEBRUARY 23 | Read Numbers 20–21

20:1–13 In anger, Moses strikes a rock at Meribah to produce water for the Israelites. God punishes him and Aaron for disobeying His directions, refusing to let them enter the Promised Land (Num. 27:12–14).

20:14–22 The king of Edom refuses to allow the Israelites to pass through his territory (Deut. 2:8).

20:23–29 Aaron dies on Mount Hor.

21:1–9 God punishes the Israelites for their rebellion by sending poisonous snakes to bite them. Then God delivers the people by means of a brass serpent on a pole erected by Moses (John 12:32).

21:10–20 Several camping sites of the Israelites are listed.

21:21–32 The Israelites defeat Sihon, king of the Amorites.

21:33–35 The Israelites defeat Og, king of Bashan.

. . . .

Massah and Meribah A site in the wilderness where the Israelites rebelled against Moses and Aaron (Exod. 17:4–7). Their complaints provoked the wrath of the Lord (Deut. 6:16).

Edom The land where the descendants of Esau settled. It was in extreme southern Palestine in the barren territory below the Dead Sea. Mount Seir was located in this territory (Gen. 36:8). Edom was referred to by the Greeks and Romans as *Idumaea* (Mark 3:8).

King's Highway An important road linking Damascus and Egypt that ran through Israel. While in the wilderness, the Israelites were denied passage on this road as they traveled toward Canaan (Num. 20:17–21).

. . . .

Eleazar Succeeds Aaron *Moses stripped Aaron of his garments, and put them upon Eleazar his son; and Aaron died there in the top of the mount* (Num. 20:28).

At Aaron's death the special clothes that he wore as high priest of Israel (Exod. 40:13) were transferred to his son Eleazar. This showed that Eleazar was the legitimate successor to his father in this role. Eleazar served as high priest for the rest of Moses' life and also for a time after Joshua succeeded Moses as leader of the Israelites. Eleazar assisted in the division of the land of Canaan among the twelve tribes (Josh. 14:1).

FEBRUARY 24 | Read Numbers 22–24

22:1–21 Balak, king of Moab, sends messengers to hire Balaam the soothsayer to curse the Israelites.

22:22–35 On his way to meet Balak, Balaam encounters the angel of the Lord, who gets Balaam's attention through his stubborn donkey. The angel tells Balaam to meet Balak but to speak only the words that God will direct him to speak.

22:36–41 Balaam meets Balak and prepares to curse the Israelites.

`23:1–24:25` On three separate attempts, Balaam fails to curse the Israelites, blessing them instead.

`Moab` The country of the Moabites, lying east of the Jordan River and the Dead Sea and south of the Arnon River (Deut. 1:5–7). Its earliest name was *Lotan* or *Lot,* since the inhabitants were descended from Lot (Gen. 19:37).

`Balaam` A soothsayer or magician hired by the king of Moab to curse the Israelites to drive them out of his territory. Prevented from doing so by an angel, Balaam blessed the Israelites instead (Num. 22–24).

`Baal Worship` *Balak took Balaam, and brought him up into the high places of Baal* (Num. 22:41).

King Balak of Moab enlisted a wizard named Baalam to pronounce a curse against the Israelites. Balak and Baalam went up into the "high places" devoted to worship of the pagan god Baal to get a panoramic view of the Israelites as they camped in the valley below. Baal was a major pagan god of the Canaanites that was thought to provide fertility for crops and livestock. Stone carvings discovered by archaeologists show Baal holding a bolt of lightning. This probably shows that he was thought to bring the rain, which caused crops to grow. Baal is also shown in other carvings as a mating bull—another fertility symbol.

After settling in Canaan, some of the Israelites were influenced by their pagan neighbors to worship this false god. During the days of King Ahab of Israel, one of his wives, Jezebel, actually promoted Baal worship throughout the land. With King Ahab looking on, the prophet Elijah won a decisive victory over the prophets of Baal in a dramatic contest on Mount Carmel (1 Kings 18).

FEBRUARY 25 | Read Numbers 25–27

`25:1–18` Some of the Israelites commit idolatry because of the temptations of Moabite women.

`26:1–56` All able-bodied Israelite males twenty years old and above are counted again at the end of the forty years of wandering in the wilderness. This census is to be used as the basis for assigning land to the tribes after they conquer the territory of the Canaanites (Num. 1:1–3).

`26:57–65` A separate count is made of the tribe of Levi, or the Levites.

`27:1–11` The five daughters of Zelophehad are allowed to inherit his property, since he died with no male heirs; principles of inheritance are established.

`27:12–14` God reminds Moses that he will not be allowed to enter the Promised Land with the other Israelites (Num. 20:1–13).

`27:15–23` Joshua is selected by the Lord as Moses' successor (Deut. 34:9).

Zelophehad A member of the tribe of Manasseh whose five daughters petitioned for the right to inherit his property because he had no sons. Their request was granted on the condition that they not marry outside the tribe (Num. 26:33; 27:1–8).

Inheritance A gift of property or rights passed from one generation to another. In ancient Israel, a father's possessions were passed on to his living sons, with the oldest receiving a double portion (Deut. 21:17). Reuben lost his inheritance because he committed incest with Bilhah (Gen. 35:22; 49:4). Esau traded his birthright as the oldest son to his brother, Jacob, for a bowl of stew (Gen. 25:29–34).

Christians enjoy a spiritual birthright (Eph. 1:13–14). All the redeemed, including Gentiles, become God's adopted children with full inheritance rights (Gal. 4:5–7).

FEBRUARY 26 | Read Numbers 28–30

28:1–29:40 Regulations and procedures for various types of offerings are prescribed by the Lord.

30:1–16 Vows made to the Lord are a serious matter, but people may be excused from their vows in special circumstances (Gen. 28:20–22).

Vow A pledge or agreement to perform a service for God in return for some expected benefit (Gen. 28:20–22).

Oath A solemn promise, often used to appeal to God to attest that a statement was true or to affirm a covenant (2 Sam. 21:7). The taking of an oath was accompanied by raising the hand or placing the hand under the thigh (Gen. 24:2–3). Jesus warned against careless oaths (Matt. 5:34–36).

FEBRUARY 27 | Read Numbers 31–32

31:1–54 Israel defeats the Midianites, and all the people share in the spoils of war.

32:1–42 Moses allows the tribes of Reuben and Gad and half the tribe of Manasseh to settle on the fertile pasturelands east of the Jordan River across from Canaan (Josh. 12:1–6). In return, these three tribes promise to help the other tribes in their campaign against the Canaanites.

Midianites Nomadic traders who occupied the land of Midian. A band of Midianites probably bought Joseph and sold him as a slave in Egypt (Gen. 37:28). This tribe joined the Moabites in attacking Israel but failed (Num. 22). The Midianites were probably absorbed into the Moabites and the Arabs.

Reuben The oldest son of Jacob and Leah and founder of one of the twelve tribes of Israel (Gen. 29:32). He lost his birthright by committing adultery with his father's concubines (Gen. 35:22; 49:3–4). Reuben likely saved Joseph's life when his brothers proposed to kill him (Gen. 37:21–22). The tribe of Reuben settled east of the Jordan River, along with Gad and Manasseh (Num. 32:1–25).

Gad The seventh son of Jacob, born of Zilpah (Gen. 30:10–11), and ancestor of one of the twelve tribes of Israel. Known as a fierce, warlike people, the Gadites settled east of the Jordan River (Josh. 13:24–28).

Jordan River The largest and most important river in Palestine. It runs the length of the country, from the Sea of Galilee in the north to the Dead Sea in the south. Jesus was baptized by John in the Jordan (Matt. 3:13).

FEBRUARY 28 | Read Numbers 33–34

33:1–49 The places where the Israelites camped in the wilderness for forty years after they left Egypt are listed.

33:50–56 God repeats His promise to give the land of Canaan to the Israelites. He urges them to drive out all the pagan Canaanites, lest they become a stumbling block to His people.

34:1–15 God establishes the boundaries of the territory in which the Israelite tribes will settle.

34:16–29 Tribal representatives are selected to serve with Joshua and Eleazar the priest to divide the land among the various tribes.

....

Stumblingblock A hindrance to belief or understanding. Israel's iniquity and idolatry were a stumblingblock (Jer. 6:21; 18:15). Paul urged Christians not to offend or serve as a hindrance to a weak brother (Rom. 14:13; 1 Cor. 8:9). The preaching of "Christ crucified" was a stumblingblock to the Jews (1 Cor. 1:23).

Dead Sea A body of water (about fifty miles long by ten miles wide) into which the Jordan River empties at the lowest point on earth in southern Palestine. Because of the hot, dry climate, the water evaporates, leaving a high concentration of salt and other minerals. *Salt sea*: Josh. 3:16; *East sea*: Joel 2:20.

Mediterranean Sea The sea on Israel's western border that was also called the *Great Sea* (Josh. 9:1). Solomon used the Phoenicians to provide import/export services for Israel across this body of water (1 Kings 9:27). Paul often sailed the Mediterranean during his missionary journeys (Acts 9:30; 18:18; Acts 27).

MARCH 1 | Read Numbers 35–36

35:1–34 The tribe of Levi will not receive a specific land inheritance like the other tribes because of their religious function. Rather, Levites are to live among all the other tribes in forty-eight designated cities. Six of these cities are to be known as cities of refuge—places to which a person can go after killing another person to keep from being killed by an avenging relative. In these refuge cities, guilt or innocence of the person accused of murder will be determined through due process (Deut. 19:1–13).

36:1–13 Once the land is divided among the tribes, each tribal allotment is to remain intact. The daughters of Zelophehad (Num. 27:1–11) are to marry within their tribe to ensure that the land they inherited from their father does not pass to another tribe.

Cities of Refuge These cities, scattered throughout Palestine, were Bezer, Golan, Hebron, Kedesh, Ramoth-gilead, and Shechem (Josh. 20:7–9).

MARCH 2 | Read Deuteronomy 1–2

1:1–18 Moses recalls the experiences of the Israelites after they first came out of Egypt, including his appointment of officials to help him lead the people (Exod. 18:1–27).

1:19–46 Moses reminds the people of their rebellion and refusal to enter Canaan after spies were sent to investigate the land (Num. 13:17–33).

2:1–23 Moses recounts the marching orders given the Israelites by the Lord after their forty years of wandering in the wilderness came to an end.

2:24–37 Moses recalls the victory of the Israelites over King Sihon of Heshbon (Num. 21:21–32).

Kadesh A wilderness region between Canaan and Egypt that served as the southern boundary of the Promised Land (Num. 34:4). The Israelites camped in this area during the wilderness wandering years before they entered the Promised Land (Num. 32:8; 27:14). *Kadesh-barnea*: Josh. 14:7.

Anakims A tribe of giants, descended from Anak, who inhabited Canaan and were greatly feared in Joshua's time (Num. 13:28, 33; Deut. 9:2). The term may also refer to prominent people, or men of renown. Joshua divided their forces and captured their major walled city, Hebron, or Kirjath-arba (Josh. 14:12–15). The remnants of the Anakim may have been absorbed into the Philistine people. *Anakim*: NRSV; *Anakites*: NIV.

Camping Grounds *The Avims which dwelt in Hazerim* (Deut. 2:23).

This verse is part of an extended review by Moses of the different tribes and ethnic groups encountered by the Israelites during their years of wandering in the wilderness. The Hebrew word *Hazerim* is not the name of a specific place. In this context it should be translated as "camping grounds." The Avims were probably a nomadic people who moved from place to place with their grazing livestock.

MARCH 3 | Read Deuteronomy 3–4

3:1–22 Moses reminisces about the victory of the Israelites over King Og of Bashan and the settlement of the tribes of Reuben, Gad, and one-half of the tribe of Manasseh in Og's territory (Num. 21:33–35; 32:1–42).

3:23–29 Moses reminds the people of God's decision that he—Moses—would not be allowed to enter the Promised Land (Num. 20:1–13).

4:1–49 Moses challenges the Israelites to remain faithful to the covenant that God established with His people and to follow the teachings of the law that God handed down through Moses at Mount Sinai.

- -

Bedstead or Coffin? *Only Og king of Bashan remained of the remnant of giants; behold, his bedstead was a bedstead of iron. . . . Nine cubits [thirteen feet, NIV] was the length thereof, and four cubits [six feet, NIV] the breadth of it* (Deut. 3:11).

King Og was apparently the last of a giant race that once occupied the territory of Bashan. This description of his iron bed leaves no doubt that he was a person of superhuman size. Some interpreters believe the Hebrew word behind "bedstead" (literally, "resting place") should be translated as "coffin" or "sarcophagus." Thus, Og may have been laid to rest in a huge coffin that reflected his large size as well as his position as the king.

Worship of the Sun, Moon, and Stars *Lest thou lift up thine eyes unto heaven, and when thou seest the sun, and the moon, and the stars, even all the host of heaven [all the heavenly array, NIV], shouldest be driven [enticed, NIV] to worship them, and serve them* (Deut. 4:19).

Worship of the sun and other heavenly bodies was common among the pagan nations of the ancient world. For example, the city of Ur in Mesopotamia from which Abraham migrated was a center of moon worship. The Egyptians worshiped the sun god known as Ra. The Lord, speaking through Moses, specifically prohibited this form of idolatry. Worship of the heavenly bodies is also referred to in Deut. 17:3; 2 Kings 17:16; 21:3; 23:5; and Jer. 8:2.

The title "the LORD of hosts" applied to God throughout the OT (Psalm 24:10; Isaiah 19:16) is actually a declaration that He is superior to all of the heavenly bodies, since He brought them into being (Genesis 2:1).

MARCH 4 | Read Deuteronomy 5–7

5:1–22 Moses restates the Ten Commandments, which God delivered to him at Mount Sinai (Exod. 20:1–17).

5:23–33 Moses reminds the people that the awesome, unapproachable God of the universe has chosen to reveal Himself to the nation of Israel.

6:1–25 Moses reminds the people of their responsibility to teach the laws and commandments of God to their children.

7:1–26 God promises to give the Israelites victory over the pagan peoples who inhabit Canaan and bring prosperity to His people when they are settled in the land.

Law (Law of Moses) The authoritative rule of conduct spelled out in the Ten Commandments and the Pentateuch—the books of Genesis, Exodus, Leviticus, Numbers, and Deuteronomy. This code was revealed to Moses by the Lord on Mount Sinai (Deut. 5:1–2). While many of the regulations are ceremonial or procedural in nature, the moral law embodied in the Law of Moses is eternal and unchangeable (Rom. 7:7–12). It was fulfilled by the Gospel and confirmed by Christ (Matt. 5:17–18).

Shema, The The noted confession of faith quoted by faithful Jews each day: "Hear, O Israel: The LORD our God is one LORD" (Deut. 6:4–9). The complete Shema also includes Num. 15:37–41 and Deut. 11:13–21.

Abomination Something considered repulsive by the Hebrews. Examples of these despised practices are heathen idolatry (Deut. 7:25–26), blemished animal sacrifices (Deut. 17:1), sexual transgressions (Lev. 18), child sacrifice (Deut. 12:31), and the practice of witchcraft, magic, and spiritism (Deut. 18:9–12).

Writing on the Door *Thou [Israelites] shalt write them upon the posts [doorframes, NIV] of thy house, and on thy gates* (Deut. 6:9).

The Israelites were commanded by the Lord to write passages from His law on the doorframes of their houses after they settled permanently in the land of Canaan. Every time they entered or left their dwellings, they would be reminded of God's Word and their promise to obey His commands.

MARCH 5 | Read Deuteronomy 8–11

8:1–20 The Lord warns the people of the perils of prosperity. They must not forget Him after they have become comfortable and affluent in the land He is giving them.

9:1–29 Moses warns the people not to become overconfident after they settle in Canaan. They are capable of ignoring and rejecting God and turning to false gods, just as they did at Mount Sinai and during their years of wandering in the wilderness.

10:1–5 Moses recalls how God wrote the Ten Commandments a second time on two tablets of stone, which Moses placed in the ark of the covenant (Exod. 34:1).

10:6–22 Moses reminds the Israelites of the awesome God whom they serve and the signs and wonders He has performed on behalf of His people.

11:1–32 God places two choices before the Israelites. If they remain faithful to Him, He will bless them. But if they turn to false gods, He will curse them (Josh. 24:1–15).

Anak The son of Arba and ancestor of a tribe of giants (Deut. 9:2), or men of renown.

Irrigation of Egyptian Crops *The land, whither thou [Israelites] goest in to possess it, is not as the land of Egypt, from whence ye came out, where thou sowedst thy seed, and wateredst it with thy foot* (Deut. 11:10).
This verse contrasts the land of Egypt, where the Israelites had been enslaved, with the land of Canaan, which God had promised to His people. Egyptian crops grew in the fertile flood plain along the Nile River. But Canaan was a land of hills and valleys. Here the crops of the Israelites would flourish from the "waters of the rain of heaven" (Deut. 11:11). Watering crops "with thy foot" in Egypt probably refers to the small waterwheels that were turned by foot to pump water from the Nile River into irrigation canals. This artificial watering system was essential for crop production in Egypt's hot, dry climate.

MARCH 6 | Read Deuteronomy 12–14

12:1–32 After the Israelites settle in the land, God promises to give the nation a central place of worship, where they will present various offerings and sacrifices.

13:1–18 A false prophet or any other Israelite who causes people to worship pagan gods is to be put to death.

14:1–21 The Lord reminds the Israelites of the animals that may be eaten and those that are prohibited as food (Lev. 11).

14:22–29 A tithe, or one-tenth of one's crops or livestock, is to be presented as an offering to the Lord (Num. 18:20–32).

Tithe One-tenth of a person's income presented as an offering to God. Abraham paid tithes to Melchizedek (Gen. 14:18–20), and Jacob vowed to give tithes in accordance with God's blessings (Gen. 28:20–22). In NT times, the Pharisees were scrupulous tithers (Matt. 23:23). Jesus encouraged generosity and promised to bless sacrificial giving (Luke 6:38). Paul endorsed the principle of proportionate giving (1 Cor. 16:2).

Eating Blood Forbidden *Be sure that thou [Israelites] eat not the blood: for the blood is the life; and thou mayest not eat the life with the flesh. Thou shalt not eat it; thou shalt pour it upon the earth as water* (Deut. 12:23–24).

These verses occur in the context of presenting a sacrificial animal as an offering to the Lord. The Israelites believed the blood of such an animal was sacred, since it carried the very essence of life itself. In a sense, the blood was the ransom price that atoned for their sins. It was to be drained from the animal and poured on the ground at the base of the altar. The meat from some sacrificial animals could be eaten by the priests (Lev. 6:19–30). But the blood of such animals was considered sacred and was never to be eaten.

Perhaps another reason for this prohibition against eating blood is that this was practiced in some pagan religious systems. Pagan priests would drink the blood of sacrificial animals to symbolize their devotion to the false gods they worshiped. God made it clear that His people were to avoid such pagan customs.

MARCH 7 | Read Deuteronomy 15–17

15:1–18 God establishes guidelines for fair and just treatment of the poor.

15:19–23 Firstborn animals from herds of livestock are to be presented as offerings to God.

16:1–17 God reminds the people of the regulations for observing three major festivals or religious holidays: Passover and Feast of Unleavened Bread (vv. 1–8), Feast of Weeks (vv. 9–12), and Feast of Tabernacles (vv. 13–15) (Lev. 23).

16:18–20 Judges are expected to be fair and just in their decisions.

16:21–22 The making of idols or images of false gods is prohibited (Exod. 20:3–4).

17:1–7 A person found guilty of idolatry—on the testimony of at least two witnesses—is to be put to death.

17:8–13 A sentence handed down by judges and priests through due process is considered a binding judgment. Refusal to abide by the verdict will result in the death penalty.

17:14–20 If a king is ever appointed to rule over Israel, he must not trust in military might or marry many wives. He is expected to rule with justice and to fear God and obey His commandments.

Alms Voluntary gifts to the needy. The Israelites were commanded to be generous to the poor (Deut. 15:11; Luke 12:33). Jesus cautioned His disciples not to give alms for show or the praise of others (Matt. 6:2–4).

Solemn Assembly A religious gathering, usually occurring during a major Jewish festival, that was devoted to repentance, confession, and prayer (Lev. 23:36; Deut. 16:8).

No Trees around Altars *Thou [Israelites] shalt not plant thee a grove of any trees near unto the altar of the Lord thy God* (Deut. 16:21).

Shrines devoted to worship of false gods were surrounded by thick groves of trees, perhaps to hide the immoral acts that occurred around these altars. The Lord prohibited the planting of trees around His altars to avoid any hint of idol worship among His people.

MARCH 8 | Read Deuteronomy 18–20

18:1–8 Since the Levites will not receive an inheritance of land in Canaan, they are to be supported by tithes and offerings from the people (Num. 18:20–32).

18:9–14 All forms of "black magic"—witchcraft, fortune-telling, and communing with the dead—are prohibited for God's people.

18:15–22 God promises to send prophets—particularly a special Prophet after the pattern of Moses—to declare His will to His people. True prophets are those whose predictions come true.

19:1–13 God repeats His instructions that cities of refuge are to be established throughout the land after the Israelites have settled in Canaan. These cities are to serve as safe harbors for innocent people who are accused of murder (Num. 35).

19:14–21 Bearing false witness is a serious matter. Any person who wrongly accuses another of a crime is to bear the penalty the innocent person would have received if convicted (Exod. 20:16).

20:1–8 Any man who has just built a house, planted a new vineyard, or married a wife may be excused from military duty (Luke 14:16–20).

20:9–20 Israelite armies are expected to observe specific "rules of war" when engaging their enemies in battle.

No Black Magic *There shall not be found among you [Israelites] any one. . .that useth [practices, NIV] divination, or an observer of times, or an enchanter, or a witch, or a charmer, or a consulter with familiar spirits, or a wizard, or a necromancer* (Deut. 18:10–11).

The term *divination*, as used in this passage, refers to attempts to control evil spirits, to penetrate the mysteries of the universe, or to foretell the future by using magical acts, pronouncing superstitious incantations, or interpreting natural signs. Today we refer to such practices as the occult. "Black magic" was a prominent feature of pagan religious systems in Bible times. But God prohibited the Israelites from participating in these practices. Seven different types of divination are mentioned in this passage.

Observer of times. The Hebrew word behind "observer of times" is translated by the New International Version as one who practices "sorcery." They often made their predictions by "reading" the clouds in the sky. The practitioners of this art specialized in distinguishing lucky days from unlucky days and recommending to people the best times to plant crops, make a purchase, take a trip, and so on.

Enchanter. The New International Version translates the Hebrew word behind "enchanter" as one who "interprets omens." This person predicted the future or told people's fortunes by reading certain signs. One way of doing this was to use a magic cup. The cup of Joseph was referred to as a "divining cup." Another method was to interpret the pattern formed by birds in flight. The art of enchantment is referred to several times in the OT (Lev. 19:26; Num. 23:23; 24:1; 2 Kings 17:17; 21:6; 2 Chron. 33:6).

Witch. A witch was a person who cast spells or used other supernatural "black magic" tricks to commit evil or wicked acts. The Hebrew word for "witch" or "witchcraft" is used to describe Jezebel and her associates who promoted the worship of the false god Baal throughout the Northern Kingdom during the reign of King Ahab (2 Kings 9:22).

Charmer. The Hebrew word behind "charmer" is translated as one who "casts spells" by the New International Version. It is not clear how a charmer differed from a witch. Some interpreters believe charmers practiced their craft by tying magic knots or using a magic ring.

Consulter with familiar spirits. Consulters with familiar spirits claimed to be able to call up the spirits or ghosts of dead people. They did this at the request of friends or loved ones who sought advice or guidance from the deceased. King Saul sought out "a woman that hath a familiar spirit" (1 Samuel 28:7) when he wanted to communicate with the prophet Samuel, who had died. This woman was shocked when the spirit of Samuel actually appeared and gave the king some bad news about his forthcoming battle with the Philistines (1 Samuel 28:11–19). Her surprise indicates that these consulters with familiar spirits probably used trickery—perhaps ventriloquism—to convince people that they were talking with their departed friends and loved ones.

Wizard. The Hebrew word behind "wizard" means "the knowing one." Thus, a wizard may have been an expert in all of the magical tricks associated with sorcery and divination.

Necromancer. The New International Version translates the Hebrew word behind "necromancer" as one who "consults the dead." This practitioner of the occult apparently claimed to be able to conjure up the spirits of the dead, just like a consulter with familiar spirits. In addition, necromancers may have used corpses to foretell the future. Some interpreters believe they "read" dead people's bones or veins to determine the future of the survivors of the deceased.

Boundary Stones *Thou [Israelites] shalt not remove thy neighbour's landmark [boundary stone, NIV], which they of old time have set in thine inheritance* (Deut. 19:14).

After the Israelites settled in Canaan and received their land allotments, they marked their property by placing small stones around the edges of their plots. Unlike permanent fences, these stones could be moved easily. A dishonest person on an adjoining plot could move these markers and encroach on his neighbor's property. The Lord specifically prohibited this practice because it was a form of stealing (Exod. 20:15). Moving boundary stones is also forbidden in Proverbs 22:28; 23:10.

MARCH 9 | Read Deuteronomy 21–23

21:1–9 The elders of a city are given a hand-washing ritual by which they can proclaim their innocence when the body of a person is found near their city.

21:10–14 An Israelite man may marry a woman who is captured from their enemies in times of war, but specific guidelines are prescribed by the Lord for such a marriage.

21:15–17 If a man is married to more than one wife, he cannot play favorites by transferring inheritance rights from his firstborn son to a son born later to a favorite wife. The father's true firstborn son should receive a double portion when his property is divided at his death.

21:18–21 A son who is stubborn and rebellious toward his parents may be stoned to death if they bring charges against him before the elders of the city.

21:22–23 To avoid defiling the land, a person executed by hanging must be taken down and buried before nightfall.

22:1–23:25 The Lord issues regulations for the conduct of Israelites in various situations: the provision of a protective railing on the roof of a house, the treatment of borrowed property, physical disabilities that prevent a person from entering the sanctuary, the restoration of an unclean person to cleanliness, the lending of money, and fair and just treatment of the poor (Exod. 21–23).

Fringe An ornament worn on the edges of one's robe as a profession of piety and commitment to God (Deut. 22:12). *Tassel*: NIV, NRSV.

Debt Borrowed property or money that must be repaid. The Hebrews were encouraged not to charge interest to their own countrymen (Lev. 25:35–38), but foreigners could be charged (Deut. 23:20).

Justice at the City Gate *Then shall his father and his mother lay hold on him [a rebellious son], and bring him out unto the elders of his city, and unto the gate of his place [town, NIV]* (Deut. 21:19).

The gates of ancient walled cities were places where people gathered to conduct business and catch up on the latest news. The elders or rulers of the city also held court at this location, rendering judgments in cases brought before them by the people. This verse specifies that parents with a rebellious son could bring charges against him before the elders at the city gate. A son who was found guilty of consistent disobedience, gluttony, and drunkenness could actually have the death penalty pronounced against him (Deut. 21:20–21).

Guardrails on the Roof *When thou [Israelites] buildest a new house, then thou shalt make a battlement [parapet, NIV] for thy roof, that thou bring not blood upon thine house, if any man fall from thence* (Deut. 22:8).

This verse is something of an ancient "building code." A house was to be built with a guardrail around the edge of the roof to protect people from accidental falls. In Bible times the roofs of houses were flat. A stairway on the outside of the house allowed the residents to use the roof much like a patio or deck is used today. Particularly at night, the roof was a good place to relax and catch a cooling breeze. Sometimes a family would even sleep on the roof to escape the oppressive heat (2 Sam. 11:2). Perhaps the most famous "rooftop incident" in the Bible was King David's chance encounter with Bathsheba. The king was tempted to commit adultery with her when he looked down from the roof of his palace and saw her taking a bath (2 Sam. 11:2).

MARCH 10 | Read Deuteronomy 24–26

25:5–10 If an Israelite man should die without children, his brother is encouraged to marry his widow to produce children so the dead man's family name will continue. A brother who dodges this responsibility will be ridiculed and humiliated by the elders of the city.

25:11–19 Israelites are charged to be honest in all their business dealings, not using one pair of scales for buying and another for selling (Lev. 19:35–36).

26:1–19 The people are to present the firstfruits of their harvest as a special offering to God (Exod. 23:19).

. . . .

Divorce A breaking of the ties of marriage. The divine ideal is for permanence in marriage (Matt. 19:3–6), and divorce violates the oneness that God intended (Gen. 2:24). Under the Mosaic Law, divorce was permitted in certain situations (Deut. 24:1–4), but this provision was greatly abused (Matt. 19:8). Christ regarded adultery as the only permissible reason for divorce (Matt. 5:31–32; 19:9; Mark 10:11; Luke 16:18), and He reprimanded the Jews for their insensitive divorce practices (Matt. 19:3–9). Unfaithfulness to God was regarded as spiritual adultery (Hosea 2:2).

. . . .

Threshing by Oxen *Thou [Israelites] shalt not muzzle the ox when he treadeth out the corn [grain, NIV]* (Deut. 25:4).

The heads of grain such as wheat and barley were sometimes separated from the stalks by driving an ox or a team of oxen back and forth over the stalks on a flat surface. An unmuzzled ox would be able to eat some of the grain while it worked, thus renewing its strength. The apostle Paul cited this verse to show that churches have a responsibility to contribute to the financial support of their ministers (1 Corinthians 9:9–14).

Marriage of a Brother's Wife *If brethren dwell together, and one of them die, and have no child, the wife of the dead shall not marry without [outside the family, NIV] unto a stranger: her husband's brother shall go in unto her, and take her to him to wife, and perform [fulfill, NIV] the duty of an husband's brother unto her* (Deut. 25:5).

The custom described in this verse is known as the law of levirate marriage. If a man died and he and his wife had no children, his brother was expected to take his widow as his wife. This would keep the deceased man's property in the family and possibly produce sons who would carry on his family name (Deut. 25:6). This custom was not binding in an absolute sense on a dead man's brother. But if he refused to marry his brother's widow, he was branded by having one of his sandals removed (Deut. 25:9–10). This signaled to others that he had failed to assume his family responsibilities.

MARCH 11 | Read Deuteronomy 27–28

27:1–10 Moses instructs the people to build an altar of stones after they cross the Jordan River to enter the Promised Land (Josh. 4:1–9). On this altar, sacrifices of thanksgiving are to be offered to God.

27:11–26 The Levites are instructed to issue a series of warnings to the Israelites after they enter the Promised Land. These warnings will remind the people to obey God's commands.

28:1–68 If God's people obey Him, they will live long and prosper in their new land. But if they turn away from Him and worship other gods, they will be afflicted with pain and disaster.

Ebal A rocky mountain in Samaria, or the territory of Ephraim, where Joshua built an altar after destroying the city of Ai (Josh. 8:30).

Emerods A strange disease, exact nature unknown, that struck the Philistines when they placed the stolen ark of the covenant next to their false god Dagon (Deut. 28:27). *Tumors*: NIV; *ulcers*: NRSV.

MARCH 12 | Read Deuteronomy 29–31

29:1–30:13 Moses calls upon the Israelites to be brave and courageous, since the time for them to do battle with the Canaanites is drawing near. He charges them to be diligent in obedience to God's laws.

31:14–30 Moses recalls how the Lord directed him to write a song for the Israelites to remind them to remain loyal to the powerful God who brought them out of slavery and sustained them in the wilderness.

Wormwood A plant noted for its bitter taste (Jer. 9:15). The phrase "gall and wormwood" describes something offensive or sorrowful (Deut. 29:18).

Cities of the Plain Five cities on the plain of Jordan destroyed in Abraham's time because of the great sin of their inhabitants. These cities were Admah, Bela or Zoar, Gomorrah, Sodom, and Zeboiim (Gen. 14:1–2).

Book of the Law A term for the Law of Moses or the Pentateuch, the first five books of the OT. After receiving and recording these instructions from God, Moses delivered the law to the priests for public reading (Deut. 31:9–11). In later years, the Book of the Law became the basis for King Josiah's religious reforms (2 Kings 23:1–25).

MARCH 13 | Read Deuteronomy 32–34

32:1–47 Moses reminisces about how he delivered a song he wrote to the people of Israel. He praised the Lord for His faithfulness and graciousness to His chosen people, in spite of their rebellion and worship of false gods (Exod. 15:1–22).

32:48–52 God commands Moses to climb to the top of Mount Nebo, the highest peak in the Abarim Mountains, and look across the Jordan River to view the land He has promised to Israel.

33:1–29 Moses blesses the people of Israel tribe by tribe, just as Jacob had spoken hundreds of years before to each of his sons (Gen. 49). The descendants of Jacob's sons have grown into the twelve tribes of Israel.

34:1–12 Moses dies in Moab after viewing the Promised Land and is succeeded by Joshua.

Nebo The highest point of Mount Pisgah in Moab near Jericho where Moses died after viewing the Promised Land and where he was buried (Deut. 32:49; 34:5–6).

BOOKS OF HISTORY

The second major section of the Old Testament contains twelve books classified as historical writings: Joshua, Judges, Ruth, 1 and 2 Samuel, 1 and 2 Kings, 1 and 2 Chronicles, Ezra, Nehemiah, and Esther.

These books trace the history of the nation of Israel across a period of more than 800 years—from the conquest of Canaan under Joshua about 1400 BC to their return from captivity by the Babylonians and Persians about 530 BC. In between these two pivotal events were such happenings as rule by charismatic judges after the death of Joshua, the establishment of a central kingship form of government, the glory days of the Israelites under King David and his son Solomon, the division of the nation into northern and southern factions, the destruction of the Northern Kingdom by Assyria, and the fall of the Southern Kingdom to Babylonia.

MARCH 14 | Read Joshua 1–2

1:1–10 God orders Joshua, Moses' successor, to lead the people across the Jordan River and into the land of Canaan.

1:11–18 Joshua spreads the word for the people to get ready to move out. He reminds the tribes of Reuben and Gad and one-half of the tribe of Manasseh of their promise to help the other tribes when the time comes for them to conquer the Canaanites (Num. 32).

2:1–24 Joshua sends two spies to investigate the Canaanite city of Jericho. Rahab the prostitute hides them in her house and helps them escape over the city wall. They report to Joshua that conditions are right for conquest of the land.

....

Rahab A harlot in Jericho who hid the spies sent by Joshua to scout the city (Josh. 2:1–6). Later she and her family were spared when Jericho fell to the invading Israelites (Josh. 6:22–25). In the NT, Rahab was commended for her faith (Heb. 11:31). *Rachab*: Jesus' ancestry (Matt. 1:5).

....

A House on a Wall *She [Rahab] let them [Israelite spies] down by a cord through the window: for her house was upon the town wall, and she dwelt upon the wall* (Josh. 2:15).

Some walled cities of Bible times had an inner wall and an outer wall for maximum protection. To strengthen these walls, the space between them was filled with dirt and rubble at selected points. Houses were sometimes built right into the city wall by placing them on top of these piles of rubble. Since Rahab "dwelt upon the wall" of Jericho, she must have lived in one of these "wall houses." She helped the Israelite spies escape over the city wall by lowering them with ropes from her window. A similar escape was made in NT times by the apostle Paul. Believers in the city of Damascus delivered him from his enemies, who were watching the city gates "day and night to kill him" (Acts 9:24). They placed Paul in a basket and lowered him over the city wall.

MARCH 15 | Read Joshua 3–5

3:1–17 Led by the priests carrying the ark of the covenant, the people cross the flooded Jordan River on dry land as God miraculously stops the flow of water (Exod. 14).

4:1–24 Twelve stones are taken from the Jordan River and set up as a memorial in Gilgal to remind the Israelites of God's presence and protection (Deut. 27:1–10).

5:1 The Canaanites are frightened when they learn about the miraculous crossing of the Jordan River by the Israelites.

5:2–12 Joshua performs the rite of circumcision on all male Israelites who have not been circumcised (Gen. 17:9–14).

5:13 15 At Jericho, the mysterious captain of the host of the Lord meets and encourages Joshua.

Gilgal A site between the Jordan River and the city of Jericho where the Hebrew people erected memorial stones to commemorate God's faithfulness in leading them into the Promised Land (Josh. 4:19–20). Gilgal apparently served as Joshua's headquarters in his campaign against the Canaanites (Josh. 10). In later years, Saul was crowned as Israel's first king at Gilgal (1 Sam. 11:15).

MARCH 16 | Read Joshua 6–8

6:1–27 God miraculously delivers the city of Jericho to Joshua and his warriors by causing the walls to collapse. Rahab the prostitute and her family are spared because she helped the two Israelite spies when they investigated the city (Josh. 2).

7:1–26 The Israelites fail to conquer the city of Ai because one of their own warriors, Achan, disobeyed the Lord by keeping some of the spoils of war for himself. The people stone Achan to death when they discover his sin.

8:1–29 After dealing with Achan, Joshua and his warriors capture the city of Ai by pretending to retreat, then ambushing Ai's pursuing army.

8:30–35 Joshua builds an altar on which sacrifices are offered. He reads to all the Israelites the book of the law that God delivered to Moses.

Jericho A fortified Canaanite city near the Jordan River and the Dead Sea (Deut. 32:49) that was captured by Joshua when the Israelites entered the Promised Land (Josh. 6:1–22).

Stoning The Jewish mode of capital punishment, specified in the law for these offenses: sacrificing of children to idols (Lev. 20:2–5), breaking of the Sabbath (Num. 15:32–36), idolatry (Deut. 17:2–7), rebellion of children against parents (Deut. 21:18–21), and adultery (Deut. 22:23–24). Godly men who were stoned for their faith included the prophets (Heb. 11:37), Stephen (Acts 7:59), and Paul, who was presumed dead from stoning (Acts 14:19–20).

Monument to a Crime *They [Joshua and the Israelites] raised over him [Achan] a great heap of stones* (Josh. 7:26).

Achan was executed because he kept some of the spoils of war taken in battles against the Canaanites for himself (Josh. 7:20–21). This was a violation of the Lord's command (Josh. 6:19). To commemorate Achan's crime, Joshua and other Israelite leaders piled stones on his grave. This makeshift monument served as a constant reminder to others of the seriousness of disobeying God. Throughout Israel's history, stones were also heaped up to serve as memorials of positive events in the life of the nation (Exod. 24:4; Josh. 4:3–9; 24:26; 1 Sam. 7:12).

MARCH 17 | Read Joshua 9–11

9:1–27 The Gibeonites trick Joshua into making a peace treaty with them. Joshua makes good on his promise not to harm them, but they become menial servants of the Israelites (2 Sam. 21:1–9).

10:1–11:23 Joshua and his army defeat the united forces of several Canaanite kings and occupy their territories.

Aijalon A city in the territory of Dan (1 Sam. 14:31) where Joshua battled the five Amorite kings. During this battle the sun stood still (Josh. 10:12–13). *Ajalon:* Josh. 19:42.

Trickery of the Gibeonites *When the inhabitants of Gibeon heard what Joshua had done unto Jericho and to Ai, they did work wilily [resorted to a ruse, NIV], and went and made as if they had been ambassadors, and took old sacks upon their asses [donkeys, NIV], and wine bottles [wineskins, NIV], old, and rent, and bound up; and old shoes and clouted upon their feet, and old garments upon them; and all the bread of their provision was dry and mouldy (Josh. 9:3–5).*

The Gibeonites were Canaanites, just like the other tribal groups that Joshua was defeating and executing. But the Gibeonites were smart. They used trickery to save their lives: By wearing worn-out clothes and carrying torn wineskins and stale bread, the Gibeonites pretended that they were travelers from a distant country rather than residents of Canaan. Fooled by their trickery, Joshua agreed to grant them asylum and to let them live in peace in the land (Josh. 9:15). After he discovered the truth, Joshua honored the covenant he had made with the Gibeonites. But he sentenced them to a life of servitude as woodcutters and water carriers for the Israelites (Josh. 9:21–23). The task of carrying water must have been particularly degrading to the Gibeonites. This chore was normally done by women.

Feet on the Necks of Enemies *When they [Israelite warriors] brought out those kings unto Joshua. . .Joshua. . .said unto the captains [commanders, NIV] of the men of war. . . Come near, put your feet upon the necks of these kings (Josh. 10:24).*

Joshua directed that this action be taken against the five Amorite kings whom his military forces had defeated (Josh. 10:5–10). Putting one's foot on the neck of an enemy was not an act of hostility or violence but a symbolic action that showed total subjection. There was no doubt that these kings and their people were now under Israel's control.

MARCH 18 | Read Joshua 12–13

12:1–6 The territories east of the Jordan River—those captured by the Israelites under Moses' leadership—are listed. This area had already been settled by the tribes of Reuben and Gad and one-half of the tribe of Manasseh (Num. 32).

12:7–24 The kings and their territories west of the Jordan River in Canaan—those captured under Joshua's leadership—are listed.

13:1–7 The Lord reminds Joshua in his old age that the Canaanites still occupy parts of the land that He has promised to the Israelites.

13:8–14 God gives a general description of the territories east of the Jordan River that have already been settled by the tribes of Reuben and Gad and one-half of the tribe of Manasseh.

13:15–23 The territory east of the Jordan River assigned to the tribe of Reuben is listed.

13:24–28 The territory east of the Jordan River assigned to the tribe of Gad is listed.

13:29–31 The territory east of the Jordan River assigned to one-half of the tribe of Manasseh is listed (1 Chron. 5:23).

13:32–33 A summary statement about the territories east of the Jordan River assigned to the Israelites and a reminder that the Levites received no land inheritance.

Waters of Merom A lake ten miles north of the Sea of Galilee through which the Jordan River flows on its southward passage (Josh. 11:5–7).

Amorites One of the tribal groups of Canaan defeated by the Israelites. Descendants of Ham through his son Canaan (Gen. 10:6), the Amorites were a formidable enemy, but Joshua broke their strength with victories over the armies of Sihon and Og (Josh. 12:1–6). Remnants of the Amorites were reduced to servitude under King Solomon (1 Kings 9:19–21).

Tirzah A Canaanite town captured by Joshua (Josh. 12:24). In later years it served as a capital of the Northern Kingdom until Samaria was built (1 Kings 14:17).

Philistia A coastal region about forty miles long beside the Mediterranean Sea that served as the land of the Philistines in OT times (Gen. 21:32–34). The name *Palestine* was derived from *Philistia*. The chief cities of Philistia were Ashdod, Askelon, Ekron, Gath, and Gaza (Josh. 13:3).

MARCH 19 | Read Joshua 14–16

14:1–5 A general statement about the division of the land of Canaan among the Israelite tribes.

14:6–15 Caleb receives a special inheritance of land, which includes the city of Hebron. Moses had made this promise of land to Caleb forty years before. Caleb was one of the twelve spies who investigated the land. Only he and Joshua had trusted God and recommended that the Israelites move forward immediately to conquer the land (Num. 14:5–10).

15:1–63 The territory, including cities, assigned to the tribe of Judah is listed.

16:1–4 A general statement about the territories assigned to the two tribes that sprang from Joseph's two sons, Ephraim and Manasseh.

16:5–10 The territory assigned to the tribe of Ephraim is listed.

Hebron An ancient town in Canaan where Abraham lived and where Sarah died (Gen. 23:2–6). After the conquest of Canaan, it was designated as one of the six cities of refuge. *Kirjath-arba*: Josh. 14:15.

Caleb's Delayed Reward Caleb must have been more than eighty years old when he was finally rewarded for his faithfulness with a tract of land in the Promised Land (Josh. 14:6–15). He was forty when he served on the scouting expedition into Canaan (Josh. 14:7), and another forty years had passed while the Israelites wandered in the wilderness (Num. 14:33). God's promised reward may be slow in coming, but He always delivers.

MARCH 20 | Read Joshua 17–19

17:1–13 The territory, including cities, assigned to the tribe of Manasseh is listed.

17:14–18 The tribes of Ephraim and Manasseh ask for additional land, and Joshua grants their request.

18:1–10 Joshua sends representatives from each tribe to survey the remaining land so it can be divided among the tribes that have not yet received an inheritance.

18:11–28 The territory, including cities, assigned to the tribe of Benjamin is listed.

19:1–9 The territory, including cities, assigned to the tribe of Simeon is listed.

19:10–16 The territory, including cities, assigned to the tribe of Zebulun is listed.

19:17–23 The territory, including cities, assigned to the tribe of Issachar is listed.

19:24–31 The territory, including cities, assigned to the tribe of Asher is listed.

19:32–39 The territory, including cities, assigned to the tribe of Naphtali is listed.

19:40–48 The territory, including cities, assigned to the tribe of Dan is listed.

19:49–51 The tribes of Israel grant Joshua a city as a reward for his faithful leadership.

.....

Machir The oldest son of Manasseh (Josh. 17:1), a grandson of Joseph (Gen. 50:23), and a military hero who became the ancestor of the Macherites (1 Chron. 7:17–18). The Macherites won significant victories over the Amorites during the conquest of Canaan (Num. 32:39). *Makir*: NIV.

Casting of Lots The practice of making decisions by casting small stones out of a container, similar to our modern practice of "drawing straws" (Josh. 18:6). It was believed that God made His will known through this method (Prov. 16:33). Matthias was chosen as an apostle to succeed Judas by the casting of lots (Acts 1:26).

Arabah The valley on both sides of the Jordan River that stretches for about 240 miles from Mount Hermon in the north to the Red Sea in the south (Josh. 18:18).

Timnath-serah A town in the territory of Ephraim given to Joshua as an inheritance and the place where he was buried (Josh. 24:29–30). *Timnath-heres*: Judg. 2:9.

MARCH 21 | Read Joshua 20–22

20:1–9 Six cities throughout the territory of the tribes are designated as cities of refuge (Num. 35; Deut. 19:1–13). Three of these are to be on the western side and three on the eastern side of the Jordan River.

21:1–45 The Levites receive no land inheritance, so they are given forty-eight cities throughout the territory of the tribes. These cities are assigned to the three branches of the Levites: Kohathites (vv. 10–26), Gershonites (vv. 27–33), and Merarites (vv. 34–40) (see Num. 35).

22:1–9 Now that the war with the Canaanites is over, Joshua allows the warriors from the tribes of Reuben and Gad and one-half of the tribe of Manasseh to return to their homes on the eastern side of the Jordan River. They have made good on their promise to help the other tribes conquer the land (Num. 32).

22:10–34 The tribes of Reuben and Gad and one-half of the tribe of Manasseh build a huge altar on their side of the Jordan River. The tribes on the other side of the river fear this is an altar for pagan worship. But they are assured it has been built as a gesture of praise and thanksgiving to God.

.....

Kedesh One of the six cities of refuge, situated in the territory of Naphtali in northern Palestine (Josh. 20:1–7). This city is now called *Keder*.

Levitical Cities Forty-eight cities assigned to the tribe of Levi instead of one specific territory (Num. 35:2–7). This arrangement gave the priestly class access to the spiritual needs of the other tribes. Six of these cities were designated as cities of refuge to protect those who accidentally killed persons from avenging relatives (Josh. 20:1–6).

Safety in the Cities *Speak to the children of Israel, saying, Appoint out for you cities of refuge* (Josh. 20:2).

In the six cities of refuge (Josh. 20), Jewish citizens were protected from revenge by relatives of the deceased while a system of due process was put into motion. After investigating the matter, city officials issued the final judgment on whether a person was innocent or guilty of murder.

MARCH 22 | Read Joshua 23–24

23:1–16 In his old age, Joshua gathers the people and reminds them that God has fulfilled His promise to give them a land of their own. He challenges them to love the Lord and to keep His commandments.

24:1–28 In his farewell speech to Israel, Joshua gives the people a history lesson to show how gracious God has been to His people. He challenges them to remain faithful to God and to put away the worship of false gods; then he leads them to renew the covenant with the Lord.

24:29–33 Joshua dies and his accomplishments are summarized.

Intermarriage Marriage between members of different races or religions. Intermarriage of the Israelites with the idolatrous Canaanites was forbidden by God (Josh. 23:12–13). Paul counseled the Corinthian Christians not to marry unbelievers (2 Cor. 6:14–17).

Mount Gaash A mountain in the hill country of Ephraim where Joshua was buried (Josh. 24:30).

MARCH 23 | Read Judges 1–3

1:1–36 When Joshua dies, pockets of Canaanites still live in the territory settled by the tribes of Israel. Battles with the Canaanites and other enemies continue.

2:1–5 An angel of the Lord reveals that God is not pleased because the Israelites have not driven all the Canaanites out of the land. They have allowed the pagan worship practices of the Canaanites to continue.

2:6–23 After Joshua's death, a new generation of Israelites that does not obey the Lord comes on the scene. They are corrupted by worshiping the false gods of their enemies. As punishment, God raises up a group to oppress them. The people then repent of their idolatry and cry out to God for deliverance. Then God empowers a judge, or military leader, to lead the Israelites to defeat the enemy.

3:1–6 Some of the nations or tribal groups that oppressed the Israelites during the period of the judges are listed.

3:7–11 The Lord empowers the judge Othniel, Caleb's brother (Josh. 14:6–15), to deliver the Israelites from oppression by King Chushan-rishathaim of Mesopotamia.

3:12–15 The Lord empowers the judge Ehud to deliver the Israelites from oppression by the Moabites (2 Sam. 8:2).

3:16–26 Ehud, pretending to bring a gift, assassinates King Eglon of Moab in his own house.

3:27–30 Ehud leads the Israelite army to victory over the Moabites.

3:31 The judge Shamgar leads Israel to defeat the Philistines (2 Sam. 5:17–25).

. . . .

Judges of Israel Popular military leaders or deliverers who led Israel between the time of Joshua's death and the beginning of the kingship (about 1380–1050 BC). Israel's judges served in times of disunity and spiritual decline among the twelve tribes (Judg. 17:6; 21:25) as well as times when all the tribes were oppressed by their enemies. While some judges were weak or wicked, noteworthy exploits include Deborah and Barak's defeat of the Canaanite king Jabin (4:4–24), Gideon's 300 warriors who subdued the Midianites (7:1–8:21), and Samson's massacre of the Philistines (15:14–16).

. . . .

Mutilation of Captives *They [tribe of Judah] pursued after him [King Adoni-bezek], and caught him, and cut off his thumbs and his great [big, NIV] toes* (Judg. 1:6).

Adoni-bezek, a Canaanite king, was defeated by warriors from the tribe of Judah. In ancient warfare captive soldiers were sometimes mutilated like Adoni-bezek was to take away their fighting abilities. With both thumbs and both big toes missing, the king would not be able to move quickly or handle a bow or spear. The ancient Assyrians were known to mutilate captives just for sport, cutting off body parts that had nothing to do with waging war. One monument left by an Assyrian king testifies to their military cruelty: "Their men, young and old, I took prisoners. Of some I cut off the feet and hands; of others I cut off the noses, ears, and lips; of the young men's ears I made a heap."

An Ox Goad as a Weapon *After him [Ehud] was Shamgar the son of Anath, which slew of the Philistines six hundred men with an ox goad* (Judg. 3:31).

As one of the judges, or military deliverers, of Israel, Shamgar used an ox goad as an efficient weapon against the Philistines. An ox goad was a pole about eight feet long and two inches in diameter. It was sharpened to a point on one end. A farmer used this end when plowing an ox to prod him into a faster gait. The other end had a metal blade that he used to clean roots or clay from the tip of the plow. Jesus referred to an ox goad when He appeared to the apostle Paul on the road to Damascus: "Saul, Saul, why persecutest thou me? It is hard for thee to kick against the pricks [goads, NIV]" (Acts 26:14).

MARCH 24 | Read Judges 4–5

4:1–5 The Lord empowers the judge Deborah, a prophetess, to deliver the Israelites from oppression by the Canaanites.

4:6–9 Deborah enlists Barak (Heb. 11:32) to lead the army of Israel against the Canaanites.

4:10–17 Barak gathers an army from the tribes of Zebulun and Naphtali. They defeat the Canaanites, whose commander, Sisera, escapes on foot.

4:18–24 Victory over the Canaanites is sealed by the assassination of Sisera. A woman named Jael drives a tent stake through his skull while he is in a deep sleep from exhaustion.

5:1–31 Deborah and Barak celebrate the defeat of the Canaanites with a song of praise to the Lord, "The Song of Deborah."

. . . .

Deborah A prophetess and judge of Israel who, along with Barak, defeated the Canaanite forces of Sisera (Judg. 4:4–14). She celebrated the victory in a triumphant song (Judg. 5).

Barak A general under Deborah and judge of Israel. He and Deborah were victorious against the Canaanites (Judg. 4).

Hazor A royal Canaanite city destroyed by Joshua (Josh. 11:1–13). The rebuilt fortress city was later ravaged by Deborah and Barak during the period of the judges (Judg. 4:2–24). Hazor was ultimately destroyed by King Tiglath-pileser of Assyria (2 Kings 15:29).

MARCH 25 | Read Judges 6–8

6:1–6 The combined forces of the Midianites and the Amalekites oppress Israel, destroying their crops and stealing their livestock.

6:7–10 A prophet arrives in Israel to remind the people that they are suffering because they have disobeyed the Lord.

6:11–16 The judge Gideon (Heb. 11:32) learns from an angel of the Lord that he has been selected to deliver Israel from oppression by the Midianites.

`6:17–24` The angel disappears after proving to Gideon through a miracle that he is God's messenger. Gideon builds an altar to the Lord to show he accepts God's call.

`6:25–32` Obeying God's orders, Gideon tears down an altar devoted to the pagan god Baal. He builds in its place an altar dedicated to the Lord.

`6:33–35` The combined forces of the Midianites and the Amalekites gather at the valley of Jezreel. Gideon raises an army from the tribes of Manasseh, Asher, Zebulun, and Naphtali.

`6:36–40` Gideon asks God for two miraculous signs involving a fleece, or a piece of wool, to prove that He will use Gideon to deliver Israel.

`7:1–8` The Lord trims Gideon's army—from 32,000 to 22,000 to 10,000 and finally to just 300—to show that the battle will not be won through military might but by dependence on the Lord to deliver on His promise.

`7:9–15` Gideon hears two enemy soldiers discussing a dream about a battle in which the Midianites are defeated. This is another sign from the Lord that victory over the Midianites is assured.

`7:16–25` Using torches, pitchers, and trumpets, Gideon and his 300 warriors launch a surprise attack on the Midianite army at night. The resulting chaos causes the warriors to attack and kill one another. Gideon seals the victory by capturing and executing two Midianite princes.

`8:1–3` Warriors from the tribe of Ephraim complain because they were not summoned to join the battle against the Midianites. Gideon uses diplomacy to soothe their wounded pride.

`8:4–21` Gideon captures and executes two kings of Midian, Zebah and Zalmunna, to break the power of the Midianite kingdom.

`8:22–23` The Israelites ask Gideon to become their king, but he refuses.

`8:24–27` Gideon makes a golden ephod, or apron, which apparently becomes an object of worship in the city where he lives.

`8:28–35` After Gideon dies, the Israelites again turn away from God and begin to worship the pagan Canaanite god Baal.

`Gideon` Gideon came from an obscure family of the tribe of Manasseh, but he trusted God at every step of his military campaign and thus was successful (see Judg. 6–8). He is listed in the NT as one of the heroes of the faith (Heb. 11:32; *Gedeon*). *Jerubbaal*: Judg. 6:25–32.

`Angel of the Lord` A heavenly being sent by God to human beings as His personal agent or spokesman. This messenger appeared to Hagar in the wilderness (Gen. 16:7–12), to Moses (Exod. 3:2–3), and to Gideon (Judg. 6:11–12).

Gideon's Secret Weapons *He [Gideon] divided the three hundred men into three companies, and he put a trumpet in every man's hand, with empty pitchers, and lamps within the pitchers* (Judg. 7:16).

Gideon relied on the Lord, as well as shock and surprise, to defeat the huge Midianite army with a force of only three hundred warriors. He and his men advanced on the enemy camp at night while most of the Midianites were still asleep. Then, at Gideon's signal, they blew their trumpets and broke their pitchers with torches inside, suddenly bathing the camp in light. All the noise and light convinced the Midianites that they were being attacked by a huge army. In the shock and confusion, they "set every man's sword against his fellow" (Judg. 7:22) and fled into the night. Their disorganization made them easy prey for the pursuing Israelites.

MARCH 26 | Read Judges 9

9:1–6 Abimelech, a son of Gideon, is appointed king by the people of the city of Shechem. He kills the other sons of Gideon to eliminate any challengers for the throne. Only Gideon's youngest son, Jotham, escapes the slaughter.

9:7–21 Jotham ridicules Abimelech by telling a parable about the bramble, or thornbush, and the trees. Abimelech, just like the thornbush, isn't worthy of the kingship.

9:22–57 The people of Shechem turn against Abimelech. He is eventually killed by a woman who drops a piece of millstone on his head while he is leading a siege against a walled city.

Abimelech A rebellious son of Gideon who killed all his brothers after his father's death in an attempt to become king over all Israel (Judg. 9:5–22). He was killed by his armorbearer after a woman dropped a stone on his head from a city wall (Judg. 9:50–54).

Shechem A city of refuge on a trade route in the territory of Ephraim (Josh. 20:7). *Sichem*: Gen. 12:6. *Sychem*: Acts 7:16.

MARCH 27 | Read Judges 10–12

10:1–5 Tola and Jair serve as judges to deliver Israel from their enemies.

10:6–18 The people of Israel turn to idol worship; God punishes them by raising up the Philistines and the Ammonites as their oppressors.

11:1–33 The judge Jephthah leads Israel to victory over the Ammonites (Deut. 23:3).

11:34–40 Jephthah is obligated to offer his own daughter as a sacrifice because of his rash vow to give God the first thing that came out to meet him when he returned from battle (see v. 31).

12:1–6 Jephthah leads his forces in a civil war against the tribe of Ephraim.

12:7 Jephthah dies and is buried in Gilead.

12:8–15 Three different men—Ibzan, Elon, and Abdon—serve for a brief time as judges over Israel.

. . . .

Ammonites A race or tribe descended from Ammon who became enemies of the Israelites during the Exodus (Deut. 23:3). Their chief pagan god was Chemosh (Judg. 11:24), and the Israelites often indulged in their idolatrous practices (Ezra 9:1). Tobiah, an Ammonite, tried to prevent Nehemiah from rebuilding the walls of Jerusalem (Neh. 2:10, 19).

Chemosh The chief pagan god of the Moabites and Ammonites to which children were sacrificed (Judg. 11:24; 2 Kings 23:13).

Jephthah A judge of Israel who delivered the nation from the Ammonites. After making a rash and foolish vow, Jephthah sacrificed his only child as an offering to God (Judg. 11). *Jephthae*: Heb. 11:32.

MARCH 28 | Read Judges 13–16

13:1–25 The judge Samson (Heb. 11:32) is born to godly parents in the tribe of Dan. Consecrated as a Nazarite (Num. 6:1–21), his mission is to deliver Israel from oppression by the Philistines.

14:1–20 Samson selects a Philistine woman as his wife. He taunts his friends by giving them a riddle to solve.

15:1–20 Samson burns the crops of the Philistines and slaughters 1,000 men with the jawbone of a donkey.

16:1–3 Samson escapes from a Philistine trap by tearing a city gate out of the wall and carrying it off to Hebron.

16:4–21 Samson reveals to Delilah, a Philistine woman, that the source of his superhuman strength is his long hair that has never been cut. Delilah shaves his head while he is asleep. Samson is captured, blinded, and sentenced to a life of hard labor as a prisoner of the Philistines.

16:22–31 Samson dies, along with thousands of the Philistines, when he pushes down the support columns of a building where he was being taunted by his captors.

. . . .

Delilah A woman, probably a Philistine, who cut off Samson's long hair—the source of his strength—so he could be captured by his Philistine enemies (Judg. 16:13–21).

Dagon of the Philistines *The lords of the Philistines gathered them [the Philistines] together for to offer a great sacrifice unto Dagon their god, and to rejoice: for they said, Our god hath delivered Samson our enemy into our hand* (Judg. 16:23).

This pagan god to whom the Philistines attributed such power was their primary, national god. They must have gathered often in ceremonies such as this—probably in a temple devoted to Dagon—to worship and pay tribute to him. Stone carvings of Dagon portray him with the head, hands, and upper body of a man and the lower part of his body as a fish. The Hebrew word for Dagon actually means "little fish." This pagan god represented the reproductive powers of nature. The fish was an appropriate image because of its ability to reproduce rapidly and in great numbers. The Philistines boasted that Dagon had delivered their enemy Samson into their hands. But when he pushed down the pillars that held up Dagon's temple (Judg. 16:29–30), he proved that Israel's God was superior to this pagan idol.

Samson the Nazarite *Thou [Manoah's wife] shalt conceive, and bear a son; and no razor shall come on his head: for the child shall be a Nazarite unto God from the womb* (Judg. 13:5).

A Nazirite was a person who took an oath known as the Nazirite vow. He promised to avoid worldly things and to devote himself totally to the Lord. As evidence of this commitment, a Nazirite was not to drink wine or any intoxicating beverages and he was not to cut his hair (Num. 6:5). The Nazirite vow was voluntary, and it was generally taken for a limited time, perhaps thirty or sixty days. But Samson was designated as a Nazirite for life; this choice was made for him by the Lord and his parents even before he was born. Samson failed to live up to the vow that others had made for him. He indulged in worldly pleasures and sinned against the Lord. When Delilah succeeded in cutting his hair, the spirit of the Lord left him and his great strength was taken away (Judg. 16:19).

MARCH 29 | Read Judges 17–19

17:1–13 Micah fashions several objects of idol worship and hires a Levite as his household priest.

18:1–6 The tribe of Dan sends out scouts to find a territory or city they can claim as their own. Micah's household priest assures them that God will bless their efforts.

18:7–31 The Danite scouts recommend that Laish, a city of the Zidonians, be taken. Danite warriors stop at Micah's house on their way to Laish, stealing Micah's objects of idol worship and taking away his household priest. These become part of the worship system of the Danites after they occupy Laish.

19:1–30 A Levite's concubine is violated and killed by perverted residents of the city of Gibeah in the territory of the tribe of Benjamin. The Levite informs the other Israelite tribes of this outrage and urges them to take action against the city of Gibeah and the Benjaminites.

Teraphim Small images representing human figures that were venerated in households as guardians of good fortune (Judg. 17:5). Rachel stole her father's teraphim when Jacob left for Canaan (Gen. 31:19, 35).

Dan (1) Jacob's fifth son and ancestor of one of the tribes of Israel (Gen. 30:6; Num. 1:38–39). (2) A village in the territory allotted to the tribe of Dan. It was located farther north than any other city of Palestine during most of the OT era. The phrase "from Dan even to Beersheba" (Judg. 20:1) described the entire territory of the Hebrew nation from north to south. *Laish:* Isa. 10:30.

MARCH 30 | Read Judges 20–21

20:1–21:25 The tribes of Israel raise an army and attack the Benjaminites at Gibeah. They wipe out most of the tribe, including the women. Because of its great losses, the tribe of Benjamin is in danger of going extinct, especially since the other tribes made a vow not to give their daughters in marriage to the few remaining Benjaminite men. But the tribes find a way to produce wives for Benjamin so this tribe will not be "cut off from Israel" (v. 6).

Beer-sheba The name of a well in southern Judah that Abraham and Abimelech dug to seal their covenant of friendship (Gen. 21:31). The name was also applied to the surrounding wilderness (Gen. 21:14) and an important city that grew up around the well (Gen. 26:32–33; Judg. 20:1).

Saving Benjamin *And the children of Israel repented them for Benjamin their brother, and said, There is one tribe cut off from Israel this day. How shall we do for wives for them that remain, seeing we have sworn by the Lord that we will not give them of our daughters to wives?* (Judg. 21:6–7).

At one point in Israel's history, the tribe of Benjamin was almost wiped out. Thousands of Benjaminite men were killed by the other tribes in retaliation for a heinous crime they committed (Judg. 20). To save the tribe from extinction, the other tribes provided women from the clan of Jabesh-gilead to marry the remaining Benjaminite men. This paid off for the entire nation in future years. Israel's first king, Saul, was from the tribe of Benjamin (1 Sam. 9:1–2). The apostle Paul also traced his lineage through this tribe (Rom. 11:1).

MARCH 31 | Read Ruth 1–4

1:1–5 Elimelech and his wife and two sons move to Moab from Judah to escape a famine in their homeland. Then Elimelech and his two sons die, leaving three widows in distress: his wife, Naomi, and the two Moabite women whom his sons had married.

1:6–22 Naomi decides to return to her homeland. One of her widowed daughters-in-law, Ruth, insists on going with her.

2:1–23 Ruth goes into the barley fields to gather left-behind stalks of grain to make bread for herself and Naomi. By chance, this field belongs to Boaz, a distant relative of Naomi's late husband, Elimelech. Ruth meets Boaz, who arranges with his harvesters to leave many stalks in the field for her to glean. Naomi is pleased when she learns that Ruth has met Boaz.

3:1–18 Naomi sends Ruth to lie at the feet of Boaz at night, a custom that indicates she is willing to marry Boaz. The law of levirate marriage encouraged relatives of deceased males who had no children to marry their widows in order to produce children to carry on the family name (Deut. 25:5–10). Boaz, as a distant relative of Naomi's late husband, Elimelech, is willing to marry Ruth but indicates there is a relative closer to Elimelech who has first choice in the matter.

4:1–12 With the elders of the city looking on as witnesses, Boaz sits down with this relative at the city gate. The man gives up the right to marry Ruth, leaving Boaz free to take her as his wife.

4:13–22 Boaz marries Ruth, who gives birth to a son named Obed. Obed becomes the father of Jesse and the grandfather of the great King David of Judah (Matt. 1:5).

- -

Naomi The mother-in-law of Ruth. After marrying Elimelech, Naomi moved to Moab to escape a famine. Her husband and two sons died, leaving Naomi and her two daughters-in-law alone. She returned to Bethlehem with Ruth and helped arrange Ruth's marriage to Boaz (see Ruth 1–4).

Ruth A Moabite woman who remained loyal to her Jewish mother-in-law, Naomi, after the death of their husbands. Ruth moved with Naomi to Bethlehem (Ruth 1:16–19), where she gleaned grain in the fields of Boaz. She eventually married Boaz and became an ancestor of David and Christ (Ruth 4:9–22).

Boaz The husband of Ruth and an ancestor of Christ. He married Ruth, who gave birth to Obed, grandfather of David (Ruth 4:17). *Booz*: Jesus' ancestry (Matt. 1:5).

- -

Gleaning in the Fields of Boaz *She [Ruth] went, and came, and gleaned in the field after the reapers* (Ruth 2:3).

Ruth's gathering of grain in the fields of Boaz is the best example in the Bible of the practice of gleaning. After crops had been harvested, poor people were allowed in the fields and orchards to pick up any grain or fruit that had been left behind.

Old Testament law specified that the corners of fields were not to be harvested by landowners. Grain in these spots was to be left for the poor (Lev. 23:22). Likewise, a sheaf of grain left accidentally in the field was to remain there as provision for the poor (Deut. 24:19). Some generous landowners went beyond the letter of the law and deliberately left part of the harvest in the fields for the poor. For example, when Boaz learned about Ruth gleaning on his property, he instructed his workers, "Pull out some stalks for her from the bundles [of grain] and leave them for her to pick up" (Ruth 2:16 NIV).

Sign of the Shoe *Now this was the manner in former time in Israel concerning redeeming and concerning changing, for to confirm all things; a man plucked off his shoe, and gave it to his neighbour: and this was a testimony in Israel* (Ruth 4:7).

Naomi's deceased husband, Elimelech, had some land in Bethlehem that she had been forced to sell because of her poverty conditions (Ruth 4:3). Elimelech had a relative who, as his next of kin, had the right to buy back or redeem this property to keep it in the family. But this unnamed relative gave up that right by removing his sandal. Only the owner of a plot of land had the right to walk on it. Removal of his sandal symbolized that he was giving up his ownership rights and transferring them to Boaz, who could then proceed to buy back the property from the current owner.

APRIL 1 | Read 1 Samuel 1–3

1:1–8 Hannah expresses her sorrow over her childlessness by weeping and refusing to eat.

1:9–18 Hannah prays for a son and promises to devote him to the Lord.

1:19–28 Samuel is born as an answer to Hannah's prayer. She follows through on her promise to devote him to the Lord by presenting him to the priest Eli at Shiloh.

2:1–10 Hannah prays and sings a song of thanksgiving to God for the birth of Samuel and His continuing faithfulness to Israel.

2:11 The boy Samuel lives with the priest Eli at Shiloh and helps him with his ceremonial religious duties.

2:12–17 The dishonest sons of Eli cheat people when they offer sacrifices to the Lord at Shiloh.

2:18–21 The boy Samuel continues his work with Eli at Shiloh. Samuel's mother and father are blessed with other children.

2:22–36 A prophet warns Eli that he and his household will be judged by the Lord because of the wicked behavior of his two sons, Hophni and Phinehas.

3:1–9 The Lord speaks to the boy Samuel three times; he assumes he is being called by the priest Eli.

3:10–21 God speaks to Samuel for the fourth time, revealing that He will punish Eli and his descendants because he has failed to deal with his wicked sons. Samuel is recognized throughout the land as a true prophet of the Lord.

Hannah The mother of Samuel the prophet. She prayed earnestly for Samuel to be born (1 Sam. 1:5–11), devoted him to God's service (1 Sam. 1:24–28), and offered a beautiful prayer of thanksgiving for God's blessings (1 Sam. 2:1–10).

Barren Unable to bear children. In the OT, barrenness was seen as a sign of God's judgment (1 Sam. 1:5–7). Women in the Bible who had this problem—but who were eventually blessed with children—were Sarah (Gen. 11:30), Rachel (Gen. 29:31), Hannah (1 Sam. 1:5), and Elisabeth (Luke 1:7).

Eli's Seat of Judgment *Eli the priest sat upon a seat by a post of the temple of the Lord* (1 Sam. 1:9).

Since Eli was the high priest of Israel, the seat on which he sat was probably a "seat of judgment" from which he advised the people. As the final judge in religious matters, he helped people solve their problems by subjecting themselves to the Lord's will. Hannah, a godly woman who had been unable to have children, brought this problem before Eli for his advice and counsel. Eli told Hannah, "Go in peace: and the God of Israel grant thee thy petition" (1 Sam. 1:17). She eventually did give birth to a son—the prophet Samuel.

APRIL 2 | Read 1 Samuel 4–6

4:1–11 Eli's sons, Hophni and Phinehas, are killed in a battle with the Philistines. The Philistines carry away the Israelites' sacred chest known as the ark of the covenant (Exod. 37:1–9).

4:12–18 The aged priest Eli dies at the news that his sons have been killed and the ark of the covenant has been captured by the Philistines.

4:19–22 Eli's daughter-in-law names her newborn child Ichabod, symbolizing that God's glory has left Israel.

5:1–12 God punishes the Philistines for capturing the ark. He works miracles and sends plagues upon them in three different cities where it is being kept.

6:1–21 After keeping the ark for seven months, the Philistines return it to Israel, along with gifts of gold as a trespass offering.

Hophni A sinful and immoral son of Eli the high priest who was not considered worthy of conducting priestly duties (1 Sam. 1:3; 2:22–25). Along with his evil brother Phinehas, he was killed by the Philistines (1 Sam. 4:1–11).

I-chabod The son of Phinehas and grandson of Eli. He was given this symbolic name, meaning "inglorious," by his dying mother when she learned the ark of the covenant had been captured by the Philistines and that Eli and Phinehas were dead (1 Sam. 4:19–22).

Beth-shemesh A border town between the territories of Judah and Dan taken by the Philistines. Later the ark of the covenant was kept here (1 Sam. 6:1–7:2). *Irshemesh*: Josh. 19:41.

Pagan Charms *Ye [Philistines] shall make images [models, NIV] of your emerods [tumors, NIV], and images of your mice that mar the land* (1 Sam. 6:5).

The Philistines captured the ark of the covenant from the Israelites and carried it to the city of Ashdod (1 Sam. 5:1). God punished the Philistines by sending swarms of mice throughout their land. These mice apparently carried a disease that caused the Philistines to break out in sores, or tumors. Pagan priests among the Philistines recommended that they send the ark back to the Israelites, along with images of the mice and tumors that were causing their suffering. They thought these images would serve as magic charms to cure their sores and ward off evil spirits.

APRIL 3 | Read 1 Samuel 7–9

7:1–2 The ark is kept at the Israelite city of Kirjath-jearim for twenty years.

7:3–6 Samuel calls on the Israelites to turn from their idolatry back to God and offers sacrifices to the Lord at Mizpeh.

7:7–14 Israel wins a victory over the Philistines after Samuel prays and makes a special offering to the Lord.

7:15–17 Samuel serves as a priest and judge for all Israel from his home at Ramah.

8:1–3 In his old age, Samuel appoints his two sons as judges over Israel, but they become dishonest and corrupt.

8:4–9 The elders of Israel ask Samuel to appoint a king to rule over all the tribes (Hosea 13:10).

8:10–22 At God's command, Samuel informs the people about the suffering they will experience under a human king. But his warnings fall on deaf ears. God tells Samuel to proceed to select a king to rule over Israel.

9:1–27 Saul, a handsome young man from the tribe of Benjamin, encounters Samuel while searching for his father's lost donkeys. The Lord informs Samuel that Saul is the person who should be anointed as Israel's king.

Samuel A prophet and the last judge of Israel who anointed the first two kings of Judah—Saul (1 Sam. 10:1) and David (1 Sam. 16:1–13). Samuel was dedicated to God's service by his mother, Hannah, even before his birth (1 Sam. 1:11–22), and he grew up under the tutelage of Eli the priest to prepare for priestly service (1 Sam. 3:1–20). A popular leader, he was mourned by the entire nation at his death (1 Sam. 25:1). *Shemuel*: 1 Chron. 6:33.

Rama A Benjamite city near Jerusalem and the probable site of Rachel's tomb (Matt. 2:18). *Ramah*: NIV, NRSV.

Saul The first king of Israel who displeased God by his disobedience and his insane jealousy against David. Anointed privately by Samuel (1 Sam. 10:1) and publicly proclaimed king at Gilgal (1 Sam. 11:15), he waged war against the Philistines during his administration (1 Sam. 17–18). He kept the spoils of war from at least one battle, assumed duties of the priestly office, and murdered Ahimelech and eighty-four other priests (1 Sam. 22:11–19)—acts that brought God's judgment. After his sons were killed, Saul committed suicide rather than be captured by the Philistines (1 Sam. 31:1–6).

APRIL 4 | Read 1 Samuel 10–12

10:1 Samuel pours oil on Saul's head to anoint him as king over the Israelites.

10:2–16 Samuel tells Saul to look for several miraculous signs to show that he is the Lord's anointed to rule over Israel.

10:17–27 Samuel calls the tribes of Israel together for a public presentation of Saul as their new king. The reluctant Saul is summoned from his hiding place to begin his duties.

11:1–15 Saul gathers an army from among all the tribes and defeats the Ammonites at Jabesh-gilead. This quiets minority opposition to his kingship, and he is acclaimed king by all Israel at Gilgal.

12:1–25 Samuel reminds the people of how God has blessed them in past years; he challenges them to remain faithful to Him during this new era of their history under a human king (Josh. 24:1–28).

Anoint To set a person apart for a specific work or task. In OT times kings, priests, and prophets were anointed by having oil poured on their heads (Exod. 29:7). Anointing for healing was practiced in NT times with the application of oil (Mark 6:13).

King The monarch or supreme ruler of a nation. Beginning with the first king, Saul, who was anointed with God's authority (1 Sam. 10:1), Judah and Israel had a succession of kings across several centuries until both nations were overrun by foreign powers. The books of 1 and 2 Samuel, 1 and 2 Kings, and 1 and 2 Chronicles report on the reigns of many of these kings. A few were godly and kind rulers who honored God and followed His law, but most were evil and corrupt. They led God's people into sin and idolatry. The believer should remember that God is our eternal

King, worthy of all honor (1 Tim. 1:17). Christ, our ultimate ruler, is Lord of lords and King of kings (John 18:37; Rev. 17:14).

APRIL 5 | Read 1 Samuel 13–14

13:1–14 Preparing for battle with the Philistines, Saul offers a sacrifice to God on his own rather than waiting for Samuel the priest to present the offering with the prescribed ritual. Samuel informs him that this act of impatience and obedience will cost him the kingship.

13:15–23 Saul's warriors have only a few iron weapons to fight with. Their Philistine enemies have developed a monopoly on making and sharpening iron weapons throughout the entire territory of Israel (2 Kings 24:14).

14:1–19 Saul's son Jonathan, accompanied by his armorbearer, leads a secret mission against a company of Philistines, causing panic throughout the enemy camp.

14:20–23 Saul and his army join the battle and chase the Philistine garrison from the area.

14:24–42 Saul warns all Israelite warriors against partaking of food during the day when a great battle rages against the Philistines. His own son Jonathan violates the command.

14:43–46 Saul prepares to execute Jonathan for his disobedience, but other Israelite warriors intervene to save Jonathan's life.

14:47–52 Saul's victories over Israel's enemies are listed, along with the members of his family (1 Chron. 8:33).

Gibeah The native city of King Saul and capital of his kingdom (1 Sam. 14:16; 15:34). This was apparently the same city destroyed by the Israelites during the period of the judges (Judg. 20:19–36). *Gibeath*: Josh. 18:28.

Jonathan King Saul's oldest son (1 Sam. 14:49), who was a loyal friend of David, even while his father was trying to kill David (1 Sam. 20). David mourned Jonathan (2 Sam. 1:17–26) after he was killed by the Philistines (1 Sam. 31:2).

Armourbearer An aide or attendant who carried the armor and weapons of a military officer or warrior of high rank (Judg. 9:54).

APRIL 6 | Read 1 Samuel 15–16

15:1–9 The prophet Samuel directs Saul to destroy the Amalekites and all their livestock (Exod. 17:8–16). But Saul spares the life of King Agag and keeps some of the choice spoils of war.

15:10–35 Samuel reprimands Saul for his disobedience. He declares that the kingship has been taken away from him by the Lord and will be given to another.

16:1–13 At the Lord's command, Samuel anoints the shepherd boy David—the youngest son of Jesse—as Saul's replacement as king of Israel.

16:14–23 Saul selects David to serve as his armorbearer and to play the harp to soothe his troubled mind.

Jesse The father of David and an ancestor of Christ. Jesse presented his eight sons to the prophet Samuel, who anointed David as the future king of Israel (1 Sam. 16:10–13). Jesse is mentioned in scripture as the root or shoot that would produce the royal line of David (Isa. 11:1, 10; Rom. 15:12) and ultimately the Savior (Matt. 1:5–6).

David The popular king of Judah described by the Lord as "a man after mine own heart" and an earthly ancestor of the promised Messiah, Jesus Christ (Luke 2:4–7). A descendant of the tribe of Judah (1 Chron. 28:4), he was a native of Bethlehem (1 Sam. 17:12). As a shepherd boy, he defeated the Philistine giant Goliath (1 Sam. 17:44–52). David then served as King Saul's musician and armorbearer (1 Sam. 16:14–21) and was anointed king after Saul's sin and disobedience (1 Sam. 16:11–13). Forced to flee from Saul's jealousy and wrath (1 Sam. 21:10), he was befriended by Saul's son Jonathan (1 Sam. 19:1–3). After he became king, he united the Hebrew tribes into one nation with Jerusalem as the capital city (2 Sam. 5:1–10) and defeated many enemy nations (2 Sam. 8:1–15). Later in life, in a moment of weakness, David committed adultery with Bath-sheba (2 Sam. 11:1–4), but he later repented (Pss. 32; 51). He was forgiven and restored, but the consequences of his sin remained (2 Sam. 12:13–14). He suffered family tragedies (2 Sam. 12:15–20; 18:31–33) and wrote many psalms (see Pss. 54; 59; 65). He was succeeded as king by his son Solomon (1 Kings 2:12). In the NT, Jesus is called the "son of David" (Matt. 1:1; Mark 10:48).

APRIL 7 | Read 1 Samuel 17–18

17:1–22 Saul's army is stationed for battle against the Philistines, but they are bullied into inaction by the taunts of a Philistine giant named Goliath.

17:23–39 The shepherd boy David arrives on the scene and prepares to fight Goliath, since no Israelite warrior will accept his challenge. David refuses to wear the armor of Saul for the battle.

17:40–51 David fells Goliath with a single stone from his sling, then executes the giant with his own sword.

17:52–58 At the death of their champion, the Philistine army flees in panic and suffers a humiliating defeat by the army of Israel.

18:1–4 David and Saul's son Jonathan make a pact of everlasting friendship.

18:5–16 David becomes a commander in Saul's army and is praised by the Israelites for his bravery. In a fit of jealousy, Saul tries to kill David.

18:17–30 David takes Saul's daughter Michal as his wife after leading a successful campaign against the Philistines.

Philistines The people of Philistia who were enemies of the Israelites, especially during the days of Saul and David. After settling in Canaan, the Philistines often battled the Israelites (2 Sam. 5:17–25). Their chief pagan gods were Dagon (Judg. 16:23) and Baalzebub (2 Kings 1:2–3). Their kingdom disappeared after the Babylonian Exile. *Philistim*: Gen. 10:14.

Goliath's Battle Gear *He [Goliath] had an helmet of brass [bronze, NIV] upon his head, and he was armed with a coat of mail [scale armor, NIV]. . . . He had greaves of brass upon his legs, and a target of brass [bronze javelin, NIV] between his shoulders. . . . The staff [shaft, NIV] of his spear was like a weaver's beam [rod, NIV]; and his spear's head weighed six hundred shekels of iron: and one bearing a shield went before him* (1 Sam. 17:5–7).

Goliath, the Philistine giant whom David faced in battle, was equipped for close-quarter combat. Several implements of attack and defense are mentioned in these three verses.

Helmet. Goliath's helmet was designed to protect him from blows by a sword in hand-to-hand fighting. Some ancient helmets were made from wood, closely woven tree branches, or tough animal hide. But the Philistine army was well equipped with helmets of bronze, a hard metal that was probably an alloy of copper and zinc. Helmets are also mentioned in 2 Chronicles 26:14; Jeremiah 46:4; and Ezekiel 23:24; 27:10; 38:5.

Body armor. Goliath also wore scale armor, or body armor—probably from his neck to his waist—to protect himself in battle. Scale armor was made of small pieces of metal attached to a solid piece of linen or felt. These small metal pieces moved independently of one another, giving a warrior greater mobility in combat. Body armor like this must have been heavy, cumbersome, and clumsy to someone who wasn't accustomed to wearing it. When King Saul put his armor on David to send him out to fight Goliath, David took it off with the words, "I cannot go in these . . .because I am not used to them" (1 Sam. 17:39 NIV).

Greaves. To protect his lower legs, Goliath wore greaves, or leg armor, from his knees down to his feet. These were usually made of leather or wood, but Goliath had heavy-duty greaves of brass, or bronze.

Javelin. The Hebrew word behind "target" is more correctly translated as "javelin." As a matter of fact, this word is rendered as "spear" (Job 41:29) and "lance" (Jer. 50:42) in other places in the King James Version. A javelin was a shorter and lighter version of the spear. Slung over a soldier's back so it could be reached quickly, it was particularly useful in hand-to-hand battles.

Spear. Goliath carried both a javelin and a spear—the javelin for close-quarter combat and the spear for thrusting close in as well as throwing from a distance. A spear's sharp point was not the only thing that made it a formidable weapon. Apparently its butt end was sharpened or strengthened so it could also be used in battle. Abner killed Asahel with the "hinder end" ("butt," NIV) of his spear by thrusting it through his stomach (2 Samuel 2:23).

Shield. The final piece of Goliath's battle gear was a large shield that a carrier held in front of the giant. This protected Goliath from arrows or spears that might be shot or hurled by the enemy. The Hebrew word behind "shield" in this verse makes it clear that it provided full-body protection. This word is also rendered as "buckler" (1 Chronicles 5:18). These shields were about five feet tall for a normal man, but Goliath's may have been bigger because of his giant size. Made of wood and covered with animal skin, shields like this provided good protection when warriors knelt behind them. They were often pulled together in tight formation to serve as movable breastworks.

David's Sling | *His [David's] sling was in his hand* (1 Sam. 17:40).

The sling that David carried was a simple but effective weapon used by shepherds, farmers, and even soldiers in Bible times. It was similar to the slingshot in its design and how it was used. Like a slingshot, the sling had a pocket in which a small stone was placed. Attached to this pocket were two leather straps. The slinger grasped the ends of the straps, twirled the stone around several times in a circular motion, then released one of the straps at just the right time to hurl the stone toward its target. In skilled hands, the sling was a formidable weapon. The force of the stone was strong enough to kill wild animals and—in Goliath's case—even a giant of a man (1 Sam. 17:49). During the time of the judges, the tribe of Benjamin had a unit of seven hundred soldiers who specialized in use of the sling. All the slingers in this elite corps were left-handed, and they "could sling a stone at a hair and not miss" (Judg. 20:16 NIV).

APRIL 8 | Read 1 Samuel 19–20

19:1–7 Jonathan intercedes with his father, Saul, on behalf of David, receiving Saul's assurance that he will not harm David.

19:8–18 Saul breaks his promise and attempts to kill David again. David seeks sanctuary with the prophet Samuel.

19:19–24 Saul sends soldiers to capture David, but they are moved by God's Spirit to prophesy instead. The same thing happens to Saul when he comes looking for David in Samuel's household.

20:1–42 Jonathan warns David that Saul intends to kill him and that he should flee for his life. Then David and Jonathan bid each other a sorrowful farewell.

Not Quite Naked *He [Saul] stripped off his clothes also, and prophesied before Samuel in like manner, and lay down naked all that day and all that night* (1 Sam. 19:24).

The basic dress for both men and women of Bible times was a full-length outer garment, or robe, as well as a full-length undergarment of lighter material. Thus, the term *naked* as rendered by the KJV in this verse does not mean totally nude. A person who took off his outer robe was considered "naked," although he might still be wearing his undergarment. This is the sense in which the prophet Isaiah went around "naked" (Isa. 20:2) at the Lord's command to symbolize the fate of the people of Judah unless they turned from their idolatry. The NIV says that Isaiah went around "stripped"—without his outer robe.

APRIL 9 | Read 1 Samuel 21–23

21:1–9 David visits the priest Ahimelech at Nob. Ahimelech gives him food and the sword of the Philistine giant Goliath to use as his own weapon.

21:10–15 David pretends to be insane in order to find sanctuary with Achish, king of Gath, in Philistine territory.

22:1–5 David gathers an army of 400 warriors while hiding from Saul.

22:6–23 Saul slaughters Ahimelech and scores of other priests at Nob for providing assistance to David.

23:1–5 David and his fighting men defeat a Philistine force to save the city of Keilah.

23:6–29 David eludes Saul and his army by hiding in various places in the wilderness.

Nob A Levitical city near Jerusalem (Isa. 10:32) where David fled to escape King Saul's wrath (1 Sam. 21:1–6). Saul ordered the slaughter of eighty-five priests here in retaliation for their kindness to David (1 Sam. 22:13–19).

Wrapped in a Cloth *The priest [Ahimelech] said, The sword of Goliath the Philistine, whom thou [David] slewest [killed, NIV] in the valley of Elah, behold, it is here wrapped in a cloth* (1 Sam. 21:9)

David was forced to flee when King Saul sought to kill him. He had left hurriedly with no weapons. A priest named Ahimelech befriended David by giving him the sword that David had taken from the giant Goliath (1 Samuel 17:50–51). The priest had wrapped the sword in a cloth and was apparently keeping it in a holy place. Items that were especially valuable or sacred were kept hidden away and wrapped in this fashion.

APRIL 10 | Read 1 Samuel 24–25

24:1–15 David gets close enough to Saul in a dark cave to cut off a piece of his robe, but he refuses to kill him. From a distance, David condemns Saul for wasting his time by chasing him and trying to kill him.

24:16–22 Saul admits that David is a righteous man and that he is destined to become the new king of Israel. He secures David's promise that he will not murder all of Saul's descendants after he is anointed king.

25:1 Samuel dies and is buried at Ramah.

25:2–13 David asks a wealthy livestock owner named Nabal for food supplies for his hungry army, but Nabal insults David and refuses his request. David prepares to take the needed supplies by force.

25:14–35 Nabal's wife, Abigail, gathers food supplies and presents them to David to appease his anger.

25:36–44 Nabal dies, and David takes Abigail as one of his wives.

Abigail A wife of David and the mother of Chileab (2 Sam. 3:3). While married to Nabal, Abigail appeased David's anger after Nabal rejected David's servants (1 Sam. 25:14–35).

Samuel's Tomb *Samuel died; and all the Israelites were gathered together, and lamented him, and buried him in his house at Ramah* (1 Sam. 25:1).

Some interpreters believe this verse means that Samuel was buried in a tomb in the house he lived in at Ramah. But it is likely that the term *house* was just a poetic way of referring to a tomb. Job spoke of the grave as a "house appointed for all living" (Job 30:23).

APRIL 11 | Read 1 Samuel 26–28

26:1–16 David and one of his warriors slip into Saul's camp at night. David gets close enough to Saul to kill him, but he refuses—once again (1 Sam. 24:1–15)—to do so.

26:17–20 From a distance, David again condemns Saul for trying to kill him (1 Sam. 24:9–15).

26:21–25 Saul again admits his wrongdoing (1 Sam. 24:16–22) and predicts that David will be victorious and successful as king of Israel.

27:1–4 David and his army of 600 warriors again seek sanctuary with Achish, king of Gath, in Philistine territory (1 Sam. 21:10–15).

27:5–12 David lives among the Philistines for sixteen months. From his headquarters at the city of Ziklag, he conducts raids against several tribal enemies of the Israelites, including the Geshurites, Gezrites, and Amalekites.

28:1–4 A coalition of several Philistine armies assembles against Saul's forces at Gilboa.

28:5–25 Saul asks for the Lord's direction but gets no response. He hires a medium to conjure up the spirit of Samuel, who predicts that Saul's army will be defeated by the Philistines.

. . . .

Endor A city in the territory of Issachar (Josh. 17:11). King Saul sought advice from a witch in this city (1 Sam. 28:7–10).

Witchcraft The practice of sorcery or black magic by witches and wizards—an activity denounced by God (Deut. 18:10; Mic. 5:12). King Saul displeased God by asking the witch of Endor to summon the spirit of Samuel from the dead (1 Sam. 28:3–25).

APRIL 12 | Read 1 Samuel 29–31

29:1–11 The commanders of the allied Philistine forces do not trust David. They insist that he and his fighting men not be allowed to go into battle against Saul, lest they turn against the Philistines. David is dismissed by his Philistine friend Achish, king of Gath.

30:1–21 David and his army defeat the Amalekites, who had raided his headquarters city of Ziklag and carried away captives and spoils of war.

30:22–31 David shows his kindness and fairness by sharing the spoils of war with 200 of his warriors who were too weak to pursue the battle with the Amalekites to the end. He shows his political astuteness by sharing the spoils with his fellow Israelites in several selected cities.

31:1–13 The Philistines defeat Saul's forces at Mount Gilboa (1 Chron. 10:1–4). Among the dead are Saul and his three sons, whose corpses are displayed on the wall of a Philistine city. Some brave Israelite warriors take the bodies down under the cover of darkness and give them a decent burial.

. . . .

Spoil Plunder taken in war or seized by bandits (Num. 31:9). David established strict regulations for division of the spoils of war among his soldiers (1 Sam. 30:20–25). *Plunder*: NIV; *booty*: NRSV.

Mount Gilboa A mountain range in the territory of Issachar where King Saul died after his defeat by the Philistines (1 Chron. 10:1–8).

Bethshan A Philistine city where King Saul's corpse was displayed (1 Sam. 31:10–13). In later years, Solomon stationed troops in this city (1 Kings 4:12). *Beth-shean*: Josh. 17:11.

APRIL 13 | Read 2 Samuel 1–2

1:1–16 David is informed of the death of Saul and Saul's son Jonathan at the hands of the Philistines.

1:17–27 David laments the death of Saul and Jonathan.

2:1–7 David is recognized as king by the tribe of Judah in southern Israel. He makes Hebron his headquarters city.

2:8–11 Abner, commander of Saul's army, makes Saul's son Ish-bosheth king over the other tribes of Israel. For seven and one-half years, two opposing kingships exist in Israel. One faction recognizes David, and the other recognizes Ish-bosheth.

2:12–32 In an initial battle between the two factions, Ish-bosheth's forces under Abner are defeated by David's army under the leadership of Joab.

Judah The Southern Kingdom, or nation of Judah. Founded after Solomon's death, the Southern Kingdom was composed largely of the tribes of Judah and Benjamin, while the rebellious ten northern tribes retained the name of Israel. Solomon's son Rehoboam was the first king of Judah, with the capital at Jerusalem (1 Kings 14:21). The nation of Judah drifted into paganism and idolatry under a succession of kings, turning a deaf ear to great prophets such as Isaiah and Jeremiah, who tried to bring them back to worship of the one true God. Judah was overrun and taken into exile by the Babylonians about 587 BC. A remnant returned to rebuild Jerusalem about 530 BC (2 Chron. 36:20–23).

Ish-bosheth The youngest son of Saul who became king of Israel for two years (2 Sam. 2:8–9). He was eventually defeated by David and assassinated in his bed (2 Sam. 4:8–12). *Esh-baal*: 1 Chron. 8:33.

King Saul's Bracelet *I [soldier from Saul's camp] took the crown that was upon his [Saul's] head, and the bracelet [band, NIV] that was on his arm* (2 Sam. 1:10).

After King Saul died, a warrior removed his crown and bracelet and brought a report to David about the death of the king. The bracelet worn by Saul probably signified his royal status, just like his crown. Common among kings of the ancient world, these royal arm bands were often decorated with jewels and precious stones.

APRIL 14 | Read 2 Samuel 3–4

3:1–5 David's fortunes increase, while Ish-bosheth loses ground. Six sons from several different wives are born to David while he rules over the tribe of Judah at Hebron.

3:6–21 Abner offers to desert to David and to swing the support of the tribes that follow Ish-bosheth to David.

3:22–39 Joab assassinates Abner. David makes it clear that he had nothing to do with his death.

4:1–8 Ish-bosheth is assassinated by his two brothers; they cut off his head and present it to David.

4:9–12 David executes Ish-bosheth's assassins.

Abner The commander-in-chief of Saul's army. He introduced David to King Saul (1 Sam. 17:55–58) and established Saul's son Ish-bosheth as king after Saul's death (2 Sam. 2:8–10). Later he shifted his loyalty to David and persuaded all the tribes of Israel to follow David's leadership (2 Sam. 3:17–21).

Joab The commander of King David's army during most of David's reign (2 Sam. 8:15–16). He became commander because he was the first to launch an attack against the Jebusites in their fortified city known as Jebus (later called Jerusalem; see 1 Chron. 11:6). His military exploits included victories over the Edomites (1 Kings 11:15) and the Ammonites (2 Sam. 10:6–14). Joab carried out David's plan to have Uriah the Hittite killed in battle (2 Sam. 11:14). He was murdered on orders from the king when Solomon succeeded David as ruler of Judah (1 Kings 2:5–6, 31–34).

Murder in the Gate *When Abner was returned to Hebron, Joab took him aside in the gate [gateway, NIV] to speak with him quietly, and smote him there. . .that he died* (2 Sam. 3:27).

Abner was the commander of King Saul's army. After Saul's death, David became king. Joab, a military leader who was loyal to David, killed Abner because Abner had tried to install one of Saul's sons as the new king. Joab took Abner "aside in the gate" of the city of Hebron, supposedly for a private talk. The vaulted openings through the massive walls of some ancient cities were ten to twelve feet thick. This dark passageway was an ideal place for Joab to commit this crime.

APRIL 15 | Read 2 Samuel 5–7

5:1–5 David is recognized by all the tribes as king over all Israel (1 Chron. 11:1–3).

5:6–10 David captures the city of Jerusalem from the Jebusites and turns it into his new headquarters city (Josh. 15:63; 1 Chron. 11:4–9).

5:11–16 Hiram, king of Tyre, pays honor to David as king of Israel (1 Chron. 14:1–2). Eleven sons from several different wives are born to David at Jerusalem (1 Chron. 14:3–7).

5:17–25 David defeats the Philistines in a major battle in the valley of Rephaim (1 Chron. 14:8–17).

6:1–11 David moves the ark of the covenant from the house of Abinadab to the house of Obed-edom. Uzzah is killed when he touches the ark while it is being moved (1 Chron. 13:1–14).

6:12–19 David dances before the ark of the covenant when it is moved from the house of Obed-edom to Jerusalem (1 Chron. 15:1–29).

6:20–23 David's wife Michal criticizes him for dancing before the ark of the covenant. David defends his behavior as an act of devotion and worship before the Lord.

7:1–17 God promises David that his kingship will be established forever—that a descendant of David will always occupy the throne of Israel (1 Chron. 17:1–15; Ps. 132:11).

7:18–29 David pours out his heart to God in a prayer of praise and thanksgiving (1 Chron. 16:7–36).

. . . .

Israel The Northern Kingdom. This nation was formed in 931 BC when the ten northern tribes rebelled against the two southern tribes and established their own kingship under Rehoboam (1 Kings 12). Samaria was established as the capital city. After about two centuries, the Northern Kingdom was carried into captivity by Assyria in 722 BC and Samaria was populated by foreigners (2 Kings 17:23–24).

Jerusalem The religious and political capital of the Jewish people. Situated forty-eight miles from the Mediterranean Sea and eighteen miles west of the Jordan River, Jerusalem was known as *Salem* in Abraham's time (Gen. 14:18) and as *Jebus* when the people of Israel entered Canaan, or the Promised Land (Josh. 15:8). David captured the city from the Jebusites, renamed it, and turned it into his capital (2 Sam. 5:6–9). It was often called the "city of David" (2 Chron. 32:5). Solomon built the magnificent temple in Jerusalem as the center of worship for the Jewish people about 950 BC (1 Kings 5:5–8). The city fell to the Babylonians in 587 BC, and its leading citizens were taken away as captives (Jer. 39:1–8). After the Persians defeated the Babylonians, King Cyrus of Persia allowed Jewish exiles to return to their homeland and rebuild Jerusalem, including the temple and the city wall (Ezra 1:1–4; Neh. 12:27–47; Zech. 4).

In NT times, Christ wept over the city because of its sin and spiritual indifference (Luke 19:41–42). He predicted its destruction (Luke 19:43–44), entered Jerusalem as a conquering spiritual leader (Matt. 21:9–10), and was crucified on a hill just outside the city wall (Luke 23:33). As Jesus predicted, Jerusalem was destroyed in AD 70 during a fierce battle between the Roman army and Jewish zealots. The church was launched in Jerusalem, where it experienced spectacular growth (Acts 2). The apostle John described the future heavenly city as "new Jerusalem" (Rev. 21:2).

APRIL 16 | Read 2 Samuel 8–10

8:1–14 David extends his kingdom and his influence by defeating the Philistines, Moabites, Syrians, Amalekites, and Edomites (1 Chron. 18:1–14).

8:15–18 The aides and chief officials in David's administration are listed (1 Chron. 18:15–17).

9:1–13 David provides for Mephibosheth, the lame son of his late friend Jonathan. David invites Mephibosheth to live in Jerusalem and to eat at his table like one of his own sons.

10:1–19 David's army, led by his commander Joab, defeats the allied forces of the Ammonites and the Syrians (1 Chron. 19:6–19).

. . . .

Mephibosheth The crippled son of David's friend Jonathan and a grandson of King Saul. He was dropped by his nurse and crippled at age five when she received the news that Jonathan and Saul had been killed by the Philistines (2 Sam. 4:4). David sought out Mephibosheth, restored his family's land, and gave him a place at the king's table. *Merib-baal*: 1 Chron. 8:34.

. . . .

A Dead Dog *He [Mephibosheth] bowed himself, and said, What is thy servant, that thou [David] shouldest look upon such a dead dog as I am?* (2 Sam. 9:8).

King David summoned Mephibosheth, the lame son of his deceased friend Jonathan, to his palace. This verse describes how Mephibosheth responded when the king offered to take care of him. To the Israelites, dogs were worthless and despised animals (1 Sam. 17:43; Ps. 22:16). Mephibosheth's description of himself as a "dead dog" indicates that he thought he was unworthy of King David's kindness and compassion.

A Double Insult *Hanun took David's servants, and shaved off the one half of their beards, and cut off their garments in the middle, even to their buttocks, and sent them away* (2 Sam. 10:4).

King David sent several ambassadors to Hanun, king of the Ammonites, to express his sympathy at the death of his father (2 Sam. 10:1–2). Convinced these messengers were spies, Hanun humiliated them by cutting off their beards on one side of their faces. Israelite men were fond of their beards and considered them a symbol of manhood. To have only half a beard made these messengers objects of ridicule and scorn. Israelite men also wore long outer robes and full-length undergarments. To have these clothes cut off below the waist so their lower bodies were exposed added to the embarrassment they had already endured. When David learned about these actions by Hanun, he took military action against the Ammonites (2 Sam. 10:7–9).

APRIL 17 | Read 2 Samuel 11–12

11:1–5 David commits adultery with Bathsheba, the wife of Uriah the Hittite, while Uriah is away on duty with David's army. She informs David that she is pregnant with David's child.

11:6–13 David tries to cover his sin by granting Uriah a furlough to spend time with Bathsheba. But Uriah foils the king's scheme by refusing to spend the night with his wife.

11:14–25 David directs his commander, Joab, to move Uriah to the front of the battle so Uriah will be killed.

11:26–27 With Uriah disposed of, David takes Bathsheba as his own wife. She gives birth to a son by David.

12:1–9 Nathan the prophet condemns David for his sin and his crime against Uriah. Nathan convicts David of his sin by telling him a parable about a wealthy man (representing David) who stole a lamb from a poor man (representing Uriah).

12:10–12 Nathan announces God's judgment against David because of his sin with Bathsheba: David's own family will be afflicted with trouble and violence.

12:13–23 David repents of his sin and is assured by Nathan that he will not die. But the sickly child born to Bathsheba dies within a few days.

12:24–25 David comforts Bathsheba in the loss of their first child. She later gives birth to another son by David whom they name Solomon.

12:26–31 David's commander, Joab, defeats the Ammonites at Rabbah, and they are made slaves in David's kingdom (1 Chron. 20:1–3).

. . . .

Bath-sheba The wife of Uriah who committed adultery with David and became his wife (2 Sam. 11:2–27). Because of their sin, Bath-sheba's first child died. She later gave birth to four sons, including Solomon, who succeeded David as king. *Bath-shua*: 1 Chron. 3:5.

Nathan The brave prophet who used an allegory to rebuke King David for his sin with Bath-sheba and his plot to kill Bath-sheba's husband, Uriah (2 Sam. 12:1–15). Nathan also assisted David when Adonijah attempted to seize the throne (1 Kings 1:8–45) and wrote histories of David's and Solomon's administrations (1 Chron. 29:29; 2 Chron. 9:29).

. . . .

Temptation on the Roof *David arose from off his bed, and walked upon the roof of the king's house: and from the roof he saw a woman washing herself* (2 Sam. 11:2).

In Bible times the roofs of houses were flat. People used these rooftops, particularly in the evening, to catch a cooling breeze. This is probably what King David was doing when he looked down and saw Bathsheba taking a bath. His casual "rooftop glance" turned to lust. He committed adultery with her and eventually arranged for her warrior husband to be killed in battle to cover up his sin (2 Sam. 11:4–27).

David's Bereavement Pattern *Then said his servants unto him [David], What thing is this that thou hast done? thou didst fast and weep for the child, while it was alive; but when the child was dead, thou didst rise and eat bread* (2 Sam. 12:21).

The newborn child whom King David's servants referred to had been conceived during his adulterous affair with Bathsheba. David's servants were amazed because he reversed the normal pattern of grieving in Israelite culture. Following the death of a loved one, the survivors would stop all their normal activities and mourn and fast for a period of several days. Then they would be persuaded by other family members to return to their daily routine. But David mourned for his newborn child for seven days before he died. He knew this child would die because the prophet Nathan had told him so (2 Sam. 12:13–17). He returned to his routine activities as soon as the child died.

APRIL 18 | Read 2 Samuel 13–14

13:1–19 Amnon, one of David's sons, rapes his half sister Tamar.

13:20–33 David's son Absalom, full brother of Tamar and half brother of Amnon, murders Amnon to avenge his crime against Tamar.

13:34–39 Absalom goes into hiding in Geshur and is greatly missed by his father, David.

14:1–24 David's commander, Joab, pleads with the king to let Absalom return to Jerusalem from Geshur. David agrees but refuses to have any contact with Absalom.

14:25–28 Absalom is portrayed as a handsome, vain, and arrogant man who takes great pride in his long, beautiful hair.

14:29–33 Absalom sets Joab's barley fields on fire to force him to arrange a meeting between him and the king. David and his son Absalom are finally reconciled after years of estrangement.

Absalom The vain, rebellious son of David (2 Sam. 3:3). He killed his brother Amnon for molesting their sister Tamar (2 Sam. 13:22–33). Absalom conspired against David and seized Jerusalem (2 Sam. 15:1–29). Massing an army against David (2 Sam. 17:24–26), he was killed by David's commander Joab after his hair was tangled in a tree (2 Sam. 18:9–18). David mourned grievously at Absalom's death (2 Sam. 18:19–33). *Abishalom*: 1 Kings 15:2, 10.

APRIL 19 | Read 2 Samuel 15–16

15:1–12 Absalom works behind the scenes to undercut his father's influence and to cultivate loyalty to himself throughout Israel. Absalom gathers a force at Hebron in opposition to David's kingship.

15:13–23 David and his family, his household servants, and the officials in his administration flee Jerusalem. They hide in the wilderness because of the threat from Absalom's rebellion.

15:24–29 David sends the priests Zadok and Abiathar back to Jerusalem with the ark of the covenant, since this city is considered its appropriate resting place.

15:30–37 David sends his friend and supporter Hushai the Archite into Jerusalem so he can spy on the rebellious Absalom.

16:1–4 Ziba, the servant of Mephibosheth, comes to the aid of the fleeing David and his officials by providing food and supplies.

16:5–14 Shimei, a distant relative of Saul, issues curses against David as he flees from Jerusalem.

16:15–19 Absalom enters Jerusalem with his supporters. The spy Hushai convinces Absalom he has switched loyalties from David to Absalom.

16:20–23 Ahithophel, a former aide of David, now supports Absalom's rebellion. Ahithophel advises Absalom to claim David's concubines as his own, an act that symbolizes Absalom is assuming the kingship.

. . . .

Abiathar A high priest under David who remained faithful to the king during Absalom's rebellion (2 Sam. 15:24–35). He was later banished from the royal court by Solomon for supporting Adonijah as king (1 Kings 1:7–25; 2:22–35).

. . . .

Dust on the Head *Hushai the Archite came to meet him [David] with his coat rent [torn, NIV], and earth [dust, NIV] upon his head* (2 Sam. 15:32).

Hushai was a friend and supporter of King David. During Absalom's rebellion, Hushai expressed his sorrow at David's exile by tearing his clothes and throwing dust on his head. Adam, the first man, was created by the Lord from "the dust of the ground" (Gen. 2:7), one of the most common substances on earth. Putting dust on one's head may have been a way of showing humility and helplessness in the face of sorrow. The custom of putting dust on the head is also referred to in several other passages in the Bible (Josh. 7:6; 1 Sam. 4:12; 2 Sam. 1:2; 13:19; Neh. 9:1; Job 2:12; Lam. 2:10; Ezek. 27:30; Rev. 18:19).

APRIL 20 | Read 2 Samuel 17–18

17:1–14 Ahithophel advises Absalom to attack David and his forces while they are on the run. But the spy Hushai convinces him to wait until he has gathered a large army before pressing the attack.

17:15–22 Hushai sends messengers to warn David to flee into the wilderness, in case Absalom should decide to mount a surprise attack against him.

17:23 Ahithophel commits suicide because Absalom did not follow his advice to attack David immediately.

17:24–29 David and his forces hide out near the city of Mahanaim; here they are supplied with food and other necessities by local residents.

18:1–8 David's army, under three military leaders—Joab, Abishai, and Ittai—attack Absalom's forces in the forest of Ephraim. David instructs them not to harm his son Absalom.

18:9–18 Disregarding the king's orders, Joab kills Absalom after his long hair is entangled in the branches of a tree.

18:19–33 David weeps bitterly for his son after a messenger informs him that Absalom is dead.

Hidden in a Cistern *They [Jonathan and Ahimaaz]. . .came to a man's house . . .which had a well in his court; whither they went down. And the woman took and spread a covering over the well's mouth, and spread ground corn [grain, NIV] thereon; and the thing was not known* (2 Sam. 17:18–19).

Jonathan and Ahimaaz were spies who reported on Absalom's activities to King David while David was in exile during Absalom's rebellion. The "well" in which Jonathan and Ahimaaz were hidden was probably a cistern that was used to collect rainwater. It must have been dry at this time. With containers of grain or flour placed on top of its cover, this cistern was an ideal hiding place.

David's Sad Lament *The king [David]. . .wept. . .O my son Absalom, my son, my son Absalom! would God I had died for thee* (2 Sam. 18:33).

David's outpouring of grief over his son Absalom is one of the saddest passages in the entire Bible. Apparently such expressions of sorrow over deceased loved ones were common in Bible times. When Jacob died, his family "mourned with a great and very sore lamentation" (Gen. 50:10).

APRIL 21 | Read 2 Samuel 19–20

19:1–8 David's extreme and extended grief over his son Absalom comes across to his supporters as lack of appreciation for their loyalty. Joab confronts David about this problem, and David agrees to meet with his soldiers and constituents at the city gate.

19:9–14 David builds political support throughout Israel to prepare for his return to Jerusalem as king. He names his nephew Amasa, who had commanded Absalom's army (2 Sam. 17:25), an officer in his army in order to reach out to those who had supported Absalom.

19:15–43 David is acclaimed king by several different segments of Israelite society as he crosses the Jordan River and enters the city of Jerusalem. He forgives Shimei for insulting him as he was fleeing the city (2 Sam. 16:5–14).

20:1–7 A man named Sheba of the tribe of Benjamin incites a rebellion against David among the northern tribes of Israel. David dispatches his army under Joab and Amasa to put down the rebellion.

20:8–13 Joab murders Amasa, apparently because he had doubts about Amasa's loyalty to the king.

20:14–22 Sheba's rebellion ends when he is assassinated by citizens of the city where he sought refuge from David's army.

20:23–26 The chief officials in David's administration are listed.

. . . .

Benaiah A loyal supporter of David and Solomon. A commander of David's bodyguard (2 Sam. 20:23), he later became commander-in-chief of Solomon's army (1 Kings 2:35).

Seraiah David's secretary or recorder who served also in Solomon's administration (2 Sam. 8:17). Also called *Sheva* (2 Sam. 20:25), *Shisha* (1 Kings 4:3), and *Shavsha* (1 Chron. 18:16).

. . . .

Crossing the Jordan River *There went over a ferry boat to carry over the king's household* (2 Sam. 19:18).

This verse describes David's return from exile to take up his duties as king over Israel after Absalom's rebellion had been put down. David and the rest of the royal household crossed over the Jordan River back into Israelite territory. Many interpreters question the KJV's use of the term *ferry boat* to describe this crossing. The Jordan River is not very deep in most places. It is generally crossed at shallow places known as fords by just wading across. The NIV's rendering of this verse—"they crossed at the ford to take the king's household over"—is probably a better translation.

Grasping the Beard *Joab said to Amasa, Art thou in health, my brother? And Joab took Amasa by the beard with the right hand to kiss him* (2 Sam. 20:9).

Grasping a person's beard and kissing his cheek was a customary greeting among men of Bible times. But Joab used it as a cover to assassinate Amasa (2 Sam. 20:10) because Amasa had supported Absalom's rebellion.

APRIL 22 | Read 2 Samuel 21–22

21:1–9 About 400 years before David's time, Joshua had made a treaty with the Gibeonites that guaranteed their safety (Josh. 9:3–27). But Saul had broken this treaty by killing some of the Gibeonites. David makes amends with the Gibeonites by allowing them to execute seven of the surviving descendants of Saul.

21:10–14 David retrieves the bones of Saul and his son Jonathan from the city of Jabesh-gilead and has them buried in Saul's family plot in the territory of Benjamin.

21:15–22 David's army kills several Philistine giants, some of whom were descendants of the giant Goliath whom David had killed several years before (1 Sam. 17:32–52).

22:1–51 David utters a prayer of thanksgiving to God for giving him victory over all his enemies. This psalm also appears in the Bible as Psalm 18.

Jabesh-gilead A city of Gilead about twenty miles south of the Sea of Galilee. King Saul defended this city against Nahash, king of the Ammonites (1 Sam. 11:1–11).

A Psalm Repeated *David spake unto the LORD the words of this song in the day that the LORD had delivered him out of the hand of all his enemies* (2 Sam. 22:1).

The remaining verses in 2 Samuel 22 contain the words of this psalm that David wrote. This psalm also appears in the Bible as Psalm 18. Although there are a few minor variations between these two recordings of the same psalm, it is essentially the same in both locations. This verse shows that David wrote many of the psalms in response to specific events in his life. He wrote this psalm to praise the Lord for giving him victory over the enemies of Israel and for establishing him as king throughout the land.

APRIL 23 | Read 2 Samuel 23–24

23:1–7 Apparently near the end of his life, David issues these words of praise to God for His faithfulness and His promise that David would enjoy an eternal reign on the throne of Israel (2 Sam. 7:1–17).

23:8–39 The names and brave deeds of David's "mighty men" are listed. These men may have been an elite group of warriors, perhaps David's personal body-guards (1 Chron. 11:10–47).

24:1–9 David directs his commander, Joab, to take a census of all the fighting men throughout the tribes of Israel (1 Chron. 21:1–6).

24:10–15 The Lord sends a plague upon the people because of David's sin in ordering the census. Perhaps his sin was human pride over the kingdom he had built (1 Chron. 21:7–17).

24:16–25 David buys a threshing floor from Ornan/Araunah the Jebusite as the site for an altar on which sacrifices will be offered to God. These sacrifices bring an end to the plague (1 Chron. 21:18–30).

Mighty Men The brave and loyal warriors who risked their lives for David before and after he became king (2 Sam. 23:8–39). Joshua also had the support of courageous warriors known as "mighty men of valor" (Josh. 1:14; 10:7). *Fighting men*: NIV; *warriors*: NRSV.

Threshingfloor A place where grain was threshed (or separated from the stalk and husk) after harvesting (2 Sam. 6:6).

Araunah A Jebusite from whom David bought a threshing floor as a place to build an altar (2 Sam. 24:16–24). This plot of ground was the site on which Solomon's temple was built in Jerusalem in later years (2 Chron. 3:1). *Ornan*: 1 Chron. 21:15; 2 Chron. 3:1.

APRIL 24 | Read 1 Kings 1–2

1:1–4 David's health declines with age, and he is unable to carry out his duties as king.

1:5–10 Adonijah, a son of David and brother of Absalom, plots to seize the throne as David's successor.

1:11–31 David's wife Bathsheba and Nathan the prophet persuade David to designate Bathsheba's son Solomon as the royal successor.

1:32–40 Solomon is officially anointed at Gihon as David's successor (1 Chron. 23:1).

1:41–53 Adonijah seeks sanctuary from Solomon at the altar. Solomon promises Adonijah that he will not kill him if he causes no trouble for the new king.

2:1–9 David charges Solomon to remain faithful to the Lord as the new king of Israel. David gives Solomon permission to take revenge against two of his political enemies—Joab and Shimei.

2:10–12 David dies after forty years as king—seven years as king of the southern tribe of Judah and thirty-three years as king over all the tribes of Israel (1 Chron. 29:26–27).

2:13–25 Solomon has Adonijah killed because he requested that a former wife of David be given to Adonijah as his own wife.

2:26–27 Solomon deposes Abiathar from the priesthood because he supported Adonijah's quest for the kingship.

2:28–35 Solomon assassinates Joab, former commander of David's army, because he supported Adonijah's attempt to seize the throne. Joab had also killed two innocent men: Abner and Amasa.

2:36–46 Solomon has Shimei assassinated when he disobeys the king's orders and leaves the city of Jerusalem.

....

Solomon David's son and successor as king of Israel (reigned about 970–930 BC). Solomon got off to a good start by praying for divine wisdom and insight (1 Kings 3), and he developed fame as a wise and efficient king of great wealth (1 Kings 4). At God's command, Solomon completed the building of the temple in Jerusalem (1 Kings 5–8). But he drifted away from commitment to the one true God through his marriages with pagan wives (1 Kings 11:1–8). He also oppressed his people with burdensome taxes to support his ambitious kingdom-building projects (1 Kings 12:4). After Solomon's death, the ten northern tribes rebelled under Jeroboam and formed their own nation known as Israel, or the Northern Kingdom (1 Kings 12:1–19).

....

Safety at the Altar *Adonijah feared because of Solomon, and arose, and went, and caught hold on the horns of the altar* (1 Kings 1:50).
Adonijah, a son of David, had hoped to succeed his father as king of Israel (1 Kings 1:11). But this honor went to Adonijah's brother Solomon. Adonijah sought protection from Solomon's wrath by grasping the four corners, or horns, of the altar in the tabernacle. This provided temporary asylum or protection for a person who had committed a crime until the charges against him were thoroughly investigated. This same protection could be sought in one of the cities of refuge throughout the land (Deut. 4:41–42).

Buried with Honors *David slept [rested, NIV] with his fathers, and was buried in the city of David* (1 Kings 2:10).
When King David died, he was accorded the great honor of being buried in the city of Jerusalem. The dead were usually buried outside the cities of Bible times. Several successors of David as kings of Judah were also honored with burials inside Jerusalem: Solomon (1 Kings 11:43), Ahaz (2 Chron. 28:27), Hezekiah (2 Chron. 32:33), Manasseh (2 Kings 21:18), and Amon (2 Kings 21:26). The location of David's tomb was apparently known in NT times (Acts 2:29), but the site is a mystery today.

APRIL 25 | Read 1 Kings 3–4

3:1–2 Solomon marries the daughter of the pharaoh of Egypt to seal a political alliance with that nation.

3:3–15 Solomon has a dream while offering sacrifices to the Lord at Gibeon. In the dream, Solomon asks for great wisdom so he might be a wise and just king. God promises to honor his request and to give Solomon great riches and honor, as well (2 Chron. 1:1–13).

3:16–28 Solomon's wisdom is revealed as he settles a dispute between two women who claim to be the mother of the same child.

4:1–20 The aides and officials in Solomon's administration are listed.

4:21–28 Solomon becomes wealthy and extravagant as the ruler of a kingdom that stretches from Egypt in the south to the Euphrates River in the north (Ps. 72:8–11).

4:29–34 Solomon is also acclaimed for his great wisdom. He writes thousands of songs and proverbs.

Book of Proverbs A book of wisdom in the OT filled with short, pithy sayings on how to live with maturity and integrity under the watchful eye of God—the source of all wisdom. These wise sayings, written by Solomon as well as other sages of Israel, deal with such practical matters as strong drink (23:20–21), pride (16:18), work (6:6–11), child rearing (22:6), friendship (17:17), anger (19:11), speech (15:1–4), sexual temptation (chap. 5), and honesty in business (11:1–4).

Supplies for Solomon *Solomon had twelve officers [district governors, NIV] over all Israel, which provided victuals [supplies] for the king and his household: each man his month in a year made provision* (1 Kings 4:7).

Taxes are nothing new. They existed as early as King Solomon's time (about 950 BC). He needed revenue to support his lavish building projects and the huge army and staff that he assembled. For taxation purposes, Solomon divided the nation into twelve administrative districts. Each of these districts supplied the king with what he needed to run the central government for one month out of the year. Each district had a governor or administrator appointed by the king. This official was responsible for gathering needed supplies from the people in his district.

APRIL 26 | Read 1 Kings 5–7

5:1–18 Solomon makes a trade agreement with King Hiram of Tyre, a friend and supporter of his father, David. Solomon trades food for cedar trees as well as cut stone, which are available in Hiram's territory. These building materials are to be used in the construction of a magnificent temple for worship of the Lord in Jerusalem (2 Chron. 2).

6:1–38 Solomon's temple in Jerusalem is completed in seven years (2 Chron. 3).

7:1–12 Solomon spends thirteen years constructing his own royal palace and other administrative buildings in the capital city.

7:13–22 Solomon hires a metalworker from Tyre to construct two magnificent pillars of brass, or copper, in the temple.

7:23–51 This metalworker also fashions other furnishings for the temple, including a huge water basin ("molten sea," v. 23) for sacrificial washing of the priests; candlesticks that stand before the altar; and pots, shovels, and other utensils to be used by the priests in handling sacrificial offerings (2 Chron. 4).

Molten Sea A large bronze vessel made by King Hiram of Tyre for ceremonial use by the priests in Solomon's temple at Jerusalem (1 Kings 7:23).

Solomon's Temple *The house which king Solomon built for the* LORD, *the length thereof was threescore cubits, and the breadth thereof twenty cubits, and the height thereof thirty cubits* (1 Kings 6:2).

The idea of the temple did not originate with Solomon, but with David, who was not permitted to build it because he had been a man of war (1 Chron. 28:2–3). God gave David a plan for the temple, just as He had given Moses the plan for the tabernacle. David communicated this plan to Solomon, directing him to construct the building (1 Chron. 28:11–19). The temple was built on Mount Moriah, on the site of the altar that David raised up on the threshing floor of Araunah the Jebusite (2 Sam. 24:21–25). It had the same general arrangements as the tabernacle, since it was a place where God would meet with His people and where they would worship Him. The dimensions of the temple were double those of the tabernacle. Using eighteen inches as the length of a cubit, the temple was ninety feet long, thirty feet wide, and forty-five feet high.

APRIL 27 | Read 1 Kings 8–9

8:1–11 The ark of the covenant is placed in the Most Holy Place in the inner court of the temple. The Lord shows His pleasure and His presence by filling the Most Holy Place with a cloud.

8:12–66 In an elaborate ceremony of dedication for the temple, Solomon prays a prayer of gratitude to the Lord and leads the people to make sacrificial offerings to show their dedication and obedience (2 Chron. 5–6).

9:1–9 God makes Solomon the same conditional promise He had made to his father, David. If Solomon follows the Lord, his kingship over Israel will be established forever. But if Solomon turns away from God and leads His people astray, the Lord will reject Solomon and bring punishment upon the land (2 Chron. 7:12–22).

9:10–28 Solomon builds supply cities and chariot cities for military purposes and establishes a port for conducting trade with other nations (2 Chron. 8).

Zion One of the hills on which Jerusalem was built and the site of an ancient Jebusite fortress before the city was captured by David. In Solomon's time this section of Jerusalem was extended to include the temple area. Sometimes all of Jerusalem is referred to as "Zion" (1 Kings 8:1). *Sion*: Rev. 14:1.

Ship A seagoing vessel propelled by oars or sails (Jon. 1:4–5). The Jews were not mariners, since most of the Mediterranean coast was controlled by the Phoenicians and Philistines. Solomon's fleet was manned by Phoenicians (1 Kings 9:26–28).

The Month of Ethanim *All the men of Israel assembled themselves unto king Solomon at the feast in the month Ethanim, which is the seventh month* (1 Kings 8:2).

The "feast" referred to in this verse is the Feast of Tabernacles. Solomon chose this important celebration as the perfect time to dedicate the newly constructed temple. The month of Ethanim parallels our September/October.

Hands Lifted in Prayer *Solomon stood before the altar of the Lord in the presence of all the congregation of Israel, and spread forth his hands toward heaven* (1 Kings 8:22).

When King Solomon dedicated the newly constructed temple with a prayer to the Lord, he stood with his hands open and the palms lifted toward heaven. This stance was often taken when praying, especially in OT times (Exod. 9:33; Ezra 9:5; Ps. 28:2; Isa. 1:15).

APRIL 28 | Read 1 Kings 10–11

10:1–13 The Queen of Sheba visits Solomon and is impressed with his wisdom and great riches (2 Chron. 9:1–12).

10:14–29 Solomon's riches multiply as he develops trade relationships with other nations. Other rulers honor him for his wisdom and power (2 Chron. 9:13–28).

11:1–8 Solomon's dozens of foreign wives, many of whom he married to seal political alliances, cause him to turn from the Lord and worship pagan gods.

11:9–13 God declares that He will divide Solomon's kingdom because of his sin of idolatry. But He will allow one tribe to remain under the kingship of Solomon's son and successor because of His promise of an eternal kingship to Solomon's father, David (2 Sam. 7:1–17).

11:14–25 Several Israelite leaders oppose Solomon's kingship. These include Hadad and Rezon.

11:26–40 The most serious threat to Solomon arises from within his own administration. Jeroboam, one of Solomon's officials, rebels against the king. The prophet Ahijah promises Jeroboam that Solomon's kingdom will be split into two factions. The northern tribes will unite under Jeroboam against Solomon. The southern tribe of Judah will remain loyal to the dynasty of David and will be ruled by Solomon's son.

11:41–43 Solomon dies and is succeeded by his son Rehoboam (2 Chron. 9:29–31).

Sabeans Natives or inhabitants of ancient Sheba in southwest Arabia, a country now known as Yemen. Job's livestock was stolen by Sabeans (Job 1:13–15). The wealthy queen of Sheba visited King Solomon (1 Kings 10).

Jeroboam I The first king of Israel (reigned about 931–910 BC) after the kingdom of Solomon split into two separate nations following Solomon's death. An official in Solomon's administration, Jeroboam led the ten northern tribes to rebel against the two southern tribes when Rehoboam succeeded his father, Solomon, as king (1 Kings 12:17–20). Jeroboam established idol worship in the cities of Bethel and Dan (1 Kings 12:26–30) and was ultimately defeated by King Abijah of Judah and struck down by the Lord (2 Chron. 13:19–20).

APRIL 29 | Read 1 Kings 12–13

12:1–15 Rehoboam disregards the complaints of the northern tribes under Jeroboam and vows to intensify the harsh practices of his father, Solomon (2 Chron. 10:1–15).

12:16–24 The northern tribes revolt against Rehoboam and acclaim Jeroboam as their king. For the next several centuries of Israel's history, two opposing nations of the Jewish people exist—the northern tribes known as the nation of Israel (or the Northern Kingdom) and the southern tribes known as the nation of Judah (or the Southern Kingdom). God's promise of an eternal kingship through David and his descendants continues through the Southern Kingdom (2 Chron. 10:16–19).

12:25–33 King Jeroboam of Israel (Northern Kingdom) sets up sanctuaries for worship at the cities of Bethel and Dan in his territory. He wants to remove the temptation for the people of his kingdom to return to the temple at Jerusalem in Judah (Southern Kingdom) to worship God and offer sacrifices (2 Chron. 11:14–17).

13:1–10 God sends a prophet from Judah to King Jeroboam of Israel. This prophet delivers the prediction that Josiah, a descendant of King David, will burn the bones of Jeroboam's priests upon the altar at Bethel at a distant future time.

13:11–32 The prophet who delivers this message to King Jeroboam is killed by a lion after he disobeys God's commands to return immediately to Judah.

13:33–34 King Jeroboam continues his practice of using unauthorized and unqualified persons as priests in the sanctuaries he has established in the Northern Kingdom.

Rehoboam The son and successor of Solomon as king of Judah (reigned about 931–913 BC). He refused to implement the reform measures called for by northern leaders after Solomon's death—a foolish act that resulted in the split of the ten northern tribes into the Northern Kingdom (1 Kings 12:1–24). *Roboam*: Jesus' ancestry (Matt. 1:7).

APRIL 30 | Read 1 Kings 14–15

14:1–18 A prophet at Bethel predicts that King Jeroboam's ill son will die and that Jeroboam will be punished for his sin and idolatry.

14:19–20 Jeroboam dies after reigning over Israel for twenty-two years and is succeeded by his son Nadab.

14:21–31 Rehoboam dies after serving as king of Judah for seventeen years and is succeeded by his son Abijam (2 Chron. 12:13–16).

15:1–8 Abijam dies after reigning over Judah for three years and is succeeded by his son Asa (2 Chron. 13:21–14:2).

15:9–24 King Asa pleases the Lord while ruling Judah. He removes the idols and pagan shrines that had been established in the land. After reigning for forty-one years, Asa dies and is succeeded by his son Jehoshaphat (2 Chron. 15; 16:13–17:1).

15:25–31 King Nadab of Israel is assassinated and succeeded by Baasha after a reign of only two years.

15:32–16:7 The prophet Jehu predicts that the dynasty of King Baasha of Israel will end. Baasha dies and is succeeded by his son Elah.

Abijah The son and successor of Rehoboam as king of Judah (reigned about 913–911 BC; 2 Chron. 11:20–22). *Abijam*: 1 Kings 14:31; *Abia*: Jesus' ancestry (Matt. 1:7).

Asa Third king of Judah (reigned about 911–869 BC) who led in a national religious revival. He destroyed the places of idol worship (2 Chron. 14:2–5) and fortified Judah to usher in a period of peace (2 Chron. 14:6–8). Reproved by Hanani the prophet for not relying on the Lord, he died from a foot disease (2 Chron. 16:7–14).

Food for a Journey *Take with thee [King Jeroboam's wife] ten loaves, and cracknels [cakes, NIV], and a cruse of honey, and go to him [the prophet Ahijah]* (1 Kings 14:3).

When King Jeroboam's son became sick, he sent his wife to ask the prophet Ahijah whether his son would get well. The journey to Ahijah's house must have been long, since the king's wife carried enough food for several days. Cracknels were bread that had been baked into thin, hard biscuits. They probably held up better under traveling conditions than soft-baked bread.

MAY 1 | Read 1 Kings 16–17

16:8–14 Elah is assassinated and succeeded as king of Israel by Zimri, one of his chariot commanders. Zimri also murders all the relatives of Baasha and Elah to end the royal dynasty of Baasha, as the prophet Jehu had predicted (1 Kings 16:1–7).

16:15–20 Zimri commits suicide after he realizes his forces face defeat at the hands of Omri. He is succeeded as king of Israel by Omri.

16:21–30 Omri builds Samaria and makes it the capital city of Israel. After an evil reign of twelve years, he dies and is succeeded by his son Ahab.

16:31–34 Ahab marries Jezebel, a worshiper of the pagan god Baal, and sets up a shrine to Baal in the capital city of Samaria.

17:1 The prophet Elijah predicts that a drought will strike Israel as punishment for Ahab's sins.

17:2–7 Elijah is kept alive by ravens as he hides from Ahab beside the brook Cherith.

17:8–16 During the drought, Elijah and a widow and her son are kept alive miraculously by the Lord through a small amount of meal and oil that never runs out.

17:17–24 The son of the widow dies, and Elijah restores him miraculously to life.

Samaria The capital city of Israel, or the Northern Kingdom, and a name often applied to the surrounding region. The city was built by Omri, king of Israel, about 900 BC. It was destroyed about 722 BC when the Assyrians overran the Northern Kingdom (2 Kings 17:3–24).

Ahab The wicked king of Israel (reigned about 874–853 BC) and husband of Jezebel. Ahab was known as an aggressive builder (1 Kings 22:39). Influenced by Jezebel, he introduced Baal worship into Israel (1 Kings 16:31–33). His pagan practices were denounced by the prophet Elijah (1 Kings 17:1). Ahab waged war against King Ben-hadad of Syria (1 Kings 20) and was killed in a battle at Ramoth-gilead (1 Kings 22:34–38).

Jezebel The scheming wife of King Ahab who promoted Baal worship in the nation of Israel (Northern Kingdom). She led Ahab to erect pagan altars (1 Kings 16:32–33), killed several prophets of the Lord (1 Kings 18:4–13), and plotted the death of the prophet Elijah (1 Kings 19:1–2), who prophesied her death (1 Kings 21:23). King Jehu had Jezebel assassinated when he came into power, in fulfillment of Elijah's prophecy (2 Kings 9:7–37).

Elijah A courageous prophet who opposed King Ahab and his successor, Ahaziah, because of their encouragement of Baal worship throughout the Northern Kingdom. Because of Ahab's wickedness, Elijah predicted a drought would afflict the land (1 Kings 17). He wiped out the prophets of Baal after a dramatic demonstration of God's power on Mount Carmel (1 Kings 18:17–40).

After selecting Elisha as his successor, Elijah was carried into heaven in a whirlwind (2 Kings 2:1–11). The coming of the Messiah was often associated in Jewish thought with Elijah's return. Some people even thought Jesus was Elijah (Luke 9:8). *Elias*: Greek form (Matt. 17:4).

MAY 2 | Read 1 Kings 18–19

18:1–14 God commands Elijah to meet King Ahab. The Lord assures Elijah that He will end the drought by sending rain. Elijah sends word through one of Ahab's servants that he wants to meet with the king.

18:15–19 Elijah talks with King Ahab and asks him to send the prophets of Baal to meet him on Mount Carmel.

18:20–40 Elijah prevails over the prophets of Baal in a dramatic encounter on Mount Carmel. The Lord sends a miraculous sign to show His superiority over all pagan gods. Elijah kills the prophets of Baal at the brook Kishon.

18:41–46 God ends the drought by sending rain in response to the prayer of Elijah (1 Kings 17:1).

19:1–18 Elijah flees to Mount Horeb to escape Jezebel's threat against his life. God directs him to return to Israel to anoint new kings for Syria and Israel and to select the prophet Elisha as his successor. The Lord assures Elijah in a still, small voice that many people in Israel remain faithful to Him.

19:19–21 Elisha follows Elijah after he is selected as the prophet's successor.

. . . .

Baal The chief Canaanite god (Judg. 2:13) who, as the god of rain, was thought to provide fertility for crops and livestock. Baal worship was associated with immorality (Hosea 9:10) and child sacrifice (Jer. 19:5)—pagan rituals considered especially offensive to the one true God of the Israelites. During their history, the Hebrew people often committed idolatry by worshiping this god of their Canaanite neighbors. The prophet Elijah denounced the prophets of Baal, and the God of Israel won a decisive victory over this pagan god on Mount Carmel (1 Kings 18:17–40). *Baalim:* plural form (1 Sam. 12:10).

Mount Carmel A prominent mountain in northern Palestine where the prophet Elijah demonstrated the power of God in a dramatic encounter with the priests of the pagan god Baal (1 Kings 18:17–39).

. . . .

A God Who Hears and Acts *Elijah mocked them [the prophets of Baal], and said, Cry aloud: for he [Baal] is a god; either he is talking, or he is pursuing, or he is in a journey, or peradventure he sleepeth, and must be awaked* (1 Kings 18:27).

The prophet Elijah challenged the prophets of the pagan god Baal to a contest on Mount Carmel. They laid a sacrificial animal on a pile of wood. The prophets of Baal would call on their god, and Elijah would call on his. The god who answered by sending fire to consume the sacrifice would be declared the superior god (1 Kings 18:22–25). Elijah ridiculed Baal because he did not answer the cry of his priests, even though they called to him for several hours. Perhaps he was silent, Elijah suggested, because he was preoccupied with other matters, was away on a journey, or was taking a nap. When Elijah called on the Lord, fire fell immediately from heaven and consumed the sacrificial animal on the altar (1 Kings 18:38). This proved that God heard the prayers of His people and was superior to Baal.

MAY 3 | Read 1 Kings 20–21

20:1–12 King Ben-hadad of Syria prepares to attack the forces of King Ahab of Israel at the capital city of Samaria.

20:13–21 Although outnumbered, Ahab's army defeats Ben-hadad because of the Lord's miraculous intervention.

20:22–34 Ahab defeats Ben-hadad a second time and spares his life.

20:35–43 A prophet of the Lord condemns King Ahab for not killing Ben-hadad when he had the opportunity.

21:1–4 Naboth refuses to sell his land with a vineyard to King Ahab.

21:5–16 Jezebel and Ahab have Naboth executed on a false charge so they can take over his property.

21:17–29 The prophet Elijah announces to King Ahab that he and Jezebel will be killed and that dogs will lick up his blood and ravage Jezebel's corpse. This will be the Lord's punishment for their crime against Naboth and their encouragement of idol worship throughout Israel.

. . . .

Rope A heavy cord. Ropes on the head or neck signified distress (1 Kings 20:31–32) and perhaps submission, since cords were used to bind prisoners. *Cord*: Judg. 15:13.

Belial A word for wickedness or wicked people (1 Kings 21:10). The word also means wickedness personified—a reference to Satan (2 Cor. 6:15).

. . . .

No Sale *Naboth said to Ahab, The LORD forbid it me, that I should give the inheritance of my fathers unto thee* (1 Kings 21:3).

Naboth's refusal to sell his land in which his vineyard grew shows the dedication of the Israelites to the land they had inherited from their ancestors. By law, Israelites were not to sell their land inheritance, except in cases of extreme poverty or financial hardship (Lev. 25:23, 25; Num. 36:7). King Ahab eventually brought false charges against Naboth, had him killed, and took his land (1 Kings 21:7–13). The Lord sent the prophet Elijah to condemn these brazen acts and to tell the king that he would pay for these crimes with his life (1 Kings 21:17–22).

MAY 4 | Read 1 Kings 22

22:1–4 The kings of Israel (Ahab) and Judah (Jehoshaphat) propose a joint campaign against the Syrians to capture the city of Ramoth-gilead (2 Chron. 18:1–3).

22:5–12 Several false prophets assure King Ahab of a great victory if he and Jehoshaphat attack the Syrian forces (2 Chron. 18:4–11).

22:13–28 Micaiah, a true prophet of the Lord, announces that Ahab will be defeated if he goes against the Syrians (2 Chron. 18:12–27).

22:29–40 King Ahab is killed in the battle at Ramoth-gilead. Dogs lick up his blood when it is washed from his chariot, in fulfillment of the prediction of the prophet Elijah (1 Kings 21:19; 2 Chron. 18:28–34).

22:41–50 After twenty-five years as king of Judah, Jehoshaphat dies and is succeeded by his son Jehoram (2 Chron. 20:31–21:1).

22:51–53 Ahaziah succeeds his father, Ahab, as king of Israel and continues his evil and sinful policies.

. . . .

Micaiah An OT prophet who predicted that King Ahab of Israel would be killed in a battle at Ramoth-gilead, in contrast to false prophets who assured the king he would be victorious (1 Kings 22:8–28). Micaiah was imprisoned for his stinging message, but his prediction was correct (1 Kings 22:29–39).

Ivory Decorative trim from the tusks of elephants that was a symbol of luxury. King Ahab's house was known as the "ivory house" (1 Kings 22:39).

Ahaziah A king of Israel (reigned about 853–852 BC) and son of Ahab. A Baal worshiper (1 Kings 22:52–53), he was injured in a fall from the balcony of his palace. After consulting a pagan god for help, he died, in fulfillment of Elijah's prophecy (2 Kings 1:2–17).

MAY 5 | Read 2 Kings 1–3

1:1–18 Ahaziah, son and successor of Ahab as king of Israel, dies after suffering injuries in an accident. Since he has no son, he is succeeded by his brother Jehoram, another son of Ahab.

2:1–11 Elisha asks that a double portion of Elijah's spirit be given to him as Elijah's successor. Elijah is taken into heaven by a whirlwind.

2:12–18 Elisha is recognized by the sons of the prophets as Elijah's legitimate successor, with the Spirit of the Lord that filled Elijah.

2:19–22 Elisha miraculously purifies the bad waters of a spring at Jericho.

2:23–25 Elisha curses several children who were mocking and taunting him as God's prophet; they are attacked by two bears.

3:1–3 Ahab's son Jehoram becomes king of Israel and continues his father's evil practices.

3:4–20 Elisha predicts that the combined forces of Israel, Judah, and Edom will be victorious over the Moabites.

3:21–27 As Elisha predicts, the Moabites are defeated.

Chariot of Fire The fiery chariot with blazing horses that came between Elijah and Elisha as Elijah was taken into heaven by a whirlwind (2 Kings 2:11).

Elisha The prophet selected and anointed by Elijah as his successor (1 Kings 19:16–21). He followed Elijah for several years and was present at his ascension into heaven when the mantle of leadership fell upon him (2 Kings 2:9–14). Elisha served as a counselor and adviser to four kings of the Northern Kingdom—Jehoram, Jehu, Jehoahaz, and Joash—across a period of about fifty years (850–800 BC). *Eliseus*: Greek form (Luke 4:27).

Sons of the Prophets *And the sons of the prophets that were at Bethel came forth to Elisha* (2 Kings 2:3).

These "sons of the prophets" knew that Elisha had been chosen as Elijah's successor, so they came out to see the two prophets together when Elijah and Elisha approached the city of Bethel. Several different groups of "sons of the prophets" are mentioned in the book of 2 Kings (2:5, 7; 4:38, 43; 6:1–2). They were apparently disciples or followers of prophets such as Elijah and Elisha who assisted the prophets in their work and learned from their example and instruction. A "company of prophets" is also mentioned in connection with the ministry of the prophet Samuel (1 Sam. 19:19–20). Samuel may have been the founder of this prophetic guild.

MAY 6 | Read 2 Kings 4–5

4:1–7 Elisha works a miracle for a poor widow whose sons are about to be sold into slavery. A jar of oil is multiplied until she has enough to pay her debts.

4:8–37 Elisha brings back to life the only son of a woman at Shunem who had provided food and lodging for the prophet.

4:38–44 Elisha miraculously purifies and multiplies a meager supply of food to feed a large group of the sons of the prophets.

5:1–14 Naaman, commander of the Syrian army, is miraculously cured of his leprosy by the prophet Elisha (Luke 4:27).

5:15–27 Elisha refuses to accept the gifts of thanks offered by Naaman. But his servant Gehazi follows Naaman and claims the gifts. As punishment, Elisha declares that the leprosy that afflicted Naaman will fall on Gehazi.

Loins The midsection of the human body, just below the stomach. The Jewish people wrapped their loose garments around their loins when working or traveling to give greater freedom of movement (2 Kings 4:29). The word is used figuratively by Peter to advise his readers to be ready for Christ's return (1 Pet. 1:13).

MAY 7 | Read 2 Kings 6–8

6:1–7 Elisha miraculously causes an ax head to float so it can be retrieved from the Jordan River.

6:8–23 Elisha is miraculously delivered from a company of Syrian soldiers when the Lord strikes them blind.

6:24–7:20 The Syrians besiege Israel's capital city of Samaria, and the people begin to run out of food. But Elisha predicts that the city will be saved through a miracle. The Lord sends panic and confusion among the Syrian army; the city is delivered, just as Elisha predicted.

8:1–6 The king of Israel restores the property of the woman of Shunem who had befriended Elisha (2 Kings 4:8–37) because of the prophet's reputation and influence.

8:7–15 Hazael assassinates and succeeds Ben-hadad as king of Syria. Elisha predicts that Hazael will commit many cruel acts against the nation of Israel.

8:16–24 Jehoram succeeds his father, Jehoshaphat, as king of Judah. After a reign of eight years, Jehoram dies and is succeeded by his son Ahaziah.

8:25–29 The allied forces of Israel and Judah go to war against King Hazael of Syria. King Jehoram of Judah is wounded in a battle at Ramoth-gilead.

Cab The smallest unit of measure for dry material, equal to about three pints (2 Kings 6:25). *Kab*: NRSV.

Hazael A leader who was anointed king of Syria at God's command by the prophet Elijah (1 Kings 19:15). He murdered Ben-hadad in order to take the throne (2 Kings 8:7–15). Hazael conducted military campaigns against both Judah (2 Kings 12:17–18) and Israel (2 Kings 10:32).

Showing Off with Gifts *So Hazael went to meet him [Elisha], and took a present with him, even of every good thing of Damascus, forty camels' burden, and came and stood before him* (2 Kings 8:9).

Hazael was a servant of Ben-hadad, king of Syria. When the prophet Elisha visited Damascus, Ben-hadad sent Hazael to meet him with royal gifts. Since the king was sick, he may have been trying to get Elisha to exercise his healing powers on his behalf. In OT times, even small gifts were often accompanied by great pomp and ceremony. The forty camels that greeted Elisha were probably not loaded down with all they could carry. Each camel may have carried only a small part of the total gift. The king wanted to impress Elisha with an extravagant outward display.

MAY 8 | Read 2 Kings 9–10

9:1–13 Elisha sends a prophet to Ramoth-gilead to anoint Jehu, a commander in Israel's army, as the new king of Israel. Jehu is directed to execute all claimants to the throne from the line of Ahab.

9:14–29 Jehu assassinates King Jehoram of Israel, the son of Ahab. Jehu also kills Jehoram's ally and friend, King Ahaziah of Judah (2 Chron. 22:2–9).

9:30–37 Jehu kills Jezebel, the wife of Ahab. Her body is eaten by dogs, in fulfillment of the prophecy of Elijah (1 Kings 21:17–29).

10:1–17 Jehu assassinates all the descendants of Ahab to end the royal dynasty of this wicked and idolatrous king. Jehu also murders several relatives of King Ahaziah of Judah because of their connection with Ahab.

10:18–28 Jehu kills the worshipers of Baal throughout Israel and destroys the images of this pagan god.

10:29–31 Jehu fails to abolish the golden calves that King Jeroboam of Israel had established at Bethel and Dan. God promises to extend Jehu's royal dynasty to the fourth generation because of his obedience of God's command to end the dynasty of Ahab.

10:32–36 King Hazael of Syria wins many victories in Israel. Jehu dies and is succeeded as king of Israel by his son Jehoahaz.

Beautifying the Eyes *When Jehu was come to Jezreel, Jezebel heard of it; and she painted her face [eyes, NIV], and tired her head [arranged her hair, NIV], and looked out at a window* (2 Kings 9:30).

When Queen Jezebel heard that her husband, King Ahab, had been assassinated by Jehu, she knew her days were numbered. But she showed great composure by putting on her makeup and fixing her hair to prepare for Jehu's arrival. This verse shows that beauty aids for the eyes of women have existed for centuries. To put it in modern terms, we would say that Queen Jezebel "put on her eye shadow and applied her mascara." The eye-beautification aid of Queen Jezebel's time was a black powder known as kohl. It served the same purpose as modern cosmetics. When applied, it contrasted with the white of the eyes, causing them to look brighter and wider. The custom of beautifying the eyes is also referred to in Ezekiel 23:40 and perhaps Proverbs 6:25.

MAY 9 | Read 2 Kings 11–13

11:1–3 After King Ahaziah of Judah is killed by King Jehu of Israel (2 Kings 9:27–29), Ahaziah's mother, Athaliah, seizes the throne. She does so by murdering her own grandsons, who were legitimate claimants to the throne. Joash, one of Ahaziah's sons, is saved from Athaliah's massacre and hidden away in the temple for six years (2 Chron. 22:10–12).

11:4–21 When Joash is seven years old, he is brought out of hiding by Jehoiada the priest and acclaimed as the new king of Judah. Athaliah is deposed as queen and assassinated (2 Chron. 23).

12:1–16 Joash follows the Lord under the counsel of the priest Jehoiada. Joash authorizes a special offering to be taken among the people designated for making needed repairs to the temple (2 Chron. 24:1–14).

12:17–18 Joash pays tribute to King Hazael of Syria to keep him from invading Judah's capital city of Jerusalem.

12:19–21 Assassinated by his own servants, Joash is succeeded as king of Judah by his son Amaziah (2 Chron. 24:25–27).

13:1–9 In the Northern Kingdom (Israel), Jehoahaz succeeds his father, Jehu, as king. Israel is ravaged by the Syrians during Jehoahaz's administration. After a reign of seventeen years, Jehoahaz is succeeded by his son Joash.

13:10–13 The evil reign of Joash ends after sixteen years, and he is succeeded as king of Israel by his son Jeroboam II.

13:14–19 The prophet Elisha predicts from his deathbed that the Northern Kingdom will win several key battles against the Syrians.

13:20–21 After Elisha's death and burial, a dead man is revived when his body touches the prophet's bones.

13:22–24 After oppressing Israel for several years, King Hazael of Syria dies and is succeeded by his son Ben-hadad.

13:25 King Joash of Israel takes back from the Syrians the cities they had captured when his father, Jehoahaz, reigned in Israel. This fulfills Elisha's prophecy (2 Kings 13:14–19).

Athaliah The daughter of Ahab and Jezebel who murdered the royal heirs of Judah and claimed the throne (reigned as queen of Judah about 841–835 BC; 2 Kings 11).

Joash The eighth king of Judah (reigned about 798–782 BC) who succeeded his father, Ahaziah (2 Kings 11:20), at age seven. He was hidden by his aunt from wicked Queen Athaliah to prevent his assassination (2 Kings 11:1–3). Jehoiada the priest served as his counselor (2 Kings 11:12, 17). Joash brought needed religious reforms to Judah (2 Kings 12:4–5), but he turned to idol worship after Jehoiada's death (2 Chron. 24:17–19). He was assassinated by his own officers (2 Chron. 24:24–25). *Jehoash*: 2 Kings 11:21.

. . . .

A Royal Coronation *He [Jehoiada] brought forth the king's son [Joash], and put the crown upon him, and gave him the testimony [presented him with a copy of the covenant, NIV]; and they [the people] made him king, and anointed him; and they clapped their hands, and said, God save the king* (2 Kings 11:12).

This verse gives us insight into a royal coronation ceremony in OT times. After the royal crown was placed on Joash's head, the king was presented with a copy of God's law. This was to serve as his guide in governing the people. He was then formally anointed for his task by having oil poured on his head (1 Sam. 16:13). A royal coronation must have been a public affair. The people showed their approval of Joash's coronation by clapping and shouting, "God save the king [Long live the king, NIV]."

MAY 10 | Read 2 Kings 14–15

14:1–7 Amaziah defeats the Edomites during his reign as king of Judah.

14:8–14 The kingdoms of Judah and Israel go to war against each other. Israel's king, Joash, seizes gold and silver items from Judah's capital city, Jerusalem, and carries them to Israel's capital, Samaria (2 Chron. 25:17–24).

14:15–22 King Joash of Israel dies; King Amaziah of Judah dies.

14:23–29 Jeroboam II succeeds his father, Joash, as king of Israel (2 Kings 13:10–13). His evil reign displeases the Lord.

15:1–7 Azariah (Uzziah) succeeds his father, Amaziah, as king of Judah. Azariah dies and is succeeded by his son Jotham (2 Chron. 26:16–23).

15:8–12 Zachariah succeeds his father, Jeroboam II, as king of Israel. Zachariah is assassinated and succeeded by Shallum after a brief reign. This fulfills God's promise to Jehu that his royal dynasty would extend to the fourth generation (2 Kings 10:29–31).

15:13–16 After a reign of only one month, Shallum is assassinated and succeeded by Menahem as king of Israel.

15:17–22 During his reign as king of Israel, Menahem is forced to pay tribute to King Pul (Tiglath-pileser) of Assyria. Menahem dies and is succeeded by his son Pekahiah.

15:23–26 After a reign of two years, Pekahiah is assassinated and succeeded as king of Israel by Pekah, a commander in Pekahiah's army.

15:27–31 During Pekahiah's reign over Israel, King Tiglath-pileser of Assyria invades his territory and enslaves some of his subjects. Pekah is assassinated and succeeded by Hoshea as king of Israel.

15:32–38 Azariah's son Jotham becomes king of Judah (2 Kings 15:1–7). Jotham dies and is succeeded by his son Ahaz.

....

Edomites The descendants of Esau who were enemies of the Israelites. The king of Edom refused to allow the Israelites to pass through his territory after the Exodus (Num. 20:14–21). In later years, David conquered the Edomites (2 Sam. 8:14). But they apparently existed with a distinct territory and culture for several centuries (see Ps. 137:7).

Jotham The son and successor of Azariah (Uzziah) as king of Judah (reigned about 750–732 BC). A contemporary of the prophets Isaiah, Hosea, and Micah (Isa. 1:1; Mic. 1:1), he was a good king but failed to destroy places of pagan worship (2 Kings 15:34–35). Jotham improved the temple, strengthened the city wall, and fortified buildings throughout Judah (2 Chron. 27:3–4). *Joatham*: Matt. 1:9.

MAY 11 | Read 2 Kings 16–17

16:1–4 King Ahaz encourages worship of false gods throughout Judah, even committing the abominable practice of child sacrifice to pagan gods (2 Chron. 28:1–4).

16:5–9 Ahaz pays tribute to the Assyrian king, Tiglath-pileser, who rescues Ahaz from his enemies.

16:10–18 Ahaz offers sacrifices on the altar of a pagan god and dismantles the altar in the temple devoted to worship of the one true God.

16:19–20 Ahaz dies and is succeeded as king of Judah by his son Hezekiah (2 Chron. 28:26–27).

17:1–4 Ahaz's son Hoshea reigns over Israel as a puppet king under the thumb of King Shalmaneser of Assyria. Hoshea is imprisoned by Shalmaneser after he quits paying tribute to Assyria and tries to form an alliance with Egypt to resist the Assyrian threat.

17:5–6 Assyria defeats Israel and carries away many of its citizens as captives to several Assyrian cities.

17:7–23 The end of Israel as a separate kingdom is attributed to the people's sin and rebellion against God and their worship of false gods.

17:24–41 Assyria settles people from pagan lands in the territory previously occupied by the citizens of Israel. The Israelites left in the land eventually adopt the pagan worship practices of these foreigners.

Tiglath-pileser A powerful Assyrian king (reigned about 745–727 BC) who defeated the Northern Kingdom and carried Jewish captives to Assyria (2 Kings 15:29). *Tilgath-pilneser*: 2 Chron. 28:20. *Pul*: 1 Chron. 5:26.

MAY 12 | Read 2 Kings 18–19

18:1–12 Hezekiah becomes king of Judah. Unlike his father, Ahaz (2 Kings 16:10–18), Hezekiah follows the Lord, tears down pagan altars, and leads the people to worship the Lord. At first, Hezekiah is able to resist the threat to his kingdom from Assyria.

18:13–37 Sennacherib, king of Assyria, captures several fortified cities of Judah. He stations his army outside Jerusalem and threatens to attack the city with a prolonged siege unless Hezekiah surrenders (2 Chron. 32:1–19).

19:1–7 King Hezekiah sends word about Judah's plight to the prophet Isaiah, who assures the king that God will deal with this threat from Assyria.

19:8–19 King Hezekiah receives a written threat from the Assyrian forces; he prays earnestly to the Lord for Judah's deliverance.

19:20–37 The prophet Isaiah assures King Hezekiah again of the Lord's protection. A mysterious plague strikes the Assyrian army, wiping out 185,000 warriors. Sennacherib returns to Assyria without attacking Jerusalem (2 Chron. 32:20–23; Isa. 37).

Hezekiah The godly king of Judah (ruled about 716–686 BC) who implemented religious reforms by abolishing idol worship, restoring and reopening the temple in Jerusalem, and leading in celebration of major religious festivals, such as the Passover (2 Kings 18:4; 2 Chron. 29). Preparing for a siege against Jerusalem by the Assyrians, he cut a tunnel through solid rock to bring water from a spring outside the city wall into the city (2 Kings 20:20). *Ezekias*: Matt. 1:9.

Deportation to Assyria *The king of Assyria did carry away Israel unto Assyria, and put them in Halah and in Habor by the river of Gozan, and in the cities of the Medes* (2 Kings 18:11).

The Northern Kingdom of Israel was overrun by the Assyrians in about 722 BC. The Assyrians were generally cruel and inhumane to enemy soldiers. But they used a different approach with the civilian populations of the nations they conquered. The skilled workers and other members of the privileged classes were carried away to Assyria, where they were put to work in the king's service as administrators, craftsmen, and farmers. Conquered territories were also resettled with people of different ethnic stock who were loyal to the Assyrian king (2 Kings 17:24). This was done to keep down rebellion and hostility toward the Assyrian government among the poor people of the land who were left behind.

MAY 13 | Read 2 Kings 20–21

20:1–11 King Hezekiah falls seriously ill and prays fervently to the Lord. The prophet Isaiah assures him that he will recover and live to reign as king of Judah for fifteen more years (Isa. 38). To confirm His promise of miraculous healing to the king, the Lord moves a sundial backwards by ten degrees (2 Chron. 32:24–26).

20:12–19 The prophet Isaiah reprimands King Hezekiah for showing his vast treasures of gold and silver to envoys from Babylonia. Isaiah predicts that these treasures will be captured and carried away someday by the Babylonians (2 Chron. 32:27–31).

20:20–21 King Hezekiah dies and is succeeded as king of Judah by his son Manasseh (2 Chron. 32:32–33).

21:1–9 As king of Judah for fifty-five years, Manasseh constructs altars for idol worship, performs child sacrifice to pagan gods, and participates in black magic and witchcraft. His long reign and acts of evil make him perhaps the worst king in the history of Judah (2 Chron. 33:1–10).

21:10–16 Because of Manasseh's wickedness and encouragement of pagan worship, God vows that He will punish the nation of Judah.

21:17–18 Manasseh dies and is succeeded as king of Judah by his son Amon (2 Chron. 33:20).

21:19–26 Amon continues the evil practices of his father, Manasseh. Amon is assassinated by his own servants after a reign of only two years and is succeeded by his son Josiah (2 Chron. 33:21–25).

....

Berodach-baladan A king of Babylonia (reigned about 721–704 BC) who sent ambassadors to visit King Hezekiah of Judah. Hezekiah showed them his vast wealth—an act condemned by the prophet Isaiah (2 Kings 20:12–19).

Siloam A reservoir in Jerusalem supplied with water through King Hezekiah's underground tunnel from a spring outside the city (2 Kings 20:20). Jesus commanded a blind man to wash in the Pool of Siloam for healing (John 9:6–7). *Shiloah*: Isa. 8:6; *Siloah*: Neh. 3:15.

Manasseh The son and successor of Hezekiah as king of Judah (reigned about 687–642 BC; 2 Kings 20:21). A wicked ruler who encouraged pagan worship throughout Judah, Manasseh was captured and taken to Babylonia (2 Chron. 33:10–11). He later repented and was allowed to return to Jerusalem (2 Chron. 33:12–13). He was succeeded as king by his son Amon (2 Chron. 33:20).

Josiah The son and successor of Amon as king of Judah (reigned 640–609 BC; 2 Kings 21:26). Crowned at age eight, he made a covenant to obey God (2 Kings 23:3) and led an important reform movement to reestablish God's law, repair the temple (2 Kings 22:3–9), and abolish idolatry (2 Kings 23:4–24). *Josias*: Jesus' ancestry (Matt. 1:10–11).

MAY 14 | Read 2 Kings 22:1–23:30

22:1–7 As a faithful follower of the Lord, King Josiah authorizes repairs to the temple in Jerusalem (2 Chron. 34:8–13).

22:8–14 During the temple repairs, a copy of the Book of the Law (Genesis, Exodus, Leviticus, Numbers, and Deuteronomy) is discovered. Josiah realizes when this book is read that the people of Judah have wandered away from God's commands. He sends several priests to confer with a prophet to find out how God will deal with the sins of His people (2 Chron. 34:14–21).

22:15–20 Huldah the prophetess declares that the Lord will deal kindly with Josiah because of his determination to follow His will. But God will punish the nation of Judah for its waywardness and rebellion (2 Chron. 34:22–28).

23:1–3 King Josiah calls the leaders of Judah together to renew the covenant with the Lord (2 Chron. 34:29–33).

23:4–27 King Josiah launches a religious reform movement throughout Judah. He tears down pagan altars, destroys images of idols, puts to death pagan priests who were leading people astray, and reinstates observation of the Passover—a festival celebrating their deliverance from slavery in Egypt.

23:28–30 Killed in a battle with the Egyptians, Josiah is succeeded as king of Judah by his son Jehoahaz (2 Chron. 35:20–36:1).

. . . .

Hilkiah A high priest during the reign of King Josiah of Judah who found the lost Book of the Law and used it to bring about religious reforms (2 Kings 22:8–23:4).

Huldah The wife of Shallum and a prophetess who foretold the collapse of Jerusalem (2 Kings 22:14–20).

MAY 15 | Read 2 Kings 23:31–25:30

23:31–37 After a reign of only three months, King Jehoahaz is captured and imprisoned by the Egyptians. The Egyptians put Eliakim, another son of Josiah, on the throne as a puppet king and demand that he pay tribute to the

Egyptian government. The Egyptians also give Eliakim another name, Jehoiakim (2 Chron. 36:2–4).

24:1–7 During the reign of Eliakim/Jehoiakim, the Babylonians invade Judah. He dies and is succeeded by his son Jehoiachln.

24:8–19 King Nebuchadnezzar of Babylonia invades and subdues the nation of Judah. He takes King Jehoiachin and his royal household as well as all the key leaders of Judah to Babylon as captives. Nebuchadnezzar also places Mattaniah on the throne of Judah as a puppet king and renames him Zedekiah (2 Chron. 36:9–10).

24:20–25:7 Mattaniah (Zedekiah) rebels against Babylonia. Nebuchadnezzar invades Jerusalem and takes the king to Babylon as a prisoner after forcing him to watch the murder of his sons.

25:8–21 Nebuchadnezzar ransacks the city of Jerusalem, breaking down the city wall, burning the temple and other buildings, and carrying away gold and silver from the temple furnishings. Key leaders of Judah are murdered or enslaved and taken to Babylon, while peasants and farmers of Judah are left behind to cultivate the land.

25:22–26 A remnant of the citizens of Judah flees to Egypt after murdering Gedaliah, an official whom Nebuchadnezzar had appointed governor of Judah.

25:27–30 In Babylonia, Nebuchadnezzar is succeeded as king by his son Evilmerodach. The new king releases King Jehoiachin of Judah from prison and gives him a place of honor and privilege in the Babylonian court.

. . . .

Nebuchadnezzar The king of Babylonia (reigned about 605–561 BC) who captured Jerusalem and carried Judah into exile about 587 BC (see Dan. 1–4). The only strong Babylonian king, he was the son of Nabopolassar, founder of the empire. After a revolt by King Zedekiah of Judah, Nebuchadnezzar destroyed Jerusalem, burned the temple, and carried the nation's leading citizens into exile (2 Kings 25:1–26). *Nebuchadrezzar*: Jer. 51:34.

Babylonia A powerful nation in Mesopotamia that carried the Jewish people into exile about 587 BC. Also called *Sheshach* (Jer. 25:26), *Shinar* (Isa. 11:11), and the land of the Chaldeans (Ezek. 12:13), Babylonia reached the zenith of its power under Nebuchadnezzar (reigned about 605–560 BC). The nation was a center of idolatry dominated by worship of Merodach, the Babylonian god of war (Jer. 50:2). After holding the Jewish people captive for many years, the Babylonians were defeated by the Persians about 539 BC, fulfilling the prophecies of Isaiah and Jeremiah (Isa. 14:22; Jer. 50:9).

. . . .

Blinding of Prisoners *They [the Babylonian army] slew the sons of Zedekiah before his eyes, and put out the eyes of Zedekiah, and bound him with fetters of brass [bronze shackles, NIV], and carried him to Babylon* (2 Kings 25:7).

Zedekiah was serving as king of Judah when the nation fell to the Babylonians in 587 BC. The last thing he saw before being blinded by his captors was the death of his sons. The blinding of prisoners was a cruel punishment often meted out by the Babylonians, Assyrians, and Persians. This was done by searing the pupils with a hot copper plate or by thrusting a sword or dagger into the eyes. Samson was also blinded when he was captured by the Philistines (Judg. 16:21).

MAY 16 | Read 1 Chronicles 1–4

1:1–4 Descendants of Adam up through Noah and his sons are listed.

1:5–7 Descendants of Noah's son Japheth are listed.

1:8–16 Descendants of Noah's son Ham are listed.

1:17–27 Descendants of Noah's son Shem up through Abraham are listed.

1:28–33 Descendants of Abraham's son Ishmael and other sons born to Abraham's concubine Keturah are listed.

1:34–54 Descendants of Abraham's son Isaac through Isaac's son Esau are listed.

2:1–2 The twelve sons of Isaac's son Jacob, or Israel, are listed.

2:3–15 Descendants of Jacob's son Judah up through King David are listed.

2:16–55 Other descendants of Judah are listed.

3:1–4 Sons of David born while he reigned at Hebron are listed.

3:5–9 Sons of David born while he reigned at Jerusalem are listed.

3:10–24 Descendants of David's son Solomon are listed.

4:1–23 Descendants of Jacob's son Judah are listed.

4:24–43 Descendants of Jacob's son Simeon are listed.

MAY 17 | Read 1 Chronicles 5–7

5:1–10 Descendants of Jacob's son Reuben are listed.

5:11–17 Descendants of Jacob's son Gad are listed.

5:18–26 A brief history is given of the tribes of Israel that settled on the eastern side of the Jordan River—Reuben, Gad, and one-half of the tribe of Manasseh (Josh. 22:1–9).

6:1–30 Descendants of Jacob's son Levi are listed. The Levites assisted the priests with sacrificial duties at the tabernacle and the temple.

6:31–48 Levites who assisted with the song service after David moved the ark of the covenant to Jerusalem are listed.

6:49–53 The son and successors of Aaron as priests of Israel are listed.

6:54–81 The cities assigned to the Levites throughout the territory of Israel are listed (Josh. 21:1–45).

7:1–5 Descendants of Jacob's son Issachar are listed.

7:6–12 Descendants of Jacob's son Benjamin are listed.

7:13 Descendants of Jacob's son Naphtali are listed.

7:14–19 Descendants of Jacob's grandson Manasseh are listed.

7:20–29 Descendants of Jacob's grandson Ephraim are listed.

7:30–40 Descendants of Jacob's son Asher are listed.

Jeduthun A Levite musician and writer of psalms (1 Chron. 9:16) who led in praise services when the ark of the covenant was returned to Jerusalem (1 Chron. 16:41–42). *Ethan*: 1 Chron. 6:44.

MAY 18 | Read 1 Chronicles 8–10

8:1–40 Descendants of Jacob's son Benjamin are listed. (This is a more detailed list than that given in 1 Chron. 7:6–12.)

9:1–9 Various Jewish leaders who lived in Jerusalem are listed.

9:10–34 Various priests and Levites who ministered in Jerusalem are listed.

9:35–44 Ancestors and descendants of Saul, the first king of Israel, are listed.

10:1–14 King Saul and his sons are killed in a battle against the Philistines on Mount Gilboa (1 Sam. 31:1–13).

God Knows the News *They [Philistines] took his [Saul's] head, and his armour, and sent into the land of the Philistines round about, to carry tidings unto their idols* (1 Chron. 10:9).

When the Philistines defeated King Saul and his army, they notified their fellow citizens to carry news about their victory to their pagan gods. This shows the weakness of idols and the superiority of the one true God, who sees all and knows all: "The eyes of the LORD are in every place, beholding the evil and the good" (Prov. 15:3).

MAY 19 | Read 1 Chronicles 11–14

11:1–3 David is acclaimed king over all Israel by all the tribes (2 Sam. 5:1–5).

11:4–9 David captures the fortified city of Jebus from the Jebusites. Later it becomes his capital city and is known as Jerusalem (2 Sam. 5:6–10).

11:10–47 The brave commanders and warriors among David's "mighty men" are listed (2 Sam. 23:8–39).

12:1–40 Warriors who joined David's forces while he was hiding from King Saul at Ziklag are listed.

13:1–14 David moves the ark of the covenant from the home of Abinadab to a temporary resting place at the house of Obed-edom. Uzza/Uzzah is killed when he reaches out to steady the ark and accidentally touches it (2 Sam. 6:1–11).

14:1–2 King Hiram of Tyre provides materials and workmen to build a house for David (2 Sam. 5:11–12).

14:3–7 Thirteen children are born to David at Jerusalem (2 Sam. 5:13–16; 1 Chron. 3:5–9).

14:8–17 David defeats the Philistines in a major battle in the valley of Rephaim (2 Sam. 5:17–25).

. . . .

Jebusites Tribal enemies of the Israelites who were descended from Canaan (Gen. 10:15–16). They controlled Jerusalem (known as Jebus at that time) before David conquered the city (2 Sam. 5:6–8) and turned it into his capital. Remnants of the Jebusites became bondservants during Solomon's reign (1 Kings 9:20–21).

. . . .

David's Mighty Men *This is the number of the mighty men whom David had* (1 Chron. 11:11).

These "mighty men" were the most loyal and courageous soldiers in David's army. Known for their bravery in battle, many risked their lives for their commander. A listing of their names here (1 Chron. 11:11–47) and in 2 Sam. 23:8–39 acknowledges that David could not have risen from his humble beginnings as a shepherd boy to become the powerful king of Judah without the support of these valiant warriors.

MAY 20 | Read 1 Chronicles 15–17

15:1–29 David makes plans for a great celebration with music and dancing as the ark of the covenant is moved to Jerusalem from the house of Obed-edom. This time the ark is moved as God directed—by Levites carrying it on their shoulders on poles inserted into rings on the ark (2 Sam. 6:12–19).

16:1–6 David presents burnt offerings and peace offerings to the Lord before the ark in the tent he has prepared for its dwelling place.

16:7–36 David offers a prayer of praise and thanksgiving to God for His wonderful works on behalf of His people (2 Sam. 7:18–29).

16:37–43 David appoints a group of Levites to minister continuously before the ark, offering burnt offerings and other sacrifices to the Lord.

17:1–15 David makes plans to build a house, or temple, devoted to worship of God. Instead, the Lord promises that He will build David a house, or memorial. He promises that David's kingdom will be established forever—that his descendants will reign from generation to generation on the throne of Israel (2 Sam. 7:1–17).

17:16–27 In a prayer of humility and gratitude, David praises God for His love and goodness.

MAY 21 | Read 1 Chronicles 18–21

18:1–14 David expands his nation's territory and power by defeating the Philistines, Moabites, Syrians, Amalekites, and Edomites (2 Sam. 8:1–13).

18:15–17 Selected officials in David's administration are listed (2 Sam. 8:14–18).

19:1–5 David sends messengers to the Ammonites on a peaceful mission, but they are rejected and humiliated.

19:6–19 David's army, under the command of Joab, defeats the combined forces of the Ammonites and the Syrians (2 Sam. 10).

20:1–3 David seals his victory over the Ammonites by capturing their capital city, Rabbah (2 Sam. 12:26–31).

20:4–8 David's warriors are victorious over several Philistine giants, relatives of the giant Goliath whom David killed (1 Sam. 17:46–51).

21:1–6 David orders Joab, commander of his army, to take a census of all the fighting men throughout the tribes of Israel (2 Sam. 24:1–9).

21:7–17 God sends a plague on the nation because of David's sinful pride that led him to order the census (2 Sam. 24:10–15).

21:18–30 David buys a threshing floor from Ornan (Araunah) the Jebusite as the site for an altar on which sacrifices will be offered to the Lord. The plague ends when sacrifices are offered (2 Sam. 24:16–25).

Crippling War Horses *David also houghed [hamstrung, NIV] all the chariot horses* (1 Chron. 18:4).

David extended his kingdom as far north as Syria by defeating Hadarezer, king of Zobah. He weakened Hadarezer's ability to wage war by capturing his chariots and crippling his chariot horses, probably by cutting a muscle or tendon in their legs. Since David did not take the horses as booty, he probably had little use for chariots and horses in his own army. Chariots would have been impractical in the rocky and hilly terrain of Palestine.

MAY 22 | Read 1 Chronicles 22–24

22:1–19 God refuses to allow David to build the temple in Jerusalem because he has "made great wars," but God says Solomon, David's son and successor, will complete the task.

23:1 Solomon will succeed his father, David, as king of Israel (1 Kings 1:32–40).

23:2–32 David organizes the Levites into several different groups and assigns them specific duties as officers and judges, musicians, doorkeepers, and assistants to the priests.

24:1–19 David organizes the priests into twenty-four different groups that will officiate at the altar on a rotating basis.

24:20–31 Several different leaders of the divisions of the Levites are listed.

MAY 23 | Read 1 Chronicles 25–27

25:1–31 The Levites responsible for worship music are organized into twenty-four different groups to serve on a rotating basis.

26:1–19 Levites who serve as porters (doorkeepers and gatekeepers) for the tabernacle and temple are listed.

26:20–32 The Levites listed in these verses are responsible for storing and caring for offerings and sacrifices devoted to support and upkeep of the tabernacle and the temple.

27:1–15 David's military force is divided into twelve units of 24,000 warriors each. These units apparently served for one-month assignments on a rotating basis during the year. The captains of the twelve units are listed by name.

27:16–24 Leaders of the tribes of Israel during David's administration are listed.

27:25–34 Counselors, advisers, chief officials, and keepers of the royal herds in David's administration are listed (2 Sam. 8:14–18; 1 Chron. 18:15–17).

Music for Worship *All these were the sons of Heman the king's seer in the words of God, to lift up the horn* (1 Chron. 25:5).

David organized the priests and Levites into several different groups to serve at the tabernacle on a rotating basis. The Levites descended from Heman were to provide music for worship—specifically to play the horn, or trumpet. Other Levite musicians were assigned to play different instruments, including cymbals, psalteries [lyres, NIV], and harps (1 Chron. 25:6).

MAY 24 | Read 1 Chronicles 28–29

28:1–8 David gathers the leaders of Israel and informs them that his son Solomon will be his successor. He challenges them to remain faithful to the Lord as leaders of Israel.

28:9–21 David encourages his son Solomon to build the temple in Jerusalem, using the materials and funds that David has collected.

29:1–9 Encouraged by David, the leaders of Israel contribute additional gold and silver to pay for the temple's construction.

29:10–19 David offers a prayer of thanksgiving to God. He pledges all the money and supplies to construction of a temple that will bring glory and honor to the Lord.

29:20–25 The leaders of Israel offer sacrifices to God and acclaim Solomon as the new king of Israel.

29:26–30 David dies after forty years as king—seven years as king of the southern tribe of Judah and thirty-three years as king over all the tribes of Israel (1 Kings 2:10–12).

Parlour A room in a house for entertaining guests (1 Sam. 9:22), a secret chamber for retreat (1 Chron. 28:11), or a room on the roof for enjoying cool breezes (Judg. 3:20–25).

Doxology A brief hymn or declaration that proclaims God's power and glory (1 Chron. 29:11; Luke 2:14).

MAY 25 | Read 2 Chronicles 1–4

1:1–13 As the new king of Israel, Solomon offers sacrifices to the Lord on an altar at Gibeon. He asks God for great wisdom in order to be a good leader. The Lord promises to honor this request and to give him riches and honor as well (1 Kings 3:3–15).

1:14–17 The symbols of Solomon's wealth include his chariots, chariot cities, gold and silver, and horses.

2:1–18 Solomon prepares to build the temple by securing cedar timber from King Hiram (Huram) of Tyre (1 Kings 5). Hiram also provides skilled craftsmen for the project. Solomon presses into service thousands of non-Israelites who are living in his territory to serve as construction workers.

3:1–17 The huge, ornate temple compound built by Solomon is described (1 Kings 6).

4:1–22 The furnishings of the temple include the central altar, a huge water basin ("molten sea," v. 2), smaller basins, tables, candlesticks, and utensils used by the priests to handle sacrifices (1 Kings 7:23–51).

Alliance A treaty between nations or individuals. Alliances with conquered Canaanite nations were forbidden (Exod. 23:32; Deut. 7:2–5). The prophets warned Israel against forming alliances that might replace their dependence on God (Jer. 2:18). Nevertheless, alliances between OT personalities and foreigners were common. Examples are (1) Abraham with Abimelech of Gerar (Gen. 21:22–34); (2) King Solomon with Hiram of Tyre (1 Kings 5:1–12); and (3) Solomon's many marriage alliances (1 Kings 3:1; 11:1–3).

Tyre An ancient coastal city of Phoenicia north of Palestine. Hiram, Tyre's ruler, helped David and Solomon with their building projects (1 Kings 5:1–10). In the prophet Ezekiel's day, the city was a thriving trade center. He predicted Tyre's destruction because of its sin and idolatry (Ezek. 28:1–10). Jesus visited the city (Mark 7:24), and Paul landed here (Acts 21:3, 7). *Tyrus*: Amos 1:10.

MAY 26 | Read 2 Chronicles 5–7

5:1–6:42 In an elaborate dedication ceremony, the ark of the covenant is placed in the completed temple. God's glory fills the temple in the form of a cloud. Solomon blesses the people gathered for the ceremony and praises God for His provision for His people. He prays that Israel will always remain faithful to the one true God (1 Kings 8:12–66).

7:1–3 Fire from heaven consumes a sacrifice that had been placed on the altar of the temple.

7:4–11 Additional sacrifices to the Lord are placed on the altar of the temple. This ceremony of thanksgiving continues for eight days.

7:12–22 The Lord renews with Solomon the covenant He had made with his father, David. Solomon's kingship over Israel will be eternal if he follows the Lord. But if Solomon does not obey God's commands, God will reject him and bring catastrophe upon the land (1 Kings 9:1–9).

MAY 27 | Read 2 Chronicles 8–9

8:1–18 Solomon builds storage cities and fortifies and equips other cities as defense outposts. He also establishes a port for international trade to be conducted (1 Kings 9:10–28).

9:1–12 Solomon receives a royal visitor, the Queen of Sheba, and impresses her with his wealth and wisdom (1 Kings 10:1–13).

9:13–28 Solomon multiplies his riches through international trade. He is honored by other nations for his power and wisdom (1 Kings 10:14–29).

9:29–31 Solomon dies after reigning for forty years and is succeeded as king by his son Rehoboam (1 Kings 11:41–43).

Walled Cities *Also he [King Solomon] built Beth-horon the upper [Upper Beth Horon, NIV], and Beth-horon the nether [Lower Beth Horon, NIV], fenced cities, with walls, gates, and bars* (2 Chron. 8:5).

Cities of Bible times—like the twin cities of Upper and Lower Beth Horon—were surrounded by massive stone walls. Some of these structures were more than thirty feet high and ten to twelve feet thick. Residents of the city would retreat behind these walls when under attack by an enemy. The attacking army would either scale the wall by using ladders or try to break down the city gate. The gate was made of heavy timbers, reinforced with iron. When closed, the gate would be secured by sliding heavy timbers or iron bars across its surface from the inside. When in full lock-down mode, a heavily fortified or "fenced" city was an effective defense against an army of superior numbers. Often the besieging force would camp around the city for months and starve its citizens into submission.

MAY 28 | Read 2 Chronicles 10–13

10:1–15 Rehoboam ignores the complaints of Jeroboam and the northern tribes about the harsh and oppressive practices of King Solomon. Rehoboam tells them he plans to multiply their misery (1 Kings 12:1–15).

10:16–19 The northern tribes revolt against Rehoboam and acclaim Jeroboam as their king. For the next several centuries of Israel's history, two opposing nations of the Jewish people exist—the northern tribes, known as the nation of Israel (or the Northern Kingdom), and the southern tribes, known as the nation of Judah (or the Southern Kingdom). God's promise of an eternal kingship through David and his descendants continues through the Southern Kingdom (1 Kings 12:16–24).

11:1–4 God speaks through a prophet to prevent Rehoboam from going to war against the Northern Kingdom.

11:5–13 King Rehoboam fortifies cities as defense outposts in the Southern Kingdom.

11:14–17 Many priests and Levites in the Northern Kingdom move to the Southern Kingdom to be near the central place of worship at the temple in Jerusalem. King Jeroboam sets up rival sanctuaries for worship and appoints his own priests (1 Kings 12:25–33).

11:18–23 The wives and children of King Rehoboam of Judah are listed.

12:1–12 To punish King Rehoboam for his unfaithfulness, God allows Shishak of Egypt to invade Judah and carry away the royal treasures.

12:13–16 After reigning for seventeen years, King Rehoboam of Judah dies and is succeeded by his son Abijah (Abijam) (1 Kings 14:21–31).

13:1–20 King Abijah of Judah defeats the forces of King Jeroboam of Israel and captures several towns in the Northern Kingdom.

13:21–14:1 Abijah dies and is succeeded as king of Judah by his son Asa (1 Kings 15:1–8).

Adoram A city in southwest Judah rebuilt and fortified by King Rehoboam, son of Solomon (2 Chron. 11:5, 9). Now known as *Dura,* it is located five miles southwest of Hebron.

Beth-zur A city in the mountains of Judah fortified by King Rehoboam as a defensive outpost along the road leading to Jerusalem (2 Chron. 11:7).

Shemaiah A prophet of Judah who warned King Rehoboam not to attack Israel (1 Kings 12:22–24). He revealed that Pharaoh Shishak of Egypt was being used by the Lord to punish Judah for its sins (2 Chron. 12:5–9).

MAY 29 | Read 2 Chronicles 14–18

14:2–8 Asa is a good king who follows the Lord and removes pagan altars and idols from the territory of Judah.

14:9–15 God gives Asa a decisive victory over King Zerah of Ethiopia.

15:1–19 A prophet encourages Asa to follow the Lord. Asa responds by implementing a religious reform movement throughout Judah, tearing down pagan altars, smashing idols, and leading the people to renew the covenant with God (1 Kings 15:9–24).

16:1–6 King Asa forms an alliance with the Syrian king Ben-hadad, who delivers Judah from oppression by the forces of King Baasha of Israel.

16:7–12 The prophet Hanani rebukes Asa because he relied on the military might of Syria for deliverance rather than the power of God.

16:13–17:1 Asa dies after reigning for forty-one years and is succeeded as king of Judah by his son Jehoshaphat (1 Kings 15:9–24).

17:2–5 King Jehoshaphat continues to follow the Lord as his father, Asa, had done. God rewards him for his faithfulness.

17:6–19 Jehoshaphat sends Levites throughout the land to teach God's law to the people. His kingdom thrives, and other nations pay tribute to him and honor his accomplishments.

18:1–3 King Jehoshaphat agrees to join an alliance with King Ahab of Israel against the Syrians (1 Kings 22:1–4).

18:4–11 False prophets who served as "yes men" for the king of Israel assure Ahab and Jehoshaphat that an attack against the Syrians will be successful (1 Kings 22:5–12).

18:12–27 Micaiah, a true prophet of the Lord, warns Ahab and Jehoshaphat that their campaign against Syria will fail (1 Kings 22:13–28).

18:28–34 King Ahab of Israel is killed in the battle with the Syrians at Ramoth-gilead (1 Kings 22:29–40).

Was King Asa Cremated? *They [Israelites]. . .laid him [King Asa] in the bed [bier, NIV] which was filled with sweet odours and divers kinds of spices prepared by the apothecaries' art: and they made a very great burning for him [made a huge fire in his honor, NIV]* (2 Chron. 16:14).

Was the body of King Asa of Judah cremated by being burned on a platform, or bier, sprinkled with spices? Some interpreters say yes; others say no. Some believe the spices were first burned as an offering, then the king's body was laid in a coffin on top of the ashes from these spices. Others believe the king's body was actually burned along with the spices. This verse lends itself to either interpretation. What is certain is that cremation was practiced on occasion among the Jews in OT times. The bodies of King Saul and his sons were burned (1 Sam. 31:12). The prophets Jeremiah (Jer. 34:5) and Amos (Amos 6:10) also mentioned the practice of cremation.

MAY 30 | Read 2 Chronicles 19–21

19:1–11 King Jehoshaphat implements additional religious reforms throughout the kingdom of Judah.

20:1–30 After Jehoshaphat and the people pray fervently to God, He gives them a great victory over the combined forces of the Moabites and the Ammonites.

20:31–21:1 Jehoshaphat dies after a twenty-five year reign as king of Judah and is succeeded by his son Jehoram (Joram) (1 Kings 22:41–50).

21:2–7 On becoming king of Judah, Jehoram kills all his brothers to remove any challenge to his kingship. He fails to honor the Lord with his leadership.

21:8–10 The Edomites revolt against Judah and try to reestablish themselves as an independent kingdom.

21:11–22:1 As the prophet Elijah predicts, King Jehoram dies of a mysterious disease. His reign over Judah lasts for eight years. He is succeeded by his son Ahaziah.

Jehoshaphat The son and successor of Asa as king of Judah (reigned about 870–848 BC). A reformer like his father, Jehoshaphat attacked idolatry and sent teachers to help people learn about God (2 Chron. 17:3–9). He was rebuked by the prophet Jehu for forming an alliance with King Ahab of Israel (2 Chron. 19:1–3). *Josaphat*: Matt. 1:8.

Jehoram The wicked king of Judah (reigned about 848–841 BC) who murdered his own brothers (2 Chron. 21:1–4) in order to succeed his father, Jehoshaphat (1 Kings 22:50). Struck down by God, he died in disgrace, as predicted by the prophet Elijah, from a mysterious disease (2 Chron. 21:12–20). *Joram*: 2 Kings 8:21.

MAY 31 | Read 2 Chronicles 22–24

22:2–9 Ahaziah's reign fails to please the Lord because of his connections with Ahab, the wicked king of Israel. When Jehu assassinates Ahab and becomes the new king of Israel, he also has Ahaziah executed (2 Kings 9:14–29).

22:10–12 Athaliah seizes the throne of Judah when her son Ahaziah is assassinated. She attempts to execute all claimants to the throne. But one of Ahaziah's sons, Joash (Jehoash), is hidden in the temple for six years (2 Kings 11:1–3).

23:1–21 Jehoiada the priest brings Joash out of hiding, and the people acclaim him as the new king of Judah. Athaliah is executed (2 Kings 11:4–21).

24:1–14 Joash follows the Lord as long as the priest Jehoiada is alive. Joash authorizes a special offering to be taken among the people and designates it for making needed repairs to the temple (2 Kings 12:1–16).

24:15–22 After the death of the priest Jehoiada, King Joash turns away from the Lord and encourages idol worship in the land. He even has Jehoiada's son killed because he condemned the king's waywardness and idolatry.

24:23–24 To punish Joash, the Lord allows the Syrians to defeat Judah and carry away the king's treasures.

24:25–27 Assassinated by his own servants, King Joash of Judah is succeeded by his son Amaziah (2 Kings 12:19–21).

Amaziah A king of Judah (reigned about 796–767 BC; 2 Kings 14:1–20). He assembled an army to attack Edom and embraced the false gods of Edom (2 Chron. 25:5–15). Amaziah was assassinated by his political enemies (2 Chron. 25:25–28).

JUNE 1 | Read 2 Chronicles 25–28

25:1–16 At the beginning of his reign, Amaziah pleases the Lord. But he sins by setting up shrines for worship of pagan gods after defeating the Edomites (2 Kings 14:1–7).

25:17–24 King Jehoash of Israel invades the kingdom of Judah and carries away gold and silver from the temple in Jerusalem (2 Kings 14:8–14).

25:25–26:1 King Amaziah of Judah dies and is succeeded by his son Uzziah (Azariah) (2 Kings 15:1–7).

26:2–5 Uzziah is a good king who follows the Lord and reigns for fifty-two years in Judah.

26:6–15 Uzziah strengthens the nation of Judah during his long reign by improving Jerusalem's defenses, developing a strong army, and subduing the Philistines and the Ammonites.

26:16–23 Uzziah is struck with leprosy when he attempts to burn incense at the altar—a task reserved for priests only. After his death, he is succeeded by his son Jotham (2 Kings 15:1–7).

27:1–9 After reigning over Judah for sixteen years, Jotham dies and is succeeded by his son Ahaz.

28:1–4 Ahaz is an evil king who encourages idolatry throughout Judah. He even sacrifices his own children to a pagan god (2 Kings 16:1–4).

28:5–25 The Lord punishes Judah because of King Ahaz's abominable acts. The nation is pillaged by the Syrians, the Edomites, and the Philistines, as well as the nation of Israel (Northern Kingdom).

28:26–27 Ahaz dies and is succeeded as king of Judah by his son Hezekiah (2 Kings 16:19–20).

. . . .

Engines A word that refers to the ingenuity of a machine or apparatus. The "engines" in 2 Chron. 26:15 (*machines*: NIV, NRSV) were used to hurl objects from the walls of besieged cities upon the enemy below.

. . . .

Uzziah's War Machines *He [King Uzziah] made in Jerusalem engines [machines, NIV], invented by cunning [skillful, NIV] men, to be on the towers and upon the bulwarks [corner defenses, NIV], to shoot arrows and great stones* (2 Chron. 26:15).

King Uzziah of Judah made Jerusalem's city wall defenses even more effective by increasing the firepower of the warriors on the wall. In the defense towers on top of the wall, he placed mechanical war machines that were capable of hurling huge stones and shooting arrows in bulk on the enemy below. These "engines" were probably similar to the catapults used so effectively by the Roman army in later centuries.

JUNE 2 | Read 2 Chronicles 29–30

29:1–36 Hezekiah orders the priests to restore and purify the temple, since it had been desecrated during the reign of his father, Ahaz. Hezekiah leads the people to rededicate the temple and to resume the practice of bringing sacrifices and offerings to the altar.

30:1–27 Hezekiah leads the priests and the people to reinstate celebration of the Passover—a major religious festival that had not been observed in the land for many years.

JUNE 3 | Read 2 Chronicles 31–33

31:1 The people destroy pagan altars and idols that had been set up throughout the land.

31:2–21 Hezekiah orders the people to bring firstfruits and other offerings to provide a livelihood for the priests and Levites. He directs that the surplus goods be stored for future use.

32:1–19 King Sennacherib of Assyria surrounds the city of Jerusalem. He taunts the God of Judah and orders Hezekiah to surrender (2 Kings 18:13–37).

32:20–23 Hezekiah and the prophet Isaiah pray earnestly to the Lord. Judah is delivered miraculously from the Assyrian forces (2 Kings 19:20–37).

32:24–26 King Hezekiah is struck by a serious illness, but he recovers when he prays to God in a spirit of humility (2 Kings 20:1–11).

32:27–31 God blesses Hezekiah, and his wealth increases. But the king commits a serious error when he displays his treasures to envoys from Babylonia (2 Kings 20:12–19).

32:32–33 King Hezekiah dies and is succeeded as king of Judah by his son Manasseh (2 Kings 20:20–21).

33:1–10 Manasseh reverses the religious reforms of his father, Hezekiah, and reinstates pagan worship throughout the land. He even participates in black magic and witchcraft and sacrifices some of his own children to pagan gods (2 Kings 21:1–9).

33:11–19 As punishment, God allows the Babylonians to capture Manasseh. He eventually continues his kingship under their jurisdiction. Manasseh tries to stem the tide of idol worship in Judah that he had started, but the people continue in their misguided ways.

33:20 Manasseh dies and is succeeded as king of Judah by his son Amon (2 Kings 21:17–18).

33:21–25 King Amon continues the evil practices of his father, Manasseh. Assassinated by his own servants after a brief reign, he is succeeded by his son Josiah (2 Kings 21:19–26).

Conduit A pipe or aqueduct through which water was channeled. King Hezekiah of Judah cut a conduit through solid rock to pipe water into Jerusalem (2 Kings 20:20).

JUNE 4 | Read 2 Chronicles 34–36

34:1–7 A good and godly king like his great-grandfather Hezekiah, Josiah tears down the pagan altars and images that had been placed throughout the land.

34:8–13 King Josiah orders that needed repairs be made to the temple in Jerusalem (2 Kings 22:1–7).

34:14–21 During the temple repairs, a copy of the Book of the Law (Genesis, Exodus, Leviticus, Numbers, and Deuteronomy) is discovered. Josiah realizes when this book is read that the people of Judah have wandered away from God's commands. He sends several priests to confer with a prophet to find out how God will deal with the sins of His rebellious people (2 Kings 22:8–14).

34:22–28 Huldah the prophetess declares that the Lord will deal kindly with Josiah because he has vowed to follow His will. But God will punish the nation of Judah for its sin and rebellion (2 Kings 22:15–20).

34:29–33 Josiah calls the elders of Judah and Jerusalem to meet at the temple to renew the covenant with the Lord (2 Kings 23:1–3).

35:1–19 King Josiah orders a nationwide observance of the Passover—a religious festival celebrating the deliverance of the Israelites from slavery in Egypt.

35:20–36:1 Josiah is killed in a battle with the Egyptians. Josiah's son Jehoahaz succeeds him as king of Judah (2 Kings 23:28–30).

36:2–4 Jehoahaz reigns only three months before he is captured by the Egyptians. They put Eliakim, another son of Josiah, on the throne as a puppet king and rename him Jehoiakim (2 Kings 23:31–37).

36:5–8 Judah is invaded by the Babylonian army under King Nebuchadnezzar during the reign of Eliakim (Jehoiakim). He is succeeded as king by his son Jehoiachin.

36:9–10 Jehoiachin reigns only three months and ten days before he is captured and deported to Babylonia. The Babylonians place Jehoiachin's brother Zedekiah (Mattaniah) on the throne of Judah as a puppet king (2 Kings 24:8–19).

36:11–20 Zedekiah rebels against the Babylonians, who ransack the city of Jerusalem and carry away all the temple treasures (2 Kings 24:20–25:21).

`36:21–23` After seventy years as captives in a foreign land, the Jewish people are permitted to return to their homeland. This return is authorized by King Cyrus of Persia. This nation succeeds Babylonia as the dominant world power.

`Jehoahaz` The son and successor of Josiah as king of Judah about 610 BC. A sinful monarch, he reigned only three months before being deposed by Pharaoh Nechoh of Egypt (2 Kings 23:31–34). *Shallum*: 1 Chron. 3:15.

`From Eliakim to Jehoiakim` *The king of Egypt made Eliakim his [Jehoahaz's] brother king over Judah and Jerusalem, and turned [changed, NIV] his name to Jehoiakim* (2 Chron. 36:4).

Egypt seized control of Judah, deposed King Jehoahaz, and installed Jehoahaz's brother Eliakim as king in his place. Then the Egyptian authorities changed the new king's name to Jehoiakim. This renaming of the king sent a message to all the people that a new era in the life of their nation had begun—their subjection to Egypt. The power to change their king's name symbolized Egypt's supreme authority. The nation of Judah was eventually overrun by the Babylonians. They carried away the leading citizens as captives, installed Mattaniah as a puppet king over what was left of the nation, and changed his name to Zedekiah (2 Kings 24:16–17).

JUNE 5 | Read Ezra 1–3

`1:1–4` King Cyrus of Persia conquers Babylonia, the nation that had overrun Judah and carried away captives to Babylon about seventy years before. In the first year of his reign, Cyrus allows the Jews who want to do so to return to their homeland and rebuild the city of Jerusalem and the temple (2 Chron. 36:22–23).

`1:5–11` A group of Jewish leaders, along with priests and Levites, agree to return to Jerusalem to conduct the rebuilding project. Cyrus sends with them gold and silver and items from the temple that had been taken away by the Babylonians when they pillaged Jerusalem (2 Kings 24:13).

`2:1–67` The leaders of the first group of Jewish exiles—more than 42,000—who return to their homeland under Zerubbabel (Hag. 2:20–23) are listed.

`2:68–70` The returning exiles settle in various cities of their native land and contribute to a special rebuilding fund (1 Chron. 26:20).

`3:1–6` People gather at Jerusalem from throughout their homeland to begin rebuilding. They offer sacrifices of thanksgiving to God on the altar of the temple when it is restored.

`3:7–13` Skilled workmen are enlisted, and materials are gathered to lay the foundation of the temple. Some of the Israelites are saddened that this new temple is not as ornate and beautiful as the first temple built by Solomon.

Cyrus The founding king of the Persian empire (reigned about 559–530 BC). After defeating the Babylonians, he allowed the Jewish captives to return to their homeland about 536 BC (2 Chron. 36:22–23; Ezra 1:1–4).

Michmas A town near Jerusalem occupied by Saul's army (1 Sam. 13:2–4) and the site of Jonathan's victory over the Philistines (1 Sam. 14:6–18). Some Jewish citizens returned to this city after the Babylonian Exile (Ezra 2:27). *Michmash*: Isa. 10:28; *Micmash*: NIV.

Register A tablet on which census records or genealogical lists were inscribed, with the names of the living on one side and the dead on the other (Ezra 2:62). *Family records*: NIV; *genealogical records*: NRSV.

Temple Servants *The Nethinims: the children of Ziha, the children of Hasupha, the children of Tabbaoth* (Ezra 2:43).

This verse begins a listing of all the Nethinims, or temple servants, who returned to Jerusalem under Zerubbabel after the Babylonian captivity. The Nethinims were a distinct class of people of non-Jewish background. Many were captives of war or former Canaanites such as the Gibeonites (Josh. 9:21–27) who had been made lowly servants. The Nethinims assisted the Levites in the temple by doing such menial jobs as cleaning sacrificial utensils and carrying water and wood to the altar.

JUNE 6 | Read Ezra 4–6

4:1–3 Zerubbabel, governor of Judah under appointment by the Persian king, refuses to allow non-Israelites to join in the rebuilding project.

4:4–16 These non-Jews take revenge for this rejection by trying to stop the construction project. They send a false report to King Artaxerxes of Persia, Cyrus's successor, that the Jews are plotting a rebellion against the Persian government.

4:17–24 Artaxerxes orders the work on the reconstruction of Jerusalem to stop until this charge against the Jews is investigated. The work does not resume until the accession of Darius to the Persian throne.

5:1 The prophets Haggai and Zechariah urge the people to resume work on the temple.

5:2–17 The leaders of Israel petition King Darius of Persia to allow the work on the temple to resume.

6:1–12 Darius permits the Jews to begin building again. He orders the enemies of the Jews to quit interfering with their building efforts. He sends gold and silver and building materials to assist in the construction work so they can resume their worship in the temple.

6:13–22 The temple is completed, the priests and Levites are organized for service at the altar, and celebration of the Passover festival is reinstated.

Zerubbabel A leader of the second group of Jews who returned to Jerusalem about 520 BC after their period of exile in Babylonia and Persia (Ezra 2:2). He supervised the rebuilding of the temple and helped restore religious practices among his people (Zech. 4; Ezra 5:2). He apparently was appointed governor of Judah by King Cyrus of Persia (Hag. 2:21). *Zorobabel*: Jesus' ancestry (Matt. 1:12). *Shesh-bazzar*: Ezra 5:14.

Darius A title for the kings of Persia. Four different kings with this title are mentioned in the OT: (1) Darius I or Darius the Great (reigned about 522–485 BC). Successor to Cyrus, he continued Cyrus's policy of restoring the Jewish people to their homeland (Ezra 6:1–12). (2) Darius II or Darius the Persian (Neh. 12:22), who reigned about 424–405 BC. (3) Darius III or Darius Codomannus (reigned about 336–330 BC). He is probably the "fourth" king of Persia mentioned by the prophet Daniel (Dan. 11:2). (4) Darius the Mede, who had the prophet Daniel thrown into a den of lions. He eventually made Daniel a ruler over several provincial leaders (Dan. 6:1–2).

Zerubbabel's Temple *Cyrus the king made a decree. . . . Let the house be builded, the place where they offered sacrifices* (Ezra 6:3).

One of the reasons King Cyrus of Persia allowed the Jewish exiles to return to Jerusalem was to rebuild the temple. This central place of worship for the Jewish people had been destroyed by the Babylonian army about sixty years before. Work on this temple began under Zerubbabel, Persian-appointed governor of Jerusalem. Thus, it is known as Zerubbabel's Temple. It was built on the site of the first temple, known as Solomon's Temple (1 Kings 6).

JUNE 7 | Read Ezra 7–8

7:1–10 Ezra, a priest and scribe, prepares to leave Persia and join his countrymen who have already returned to their homeland. As an expert in the Law of the Lord, he plans to teach the law to his fellow Israelites, probably because it had been neglected during their years in exile (Neh. 2:8, 18).

7:11–26 Ezra carries with him a letter from King Artaxerxes of Persia, giving him permission to return to Israel and to lead his countrymen in renewing their commitment to the Law of the Lord. Artaxerxes also gives Ezra gold and silver and other valuable commodities to assist him in this restoration effort.

7:27–28 Ezra gives thanks to God for selecting him for this important task.

8:1–14 The exiles who returned to Jerusalem with Ezra are listed.

8:15–23 Ezra sends word for Levites to join his group of travelers. Several answer the call, and Ezra proclaims a fast of dedication to God before they begin the trip.

`8:24–36` Ezra delivers the gold and silver and vessels from the temple to a group of priests for safekeeping. These were sent to Jerusalem as a gift from the Persian king Artaxerxes.

`Ezra` A scribe and priest who led an important reform movement among the Jewish people after the Babylonian Exile. He is the author of the book of Ezra.

`Artaxerxes I` The successor of Cyrus as king of Persia and the king in whose court Ezra and Nehemiah served (Ezra 7:1, 7). About 458 BC Artaxerxes authorized Ezra to lead a large group of Jews back to Jerusalem for resettlement (Ezra 7). About thirteen years later he allowed Nehemiah to return to rebuild the walls of Jerusalem (Neh. 2:1–10; 13:6).

JUNE 8 | Read Ezra 9–10

`9:1–2` The leaders of Israel inform Ezra that many Jewish men have defiled themselves during the exile by marrying women from pagan backgrounds (Exod. 34:16).

`9:3–15` In an eloquent prayer of confession and repentance, Ezra asks the Lord to forgive His people for their transgression.

`10:1–17` All the Israelite men who have married women from pagan backgrounds gather at Jerusalem and agree to give up these wives.

`10:18–44` The names of Israelite men who gave up their pagan wives are listed.

JUNE 9 | Read Nehemiah 1–3

`1:1–3` In Persia, Nehemiah learns of the plight of the people who were left behind in Jerusalem when the Babylonians ransacked the nation of Judah many years before (2 Kings 25:1–4).

`1:4–11` Nehemiah prays for his homeland and pleads with the Lord to forgive the sin and rebellion of His people.

`2:1–10` Nehemiah is the cupbearer for King Artaxerxes of Persia (Neh. 1:11). The king gives Nehemiah permission to go to Jerusalem to help rebuild the devastated city.

`2:11–16` After arriving in Jerusalem, Nehemiah surveys the broken defensive wall of the city under the cover of darkness to determine the repairs needed.

`2:17–18` Nehemiah challenges the rulers of Jerusalem to rebuild the wall around the city.

`2:19–20` Several enemies of the Jews scoff at Nehemiah's plan to rebuild the wall. But he insists that the project will be completed with the help of the Lord.

3:1–32 The names of several people who worked with Nehemiah on this building project are listed.

Nehemiah The governor of Jerusalem (445–433 BC) who helped rebuild the city wall after the Babylonian Exile; author of the book of Nehemiah. The son of Hachaliah, he was cupbearer to King Artaxerxes of Persia (Neh. 1:11; 2:1). He received permission from the king to return to Jerusalem to assist the returned exiles in their rebuilding efforts (Neh. 2:3–6). In addition to rallying the people to rebuild the city wall, Nehemiah led a religious reform with the assistance of Ezra the priest (Neh. 8:1–13; 12:36).

Chisleu The ninth month of the Hebrew year, roughly equivalent to parts of our November and December (Neh. 1:1). *Kislev*: NIV; *Chislev*: NRSV.

Persia A great empire whose territory covered what is now western Asia and parts of Europe and Africa, reaching the height of its greatness around 486 BC under Cyrus. The Persians conquered Babylonia in 539 BC and allowed the Israelites to return to their native land (2 Chron. 36:20–23). The Persian king Artaxerxes allowed Nehemiah to return to Jerusalem to rebuild the city wall (Neh. 2:1–8). The Persians were defeated by the Greek military conqueror Alexander the Great in 330 BC (Ezek. 38:5).

A Royal Cupbearer *For I [Nehemiah] was the king's cupbearer* (Neh. 1:11).

A cupbearer was one of the most important servants in the household of a king. His task was to taste the king's wine before he drank it to make sure it had not been poisoned by his enemies. Although Nehemiah was a Jew, he had risen to a position of prominence in the Persian court. Artaxerxes, the king, trusted him and allowed him to return to Jerusalem to rebuild the walls of the city (Neh. 2:3–7).

JUNE 10 | Read Nehemiah 4–6

4:1–3 Sanballat and Tobiah, enemies of the Jews, ridicule Nehemiah's attempt to rebuild the wall of Jerusalem.

4:4–6 Nehemiah answers their taunts with a prayer for God's guidance and protection in the building project.

4:7–12 Sanballat and Tobiah and other enemies of the Jews vow to stop the building project with military force.

4:13–23 Nehemiah organizes a defensive force and arms his workers so they can protect themselves against an enemy attack. Many workers labor on the wall with their construction tools in one hand and their weapons in the other.

5:1–5 Some of the people complain to Nehemiah about their economic hardship. Their own fellow Jews are charging them excessive interest on money they have borrowed and are even holding their children in slavery as collateral against their debts (Ezra 4:13).

5:6–13 Nehemiah confronts the wealthy Jews who are exploiting their poor neighbors. They agree to restore the land and children that are being held as collateral.

5:14–19 Nehemiah is serving as governor of Judah under appointment by the Persian king. But he refuses to use his position and power to line his own pockets.

6:1–14 The enemies of the Jews continue their plots to stop the building project. They even hire a false prophet to lure Nehemiah into an error in order to undermine his leadership. But Nehemiah is not fooled by their tricks.

6:15–19 The defensive wall around Jerusalem is rebuilt in fifty-two days—to the disappointment of Tobiah and other enemies who had tried to stop the project.

. . . .

Sanballat An influential Samaritan who plotted to kill Nehemiah to stop his rebuilding projects and reform projects in Jerusalem (Neh. 4:7–8; 6:1–4).

Noadiah A prophetess who tried to frighten Nehemiah and hinder his efforts to rebuild the wall of Jerusalem (Neh. 6:14).

. . . .

An Empty Pocket *I [Nehemiah] shook my lap [shook out the folds of my robe, NIV], and said, So God shake out every man from his house, and from his labour, that performeth not this promise, even thus be he shaken out, and emptied* (Neh. 5:13).

The "lap" in this passage was a pocket in the loose outer robe where people carried items such as money or important papers. It served the same purpose as a man's wallet in modern times. Nehemiah had just received a promise from the wealthy Jews of Jerusalem that they would no longer mistreat and defraud their poorer fellow Jews. When he shook out the pocket in his robe, he was saying to the wealthy, "God will make you just as empty as this pocket if you fail to keep the promise you have made."

JUNE 11 | Read Nehemiah 7–9

7:1–4 Nehemiah selects priests and Levites to preside over sacrifices in the temple. He also appoints civil leaders to provide security for the city of Jerusalem.

7:5–69 The Jewish tribes who have returned to Judah under the leadership of Zerubbabel (Hag. 2:20–23) are listed by clans and family groups.

7:70–73 Contributors to a special fund to assist in the rebuilding effort in Jerusalem are listed.

8:1–12 The people gather in the streets of Jerusalem and listen reverently as Ezra reads the Book of the Law (Genesis, Exodus, Leviticus, Numbers, and Deuteronomy). The priests and Levites are stationed among the crowd to explain these commands from God.

8:13–18 Ezra reads God's directions from the Book of the Law on how the Feast of Booths, or Tabernacles, is to be observed (Lev. 23:39–43). The people cut branches from trees and build themselves huts, or booths, to remember their living conditions during the years of wandering In the wilderness.

9:1–38 All the people, including civil leaders, priests, and Levites, repent and confess their sins to God. They vow to keep the covenant between the Lord and Israel.

Hanani Nehemiah's brother, who became governor of Jerusalem (Neh. 7:2). Hanani brought news of the suffering citizens of Jerusalem to Nehemiah in Persia (Neh. 1:2–3).

Tirshatha The title of the governor of Judea under Persian rule. Both Zerubbabel and Nehemiah were appointed by Persian kings to this position (Ezra 2:63; Neh. 7:65). *Governor*: NIV, NRSV.

Feast of Trumpets A Jewish religious festival, also called the *Seventh Month Festival* (Lev. 16:29). It was ushered in by the blowing of trumpets and observed by reading the law and presenting burnt offerings (Lev. 23:24–25; Neh. 8:2–3, 8–12). The exact reason for its observance is not clear.

Booth A temporary shelter made of tree branches. During the Feast of Tabernacles, also called the Feast of Booths, the Israelites lived in such shelters as a reminder of their harsh life in the wilderness after their deliverance from Egyptian slavery (Neh. 8:13–18).

JUNE 12 | Read Nehemiah 10–11

10:1–27 The names of the leaders who sealed the covenant between the Lord and the Israelites are listed.

10:28–39 The people agree to follow God's commands from the Book of the Law. They agree to resume the practice of bringing tithes, offerings, and sacrifices to the priests and Levites in the temple.

11:1–2 The leaders of Israel cast lots (Matt. 27:35) to determine the settlement of the returned exiles in the land. Ten percent are to settle in Jerusalem, and the remaining 90 percent will live in other cities throughout Judah.

11:3–24 The people selected to live in Jerusalem are listed.

11:25–36 Other cities of Judah where the exiles will settle are listed.

Shekel A Jewish coin or unit of measure. The silver shekel was worth about sixty cents; the gold shekel about eight dollars (Gen. 23:15; Neh. 10:32; Jer. 32:9).

JUNE 13 | Read Nehemiah 12–13

12:1–26 The names of priests and Levites who returned from the exile under Zerubbabel are listed (Ezra 2:1–67).

12:27–43 The names of priests and Levites whom Nehemiah appointed for a special function are listed. They lead the celebration at the dedication of the restored defensive wall of Jerusalem.

12:44–47 Nehemiah appoints priests and Levites to store the goods offered by the people for the support of the priesthood. He also organizes the priests and Levites to serve at the altar in the temple on a rotating basis. This restores the procedure established by David and Solomon (1 Chron. 25:1–26:32).

13:1–31 Nehemiah institutes religious reforms throughout the land of Judah. He restores the sanctity of the Sabbath, casts foreigners out of the temple, and forbids the Jewish people from marrying people from pagan backgrounds.

. . . .

Fountain Gate A gate in the wall of Jerusalem, perhaps named for the fountain or pool of Siloam (Neh. 12:37).

Frankincense The yellowish gum of a tree, known for its pungent odor when burned as incense during sacrificial ceremonies (Neh. 13:9). Frankincense was one of the gifts presented to the infant Jesus by the wise men (Matt. 2:11). *Incense*: NIV.

. . . .

A Severe Punishment *I [Nehemiah] contended with them [Jewish men who had married pagan women], and cursed them, and smote [beat, NIV] certain of them, and plucked off [pulled out, NIV] their hair* (Neh. 13:25).

In addition to rebuilding Jerusalem in a physical sense, Nehemiah was also concerned for the spiritual rebuilding of his people. He was so angry toward the Jewish men who had married pagan women—a flagrant disobedience of God's command (Joshua 23:12–13)—that he beat some of them and pulled out their hair. This violent and serious punishment showed the severity of their sin.

People sometimes pulled out their own hair as an expression of mourning (Ezra 9:3). Sometimes the act was committed against others as an act of extreme persecution (Isaiah 50:6).

JUNE 14 | Read Esther 1–3

1:1–9 King Ahasuerus of Persia invites the leaders throughout his kingdom to a lavish banquet at his royal palace in Shushan.

1:10–12 The king asks his queen, Vashti, to appear before his guests to showcase her beauty, but she refuses.

1:13–22 On the advice of his aides, King Ahasuerus decrees that Vashti will be deposed as queen and replaced by another woman.

2:1–4 Ahasuerus begins a search throughout his kingdom for a woman to replace Vashti as queen.

2:5–18 Esther, also known as Hadassah, is a beautiful young Jewish woman who was adopted by her cousin Mordecai after the death of her parents. She wins the king's favor and replaces Vashti as the queen.

2:19–23 Mordecai, who serves in the palace of King Ahasuerus (Esther 2:5), saves the king's life when he stops an assassination plot.

3:1–6 Haman, a high official in King Ahasuerus's administration, is enraged when Mordecai refuses to bow before him and show him honor and respect.

3:7–15 In order to kill Mordecai, Haman devises a plan to destroy all the Jews. He convinces King Ahasuerus that the Jewish people are reckless and dangerous revolutionaries who refuse to abide by the king's laws. Ahasuerus issues an order that all the Jews throughout his kingdom are to be wiped out on a specific day in the future.

. . . .

Ahasuerus A king of Persia who married Esther and listened to her counsel regarding the Jewish people. He ordered his aide Haman executed—an act that saved the Jewish people from destruction (Esther 7). Most scholars agree that this Ahasuerus is the same person as King Xerxes I of Persian history (reigned 485–464 BC).

Esther A young Jewish woman who became queen under King Ahasuerus of Persia and used her influence to save her countrymen. Her Persian name was *Hadassah*.

Abib The first month of the Hebrew year, the time when barley opened (Exod. 13:4). Roughly equivalent to our modern April, this month was known as *Nisan* after the Babylonian Exile (Esther 3:7).

. . . .

Harem Caretakers *The seven chamberlains [eunuchs, NIV] that served in the presence of Ahasuerus the king* (Esther 1:10).

A chamberlain was a male servant in a king's court who was responsible for the king's harem. To minimize the danger to these women, a chamberlain was emasculated. King Ahasuerus of Persia must have had a large harem, since he had seven of these servants. Sometimes these male servants rose to positions of prominence as advisers in the king's administration. This must have been the case with two chamberlains of King Ahasuerus, since they participated in a plot to assassinate the king (Esther 2:21–23). Other references to chamberlains or eunuchs include 2 Kings 9:32; Jer. 29:2; and Dan. 1:10.

JUNE 15 | Read Esther 4–6

4:1–9 Mordecai mourns for the Jewish people in front of the royal palace. He sends word to Esther that she must use her influence with the king to save the Jews from destruction.

4:10–17 Esther reminds Mordecai of the law that any person who approaches the Persian king without authorization runs the risk of being executed. But she promises Mordecai that she will take this risk on behalf of her own people, the Jews.

5:1–2 Esther makes an unauthorized appearance before the king. He agrees to receive her by extending his royal scepter for her to touch.

5:3–8 Esther asks the king to invite Haman to a banquet that she has prepared. At this banquet, she asks the king, along with Haman, to attend another banquet that she is preparing for the next day. During this second banquet she will make known her request to King Ahasuerus.

5:9–14 Filled with pride, Haman boasts to his wife and friends about his achievements and his special invitation to attend a banquet with the king and Queen Esther the next day. But Haman admits that all these achievements mean little as long as Mordecai refuses to bow down and show him honor. At his wife's suggestion, he builds a gallows on which he plans to have Mordecai hanged.

6:1–14 While reading the royal archives, Ahasuerus discovers the account of Mordecai's intervention on the king's behalf (Esther 2:19–23). The king orders Haman to prepare and lead a tribute to Mordecai for his brave action. Haman's humiliation at being forced to honor the Jew grows deeper when his wife predicts that he will fall before Mordecai.

Haman An aide to King Ahasuerus of Persia who plotted to kill the Jewish leader Mordecai and all the Jews, only to be hanged himself on the gallows that he had built for Mordecai's execution (Esther 3:1–9:25).

Mordecai's Extreme Distress *Mordecai rent [tore, NIV] his clothes, and put on sackcloth with ashes. . .and cried with a loud and a bitter cry* (Esther 4:1).

Haman, an aide to King Ahasuerus of Persia, convinced the king to order the destruction of all of the Jewish people in his empire. When Mordecai heard the news, he expressed his distress with these four actions: tearing his clothes, wearing a rough cloth known as sackcloth, throwing ashes on his head, and lamenting with a bitter cry. Any one of these actions by itself would have been enough to show that Mordecai was distraught. But he used all four to demonstrate that he was at rock bottom in grief and despair.

Don't Bother the King *Whosoever. . .shall come unto the king. . .who is not called, there is one law. . .to put him to death, except such to whom the king shall hold out the golden sceptre* (Esther 4:11).

Mordecai asked Esther to seek an audience with King Ahasuerus of Persia to plead for the Jewish people. In this verse, Esther reminded Mordecai that anyone who approached the king without a personal invitation ran the risk of immediate execution. The purpose of this harsh law may have been to keep the king from being pestered by grumblers and favor-seekers. He had the option of granting an audience to uninvited visitors by touching them with his royal scepter. Esther did decide to approach the king—uninvited—on behalf of her people, the Jews. The king touched her with his scepter and agreed to hear her request (Esther 5:1–2).

JUNE 16 | Read Esther 7–10

7:1–10 During the banquet with Haman and the king, Queen Esther exposes Haman's plot to have the Jews destroyed. King Ahasuerus orders that Haman be put to death. He is hanged on the gallows he had prepared for Mordecai's death (Esther 5:14).

8:1–2 Mordecai is promoted to a high position in King Ahasuerus's administration.

8:3–8 Queen Esther pleads with the king to spare her countrymen, the Jewish people.

8:9–17 King Ahasuerus issues a decree that authorizes the Jews to resist when their lives are threatened under the earlier order issued by Haman (Esther 3:13).

9:1–19 Throughout the kingdom of Persia, the Jews destroy many of their enemies, including ten sons of Haman. Mordecai, on the other hand, grows in popularity and power.

9:20–32 Mordecai and Esther proclaim the fourteenth and fifteenth days of the month of Adar as an official religious holiday among the Jews. Known as Purim, it memorializes God's deliverance of His people from their enemies.

10:1–3 The Jewish Mordecai becomes an important and highly respected official under King Ahasuerus. He is also respected and honored by his own countrymen throughout the kingdom of Persia.

A Celebration of Deliverance *Wherefore they [the Jews] called these days Purim after the name of Pur* (Esther 9:26).

The Jewish people celebrated their deliverance from the death edict issued by Haman (Esther 3:5–15) with a special holiday known as the Feast of Purim. The Hebrew word *purim* means "lots." The feast was named for the lots that Haman cast to determine the time when the Jews would be annihilated (Esther 3:7). Thanks to the brave actions of Esther and Mordecai, Haman was annihilated and the Jewish people prospered throughout the land.

BOOKS OF POETRY AND WISDOM

One of the most beloved books in the entire Bible—the book of Psalms—is included among the books of poetry and wisdom of the Old Testament. Other books in this category are Job, Proverbs, Ecclesiastes, and Song of Solomon.

Old Testament poetry does not include such elements as rhyme and alliteration, which we normally associate with poetic writings. Rather, the main feature of Old Testament poetic literature is parallelism. In this form of literary construction, the content of one line is advanced, contrasted, or repeated by the content of the next line.

Writings in this section of the Old Testament that deal with issues such as the meaning of life, the nature of human suffering, and how to have a happy and successful life are known as wisdom literature. The books of Job, Proverbs, and Ecclesiastes fall into this category. Several of the individual psalms are also classified as wisdom psalms: 1, 19, 37, 49, 104, 107, 112, 119, 127, 128, 133, 147, and 148.

JUNE 17 | Read Job 1–5

1:1–5 Job is a righteous and upright man who has been abundantly blessed by the Lord. He owns large herds of livestock and has many sons and daughters.

1:6–12 In a dialogue with God, Satan charges that Job serves Him for selfish reasons—what is in it for him. God gives Satan permission to test Job to determine if his charge is true.

1:13–22 In one disastrous day, Job loses everything: his large herds of livestock, his servants, and his own sons and daughters. But Job remains faithful to God.

2:1–10 Satan tells God that Job will certainly deny Him if he is afflicted with physical suffering. With God's permission, Job is struck with boils and sores. But still he refuses to cry out against God.

2:11–13 Three of Job's friends—Eliphaz, Bildad, and Zophar—hear about Job's misfortune. They come to mourn with Job and to comfort him in his anguish and pain.

3:1–26 Before his friends say a word, Job issues a plaintive cry of self-pity. He curses the day of his birth and wishes he had never been born. This chapter begins the first cycle of debate between Job and his friends. This cycle continues through chapter 14, with Eliphaz responding to Job (chaps. 4–5); Job replying to Eliphaz (chaps. 6–7); Bildad's first speech to Job (chap. 8); Job's response to Bildad (chaps. 9–10); Zophar's first speech to Job (chap. 11); and Job's reply to Zophar (chaps. 12–14).

4:1–5:27 In his response to Job's outburst, Eliphaz reminds his friend that the innocent do not suffer like Job is suffering. He calls on Job to turn to God and repent; then his troubles will go away.

....

Job A godly man of the OT whose faith sustained him through fierce trials and sufferings. Afflicted by Satan with God's permission (Job 1:6–19), Job refused to blame or curse God for his misfortune (1:20–22; 2:10), although he did complain to God, lamenting the day he was born (3:1). Job and his three friends had long discussions about his misfortunes and what they meant. He eventually came to a greater understanding of God's ways of dealing with humans (42:3–6), and God restored his family and possessions (42:10–15). Job was praised by James in the NT for his patience and faith (James 5:11).

Satan An evil being who opposes God; the devil. In the Garden of Eden, Satan was represented as a serpent who tempted Eve (Gen. 3:1–6). He falsely accused and harassed Job (Job 1:6–12). Jesus regarded Satan as a person (Matt. 4:1–10) whom He described as a murderer and the father of lies (John 8:44). While he is called "the prince of this world" (John 16:11), Satan is subject to God's greater power (1 John 4:4) and will be cast into the bottomless pit (Rev. 20:1–3).

Bildad One of the three friends who comforted the sorrowing Job (Job 2:11). His speeches expressed the conviction that all suffering is the direct result of sin (Job 8, 18, 25).

A Man of Means His [Job's] substance also was seven thousand sheep, and three thousand camels, and five hundred yoke of oxen, and five hundred she asses [female donkeys, NKJV] (Job 1:3).

In OT times, a man's wealth was measured by the size of his flocks and herds. Job was a rich man by these standards. Female donkeys are mentioned in this passage because they were more valuable than male donkeys. The milk produced by females was a valuable food substance.

JUNE 18 | Read Job 6–10

6:1–7:21 Job protests that he is innocent. How can God be punishing him when he has done nothing wrong?

8:1–22 Bildad steps up the tempo when he enters the debate. God always acts with justice and fairness, he declares. Is Job suggesting otherwise by claiming that God is punishing an innocent man?

9:1–10:22 Job expresses his confusion and frustration. He agrees in theory with Bildad that God is just. But in Job's case He seems to be punishing a person who is righteous. Job laments his condition and again wishes he had never been born.

Messages on Foot My [Job's] days are swifter than a post [runner, NIV]: they flee away, they see no good (Job 9:25).

Job complained about the brevity of human life by declaring that his days went by faster than a swift runner. He was probably referring to the fleet-footed messengers used by OT kings to carry important messages to distant places. King Hezekiah of Judah restored several important religious practices, including observance of the Passover, which had been neglected by the people. He sent "posts [couriers, NIV]. . .with. . .letters. . .throughout all Israel and Judah" (2 Chron. 30:6), summoning all citizens to gather at Jerusalem for this solemn occasion.

JUNE 19 | Read Job 11–14

11:1–20 Zophar now jumps into the debate and turns it up a notch. He attacks Job personally and accuses him of being filled with pride and of uttering meaningless words. He charges that there must be some hidden sin in Job's life; God knows about it and is giving Job what he deserves.

12:1–14:22 Job grows angry and sarcastic with his know-it-all friends. He declares that he knows as much about God and how He works as they do. He appeals his case directly to God and calls on Him to declare him innocent. He also laments the brevity of life and the lot of all human beings on earth: "Man that is born of a woman is of few days, and full of trouble" (Job 14:1).

Prosperous Thieves *The tabernacles [tents, NIV] of robbers [marauders, NIV] prosper, and they that provoke God are secure* (Job 12:6).

Job had lost his livestock to bands of robbers (Job 1:15, 17), so he knew what he was talking about when he lamented the fact that thieves and other wicked people sometimes seem to be more prosperous than honest, God-fearing people. Robbery is a crime that has existed since ancient times. The Bible gives evidence that sometimes entire clans or tribes made their living by stealing from the unwary. During the period of the judges, one such group was associated with the city of Shechem: "The men of Shechem. . .robbed all that came along that way" (Judges 9:25). Thieves and robbers may prosper for a while, but ultimately they will be caught and punished. God commanded His people, "Thou shalt not steal" (Exodus 20:15).

JUNE 20 | Read Job 15–19

15:1–35 Eliphaz replies to Job's outburst, calling him a vain man whose stomach is filled with the east wind (in other words, a windbag!). His speech kicks off the second cycle of debate in the book of Job. This cycle continues through chapter 21, with Job's response to Eliphaz (chaps. 16–17); Bildad's second speech to Job (chap. 18); Job's reply to Bildad (chap. 19); Zophar's second speech to Job (chap. 20); and Job's response to Zophar (chap. 21).

16:1–17:16 Job continues his complaining. He calls his friends "miserable comforters" (16:2) because of their lack of sensitivity and compassion.

18:1–21 Bildad insists that Job is being punished for his sin. He describes the destiny of the wicked in graphic terms, apparently to frighten Job into repentance.

19:1–29 Broken and depressed, Job begs his friends to have pity on him. They have become accusers and tormentors instead of comforters, accusing him unfairly and providing no answers to his probing questions.

Cheek To strike a person on the cheek was considered a grave insult (Job 16:10). Jesus taught believers to react to such acts with kindness (Luke 6:29).

A Futile Attack *He [the wicked man] runneth upon him [God], even on his neck, upon the thick bosses of his bucklers [shield, NIV]* (Job 15:26).

A "buckler" or shield was used by a warrior for protection in hand-to-hand combat. The "boss" of the shield was the thickest and strongest point on its outer edge that offered maximum protection against an enemy arrow or sword. Thus, Eliphaz in this verse was pointing out the futility of a wicked man's attack against God. It would be like a warrior trying to break through the strongest point of his opponent's shield.

Caught in God's Net *God hath overthrown me [Job], and hath compassed [surrounded, NKJV] me with his net* (Job 19:6).

Birds and other animals were often trapped with nets. These were also effective weapons in combat. A warrior would restrain an enemy by throwing a thick net around him. Then he would finish him off with a sword or spear. In his suffering and struggles with God, Job compared himself to an animal or a man trapped in a net. He believed God was wielding the net. As an innocent sufferer, he thought he was being punished by God for no reason.

JUNE 21 | Read Job 20–24

20:1–29 Zophar picks up the subject that Bildad had discussed in chapter 18: the terrible fate of the wicked. The implication of his remarks is that Job is being punished by God for his wickedness.

21:1–34 Job agrees with Zophar and the others that the wicked are ultimately punished, but he insists that they often prosper and flourish during this life.

22:1–30 Eliphaz intensifies his assault on Job. He accuses him of serious sins, including oppression of the poor. His speech launches the third and final cycle of debate between Job and his friends. This cycle continues through chapter 26, with Job's response to Eliphaz (chaps. 23–24); Bildad's third speech to Job (chap. 25); and Job's reply to Bildad (chap. 26).

23:1–24:25 Job wishes he could stand in God's presence and present his case directly to Him. He protests that life is not fair—that God sometimes seems to punish the righteous and reward the wicked.

Darkness The absence of light. Darkness ruled the world before God's creation of light (Gen. 1:2). Thus, darkness is symbolic of humankind's sin, rebellion, and ignorance (Job 24:13–17).

JUNE 22 | Read Job 25–31

25:1–6 Bildad feels compelled to defend God against Job's accusations. He declares that man has no right to question God's actions.

26:1–14 Job ends the three cycles of debate with a strong affirmation about God: He is all-powerful, and His ways are beyond human understanding: "The thunder of his power who can understand?" (v. 14).

27:1–31:40 In these five chapters, Job issues his final defense against his accusers. He looks back on his days of plenty and compares them with his present state of poverty. But through it all he has kept his integrity before God. He claims, as he has throughout the debate, that he is an innocent sufferer.

East Wind A violent, scorching desert wind, also known as the sirocco (Job 27:21).

Bowels The internal digestive system of the human body. The bowels were considered the center of a person's feelings and emotions, expressive of compassion and tenderness (Job 30:27–28).

JUNE 23 | Read Job 32–37

32:1–37:24 These six chapters contain the angry outburst of a young man named Elihu. Apparently he had listened to the debate between Job and his three friends and was not pleased with what they were saying. Job was wrong because he had justified himself rather than God. And his three friends had failed to convince Job of the error of his ways. Elihu feels he needs to defend God's honor and set the record straight. In his long speech, he upholds God's works, wisdom, and justice. He declares that Job is getting what he deserves because of his sin.

Breath of God A symbolic phrase that portrays God as the source of life (Job 33:4). His breath demonstrates His power and creative ability (2 Sam. 22:14–16). In the NT, God "breathed" the Holy Spirit upon His disciples (John 20:22).

JUNE 24 | Read Job 38–42

38:1–41:34 Elihu's diatribe is not dignified by a response from either Job or God. Instead, God finally replies to Job after Job's whining throughout the book. God does not give Job an explanation for his suffering. But He reminds Job that He is the sovereign, all-powerful, omnipotent Creator of the universe whose ways are beyond human understanding. He does not have to justify and defend His actions to mere mortals (Hab. 2:2–20).

42:1–6 Job's prideful desire for understanding and justification gives way to trust and submission. With faith and humility he declares, "I have heard of thee by the hearing of the ear: but now mine eye seeth thee. Wherefore I abhor myself, and repent in dust and ashes" (vv. 5–6).

42:7–17 The Lord reprimands the three friends of Job because He is not pleased with their treatment of Job. Then He restores Job's fortunes by giving him twice as much as he had before (Isa. 40:2).

Mazzaroth A constellation of stars cited by Job as evidence of the power and sovereignty of God (Job 38:31–33).

Star A luminous body visible in the sky at night. The Hebrews regarded all heavenly bodies as stars, except the sun and moon (Gen. 1:16). The stars were considered a noble mark of God's creative power (Ps. 19:1). Stars were used symbolically for rulers, princes, angels, and ministers (Job 38:7; Dan. 8:10; Rev. 1:16–20). Christ was called "the bright and morning star" (Rev. 22:16).

Unicorn A large animal of great strength, probably the wild ox (Num. 23:22). Yoking it and harnessing its power was considered impossible (Job 39:9–11). *Wild ox*: NIV, NRSV.

Leviathan A sea monster, believed by some scholars to be the crocodile (Job 41:1). The word is also used figuratively to describe one of Israel's enemies, probably Egypt (Isa. 27:1).

....

Sealing with Clay *It [the earth] is turned as clay to the seal* (Job 38:14).
This verse is part of God's response to Job's charge against Him that He was unjust and unfair for causing Job to suffer. In Bible times clay tablets or clay bricks were often stamped or sealed with a symbol that identified their owner or creator. God declared to Job that He was the all-powerful, omnipotent Lord who had created the earth and stamped it with His own seal. He did not owe Job an explanation for His actions.

JUNE 25 | Read Psalms 1–10

Psalm 1 Blessed is the person who walks in accordance with the Word of God (Prov. 4:14).

Psalm 2 A messianic psalm that declares that God's ultimate rule over the world will be established by His Son.

Psalm 3 God is a shield who protects the believer in troublesome times. This psalm was written by David when he fled from the rebellion of his son Absalom (2 Sam. 15–16).

Psalm 4 God hears the prayers of believers and grants peace and rest in the dark experiences of life.

Psalm 5 The Lord will reward the righteous and punish the wicked.

Psalm 6 A prayer for God to show mercy to the psalmist and to punish his enemies.

Psalm 7 This psalm focuses on righteousness. David wants God to know that he has lived a righteous life. He asks God to deliver him from wicked enemies.

Psalm 8 As he meditates on the wonders of God's physical creation, the psalmist realizes that man is weak and insignificant. But God has placed him in a position of honor and glory.

Psalm 9 A psalm of praise for the mercy and grace shown by the Lord to the nation of Israel. The psalmist also declares that God will punish the pagan nations.

Psalm 10 The wicked are persecuting and cheating the poor. The psalmist calls on the Lord to rise to their defense.

. . . .

Shiggaion A musical term in the title of Ps. 7, possibly referring to an increased tempo for singing.

. . . .

A Picture of Abundance *He [the righteous man] shall be like a tree planted by the rivers [streams, NIV] of water, that bringeth forth [yields, NIV] his fruit in his season* (Ps. 1:3).

This verse compares the righteous person to a tree that flourishes in an irrigated orchard. The dry Middle East today uses irrigation for many of its crops. Artificial watering was also practiced in many countries of the ancient world. For example, Egypt used the vast water resources of the Nile River to improve its crop production. Through a series of canals, the waters of the Nile were conveyed to every part of the rich alluvial valley through which the river flowed. The prophets Isaiah and Jeremiah predicted that Israel would be like a "watered garden" because of the future blessings of the Lord (Isa. 58:11; Jer. 31:12).

JUNE 26 | Read Psalms 11–18

Psalm 11 God is in control, and the psalmist affirms his confidence in His wisdom and guidance.

Psalm 12 Surrounded by those who speak false, flattering words, the psalmist declares that "the words of the LORD are pure words" (v. 6). He can be trusted to be honest and fair.

Psalm 13 Although he is feeling lonely and abandoned, the psalmist vows to "sing unto the LORD, because he hath dealt bountifully with me" (v. 6).

Psalm 14 Wicked, depraved people who live as if God does not exist are fools (v. 1). The apostle Paul quoted the first two verses of this psalm to show that no person is sinless in God's eyes (Rom. 3:10–12).

Psalm 15 The psalmist gives a brief description of the godly person who walks in the ways of the Lord.

Psalm 16 This is a messianic psalm because of its reference to the resurrection of Christ (vv. 9–11; see Acts 13:35–37).

Psalm 17 Overwhelmed by his enemies, the psalmist looks to God for guidance and deliverance.

Psalm 18 This psalm of thanksgiving from David celebrates his deliverance by the Lord from threats against his life by King Saul. It closely parallels David's song of deliverance in 2 Sam. 22.

Michtam A word in the titles of Ps. 16 and Pss. 56–60, perhaps designating a particular type of psalm.

JUNE 27 | Read Psalms 19–27

Psalm 19 A majestic celebration of God's revelation of Himself through nature and the law, God's written Word.

Psalm 20 This is a public prayer for the king of Israel, encouraging him and the people to trust in the Lord rather than military might.

Psalm 21 A prayer for victory over Israel's enemies under the leadership of the nation's earthly, political king.

Psalm 22 A well-known messianic psalm. Christ quoted from it while He was on the cross: "My God, my God, why hast thou forsaken me?" (v. 1; see Matt. 27:46).

Psalm 23 Because it portrays God as a tender, caring shepherd, this beloved psalm is known as the "Shepherd Psalm."

Psalm 24 As worshipers traveled to the temple in Jerusalem, they may have chanted this psalm as a recessional hymn. The Lord is portrayed as "the King of glory" (v. 10).

Psalm 25 Deeply aware of his unworthiness because of his sin, the psalmist prays passionately for God's mercy and forgiveness.

Psalm 26 A prayer of a person of integrity who has always sought to walk before the Lord in trust and obedience.

Psalm 27 An affirmation of faith from a person who has found solace in worship: "That I may dwell in the house of the LORD all the days of my life" (v. 4).

Worm An insect that destroyed plants and consumed dead flesh (Job 7:5). The word is also used symbolically of human helplessness or insignificance (Isa. 41:14) and frailty (Ps. 22:6).

Meek Kind, gentle, and humble. The meek will find spiritual satisfaction (Ps. 22:26) and receive God's instruction (Ps. 25:9). Paul cited meekness as one of the fruits of the spirit (Gal. 5:22–23). Jesus declared that the meek will inherit the earth (Matt. 5:5).

Pasture   Grazing lands for livestock. The word is also used figuratively for the protection of God's people under the Good Shepherd (Ps. 23:1–2; Ezek. 45:15).

More of God's Abundant Blessing   *Thou [God] anointest my head with oil; my cup runneth over* (Ps. 23:5).

Kings were anointed by having olive oil poured on their heads (2 Kings 11:12). This was also an act of courtesy and hospitality performed by hosts for their guests. David the psalmist compared God's grace to such an anointing. He felt as if God had held nothing back—that He had blessed him beyond measure with His love and mercy. Like David, another psalmist in the book of Psalms also praised the Lord, comparing His blessings to being "anointed with fresh oil" (Ps. 92:10).

JUNE 28 | Read Psalms 28–34

Psalm 28   The psalmist appeals to God as a rock and a shield. The Lord offers protection and deliverance to those who trust in Him.

Psalm 29   God's power and majesty are displayed in the forces of nature, even in a thunderstorm (v. 3).

Psalm 30   A psalm of thanksgiving to God for deliverance from sickness and death.

Psalm 31   The psalmist cries out to God in his anguish and distress. Christ quoted from this psalm on the cross just before He died: "Into thine hand I commit my spirit" (v. 5; see Luke 23:46).

Psalm 32   Sin in the believer's life brings remorse and misery, but repentance and confession result in God's forgiveness and the restoration of joy.

Psalm 33   The psalmist issues a public call for people to praise the Lord because of the wonders of His creation and the blessings that He showers on believers.

Psalm 34   David apparently wrote this psalm out of his experience of pretending to be insane before Achish, the Philistine king of Gath (1 Sam. 21:10–15). The psalm affirms that God provides for His people.

Psaltery, Harp, and Lyre   *Praise the LORD with harp: sing unto him with the psaltery and an instrument of ten strings* (Ps. 33:2).

The King James Version translation of this verse seems to refer to three different musical instruments: the harp, the psaltery, and an instrument of ten strings. But the New International Version interprets it as a reference to only one instrument—the harp: "Praise the LORD with the harp; make music to him on the ten-stringed lyre." The words *harp, psaltery,* and *lyre* refer to the same thing—a musical instrument similar to the modern harp that was played by plucking its strings. Harps were probably made in different sizes with different string configurations. Thus, the psalmist tells us in this verse that he is referring to a specific type of harp—one with "ten strings."

JUNE 29 | Read Psalms 35–39

Psalm 35 The psalmist calls on God to pay back his enemies for their treachery and to restore his reputation and good name.

Psalm 36 This psalm paints a striking contrast between the goodness of God and the evil of human beings.

Psalm 37 Righteous people are encouraged to remain faithful to God, even though evil seems to be winning. The ultimate victory belongs to the Lord and those who are His.

Psalm 38 The psalmist is crushed and humiliated by divine discipline because of his sin. He issues an eloquent plea for God's forgiveness and deliverance.

Psalm 39 Life is fleeting and filled with suffering and disappointment. The psalmist has learned to put his ultimate hope in the Lord.

Transgression A violation of God's law that may be personal (1 Tim. 2:14), public (Rom. 5:14), or premeditated (Josh. 7:19–25). Transgression produces death (1 Chron. 10:13) and destruction (Ps. 37:38), but it may be forgiven by confession (Ps. 32:1, 5) through the atoning death of Christ (Isa. 53:5–6).

JUNE 30 | Read Psalms 40–47

Psalm 40 A psalm of praise and thanksgiving to God for answering the psalmist's prayer and coming to his aid.

Psalm 41 God is faithful, even though the psalmist has been betrayed by a close friend (v. 9). Jesus may have had this psalm in mind when He predicted that one of His own disciples would betray Him (John 13:18).

Psalm 42 The psalmist expresses despair because God seems far away, but he hopes for a restoration of their previous close relationship.

Psalm 43 The psalmist asks the Lord to plead his cause before the ungodly and to guide his life with divine light and truth.

Psalm 44 Israel had apparently suffered defeat at the hands of an enemy. The psalmist calls on God to come to their aid as He has in the past.

Psalm 45 This is a royal wedding song celebrating the marriage of an unnamed king of Israel. Considered a messianic psalm, it emphasizes God's universal rule.

Psalm 46 God and His kingdom are like a place of refuge, a stronghold, a mighty fortress that cannot be overcome by the forces of evil. This psalm was the inspiration for Martin Luther's stirring Reformation hymn, "A Mighty Fortress Is Our God."

Psalm 47 A praise psalm that exalts God as the "great King over all the earth" (v. 2).

Pierced Ears of a Servant *Mine ears hast thou [God] opened [pierced, NIV]* (Ps. 40:6).

In OT times, an indentured servant might decide to stay with his master for the rest of his life. This lifetime commitment was signified by the piercing of the servant's ear (Exod. 21:2–6; Deut. 15:12–17). David in this psalm referred to this custom to show that he was a willing servant of the Lord. He was ready to do whatever God asked of him.

Betrayal by a Friend *Yea, mine own familiar [close, NIV] friend, in whom I trusted, which did eat of my bread, hath lifted up his heel against me* (Ps. 41:9).

The ultimate insult of Bible times was betrayal by a close friend. In this psalm David may have been referring to Ahithophel, a friend and royal adviser, who joined Absalom's rebellion against the king (2 Sam. 15:12, 31). Jesus cited this psalm when He predicted that Judas, one of His disciples, would betray Him: "He that eateth bread with me hath lifted up his heel against me" (John 13:18).

JULY 1 | Read Psalms 48–55

Psalm 48 The city of Jerusalem, referred to as Zion in this psalm (v. 2) is portrayed as a place especially blessed and honored by the Lord.

Psalm 49 This psalm focuses on the folly of amassing great wealth in the belief that it will provide security. True security consists of following God and obeying His commands.

Psalm 50 Honoring God with an obedient, godly life is more important than offering sacrifices at the altar.

Psalm 51 David wrote this plea for forgiveness after he committed adultery with Bathsheba: "Create in me a clean heart, O God; and renew a right spirit within me" (v. 10; see 2 Sam. 11).

Psalm 52 This psalm grew out of Doeg's betrayal of David (1 Sam. 22). David proclaims that wicked people like Doeg will be rejected by the Lord, but the righteous will always enjoy God's blessings.

Psalm 53 This psalm, similar to Ps. 14, proclaims the universal sinfulness of humankind.

Psalm 54 In this psalm David affirms that God protected him during the time when the Ziphites told King Saul where David was hiding (1 Sam. 23:19–23).

Psalm 55 This psalm portrays a person in agony of soul after being betrayed by a close friend. But the psalmist looks to God as a never-failing friend and refuge.

Doeg An overseer of King Saul's herds who betrayed the high priest Ahimelech for assisting David and his soldiers (1 Sam. 22:9–10).

Cleansed with Hyssop *Purge [cleanse, NIV] me with hyssop, and I shall be clean* (Ps. 51:7).

Hyssop was a plant of the mint family. It grew to about three feet tall and produced clusters of yellow flowers. Bunches of this plant were used to sprinkle blood on the doorposts of Israelite houses in Egypt to keep them safe from the death angel (Exod. 12:22). Hyssop was also used in purification ceremonies. In Ps. 51 David prayed for the Lord to take away the guilt of his sins of adultery with Bathsheba and the murder of her husband (2 Sam. 11:1–27). Just as hyssop was used by priests to sprinkle lepers to show that they were free of their disease (Lev. 14:1–8), so David needed the Lord's cleansing forgiveness.

JULY 2 | Read Psalms 56–65

Psalm 56 A psalm that affirms reliance on God during a time of fear and uncertainty.

Psalm 57 David expresses his confidence in God's protection, even as he seeks refuge in a cave from the wrath of King Saul (1 Sam. 24).

Psalm 58 This psalm calls for God's judgment on leaders who use their authority to defraud and cheat the innocent.

Psalm 59 David recalls the time when King Saul posted soldiers around his house to ambush and kill him (1 Sam. 19:11–18). He denounces his enemies and affirms his trust in God.

Psalm 60 Although Israel suffers from temporary setbacks, the psalmist is convinced that God will give them the ultimate victory over their enemies.

Psalm 61 A prayer for the earthly king of Israel. He and the psalmist will find security and safety in "the rock that is higher than I" (v. 2).

Psalm 62 The psalmist urges all people to put their trust in God, not riches or prestige. He is a never-failing source of strength and power.

Psalm 63 In "a dry and thirsty land" (v. 1), David longs for God's presence rather than water. This psalm may reflect the time when David was hiding in the wilderness from King Saul (1 Sam. 24).

Psalm 64 The psalmist expresses his conviction that God will protect him from his enemies and give them what they deserve.

Psalm 65 A hymn of thanksgiving for God's physical creation (Gen. 1:1–25) and the abundant crops He provides throughout the land.

God Knows Our Tears *Thou [God] tellest my wanderings: put thou my tears into thy bottle: are they not in thy book?* (Ps. 56:8).

David may have been referring in this psalm to an ancient custom observed by mourners at funerals. They would collect the tears they shed for departed loved ones in small flasks and place them in their tombs as memorials of their love. This was David's way of saying that God knows all about us. He even keeps a record of the tears we shed in our moments of sorrow and sadness. Jesus expressed the same truth when He declared, "The very hairs of your head are all numbered" (Matt. 10:30).

The Bite of the Wicked *Their [the wicked's] poison is like the poison of a serpent [snake, NIV]: they are like the deaf adder [cobra, NIV] that stoppeth her ear; which will not hearken to the voice of charmers* (Ps. 58:4–5).

Psalm 58 declares that wicked people may seem to be flaunting the Lord and getting by with it, but eventually they will pay for their evil deeds. The psalmist compared the wicked to a snake that refused to be charmed by a snake charmer. Like these uncontrollable snakes, the wicked are always ready to bite the righteous, since they will not give in to the Lord's control. Snake charming was like a circus act in Bible times. People paid magicians and wizards to see them practice this ancient art. Solomon observed, "If a snake bites before it is charmed, there is no profit for the charmer" (Eccles. 10:11 NIV).

Thorns for Fuel *Before your pots can feel the thorns, he [the Lord] shall take them [the wicked] away as with a whirlwind* (Ps. 58:9).

Thorny shrubs and plants were plentiful in Palestine, and they were gathered and used as fuel under cooking pots (2 Sam. 23:6–7; Eccles. 7:6; Isa. 9:18; Nah. 1:10). They made a quick, hot fire. The psalmist declared that the Lord would destroy the wicked faster than the heat from a fire of thorns could reach the cooking pot. Much of Palestine is rocky and barren, so firewood was scarce. In addition to thorns, the people used grass (Matt. 6:30), sticks (1 Kings 17:10), and dried manure (Ezek. 4:12–15) for fuel.

JULY 3 | Read Psalms 66–71

Psalm 66 An eloquent expression of praise and thanksgiving for the Lord's mighty acts on behalf of His people.

Psalm 67 A call to worship that invites everyone, even the nations beyond Israel, to join in joyous praise of the Lord.

Psalm 68 This psalm is a battle march or victory hymn celebrating Israel's defeat of its enemies under the leadership of God.

Psalm 69 This messianic psalm, with its graphic description of human suffering, portrays the agony of Christ (compare Ps. 69:9 with John 2:17 and Ps. 69:21 with Matt. 27:34, 48).

Psalm 70 An urgent prayer for God's speedy deliverance. This psalm closely parallels Ps. 40:13–17.

Psalm 71 The psalmist thanks God for walking with him since his youth. He expresses confidence in the Lord's continuing presence in his senior years.

. . . .

Ascension of Christ Jesus' return to His Father after His crucifixion and resurrection (Luke 24:50–51). Foretold in the OT (Ps. 68:18), the ascension occurred forty days after the Resurrection (Acts 1:2–11). Christ will return to earth as surely as He ascended to heaven (Acts 1:11).

Jehovah A translation of *Yahweh,* a Hebrew word for God in the OT that indicated his eternity and self-existence. This word is based on a Hebrew verb meaning "to be"; thus the name "I AM" by which God revealed Himself to Moses at the burning bush (Exod. 3:14). *Yahweh* is rendered as "Lord" and printed in small capital letters (LORD) in most English versions of the Bible, although some translations use *Yahweh* or *Jehovah. Jah* is an abbreviated form of this name (Ps. 68:4).

Zeal Ardent desire and determination (Ps. 69:9; Phil. 3:6). Isaiah predicted the "zeal of the LORD" would establish the Messiah's kingdom (Isa. 9:7).

JULY 4 | Read Psalms 72–77

Psalm 72 A messianic psalm that looks toward the time when God will rule with righteousness throughout the world.

Psalm 73 Although the ungodly seem to be winning at the present time, they will eventually be judged and punished by the Lord. The righteous will be rewarded for their faithfulness.

Psalm 74 A plea for God to punish the enemies of Israel who destroyed the temple in Jerusalem (2 Kings 25:1–12). This psalm was probably written during Israel's period of exile in Babylon.

Psalm 75 A hymn of warning to the wicked. God is portrayed as the righteous judge.

Psalm 76 A hymn of victory celebrating God's deliverance of Israel from its enemies.

Psalm 77 A historical psalm that reviews the Lord's wondrous acts on behalf of His people.

. . . .

Dregs Waste that settled to the bottom of the vat in the wine-making process (Ps. 75:8). The word is also used symbolically of God's wrath and judgment (Isa. 51:17).

Right Hand A symbol of power and strength (Ps. 77:10). Jesus is exalted in power at God's right hand (Eph. 1:20).

....

Lifting Up the Horn *I said unto. . .the wicked [arrogant, NIV], Lift not up the horn.* (Ps. 75:4)

This psalm condemns the wicked for their part in flaunting the authority of the Lord. The horn of an animal symbolized its strength (Deut. 33:17; Zech. 1:18–21). The phrase "lift up the horn" referred to a stubborn animal, such as an ox, that held its head high to keep a yoke from being placed on its shoulders. Thus, the phrase expresses rebellion and stubbornness.

JULY 5 | Read Psalms 78–82

Psalm 78 Looking back on Israel's history, this psalm warns future generations to remain loyal to God and His commands.

Psalm 79 This psalm describes a time of national disaster, perhaps the destruction of Jerusalem and the temple by the Babylonians (2 Kings 25:1–12). The psalmist calls on God to deliver Israel from its shame and humiliation.

Psalm 80 Israel was once like a healthy vine (vv. 8–11; see Isa. 5:1–7), but now it has been cut down and defeated. The psalmist asks the Lord to restore the nation to its former glory.

Psalm 81 The psalmist paints a graphic contrast between God's faithfulness and the waywardness of Israel.

Psalm 82 This psalm is directed to rulers or leaders. God will judge those who use their authority to oppress and cheat others (Isa. 28).

....

Anthropomorphisms Human attributes ascribed to God. For example, God is described as having an arm of deliverance (Exod. 6:6), eyes too pure to look upon evil (Hab. 1:13), and a nature that is provoked to anger and jealousy by idolatry (Ps. 78:58).

....

Honorable Treatment of the Dead *The dead bodies of thy servants have they given to be meat unto the fowls of the heaven, the flesh of thy saints unto the beasts of the earth* (Ps. 79:2).

For a corpse to go unburied was one of the greatest dishonors imaginable. To have the body ravaged by vultures and other wild animals made the horror even worse. When the Philistines killed King Saul and his sons, they insulted the entire nation of Israel by hanging their bodies on the defensive wall of the city of Beth-shan. A group of brave Israelite warriors retrieved the bodies, cremated them, and gave their bones a decent burial (1 Sam. 31:9–13).

JULY 6 | Read Psalms 83–89

Psalm 83 The psalmist calls on God to exercise His sovereignty and defend His people against their enemies.

Psalm 84 A hymn sung by worshipers as they approached God's temple: "My soul longeth, yea, even fainteth for the courts of the LORD" (v. 2).

Psalm 85 An optimistic psalm that looks to the future under God's leadership.

Psalm 86 Out of a deep sense of spiritual need ("O LORD, hear me: for I am poor and needy," v. 1), the psalmist pleads for God's mercy and forgiveness.

Psalm 87 A short psalm on the glories of Jerusalem, referred to as Zion (v. 2).

Psalm 88 This is perhaps the most desperate of all the psalms, prayed by a person who was seriously ill. But the Lord did not seem to hear his plea. The tone of this psalm is similar to that of the book of Job.

Psalm 89 This psalm refers to the everlasting covenant that God made with David (2 Sam. 7:1–17). But tragic events since that time make the psalmist wonder if God has given up on Israel.

- -

Alone in the Pit *I am counted with them that go down into the pit* (Ps. 88:4).

Ps. 88 is the saddest psalm in the entire book of Psalms. Feeling depressed and alone, the psalmist cried out that God had forgotten him and was ignoring his pleas for help.

To "go down into the pit" was the psalmist's way of saying that he felt as though he had died and gone to the realm of the dead. To make matters worse, no one seemed to care that he had disappeared. Some people wonder why God would allow such a depressing psalm to appear in the book of Psalms. Perhaps it is included to show that depression and discouragement are as much a part of the human experience as joy and exhilaration. God does not reject us when we are feeling down and out. He wants to lift us up and restore the joy of our salvation. Notice the psalmist did begin this psalm with these words: "O lord God of my salvation" (Ps. 88:1).

JULY 7 | Read Psalms 90–99

Psalm 90 This is the only psalm in the book of Psalms attributed to Moses. He contrasts the eternity of God with the brief human life span.

Psalm 91 This is one of the most beloved of the psalms. God is a refuge and fortress for the believer: "He that dwelleth in the secret place of the most High shall abide under the shadow of the Almighty" (v. 1).

Psalm 92 A majestic hymn of praise and thanksgiving for God's goodness to His people.

Psalm 93 A short psalm that celebrates God's reign over the world in glory and majesty.

Psalm 94 The Lord is a God of justice. He will ultimately judge the wicked and reward those who follow His law.

Psalm 95 A call to worship: "O come, let us sing unto the LORD: let us make a joyful noise to the rock of our salvation" (v. 1).

Psalm 96 The psalmist calls on all the earth to sing praises to God. This psalm is one of the greatest affirmations in the Bible of the believer's missionary witness.

Psalm 97 The Lord is to be praised because He is superior to all other gods.

Psalm 98 The Lord is to be praised with music and song because of His salvation and righteousness.

Psalm 99 The Lord is to be praised because He is a holy God who has remained faithful to His people.

....

Bowing To show reverence or submission, performed by kneeling on one knee and bending the head forward. Bowing is considered appropriate for prayer and worship (Ps. 95:6). Jesus knelt or bowed to pray in Gethsemane (Matt. 26:36–39).

....

Trapping Birds *Surely he [God] shall deliver thee from the snare [trap] of the fowler* (Ps. 91:3).

This psalm celebrates God's promise that He will deliver and watch over His people, keeping them safe from danger. According to the psalmist, the Lord will not allow His people to fall into the snare, or trap, of the fowler. A fowler was a hunter who trapped birds for a living. Once a bird was caught in a fowler's net, it could not free itself, no matter how hard it struggled. It was destined to wind up as a meal on someone's table. In the OT, the perils that people face are often compared to the net of a bird trapper (Job 18:8; Ps. 141:9–10; Prov. 7:23). Only God is able to deliver us from such danger.

JULY 8 | Read Psalms 100–105

Psalm 100 A short psalm of praise to God because "the LORD is good; his mercy is everlasting; and his truth endureth to all generations" (v. 5).

Psalm 101 The psalmist pledges to remain faithful to God and not to associate with evil and ungodly people.

Psalm 102 In anguish and affliction, the psalmist pours out his heart to God. He prays that the Lord will have mercy on Jerusalem, or Zion. This psalm may have been written during Israel's period of exile under the Babylonians.

Psalm 103 This is a psalm of overflowing gratitude to God for His goodness, mercy, and love: "Bless the LORD, O my soul: and all that is within me, bless his holy name" (v. 1).

Psalm 104 The psalmist marvels at the display of God's glory in the universe that He has created (Ps. 8).

Psalm 105 This psalm reviews God's mighty acts on behalf of His people Israel, especially His dealings with Abraham and His miracles during the Exodus.

Truth That which is reliable and consistent with God's revelation. Truth is established by God's law (Ps. 119:142–144) and personified by Jesus Christ (John 14:6). Believers are purified by obedience to the truth (1 Pet. 1:22) and worshiping God in spirit and truth (John 4:23–24).

JULY 9 | Read Psalms 106–109

Psalm 106 This psalm also reviews the history of Israel's relationship with God, but it emphasizes the sin and disobedience of the people.

Psalm 107 People in many different situations experience anguish and suffering, but God is the great comforter of all who walk in His ways.

Psalm 108 A psalm of praise to the Lord, who has formed Israel into His own people. This psalm is made up of verses from Ps. 57:7–11 and Ps. 60:5–12.

Psalm 109 The psalmist describes his distress because of persecution by his enemies. He asks God to take up his case against them.

JULY 10 | Read Psalms 110–118

Psalm 110 This messianic psalm looks toward the reign of the coming Messiah, who will be exalted as "a priest for ever after the order of Melchizedek" (v. 4; see Heb. 5:6).

Psalm 111 The psalmist praises the Lord for His goodness and His gracious deeds. He reminds the people that "the fear of the LORD is the beginning of wisdom" (v. 10).

Psalm 112 The person who respects and follows the Lord will be safe and secure, having nothing to fear from the forces of evil.

Psalm 113 A psalm of praise to God because He lifts up the poor and showers them with mercy.

Psalm 114 The psalmist praises the Lord because of His deliverance of Israel from slavery in Egypt during the Exodus (Exod. 12:31–42).

Psalm 115 This psalm describes the futility of trusting in false gods and the wisdom of trusting in the Lord.

Psalm 116 Delivered from the snares of death, the psalmist vows to serve God and to present sacrifices and offerings before Him in the temple.

Psalm 117 A two-verse psalm of praise—the shortest of all the psalms.

Psalm 118 A messianic psalm. Jesus quoted this psalm to show that He had been rejected by His own people: "The stone which the builders refused is become the head stone of the corner" (v. 22; see Matt. 21:42).

Melchizedek The king of Salem who received tithes from Abraham (Gen. 14:18–20) and who is depicted as a type of Christ because of his endless priesthood (*Melchisedec*, Heb. 5:6–10; 7:15–17). The Messiah who is to come was also described as a priest "after the order of Melchizedek" (Ps. 110:4).

God Gives the Victory *Sit thou at my [God's] right hand, until I make thine enemies thy footstool* (Ps. 110:1).

A footstool was a piece of furniture, similar to a modern ottoman, on which a person rested his or her feet while in a reclining or resting position. To treat one's enemies as a footstool was to defeat them and bring them into total subjection. Thus, God assured the psalmist that he would be victorious over his enemies if he trusted in the Lord. This passage has been interpreted as a reference to the Messiah. Following His victory over death and the grave, Jesus is now seated at God's right hand as our Savior and Mediator (Acts 2:32–35; 1 Cor. 15:27).

JULY 11 | Read Psalm 119

Psalm 119 This psalm on the written Word or Law of God is the longest of the psalms and the longest chapter in the entire Bible. It is divided into twenty-two sections of eight verses each, with each section identified by a different letter of the Hebrew alphabet. The eight verses in each section begin with their respective Hebrew letter.

Meditation Contemplation of spiritual truths (Ps. 119:148) that produces understanding (Ps. 49:3) and spiritual satisfaction (Ps. 63:5–6). Meditation on God's commands encourages obedience (Josh. 1:8).

Finding Joy in the Lord *I am become like a bottle [wineskin, NIV] in the smoke; yet do I not forget thy [God's] statutes [decrees, NIV]* (Ps. 119:83).

In Bible times wine and other liquids were stored in containers made of animal skins. These skins would eventually become brittle and develop cracks, particularly when exposed to the smoke given off by fires that burned in the tents and primitive houses of that time. The psalmist compared himself to one of these useless wineskins. But even when he felt burned out and unworthy, he found comfort and joy in the Law of the Lord.

JULY 12 | Read Psalms 120–134

Psalm 120 The psalmist prays for deliverance from lies and slanderous words that are being uttered against him by his enemies.

Psalm 121 Pilgrims traveling to the temple at Jerusalem for worship may have sung this prayer for safety along the way.

Psalm 122 A prayer for the peace and prosperity of the city of Jerusalem.

Psalm 123 A short psalm imploring the Lord's mercy.

Psalm 124 The psalmist admits that Israel would not have been victorious over its enemies without the Lord's help.

Psalm 125 Just as the hills and mountains surround Jerusalem, God places His love and mercy around His people.

Psalm 126 This psalm is associated with the return of Jewish exiles to their homeland following the exile in Babylon (2 Chron. 36:22–23). The people are overwhelmed with joy.

Psalm 127 A psalm that celebrates family life, particularly the joys of children.

Psalm 128 This psalm may have been recited as a blessing on the groom at a wedding: "Thy wife shall be as a fruitful vine by the sides of thine house: thy children like olive plants round about thy table" (v. 3).

Psalm 129 This psalm celebrates the victories of the Israelites over their enemies.

Psalm 130 The psalmist waits patiently and expectantly before the Lord as he pleads for mercy and forgiveness.

Psalm 131 A brief prayer of quiet and humble trust in the Lord's goodness.

Psalm 132 This messianic psalm rejoices in God's promise to David of an eternal kingship (2 Sam. 7:1–17).

Psalm 133 A brief psalm celebrating unity and brotherly love.

Psalm 134 The psalmist encourages the priests and Levites who are on watch duty in the temple at night.

Children Children were looked upon as blessings from God (Ps. 127:3), and childlessness was considered a curse (Deut. 7:14). The word is also used symbolically of those who belong to Christ (Rom. 8:16–17).

Watching and Anticipating *As the eyes of servants look unto the hand of their masters. . .so our eyes wait upon [look to, NIV] the LORD our God* (Ps. 123:2).

Servants and slaves of Bible times were trained to anticipate the needs of their masters. Over many years they became so sensitive to what their masters wanted that they would not have to be told or commanded. A glance or a hand gesture would be enough to send them into action.

The point of the psalmist in this verse is that we as believers should be just as sensitive to the Lord's will as these household servants are to their human masters. We should be ready and willing to do the Lord's bidding, even anticipating what He desires of His servants.

Grass Growing on the Roof *Let them all be confounded and turned back that hate Zion. Let them be as the grass upon the housetops, which withereth afore it groweth up* (Ps. 129:5–6)

The psalmist describes wicked people or those who oppose God as haters of Zion, or Jerusalem. He hopes they will be as short-lived as grass that springs up on the roof of a house. Houses of Bible times had flat roofs sealed with clay. Grass would sometimes sprout and begin to grow on a flat roof. But it would wither quickly when subjected to heat, foot traffic, and the regular smoothing of the roof with a stone roller.

JULY 13 | Read Psalms 135–142

Psalm 135 God's mighty acts in history display His greatness and show that He is superior to all pagan gods.

Psalm 136 This psalm was probably a responsive hymn sung in the temple by the choir.

Psalm 137 This psalm from the exile in Babylon shows how the Israelites missed their homeland: "By the rivers of Babylon. . .we wept, when we remembered Zion" (v. 1).

Psalm 138 A prayer of thanksgiving for God's kindness, truth, and mercy.

Psalm 139 The psalmist celebrates God's unlimited knowledge and universal presence. There is nothing God doesn't know—even the psalmist's unexpressed thoughts (v. 2).

Psalm 140 Dangerous people are threatening the life of the psalmist, and he prays for God's protection.

Psalm 141 The psalmist prays that he will not use the same tactics against his enemies that they are using against him—and thus fall into sin.

Psalm 142 A prayer of David for protection when he was hiding in a cave from King Saul (1 Sam. 22:1–5).

Omnipotence The unlimited and infinite power that belongs to God. This characteristic of God's nature is expressed by His names *almighty* (Gen. 17:1) and *omnipotent* (Rev. 19:6). God controls nature (Amos 4:13) and the destiny of nations (Amos 1–2). God's omnipotence is also expressed by the Holy Spirit's power to convict and save (Rom. 15:19).

Omniscience The infinite knowledge of God. The all-wise and all-knowing God requires no counselor (Isa. 40:13–14). Christ is the key who opens all the hidden treasures of God's wisdom and knowledge (Col. 2:2–3). God's Spirit reveals the "deep things of God" to those who are spiritually receptive (1 Cor. 2:10–14).

JULY 14 | Read Psalms 143–150

Psalm 143 A plaintive cry for God's guidance and direction: "Teach me to do thy will" (v. 10).

Psalm 144 A battle song asking for victory under the leadership of the Lord. The army of Israel may have sung or chanted psalms like this as it went into battle.

Psalm 145 A psalm of pure praise to God for His wondrous works: "Great is the LORD, and greatly to be praised; and his greatness is unsearchable" (v. 3).

Psalm 146 The psalmist celebrates God's universal reign and calls on people to place their trust in Him.

Psalm 147 A hymn of praise focusing on God as protector of His people Israel and as Creator of the universe.

Psalm 148 A hymn of universal praise. Let everything praise God: angels, sun and moon, heavens, waters, mountains, animals, kings, men, women, and children.

Psalm 149 The psalmist exhorts all the people of Israel to praise the Lord, their faithful and mighty King.

Psalm 150 The book of Psalms ends with a ringing affirmation of praise to God: "Let every thing that hath breath praise the LORD" (v. 6).

Flute, Bagpipe, or Harmonica? *Praise him [God] with the timbrel [tambourine, NIV] and dance: praise him with stringed instruments and organs [flute, NIV]* (Ps. 150:4).

The exact nature of the third musical instrument mentioned in this verse is uncertain. The King James Version describes it as an "organ," while the New International Version uses the word "flute." A third translation prefers "woodwinds" (CEV). It certainly was not an instrument as sophisticated as the modern pipe organ. It probably was a wind instrument of some type, perhaps similar to the flute, the bagpipe, or the harmonica. Whatever it was, the psalmist declared that it was to be played in joyful praise to the Lord.

Praise with Cymbals *Praise him [God] upon the loud cymbals; praise him upon the high sounding cymbals* (Ps. 150:5).

The cymbals of Bible times were similar to our modern cymbals. Two circular plates of brass were struck against each other to produce a clanging or ringing sound. Two different types of cymbals are apparently mentioned in this verse. "Loud" cymbals were probably similar to the large metal plates used in modern marching bands. The "high sounding" cymbals may have been similar to our modern castanets. Worn on the fingers of both hands, these were struck together rapidly to produce a distinctive rattling or rhythmic sound.

JULY 15 | Read Proverbs 1–5

1:1–7 This brief introduction to the book of Proverbs states its purpose: to give instruction in wisdom.

1:8–33 The phrase "my son" (v. 8) is repeated often throughout Proverbs. The authors of Proverbs are imparting good advice and practical rules for living, as a father might do with his son. Those who heed the counsel of wisdom will not fall into evil.

2:1–22 The Lord is the true source of wisdom. Those who seek Him will avoid the pitfalls of sin and will not be enticed into adulterous relationships.

3:1–12 It is best to trust God for insight and direction and not to depend on human understanding: "In all thy ways acknowledge him, and he shall direct thy paths" (v. 6).

3:13–26 Happy is the person who finds wisdom and understanding. He will have nothing to fear, since his confidence is in the Lord.

3:27–35 Treat your neighbors with kindness. Do not envy or copy the ways of the wicked.

4:1–27 Avoid evil and the company of those who commit evil deeds. Follow the straight and narrow path of righteousness. Do not criticize others or speak idle words.

5:1–23 Marriage is sacred in the eyes of the Lord. Stay away from extramarital affairs, and cultivate your relationship with your spouse.

Wisdom Knowledge guided by insight and understanding. Reverence for God is the source of wisdom (Prov. 9:10). Wisdom is more valuable than riches (Prov. 8:11), and it produces good fruit (James 3:17). Christ is the key that opens the hidden treasures of God's wisdom (Col. 2:3).

JULY 16 | Read Proverbs 6–9

6:1–5 Do not enter into contracts carelessly or make foolish promises to others.

6:6–15 Idleness and laziness lead to poverty. Follow the example of the ant; it works diligently without having to be hounded by a supervisor!

6:16–19 A list of seven things that the Lord hates: pride, lying, murder, wickedness, the spreading of gossip, the bearing of false witness, and the stirring up of trouble among people.

6:20–35 A second exhortation to avoid adulterous relationships (Prov. 5).

7:1–27 A third exhortation to avoid adulterous relationships (Prov. 5; 6:20–35).

8:1–36 In this hymn of praise, wisdom is exalted as something that is more valuable than gold and silver or precious stones. Wisdom was present with God when He created the world. This is another way of saying that God is the author of all wisdom.

9:1–18 Both foolishness and wisdom are personified as women. They illustrate the two different approaches to life.

. . . .

From Naughty to Worthless *A naughty person [scoundrel, NIV], a wicked man, walketh with a froward [corrupt, NIV] mouth* (Prov. 6:12).

The word translated as "naughty person" or "scoundrel" in this verse literally means "son of Belial." In the Hebrew language, *Belial* means "worthless" or "useless." Thus, one mark of a worthless person is the evil or corrupt speech that comes from his or her mouth. People in the Bible who were called "worthless" or "son of Belial" include the evil sons of Eli the priest (1 Sam. 2:12), those who supported Jeroboam's rebellion against the southern tribes of Israel (2 Chron. 13:7), and those who gave false testimony against Naboth at the urging of Jezebel (1 Kings 21:11–13).

Shifty Signs *He [a wicked man] winketh with his eyes, he speaketh [signals, NIV] with his feet, he teacheth [motions, NIV] with his fingers* (Prov. 6:13).

We would call the person whom Solomon describes in these verses a "con man." Rather than speaking openly and forthrightly, he goes behind others' backs to cheat and deceive by using eye motions and hand signals that are understood only by his accomplices. These tactics may have been used by dishonest merchants of Solomon's time. Unfortunately, people like this are still in business today.

Wisdom's Meal *She [wisdom] hath killed her beasts [prepared her meat, NIV]; she hath mingled [mixed, NIV] her wine; she hath also furnished [set, NIV] her table* (Prov. 9:2).

This verse portrays wisdom as preparing a meal that it invites people to eat. The message is that we can achieve wisdom and understanding if only we will partake of the wisdom that God has provided for His people. The "mingled wine" or "mixed wine" was prepared by mixing two kinds of wine together—possibly an older, stronger wine with a weaker wine of more recent vintage.

JULY 17 | Read Proverbs 10–14

10:1–32 These proverbs draw a contrast between the wise/righteous/godly and the foolish/unrighteous/wicked: "The mouth of a righteous man is a well of life: but violence covereth the mouth of the wicked" (v. 11).

11:1–31 The contrast between the wise and the foolish continues: "He that trusteth in his riches shall fall: but the righteous shall flourish as a branch" (v. 28).

12:1–28 The contrast between the wise and the foolish continues: "Lying lips are abomination to the LORD: but they that deal truly are his delight" (v. 22; see Rev. 22:15).

13:1–25 The contrast between the wise and foolish continues: "Every prudent man dealeth with knowledge: but a fool layeth open his folly" (v. 16).

14:1–35 The contrast between the wise and the foolish continues. But some of these proverbs have a touch of humor: "The poor is hated even of his own neighbour: but the rich hath many friends" (v. 20).

A Hand-to-Hand Agreement *Though hand join in hand, the wicked shall not be unpunished* (Prov. 11:21).

The phrase "hand join in hand" describes the ancient custom of shaking hands—or perhaps striking hands back to back—to seal an agreement between two parties. The handshake is still used this way in modern times. The New International Version translates the verse like this: "Be sure of this: The wicked will not go unpunished." "Hand join to hand" was often used in the Hebrew language in an idiomatic sense to express certainty or agreement.

JULY 18 | Read Proverbs 15–19

15:1–33 The contrast between the wise and the foolish continues: "The thoughts of the wicked are an abomination to the LORD: but the words of the pure are pleasant words" (v. 26; see Ps. 37:30).

16:1–33 These proverbs give moral and ethical advice on various subjects: "Pride goeth before destruction, and an haughty spirit before a fall" (v. 18; see Jer. 49:16).

17:1–28 More proverbs with moral and ethical advice: "A reproof entereth more into a wise man than an hundred stripes into a fool" (v. 10).

18:1–24 More proverbs with moral and ethical advice: "Death and life are in the power of the tongue: and they that love it shall eat the fruit thereof" (v. 21; see Matt. 12:37).

19:1–29 More proverbs with moral and ethical advice: "House and riches are the inheritance of fathers: and a prudent wife is from the LORD" (v. 14).

Sluggard A lazy, inactive person. Habitual idleness leads to poverty (Prov. 13:4; 20:4). Paul declared that those who won't work shouldn't eat (2 Thess. 3:10).

Haughtiness An arrogant spirit. God's Word indicates that haughty persons will be humbled (Prov. 16:18; Isa. 2:11, 17).

Fining Pot A vessel for melting and purifying metal (Prov. 17:3).

Keep the Gate Low *He that exalteth his gate [builds a high gate, NIV] seeketh destruction* (Prov. 17:19).

The typical house of Bible times consisted of four to six rooms built around a central courtyard. This courtyard was similar to a modern hallway. First you entered the courtyard through the front door, or gateway. Then you used the courtyard to gain access to all the rooms in the house. The gateway into a house was normally only about four feet high. These low entrances may have been designed to keep thieves from riding horses into the courtyard. Thus, the writer of Proverbs states that anyone who built his gate high was asking for trouble. This was a symbolic way of saying that pride or self-exaltation also leads to destruction.

Making Decisions by Lot *The lot causeth contentions to cease, and parteth between the mighty* (Prov. 18:18).

This verse refers to the ancient custom of casting lots to settle disputes or make important decisions. We might compare the practice to flipping a coin or drawing straws in modern times. The Bible does not give us any details about the materials used in casting lots. But we can speculate that colored stones or pieces of wood may have been placed in a bag or jug. These items were then rolled around inside the container and cast out on the ground. The order in which the stones or pieces of wood lined up may have determined the course of action to follow.

JULY 19 | Read Proverbs 20–23

20:1–30 More proverbs with moral and ethical advice: "Bread of deceit is sweet to a man; but afterwards his mouth shall be filled with gravel" (v. 17).

21:1–31 More proverbs with moral and ethical advice: "The horse is prepared against the day of battle: but safety is of the LORD" (v. 31).

22:1–29 More proverbs with moral and ethical advice: "Train up a child in the way he should go: and when he is old, he will not depart from it" (v. 6; see Eph. 6:4).

23:1–35 More proverbs with moral and ethical advice: "Let not thine heart envy sinners: but be thou in the fear of the LORD all the day long" (v. 17; see Ps. 37:1).

Discipline To train or teach, as parents impart important truths to a child (Prov. 22:6). A disciplined person also controls his impulses, speech, and actions (1 Pet. 3:10). God disciplines His children through corrective actions (Heb. 12:6).

A Hut on the Roof *It is better to dwell in a corner of the housetop, than with a brawling woman [quarrelsome wife, NIV] in a wide house* (Prov. 21:9).

This verse uses humor to show that no house is big enough to accommodate two people who don't get along. If the husband and wife are always quarreling, each one could say with equal justification to the other, "I would rather be living up on the roof than in this house with you." People in Bible times sometimes built booths, or temporary shelters, on the flat roofs of their houses to provide relief from the heat during the summertime. Those huts would be cold and uncomfortable during rainy weather and the winter months. But constant squabbling in the main part of the house would tempt the residents to turn a rooftop shelter into a permanent dwelling.

JULY 20 | Read Proverbs 24–28

24:1–34 More proverbs with moral and ethical advice: "Be not a witness against thy neighbour without cause; and deceive not with thy lips" (v. 28; see Eph. 4:25).

25:1–28 More proverbs with moral and ethical advice: "Confidence in an unfaithful man in time of trouble is like a broken tooth, and a foot out of joint" (v. 19; see Job 6:15).

26:1–28 More proverbs with moral and ethical advice: "Answer not a fool according to his folly, lest thou also be like unto him" (v. 4).

27:1–27 More proverbs with moral and ethical advice: "Let another man praise thee, and not thine own mouth; a stranger, and not thine own lips" (v. 2).

28:1–28 More proverbs with moral and ethical advice: "He that covereth his sins shall not prosper: but whoso confesseth and forsaketh them shall have mercy" (v. 13; see Job 31:33).

Arrow A projectile shot from a bow. This word is also used symbolically to denote a calamity inflicted by God (Job 6:4) or to signify something injurious, such as false testimony (Prov. 25:18).

Adversity Difficult or unfavorable circumstances, perhaps caused by sin (Gen. 3:16–17) or disobedience toward God (Lev. 26:14–20). Adversity may also be used by God to test our faith (1 Pet. 1:6–7) or to chasten and correct (Heb. 12:5–11).

Dross Impurities separated from ore or metal in the smelting process (Prov. 25:4). The word is used symbolically of God's judgment against the wicked (Ps. 119:119).

Beautiful Words *A word fitly [aptly, NIV] spoken is like apples of gold in pictures [settings, NIV] of silver* (Prov. 25:11).

This verse refers to the beautiful metal engravings that were displayed in the homes of kings and the wealthy in Bible times. "Apples of gold" were probably carvings of apples that were made from gold or painted to look like gold. These were placed in a highly polished silver frame to give the entire work of art an ornate appearance. The point of this proverb is that an appropriate word spoken at just the right time is a thing of beauty. Or to put it another way, "A wholesome tongue is a tree of life" (Prov. 15:4).

Foolish to the Bone *Though thou shouldest bray [grind, NIV] a fool in a mortar among wheat with a pestle, yet will not his foolishness depart from him* (Prov. 27:22).

A mortar was a huge jar or stone container in which a substance such as grain was crushed. This was done by pulverizing the grain in an up-and-down motion with a long, heavy stick known as a pestle. This mortar-and-pestle technique was a primitive way of grinding grain if a hand-turned stone mill was not available. This proverb shows how futile it is to try to talk sense into a fool. Even grinding him like wheat in a mortar with a pestle will not turn him from his senseless ways.

JULY 21 | Read Proverbs 29–31

29:1–27 More proverbs with moral and ethical advice: "The fear of man bringeth a snare: but whoso putteth his trust in the LORD shall be safe" (v. 25).

30:1–9 God has infinite wisdom. Consider His wonderful works. By comparison, humans are weak and foolish.

30:10–33 The natural order reveals the wisdom and power of God. Humans are awestruck by many things in nature that they cannot understand (Ps. 104).

31:1–9 People in positions of authority should avoid strong drink, lest it impair their judgment. They also have the responsibility to treat the poor and helpless with fairness and compassion.

31:10–31 The book of Proverbs ends with words of praise for a wife of noble character. She works hard to take care of her household, and she performs acts of kindness in her community. A wife like this is a priceless asset to her family: "Her price is far above rubies" (v. 10).

Coney A small, furry animal that lived among the rocky cliffs of Palestine—probably the rock badger (Prov. 30:26). *Badger*: NRSV.

Lemuel An unknown king mentioned in the book of Proverbs (Prov. 31:1). Some scholars identify Lemuel as Solomon.

Churning Up Anger *The churning of milk bringeth forth butter. . .so the forcing of wrath [stirring up anger, NIV] bringeth forth strife* (Prov. 30:33).

In Bible times butter was produced by placing milk in a bag made from an animal skin and shaking it vigorously back and forth until the butter fat separated from the milk. This proverb has a "just as" construction. Just as surely as shaking milk produces butter, giving vent to one's anger will cause strife and trouble. The phrase "stirring up anger" suggests that a person can feed his or her anger until it becomes uncontrollable.

JULY 22 | Read Ecclesiastes 1–6

1:1–11 The author of the book identifies himself as the Preacher (probably Solomon). He observes that life is vain and meaningless, and it seems to go around and around in an endless circle.

1:12–18 Even the accumulation of much learning and wisdom does not give meaning and purpose to life.

2:1–3 The pursuit of fun and pleasure fails to satisfy (Prov. 14:13).

2:4–11 Great wealth and accomplishments in themselves are empty and meaningless.

2:12–23 Both the wise man and the foolish man are destined to die—and neither of them knows what will happen after they are gone. Man's brief life on earth is filled with pain and sorrow (Job 14:1–2; James 4:13–14).

2:24–26 Perhaps the most sensible thing a person can do while on earth is to enjoy life's simple pleasures and take pride in his work.

3:1–8 There is an appropriate time for everything in life: "a time to keep silence, and a time to speak" (v. 7).

3:9–15 God's gift to man is his ability to take pleasure in the daily routine and to enjoy his work.

3:16–22 God judges the righteous and the wicked. Eventually all life turns to dust, the substance from which man was originally created (Gen. 2:7).

4:1–16 The vanity of life is multiplied by man's idleness, envy, and greed.

5:1–7 Do not make a vow to God unless you intend to keep your promise and follow through on your commitment (Gen. 28:20–22).

5:8–20 A rich person doesn't sleep as soundly as a working man. The man of means is always worrying about what might happen to his possessions.

6:1–12 Another problem with wealth is that rich people are never satisfied with what they have. The more possessions they acquire, they more they want. Thus, they are ruled by their desires (Luke 18:18–30).

Pools of Solomon Water reservoirs built by King Solomon near Bethlehem to supply water for Jerusalem through a system of underground passages (Eccles. 2:6).

JULY 23 | Read Ecclesiastes 7–12

7:1–22 These verses consist of miscellaneous proverbs on many different subjects. They are similar to the sayings in the book of Proverbs.

7:23–29 While wisdom does not bring meaning to life, acting wisely is preferable to acting foolishly.

8:1–5 Wise people respect the king and bow to his authority (Dan. 4:35).

8:6–17 Solomon complains that life is not fair. Sometimes the righteous suffer while the wicked flourish and prosper.

9:1–10 Solomon laments the plight of those who have died. They are soon forgotten by the living. He exhorts the living to enjoy their brief days on earth.

9:11–18 Wisdom is better than brute strength and the weapons of war.

10:1–20 Miscellaneous proverbs on various subjects, particularly careless speech: "The words of a wise man's mouth are gracious; but the lips of a fool will swallow up himself" (v. 12).

11:1–6 Solomon's advice in these verses is twofold: Don't put all your eggs in one basket ("Give a portion to seven, and also to eight," v. 2), and have a backup strategy in case your original plan does not work out ("Thou knowest not whether [it] shall prosper," v. 6).

11:7–12:7 Old age, with the inevitable loss of physical strength, arrives sooner than one expects. In their youthful years, people should enjoy life and honor their Creator.

12:8–14 Solomon concludes his search for meaning in life with this ringing affirmation: "Fear God, and keep his commandments: for this is the whole duty of man" (v. 13).

. . . .

Pitcher An earthenware vessel used to carry water (Gen. 24:14). The word is also used symbolically of the human life span (Eccles. 12:6). *Jar:* NIV, NRSV.

Vanity Emptiness and futility. Life is vain and empty unless it is lived in obedience to God and His will (Eccles. 12:13).

. . . .

Dressed in White *Let thy garments be always white* (Eccles. 9:8).

In the hot climate of Palestine, white was a sensible color for clothes. So it was only natural for Solomon, the author of Ecclesiastes, to express this wish for others. The wearing of white clothes was also a symbol of purity and holiness—a characteristic of God and those who follow His commands. When Daniel saw God in a vision, He was dressed in white clothes (Dan. 7:9). In the end time, the redeemed are also to be "arrayed in white robes" (Rev. 7:13).

JULY 24 | Read Song of Solomon 1–8

1:1 Introduction to Solomon's Song.

1:2–7 The bride expresses her love for her groom. She is dissatisfied with her appearance, since she is a girl from the country whose skin has been darkened by the sun (vv. 5–6).

1:8–11 The groom reassures his bride that he is pleased with how she looks: "Thy cheeks are comely with rows of jewels" (v. 10).

1:12–17 Both bride and groom continue to express their affection for each other.

2:1–17 The setting for these verses is springtime in the country (vv. 11–13). The couple express their joy that they are committed in love to each other: "My beloved is mine, and I am his" (v. 16).

3:1–6 The bride dreams about her groom and expresses sorrow over their separation.

3:7–11 The groom, symbolized by King Solomon in a royal procession, arrives for the wedding ceremony.

4:1–16 The groom expresses great delight in the beauty of his bride.

5:1–8 The bride has another dream that she is separated from her groom. She asks other people to join her frantic search for him.

5:9–16 The bride takes great pleasure in the appearance of her groom: "His legs are as pillars of marble, set upon sockets of fine gold" (v. 15).

6:1–3 In answer to the question "Whither is thy beloved gone?" (v. 1), the bride says he is with her, referring to herself as "his garden" (v. 2).

6:4–13 The groom describes the beauty of his one true love. All the queens and concubines in a king's harem do not compare to her.

7:1–13 The bride and groom express their mutual love and devotion to each other. They take great delight in the time they spend together.

8:1–14 The Song of Solomon ends with the bride and groom united in their mutual love for each other. The writer declares that true love is eternal: "Many waters cannot quench love, neither can the floods drown it" (v. 7).

....

Camphire A plant that produced a valuable red dye, used by women to adorn their lips and fingernails (Song 1:14). *Henna*: NIV, NRSV.

Buckler A small piece of protective armor worn on the arm by warriors (Song 4:4). *Shield*: NIV, NLT.

....

A Midday Rest *Tell me, O thou whom my soul loveth, where thou feedest, where thou makest thy flock to rest at noon* (Song 1:7).

These are the words of King Solomon's bride as she searched for her beloved, the king. She referred to a common practice in Bible times of shepherds protecting their sheep by having them rest at midday in order to avoid the oppressive heat. David may have referred to this practice when he compared God to a watchful shepherd: "The Lord is my shepherd; I shall not want. He maketh me to lie down in green pastures" (Ps. 23:1–2).

Solomon's Portable Chair *King Solomon made himself a chariot of the wood of Lebanon. He made the pillars [posts, NIV] thereof of silver, the bottom thereof of gold, the covering of it of purple* (Song 3:9–10).

The Hebrew word translated as "chariot" in this passage actually refers to a palanquin—a portable couch or chair in which kings were carried from place to place by royal servants. Poles were fastened to each side of the palanquin. Four servants would then hoist the king in his chair and place the poles on their shoulders. Solomon's gold-and-silver palanquin had a purple awning or cover to protect him from the sun. Purple was the color that signified royalty.

BOOKS OF THE MAJOR PROPHETS

The last seventeen books of the Old Testament are classified as books of prophecy. Five of these books—Isaiah, Jeremiah, Lamentations, Ezekiel, and Daniel—are known as major prophets, while the remaining twelve are called minor prophets.

These terms do not mean that some of these books are more important than others. Rather, as the Old Testament was compiled, the longer—or major—books were placed first in the prophetic section, while the shorter—or minor—books were placed second. The exception is Lamentations, a short book of only five chapters. This book was placed after Jeremiah because the prophet Jeremiah wrote Lamentations.

The word *prophet* comes from two Greek words that mean "to speak for." The prophets of the Old Testament received God's message by direct revelation and passed it on to others in written or spoken form. They literally spoke for God and prevailed upon His people to remain obedient and loyal to Him.

JULY 25 | Read Isaiah 1–4

1:1–31 Isaiah compares the sins of idolatry in the nation of Judah to the evils committed by the cities of Sodom and Gomorrah. Judah must repent and turn back to God or suffer the Lord's punishment.

2:1–4:6 In the future, Jerusalem will become the city of God and a safe haven for all people of the earth (2:1–5). But before that happens, God will judge His people severely because of their pride, rebellion, and evil deeds (2:6–4:6).

Isaiah A major prophet of Judah whose career spanned forty years (about 740–701 BC). The son of Amoz, he was married to a "prophetess" (Isa. 8:3). Working in the capital city of Jerusalem, Isaiah was the confidant of King Uzziah (Azariah) and his successors (Isa. 1:1). He warned that the city and nation would be destroyed by Assyria, but a righteous remnant would be saved (Isa. 1:2–9; 11:11). He gave his two sons symbolic names to underscore his message (Isa. 7:3; 8:1–4). Isaiah also encouraged King Hezekiah but foretold the king's death (2 Kings 20:1). He was the author of the book of Isaiah, which prophesied the coming of the Messiah (Isa. 7:14), His rejection (Isa. 53), and the conversion of the Gentiles (Isa. 61:10–11). *Esaias*: Greek form (Matt. 4:14).

Bad News for Jerusalem *The daughter of Zion is left as a cottage [shelter, NIV] in a vineyard, as a lodge [hut, NIV] in a garden of cucumbers [melons, NIV]* (Isa. 1:8).

Farmers of Bible times had to keep a close watch on their crops to protect them from animals and thieves. They would build crude huts from tree branches in the fields to provide shelter for those who watched the crops. After the harvest these huts would soon fall and rot. Isaiah compared Jerusalem, referred to in this passage as "the daughter of Zion," to one of these abandoned and useless shelters. He declared that the city would fall to an enemy and become utterly desolate unless the people turned from their worship of false gods and renewed their commitment to the Lord.

Sitting in Despair *Her [Jerusalem's] gates shall lament and mourn; and she being desolate [destitute, NIV] shall sit upon the ground* (Isa. 3:26).

Sitting on the ground symbolized sadness and distress. So this is another image from Isaiah that expresses the fate of the nation of Judah if she continued on her present course. When Job's friends came to comfort him, they did not say a word for seven days, but "they sat down with him upon the ground. . .for they saw that his grief was very great" (Job 2:13). The same idea of despair is also expressed in these declarations: "Wallow thyself in ashes" (Jeremiah 6:26) and "roll thyself in the dust" (Micah 1:10).

JULY 26 | Read Isaiah 5–7

5:1–7 These verses are known as Isaiah's "song of the vineyard." He compares the nation of Judah to a vineyard that God has preserved and cultivated. But the people have produced nothing but bitter, useless grapes. Jesus also used this imagery of the vineyard for the Jewish people (Matt. 21:33–41).

5:8–30 Because of Judah's sins of idolatry, injustice, and rebellion, God will raise up an enemy nation to carry His people into captivity: "They shall roar, and lay hold of the prey, and shall carry it away safe, and none shall deliver it" (v. 29).

6:1–13 Isaiah is called to the prophetic ministry in a dramatic encounter with the awe-inspiring Lord in the temple.

7:1–25 Through the prophet Isaiah, God warns King Ahaz of Judah not to form an alliance with the Assyrians against other enemy nations. Assyria will eventually become an instrument of judgment in God's hands against His people.

- -

Shear-jashub A symbolic name meaning "a remnant shall return" given by Isaiah to his son to show God's promise to His people after their period of exile (Isa. 7:3).

- -

A Butter and Honey Sandwich *Butter [curds, NIV] and honey shall he eat, that he may know to refuse the evil, and choose the good* (Isa. 7:15).

Butter, or curds, and honey were often mixed together and spread on bread, much as peanut butter and jelly are eaten together as a sandwich in modern times. It may have been a staple in the diet of children, since it is mentioned in this verse as food that a young child would eat. Honey is mentioned in connection with butter or milk in several other places in the Bible (2 Sam. 17:29; Job 20:17; Song 4:11).

JULY 27 | Read Isaiah 8–10

8:1–22 Isaiah names his newborn son Maher-shalal-hash-baz, meaning "fast plunder." This signifies that the nations that oppose Assyria will fall quickly, leaving other nations an easy target for the mighty Assyrian army.

9:1–7 Although dark days are just ahead for God's people, He will eventually restore them by sending the Messiah, the Prince of Peace. As the leader of a spiritual kingdom, He will become the heir to the "throne of David" (v. 7; see 2 Sam. 7:1–17).

9:8–10:34 Israel (Northern Kingdom), with Samaria as its capital, will be overrun by the Assyrians. The people will be carried away as captives, but the Lord will preserve a remnant of His people who remain faithful to Him.

Way of the Sea A road that ran from Sidon in Phoenicia to Egypt, passing through Palestine (Isa. 9:1).

Shoulder To drop the shoulder signified servitude (Gen. 49:15); to withdraw it denoted rebellion (Neh. 9:29); to put a responsibility on a person's shoulder was to entrust it to his or her keeping (Isa. 9:6).

JULY 28 | Read Isaiah 11–14

11:1–12:6 The coming messianic King will rule with righteousness and perfect justice. Although He will spring from the lineage of David as "a root of Jesse" (11:10), He will be sought by the Gentiles and all nations of the earth.

13:1–14:23 Just as God's people will be judged for their sins, His judgment will also fall on the Babylonians. They will be defeated by the Medes and the Persians (13:17).

14:24–27 The nation of Assyria is also destined to feel God's wrath.

14:28–32 The remnants of the Philistines who still live among the Jewish people will be judged by the Lord.

Rod A staff or stick (Ps. 23:4). The word is used figuratively for a branch or offshoot of a tribe or family; for example, in reference to Christ (Isa. 11:1). *Shoot*: NIV, NLT.

Root The life-sustaining part of a plant. The word is also used figuratively to describe Christ's humiliation (Isa. 53:2) and exaltation (Isa. 11:10) and the believer's foundation in Christ (Col. 2:7).

Day of the Lord A phrase usually interpreted as a period in the end-time when God will bring His purpose for humans and the world to fulfillment. This will be a day of judgment for the rebellious and sinful (Jer. 46:10) and a time of deliverance for the godly (Joel 2:28–32). Any time—whether now or in the distant future—when the Lord acts, intervening in history for the purpose of deliverance and judgment, may also be described as the "day of the LORD" (Isa. 13:6).

Day Star A star that appears just before daybreak, signaling the beginning of a new day (2 Pet. 1:19). The word for "day star" is also translated as *Lucifer* (Isa. 14:12) and used as a name for the king of Babylon. *Morning star*: NIV.

JULY 29 | Read Isaiah 15–19

15:1–16:14 Isaiah delivers God's message of judgment against the Moabites, ancient enemies of His people.

17:1–14 The nation of Syria, with its capital at Damascus, will be punished by the Lord for its idolatry and pride.

18:1–7 God's punishment will also fall upon the Ethiopians.

19:1–25 The proud Egyptians will tremble in fear before the terrible punishment of the Lord.

....

Charmers Magicians who claimed to be able to commune with the dead (Isa. 19:3).

....

No Singing at Work *Gladness is taken away, and joy out of the plentiful field; and in the vineyards there shall be no singing* (Isa. 16:10).

The people of Bible times sang while working in the fields to escape from the monotony of farm work. Isaiah declared that the singing and gladness of the Moabites would be taken away when God judged them for their idolatry.

Ethiopia's Papyrus Boats *Woe to the land. . .beyond the rivers of Ethiopia [Cush, NIV]: that sendeth ambassadors [envoys, NIV] by the sea, even in vessels of bulrushes [papyrus boats, NIV] upon the waters* (Isa. 18:1–2).

We know that the papyrus plant that grew in abundance in the marshy areas of Lower Egypt was used to make waterproof baskets. The baby Moses was placed in such a basket on the Nile River (Exodus 2:3). But this verse shows that larger sailing vessels were also fashioned from this plant. Perhaps papyrus reeds were woven tightly together and reinforced with harder materials, then coated with tar or bitumen to make the vessel waterproof. Ethiopia, also referred to as Cush in the Bible (Isa. 11:11), was an ancient nation south of Egypt. The Ethiopians used these papyrus vessels to trade with other nations around the Mediterranean Sea.

JULY 30 | Read Isaiah 20–23

20:1–6 At God's command Isaiah walks around without his outer robe to show that Assyria will strip the Egyptians and the Ethiopians of their possessions and take them away as captives.

21:1–17 No nation will escape the marauding Assyrian army—not Babylonia (vv. 1–10), Edom ("Dumah," vv. 11–12), or the tribes of Arabia (vv. 13–17).

22:1–25 In the midst of these prophecies of judgment against foreign nations, Isaiah declares that the city of Jerusalem, Judah's capital, is also destined for destruction. This prophecy was fulfilled about 135 years after Isaiah's time when the Babylonians overran the nation of Judah (2 Kings 25:1–12).

23:1–18 Isaiah pronounces God's judgment against Tyre, a flourishing seaport and trade center north of Judah.

....

Sidon A Canaanite city about twenty miles north of Tyre founded by Sidon, the oldest son of Canaan (Gen. 10:15). Noted for its shipbuilding (Ezek. 27:8), silverware, and dyed fabrics, the city was often rebuked by the prophets for its idolatry (Isa. 23:4; Ezek. 28:21). Jesus ministered in this city (Matt. 15:21). *Zidon*: Josh. 11:8.

A Key on the Shoulder *The key of the house of David will I lay upon his [Eliakim's] shoulder; so he shall open, and none shall shut; and he shall shut, and none shall open* (Isa. 22:22).

Isaiah predicted that Shebna would be deposed from office and that he would be replaced by Eliakim. Carrying a key on his shoulder symbolized his position of power and authority, as well as his trustworthiness. The primitive locks of Bible times had to be opened with long wooden keys. These keys were often slung over the shoulders of those who had the authority to lock and unlock doors in the king's royal buildings. A key on the shoulder as a symbol of authority is probably the image behind Isaiah's famous expression about the Messiah: "The government shall be upon his shoulder" (Isaiah 9:6).

JULY 31 | Read Isaiah 24–27

24:1–23 This chapter summarizes the impact of God's judgment against Israel (Northern Kingdom) and Judah (Southern Kingdom) as well as the foreign nations. The entire earth will be shaken by His judgment against sin.

25:1–27:13 These three chapters are affirmations of hope. Although God will judge and discipline His people, He will not reject them. After they have been exiled among a foreign nation for a time, they will be restored to their homeland (2 Chron. 36:22–23). This brings a song of praise to the lips of God's people: "Trust ye in the LORD for ever: for in the LORD JEHOVAH is everlasting strength" (26:4).

Filtered Wine *The LORD of hosts [shall] make unto all people. . .a feast of wines on the lees, of fat things full of marrow, of wines on the lees well refined* (Isa. 25:6).

Isaiah referred to a future time when the Lord would restore the faithful remnant of His people and shower them with bountiful blessings. "Wines on the lees" refers to wine that had been stored with particles of grapes left in the liquid. It had to be strained through a cloth to remove the waste before it was ready to drink.

AUGUST 1 | Read Isaiah 28–31

28:1–29 Isaiah condemns both Judah (Southern Kingdom) and Israel (Northern Kingdom) because they have turned away from the Lord to worship false gods. He has harsh words especially for the leaders of these nations who have led the people astray (Jer. 8).

29:1–24 A woe is pronounced against Ariel, or Jerusalem, "the city where David dwelt" (v. 1). God is not impressed with those who flatter Him with words but refuse to obey His commands.

30:1–31:9 Through Isaiah the prophet, the Lord condemns the leaders of Judah who have formed an alliance with Egypt against the Assyrian threat. They should be turning to the Lord instead for protection against their enemies.

Ariel A symbolic name for the city of Jerusalem, meaning "lion of God" (Isa. 29:1–2, 7).

Fan A wooden pitchfork for winnowing grain (Isa. 30:24). The grain was thrown into the wind to separate it from the straw (Matt. 3:12). The fan is also spoken of as a symbol of God's judgment (Jer. 15:7). *Fork*: NIV, NRSV.

Methods of Threshing Grain *The fitches [caraway, NIV] are not threshed with a threshing instrument [sledge, NIV], neither is a cart wheel turned about upon the cummin; but the fitches [caraway, NIV] are beaten out with a staff [rod, NIV], and the cummin with a rod [stick, NIV]* (Isa. 28:27)

In this verse, Isaiah contrasted two different methods of separating grain from the stalk in Bible times. Small grains such as caraway and cummin were threshed by beating them with a stick. This method was also used when threshing a small amount of grain (Ruth 2:17). Dragging a stone threshing sledge ("threshing instrument") over the grain was the preferred method for threshing wheat or barley in large quantities. Isaiah's point is that God knows us, and He knows our needs. He will use whatever method is appropriate as His discipline to keep us focused on Him.

AUGUST 2 | Read Isaiah 32–35

32:1–20 Isaiah calls on the people to look for the Messiah, the coming King, who will "reign in righteousness" (v. 1). But before this King arrives, the people must turn from their sinful and complacent ways.

33:1–24 The Lord alone is the hope and salvation of His people: "The LORD is our judge, the LORD is our lawgiver, the LORD is our king; he will save us" (v. 22; see Ps. 77:1–2).

34:1–17 Isaiah returns to the theme of God's judgment against the foreign nations (chaps. 13–23).

35:1–10 This chapter portrays a future time when God will redeem and restore His people. They will return to Jerusalem ("Zion," v. 10) with songs of joy and gladness.

Lime Powdered limestone used for plaster and cement work (Isa. 33:12).

Rolled Like a Scroll *All the host [stars, NIV] of heaven shall be dissolved, and the heavens shall be rolled together [rolled up, NIV] as a scroll* (Isa. 34:4).

In the end times, Isaiah declared, the sky will be rolled up like a scroll when God judges the nations for their rebellion and idolatry. A scroll was the equivalent of a modern book. Writing was done on long rolls of papyrus or animal skins. The scroll was then rolled up toward the middle from both ends on two sticks. Some of these scrolls may have been sixty to seventy feet long. To read from a scroll, a person had to unroll it until he found the section he wanted to read. After reading, he rolled it up again.

AUGUST 3 | Read Isaiah 36–39

36:1–22 King Sennacherib of Assyria invades Judah and captures several walled cities. He sends word to King Hezekiah of Judah that Assyria will attack with a superior force unless Judah surrenders.

37:1–38 King Hezekiah and the prophet Isaiah pray to the Lord, asking Him to save Judah from the Assyrian threat. God miraculously delivers the nation by destroying 185,000 warriors in Sennacherib's army (2 Kings 18:13–19:37).

38:1–22 King Hezekiah of Judah is seriously ill, and Isaiah tells him he will die. But Hezekiah prays humbly to the Lord, who graciously extends the king's life for fifteen more years (2 Kings 20:1–11).

39:1–8 Hezekiah foolishly shows off his royal riches to a messenger from the king of Babylon. Isaiah predicts that the Babylonians will defeat the nation of Judah and carry off these treasures at some future time (2 Kings 20:12–19).

- -

Sennacherib The king of Assyria (reigned about 705–681 BC) who captured all fortified cities of Judah except Jerusalem and then demanded tribute from King Hezekiah (2 Kings 18:13–16). Sennacherib was eventually assassinated by his own sons as he worshiped a pagan god (2 Kings 19:36–37).

- -

Hooked and Bridled Prisoners *Because thy [Sennacherib's] rage against me, and thy tumult, is come up into mine ears, therefore will I put my hook in thy nose, and my bridle [bit, NIV] in thy lips [mouth, NIV]* (Isa. 37:29)

Sennacherib, king of Assyria, was threatening to overrun Jerusalem. But Isaiah assured the king of Judah that the Lord would deliver them from this threat. God would turn the tables on Sennacherib by putting a hook in his nose and a bit in his mouth. Hooks and bits were used in Bible times to control draft animals such as oxen and horses. But stone monuments from ancient Assyria show that this technique was also used on prisoners of war. These monuments portray prisoners with iron rings through their lower lips being pulled along by a rope.

AUGUST 4 | Read Isaiah 40–42

40:1–31 The prophet Isaiah follows his prediction of disaster for Judah with words of encouragement. The Lord is the great comforter who never stops loving His people. He gives power and strength to those who depend on Him.

41:1–29 In contrast to lifeless idols that are fashioned by human hands, God is the living, awesome Lord who brought all of creation into being (Gen. 1:1–24). He alone is worthy of worship.

42:1–9 This is one of several "Servant" passages or "Servant Songs" in Isaiah (chaps. 49–55). The nations of Judah and Israel have failed to carry out the mission of world redemption that God intended. Therefore, He will accomplish this through one person—His coming Servant, the Messiah, His Son, Jesus Christ.

42:10–16 This redemptive mission of God's Servant is reason for rejoicing: "Give glory unto the Lord, and declare his praise in the islands" (v. 12).

42:17–25 In contrast to the faithfulness of God's Servant, the nations of Judah and Israel have rejected the Lord and followed their own desires.

Myrtle A common evergreen shrub of Palestine. Its branches were used at the Feast of Tabernacles (Neh. 8:15). A myrtle tree in the desert was symbolic of God's provision for His people (Isa. 41:19; 55:13).

Get Ready for the King *Prepare ye the way of the Lord, make straight in the desert a highway for our God. . . . The crooked shall be made straight, and the rough places plain* (Isa. 40:3–4).

Roads of Bible times were little more than paths, rough and crude by modern standards. When a king traveled, his servants would go ahead of him, removing stones, filling in low places, and straightening curves so the king's journey would be more pleasant. Isaiah found in this practice a spiritual principle. The people needed to prepare the way for the coming of the Lord in a new and fresh way—a reference to the future Messiah. In the NT, this passage was applied to John the Baptist, who prepared the way for the ministry of Jesus Christ (Luke 3:4–5).

AUGUST 5 | Read Isaiah 43–45

43:1–44:5 In spite of the unfaithfulness of His people, God forgives. He will walk with them in their humiliation and suffering.

44:6–20 These are some of the most striking verses in the Bible on the worship of false gods. How foolish it is for a person to worship something he has conceived in his mind and fashioned with his hands (Jer. 10:1–25).

44:21–28 In contrast to lifeless and powerless idols, the one true God is the living and powerful redeemer of His people.

45:1–13 The Lord promises to restore His people to their homeland after a period of exile in Babylonia and Persia. This will be accomplished by the Lord, who will use King Cyrus of Persia as an instrument in His plan (v. 1; see 2 Chron. 36:22–23).

45:14–25 The entire world will eventually turn to God because He alone offers salvation: "Look unto me, and be ye saved, all the ends of the earth: for I am God, and there is none else" (v. 22).

Graven Image An image of a false god made from wood or stone and set up in a prominent place as an object of worship (Exod. 20:4). The prophets warned God's people against such idolatry (Isa. 44:9–10; Hosea 11:2). *Idol*: NIV, NRSV.

Omen A sign used to predict future events. Witchcraft and divination were forbidden by the Mosaic Law (Deut. 18:10). The Lord frustrates the efforts of fortune-tellers and astrologers (Isa. 44:25).

AUGUST 6 | Read Isaiah 46–48

46:1–13 Isaiah reminds the people that the worship of idols is futile, since they are weak and helpless and offer no hope.

47:1–15 The nation of Babylonia will be devastated by the Lord because of its wickedness and pride.

48:1–22 Throughout their history the nations of Judah and Israel have rejected God. But He continues to love them and call them back from their wayward ways.

Nebo The Babylonian god of science and knowledge. Mount Nebo was possibly a center of Nebo worship. Isaiah declared the vanity of such idols (Isa. 46:1).

No Help from Stargazers *Let now the astrologers, the stargazers, the monthly prognosticators, stand up, and save thee from these things that shall come upon thee* (Isa. 47:13).

The words *astrologers, stargazers,* and *monthly prognosticators* refer to people who studied the stars and the movement of the moon in order to foretell the future. This was especially popular among the ancient Babylonians. In Babylonia the astrologers were members of a specific caste. Persons born into this caste continued to practice the stargazing and sign-reading skills inherited from their ancestors. Astrologers were among the people with magical powers summoned by King Nebuchadnezzar of Babylonia to interpret his strange dream (Dan. 2:2). Isaiah declared that God would judge the people of Judah for their sins, and nothing could thwart His purpose. He—the Creator of the moon and stars—was more powerful than those who read the moon and stars.

AUGUST 7 | Read Isaiah 49–51

49:1–51:23 Chapters 49–55 of Isaiah contain more of the prophet's famous "Servant Songs" (see also Isa. 42:1–9). At times the prophet seems to speak of the nations of Judah and Israel as God's servant. But in other places in these passages, it is clear that he is referring to the Servant who is to come—the Messiah.

Sinim An unidentified country or region—perhaps China, Egypt, or the wilderness of Sin—from which Jewish exiles would return (Isa. 49:12). *Aswan:* NIV; *Syene:* NRSV.

A Constant Reminder *Behold, I [God] have graven [engraved, NIV] thee [Jerusalem] upon the palms of my hands; thy walls are continually before me* (Isa. 49:16).
   A figure or symbol engraved on one's hands would always be in sight and thus a perpetual reminder of a vow or promise. This is a beautiful picture of God's covenant relationship with His people. He declared through the prophet Isaiah that He would never forget the city of Jerusalem and the people whom He had set apart as His own.

AUGUST 8 | Read Isaiah 52–56

52:1–55:13 Isaiah 53 is clearly messianic in nature. It portrays the "Suffering Servant"—Jesus Christ—who gave His life to secure redemption for others: "He was wounded for our transgressions, he was bruised for our iniquities: the chastisement of our peace was upon him; and with his stripes we are healed" (v. 5).

56:1–12 God is bringing a new age of salvation for His people. But He expects them to live as people who belong to Him, keeping His laws and practicing justice.

Imputation To transfer something to another person. Adam's sin was imputed to all persons (Rom. 5:12). Our iniquity was laid on Jesus (Isa. 53:5–6), and He bore our sins (John 1:29). Jesus, the "second Adam," imputed grace and righteousness to all who put their trust in Him (Rom. 5:17–19).

God's Power Revealed *The LORD hath made bare his holy arm in the eyes [sight, NIV] of all the nations* (Isa. 52:10).
   People of Bible times wore inner tunics and outer robes that covered the entire body. The bare arm could be exposed quickly by pulling it from under this loose

clothing. "Baring the arm" was a metaphor for swift, decisive action. When God delivered His people, according to Isaiah in this verse, He would do so by baring His arm—powerfully and forcefully.

Sprinkling of the Nations *So shall he [the Messiah] sprinkle many nations* (Isa. 52:15).

The Hebrew word rendered as "sprinkle" in this verse is significant. It is the same word used of the sprinkling by priests of the blood of sacrificial animals to atone for sin (Lev. 6:25, Lev. 16:34). When the Messiah comes, according to Isaiah, He will do for the Gentile nations what He has done all along for the Jewish people. He will serve as an atonement for sin for all who receive Him as Savior and Lord.

AUGUST 9 | Read Isaiah 57–59

57:1–21 The Lord's people cannot worship the one true God and participate in idol worship at the same time. He demands their exclusive loyalty (Josh. 24:15).

58:1–14 True religion does not consist of observing rituals such as fasting and offering sacrifices. The Lord honors such things as obeying His commands and treating others with justice and fairness (Amos 5:18–27).

59:1–21 The prophet catalogs the wicked and sinful actions that have separated the people of Judah from the Lord: lying, vanity and pride, murder of innocent people, and rebellion against God.

. . . .

Worship of Stones? *Among the smooth stones of the stream is thy portion. . . even to them hast thou poured a drink offering* (Isa. 57:6).

Some interpreters have speculated that Isaiah in this verse referred to the worship of stones. But it is more likely that he was speaking with sarcasm and irony. Idolatry was so widespread in his time that some people even seemed to worship every rock they passed by!

God's Hand and Ear *The LORD's hand [arm, NIV] is not shortened, that it cannot save; neither his ear heavy [dull, NIV], that it cannot hear* (Isa. 59:1).

This verse is one of the best examples in the Bible of what theologians call an *anthropomorphism* (Greek *anthropos* [man] + *morphe* [form]). This big word describes the way biblical writers often described God in human terms. Isaiah in this verse said God has a powerful hand that can deliver His people and an ear that is always ready to hear their prayers. God is a spiritual being (see John 4:24). He does not have human characteristics. So the biblical writers are speaking metaphorically when they speak of God's mouth or eyes. But these metaphors express profound truths in words and images that we humans can understand.

AUGUST 10 | Read Isaiah 60–64

60:1–62:12 In these three chapters, Isaiah gives us a glimpse of the future glory of Jerusalem. God will take delight in His people. They will shine like a beacon of righteousness, drawing all nations of the earth to bow before the Lord. Jesus quoted from Isaiah 61:1–2 when He identified Himself as the Messiah who had been sent by God "to preach good tidings unto the meek. . .to bind up the brokenhearted, to proclaim liberty to the captives" (v. 1; see Luke 4:18–19).

63:1–64:12 But before these blessings fall upon God's people, He must punish them for their sin and rebellion. This leads Isaiah to offer a beautiful prayer that God will uphold and sustain them during their days of trouble and suffering (2 Kings 25:1–12).

Messiah The title given by the Jewish people to a future leader whom they expected to restore their honor and glory after delivering them from their oppressors (Dan. 9:25–26). Jesus fulfilled their longing but in an unexpected way by becoming a spiritual Savior who delivered believers from sin (Rom. 6:1–9). *Messias*: Greek form (John 1:41; 4:25). *Anointed one*: NIV.

Beulah A name for Israel after the Babylonian Exile when the nation would be in a fruitful relationship with God (Isa. 62:4).

An Open-Gate Policy *Therefore thy gates shall be open continually; they shall not be shut day nor night* (Isa. 60:11).
The gates of walled cities were closed and bolted at night as a security measure. Residents of the city who didn't make it back inside before darkness fell were forced to spend the night outside. Isaiah portrayed a future time under the reign of the Messiah when the city gates would never be closed. God would be all the protection His people needed.

AUGUST 11 | Read Isaiah 65–66

65:1–66:24 Isaiah ends his book by drawing a contrast between two different destinies. Total destruction awaits those who continue in their sin and refuse to turn to God. But a life of joy and peace is the destiny of those who follow the Lord.

AUGUST 12 | Read Jeremiah 1–3

1:1–3 This brief introduction to the book tells us that Jeremiah prophesied during the reigns of three different kings of Judah—Josiah, Jehoiakim, and Zedekiah—or a period of about forty years.

1:4–19 God calls Jeremiah to his prophetic ministry. His task is to proclaim God's forthcoming judgment against the nation of Judah because the people are worshiping false gods. The prophet's vision of a budding almond tree shows that God's judgment is coming soon. The vision of a boiling pot facing toward the north indicates the direction from which this judgment will come.

2:1–37 God led His people out of slavery in Egypt and brought them into the Promised Land (Exod. 12:32–42). But they have rejected Him to serve the pagan gods of the surrounding nations. God's charge against them through the prophet Jeremiah is that "they have forsaken me the fountain of living waters, and hewed them out cisterns, broken cisterns, that can hold no water" (v. 13).

3:1–25 The Lord compares the idolatry of Judah with the sin of adultery (Hosea 2:1–13). God's people promised to remain faithful to Him alone. But they have gone back on their promise and are committing spiritual adultery through their worship of idols.

- -

Jeremiah A major prophet of the OT who preached God's message of doom to the nation of Judah for about forty years during the reigns of the last five kings of the nation: Josiah, Jehoahaz, Jehoiakim, Jehoiachin, and Zedekiah (Jer. 1:2–3). Called to his prophetic ministry even before he was born (Jer. 1:4–10), he wept openly over the sins of Judah (Jer. 9:1) and declared that the nation would fall to a foreign enemy as punishment for its sin and idolatry (Jer. 16:1–13). After Judah was overrun by the Babylonians, Jeremiah remained in Jerusalem while most of his countrymen were deported to Babylonia. Eventually he was taken to Egypt, where he continued to preach to a remnant of Jewish people (Jer. 43:5–13). *Jeremias*: Greek form (Matt. 16:14); *Jeremy*: Matt. 2:17; 27:9.

Almond A small tree known for its early spring blossoms. Jeremiah visualized an almond branch as a sign of God's rapidly approaching judgment against the nation of Judah (Jer. 1:11–12).

- -

Drinking from a Cistern *They have forsaken me [God] the fountain [spring, NIV] of living waters, and hewed them out cisterns, broken cisterns, that can hold no water* (Jer. 2:13).

Cisterns of Bible times were little more than deep pits dug in the ground or shallow reservoirs carved out of limestone rock. Rainwater was directed into these holding tanks and stored for use during the dry season. Compared to a spring from which fresh groundwater flowed, a cistern left a lot to be desired. The water could get contaminated, or the cistern could lose its water supply because of a leak. Jeremiah criticized the foolish people of Judah for drinking water from a cistern when fresh springwater was available. They had forsaken the living Lord and were worshiping lifeless pagan gods.

AUGUST 13 | Read Jeremiah 4–6

4:1–31 God's declaration that He will devastate the land of Judah leads Jeremiah to inspect the destruction and to lament the fate of his fellow citizens: "I beheld, and, lo, the fruitful place was a wilderness, and all the cities thereof were broken down at the presence of the LORD, and by his fierce anger" (v. 26).

5:1–6:30 God reveals that He will use a foreign power as His instrument of judgment against His people. This mighty and ancient nation will invade Judah, destroy crops and livestock, and overrun all its walled cities.

God's Hot Judgment *The bellows are burned [blow fiercely, NIV], the lead is consumed of the fire* (Jer. 6:29)

In this verse Jeremiah compared the judgment of God against His sinful people with a fire heated by a blacksmith. The fire was intensified with air from a bellows until it became intense enough to heat metal for shaping by the blacksmith's hammer. The bellows of Bible times was a long bag made of animal skin that was placed on the ground in front of the fire. The blacksmith stepped on the bag to expel air into the fire, then pulled it open with a rope to fill it with air again.

AUGUST 14 | Read Jeremiah 7–9

7:1–34 The Lord commands Jeremiah to stand in the entrance to the temple in Jerusalem. Here he denounces their sin and calls on them to turn back to the Lord before it is too late. The people have substituted religious rituals, such as offering sacrifices at the temple, for obedience of God's commands. But God is not fooled by such practices. He demands total loyalty and commitment from His people.

8:1–22 The leaders of Judah have led the people astray. For this, they will be judged severely by the Lord: "They shall not be gathered, nor be buried; they shall be for dung upon the face of the earth" (v. 2; see Isa. 28; Zech. 10–11).

9:1–26 This chapter is a graphic portrait of the depths to which people can sink when they turn their backs on God. The sins of Judah enumerated by Jeremiah include lying, slandering, and bearing false witness against others.

Polytheism The practice of worshiping many gods, in contrast to monotheism, which emphasizes devotion to the one and only true God. The nations surrounding Israel worshiped multiple gods, a practice that led to immorality (Num. 25:1–9), prostitution (2 Kings 23:7), and child sacrifice (Jer. 7:29–34). The first two of the Ten Commandments make it clear that devotion to the one and only supreme God was not to be mixed with worship of any other false or pagan god (Exod. 20:3–5).

Tophet A place of human sacrifice in the Valley of Hinnom near Jerusalem (Jer. 7:31–32). *Topheth*: NIV, NRSV.

Not a Runaway *Oh that I [Jeremiah] had in the wilderness a lodging place of wayfaring men [travelers, NIV]; that I might leave my people, and go from them!* (Jer. 9:2).

Jeremiah is known as the "weeping prophet" because it broke his heart to see his countrymen rejecting the Lord and following false gods. In this verse he expressed his desire to leave his familiar surroundings, escape to the desert, and live among strangers. Then he would not be exposed every day to the sin and rebellion of the nation of Judah. But Jeremiah never acted on his desire. For about forty years he stayed at the prophetic task to which God had called him. He is one of the Bible's best examples of faithfulness and obedience to the Lord.

AUGUST 15 | Read Jeremiah 10–12

10:1–25 People who worship idols are vain and foolish. They bow down before a wooden statue decorated with gold that they have made with their own hands. Such gods are weak and powerless. But the Lord is the one true God, awesome in majesty and power, who is able to deliver and protect His people (Isa. 44:6–20).

11:1–17 The Lord charges His people with breaking the covenant they had formed with Him in their early history. They have turned from Him and worshiped other gods. They will be punished for their waywardness.

11:18–23 Jeremiah learns that certain "men of Anathoth" (v. 21), his hometown, have plotted to kill him because of his prophecies against Judah. But God promises to protect the prophet and to punish these people for their actions.

12:1–17 Jeremiah complains to God because the wicked people in the land seem to be prospering, while the righteous followers of the Lord are suffering. God assures the prophet that this situation will be remedied when He exercises His judgment throughout the land.

Anathoth A village about three miles north of Jerusalem and the birthplace of the prophet Jeremiah (Jer. 1:1).

AUGUST 16 | Read Jeremiah 13–15

13:1–11 The Lord commands Jeremiah to place a linen girdle (belt or sash) among the rocks on the bank of the Euphrates River. The prophet retrieves it some time later after it has rotted. Just as the girdle was ruined, God declares, He will eventually "mar the pride of Judah, and the great pride of Jerusalem" (v. 9).

13:12–27 At God's command, Jeremiah tells the people of Judah that "every bottle shall be filled with wine" (v. 12). But this is not a symbol of prosperity. It actually means that the inhabitants of Jerusalem will be as if they were drunk, helpless to defend themselves against the coming invasion from a foreign nation.

14:1–22 Jeremiah complains that false prophets are denying his message that God will punish Judah through a great disaster. They are predicting peace and prosperity for the land (1 Kings 22:1–28). God assures Jeremiah that he is the true prophet who is delivering the message He intends for His people.

15:1–21 Jeremiah reminds the Lord that he has been mocked and persecuted by his own people for proclaiming God's message of forthcoming judgment. He wonders how much longer he can stand up under the pressure. And what will happen to him when Jerusalem falls? God assures His faithful prophet of His strength and protection: "I will make thee unto this people a fenced brasen wall: and they shall fight against thee, but they shall not prevail against thee: for I am with thee to save thee and to deliver thee" (v. 20).

Divination Foretelling the future or determining the unknown through performing acts of magic or reading signs (Jer. 14:14).

No Black Magic *The prophets prophesy lies in my name: I sent them not, neither have I commanded them, neither spake unto them: they prophesy unto you a false vision and divination, and a thing of nought, and the deceit of their heart* (Jer. 14:14).

The word *divination* may also be translated as "the occult." God made it clear that all forms of the occult are off-limits to His people (Deut. 18:9–14). These practices are "an abomination" (Deut. 18:12) to Him because they are a form of idolatry. Practitioners of black magic attempt to control the so-called "spirit world" to man's advantage, but there is only one supreme power in the universe—and He cannot be manipulated.

AUGUST 17 | Read Jeremiah 16–19

16:1–21 The Lord tells Jeremiah that he will not be permitted to marry and have children. To do so would be futile, since children have no future in a land marked for destruction.

17:1–8 Jeremiah declares that the sin of the people of Judah is no surface problem. It has infected and corrupted their total being. They can be delivered from their evil only if they repent and turn to God.

17:9–27 Judah is so corrupt that the people have stopped observing the Sabbath (Exod. 20:8–11). Such ungodly behavior will be punished severely by the Lord.

18:1–17 Jeremiah watches a potter reshape a piece of clay until he makes exactly the vase or bowl he had in mind. Just like this human craftsman, God has the right to shape the nation of Judah into the people He wants them to be. If they refuse His shaping influence, He will discipline them by scattering them before their enemies.

18:18–23 The enemies of Jeremiah threaten his life again (11:18–23). He prays a bitter prayer of vengeance against them. This prayer is similar to outcries against the enemies of the psalmist in the Psalms (Ps. 59).

19:1–15 At God's command the prophet breaks a bottle, or jug, before the people of Judah. This object lesson is a warning that God will shatter the nation unless the people forsake their worship of pagan gods and turn back to God.

....

Partridge A wild bird in Palestine prized for its meat and eggs. Jeremiah compared ill-gotten wealth to a partridge sitting on eggs that will not hatch (Jer. 17:11)

....

A Lesson from the Potter *Then I [Jeremiah] went down to the potter's house, and, behold, he wrought a work on the wheels* (Jer. 18:3).

The Lord instructed Jeremiah to watch a potter at work and He would give the prophet a special message for the people. Ancient potters made pots by shaping wet clay with their hands as it turned on a foot-powered pedestal. As Jeremiah watched the potter, the vessel he was making collapsed. The potter massaged the clay into a lump and began to form it into another pot. The message for the people was that Judah was like clay in the hands of God. They should allow Him to shape them into a vessel of His own choosing (Jer. 18:6).

AUGUST 18 | Read Jeremiah 20–22

20:1–6 Pashur, son of Immer the priest, beats Jeremiah and puts him in shackles because he is proclaiming God's message of judgment against Judah. The prophet predicts that Pashur and his household as well as other citizens of Judah will be carried away as captives by the Babylonians.

20:7–18 Jeremiah cries out to God because of the burden he bears as a spokesman for the Lord against his country. This is such a difficult job for the prophet that he laments the day he was born (Job 3:1–4).

21:1–14 The setting for this chapter is apparently the final siege of Jerusalem by the Babylonians while Zedekiah was king of Judah (2 Kings 25:1–12). Resistance against the Babylonians is futile, the prophet tells the king. Their only hope for survival is to surrender.

22:1–30 This chapter contains Jeremiah's prophecies of disaster against three different kings of Judah: Shallum (vv. 11–17), Jehoiakim (vv. 18–23), and Coniah, or Jehoiachin (vv. 24–30). Chronologically, these prophecies were delivered before the events described in Jeremiah 21.

Jehoiakim The son and successor of Josiah as king of Judah (reigned about 609–597 BC). An evil ruler who exploited the people and led them into idolatry, Jehoiakim died while Jerusalem was under siege by the Babylonians (2 Chron. 36:6). The prophet Jeremiah foretold his defeat (Jer. 22:18–19). *Eliakim*: 2 Kings 23:34.

Symbols of Luxury *I will build me a wide house [great palace, NIV] and large chambers [rooms, NIV], and cutteth him out windows; and it is cieled with cedar, and painted with vermilion [red, NIV]* (Jer. 22:14).

The typical house of OT times was crude by modern standards. Jeremiah referred in this verse to the luxurious palace built by King Jehoahaz (also known as Shallum) of Judah. This palace had large rooms with windows. Adorned with red trim, it was "cieled" or paneled with cedar, which had to be imported from Lebanon. To Jeremiah, this luxurious dwelling symbolized the sinful excesses of the king, as well as of the people of Judah. Their pride and rebellion would be judged by the Lord.

AUGUST 19 | Read Jeremiah 23–25

23:1–8 Jeremiah predicts that a faithful remnant of God's people will return to their homeland after their period of captivity by a foreign nation is over. He also speaks of the future Messiah, "THE LORD OUR RIGHTEOUSNESS" (v. 6). This prophecy was fulfilled with the birth of Jesus about 600 years after Jeremiah's time (Luke 2:1–7).

23:9–40 Jeremiah denounces the false prophets of Judah who are telling the leaders of the nation what they want to hear rather than declaring the Word of the Lord (Jer. 14).

24:1–10 God shows Jeremiah a basket of good figs and a basket of spoiled figs. The good figs represent the faithful remnant of God's people whom He will return to their homeland after the Babylonian captivity is over (2 Chron. 36:22–23). But the spoiled figs represent King Zedekiah of Judah and his sons, who will be wiped out when the nation is defeated (2 Kings 25:1–12).

25:1–38 Because of their idolatry, the people of Judah will be carried away as captives to Babylon for a period of seventy years. The nations that surround Judah will also fall to the Babylonian invasion.

Jehovah-tsidkennu The name for the coming Messiah used by the prophet Jeremiah, meaning "THE LORD OUR RIGHTEOUSNESS" (Jer. 23:6).

AUGUST 20 | Read Jeremiah 26–28

26:1–19 After Jehoiakim becomes king of Judah, God sends Jeremiah to proclaim His message to the people: Jerusalem will fall because of the sin of the people. The leaders of Judah push for Jeremiah's execution, but he is spared when a group defends his prophetic ministry.

26:20–24 King Jehoiakim has Urijah the prophet executed because he is proclaiming God's forthcoming judgment just like Jeremiah. The prophet Jeremiah must have wondered if he would be next in line for the executioner.

27:1–22 The setting for this chapter is the continuing Babylonian threat against Judah. The Babylonian army had already defeated King Jeconiah/Jehoiachin, ransacked Jerusalem, carried some citizens into exile, and robbed the temple treasures (vv. 18–20). Jehoiakim was ruling over Judah (v. 1). God directed Jeremiah to put on a yoke—a symbol of submission—and to wear it in the city of Jerusalem to show that the nation's only hope for survival was unconditional surrender to Babylonia.

28:1–17 Hananiah, a false prophet, denies Jeremiah's prophecy that the Babylonians will defeat the nation of Judah. Instead, Hananiah predicts peace and prosperity for the land. As Jeremiah predicts, Hananiah dies within a short time because he delivered a false prophecy in the Lord's name and led the people astray (Jer. 14; 23:9–40).

. . . .

Jeremiah and False Prophets *The prophet which prophesieth of peace, when the word of the prophet shall come to pass, then shall the prophet be known, that the* Lord *hath truly sent him* (Jer. 28:9).

False prophets have lived in every age, but the God-called prophet Jeremiah had more than his share of trouble from "yes-men" who told the officials of Judah what they wanted to hear. They denied Jeremiah's message of certain judgment for the nation unless the people changed their ways. Hananiah was one of the worst of these misleading messengers (Jer. 28:1–17). Jeremiah declared that God would deal severely with Hananiah. He will do the same with anyone who speaks lies in His name and deliberately leads people astray.

AUGUST 21 | Read Jeremiah 29–31

29:1–9 Jeremiah writes a letter to the Jewish captives who had already been taken to Babylon. He advises them to settle down and make the best of life in Babylon, since they will be there for many years (25:11).

29:10–19 God promises that a faithful remnant of His people will eventually return from captivity to their homeland.

29:20–32 The Lord pronounces judgment against several false prophets who have been leading the people to trust in a lie.

`30:1–31:40` Even in the midst of the punishment of His people, God will show mercy. A remnant will be saved and restored to their homeland. At the same time, God will establish a new covenant with those who belong to Him. This new spiritual covenant, written on their hearts, will replace the covenant of law, which they were unable to keep. Ultimately, this promise of a new covenant was fulfilled with the coming of Jesus Christ and His sacrificial death and offer of eternal life for all who accept Him as Lord and Savior (Heb. 9:11–15).

`Remnant` A small group of God's people who remained loyal to Him in the midst of widespread sin and idolatry. The prophet Isaiah declared that Israel would be punished for its unfaithfulness (Isa. 1:9). However, a righteous remnant of His people would be preserved (Isa. 10:20–22). God continues to work through His righteous remnant, the Church (Rom. 11:5).

`Outcasts` Dispossessed people. This word was used by the prophets to describe the Jews scattered among foreign nations (Isa. 11:12; Jer. 30:17). Jesus had compassion on lepers who were social outcasts (Luke 17:11–19).

AUGUST 22 | Read Jeremiah 32

`32:1–44` While the Babylonians are attacking Jerusalem, Jeremiah buys a plot of land in Anathoth, his hometown. This shows his confidence in the promise of the Lord that the land throughout Judah will eventually be valuable again. This will happen when the remnant of God's people return from captivity to their homeland.

`Hanameel` A cousin of Jeremiah the prophet (Jer. 32:7). Jeremiah bought a field from Hanameel during the siege of Jerusalem by the Babylonians to signify hope for the future for God's people (Jer. 32:8–12). *Hanamel:* NIV, NRSV.

`Jeremiah's Show of Faith` *Take these evidences [documents, NIV], this evidence of the purchase, both which is sealed, and this evidence which is open; and put them in an earthen vessel [clay jar, NIV], that they may continue many days [last a long time, NIV]* (Jer. 32:14).

Jeremiah showed faith in the future of Judah, even while Jerusalem, the capital city, was on the verge of falling to the Babylonian army. He bought a plot of land in his hometown of Anathoth, confident that the land would be useful again after the Jewish people returned from the exile in Babylon. In Jeremiah's time two duplicate deeds to a plot of land were prepared. One copy was buried in a sealed jar in a corner of the property, and the other was left unsealed in a public place for viewing by any interested person. But the prophet was told by the Lord to place both deeds in a jar for burial on the property. All public records would be destroyed in the Babylonian invasion of Jerusalem. The deeds in the ground would be the only proof of Jeremiah's ownership of the land.

AUGUST 23 | Read Jeremiah 33–35

33:1–26 This chapter is messianic in nature. The Lord reminds His people of the promise He had made to David several centuries before—that one of David's descendants would always occupy the throne of Judah (2 Sam. 7:12–16). Jesus as the "son of David" (Matt. 1:1) is the ultimate fulfillment of this prophecy.

34:1–7 The Lord sends Jeremiah to King Zedekiah of Judah with a message while Jerusalem is under siege. The message is that the city will fall to Babylonia and Zedekiah will be captured by the enemy.

34:8–22 God expresses His displeasure that the citizens of Judah have broken His law about enslavement of their own countrymen. They are keeping Jewish slaves in perpetual slavery rather than freeing them after seven years, as the law commands (Deut. 15:12–15).

35:1–19 A group of people known as the Rechabites seeks refuge in Jerusalem because of the Babylonian threat. Their refusal to drink wine—a commitment they had made many years before—emphasizes the failure of the people of Judah to keep their covenant with the Lord.

....

Zedekiah The last king of Judah (reigned about 597–587 BC), who was renamed and placed on the throne as a puppet ruler by King Nebuchadnezzar of Babylonia (2 Kings 24:15, 17). Ignoring Jeremiah's advice, he rebelled against the Babylonians, only to be blinded and taken to Babylon in chains after seeing his sons put to death (2 Kings 25:6–7). His original name was *Mattaniah* (2 Kings 24:17).

Rechab The father of Jehonadab and founder of the Rechabites, a tribe committed to abstain from wine and to live in tents. Because of their faithfulness, the prophet Jeremiah promised they would not cease to exist (Jer. 35:8–19). The descendants of this tribe still live in Iraq and Yemen.

....

Cutting a Covenant *The men. . .have not performed [fulfilled, NIV] the words of the covenant which they had made before me [God], when they cut the calf in twain [two, NIV], and passed between the parts thereof* (Jer. 34:18).

In this verse, God charged the people of Judah with violating the covenant they had made with Him. The original covenant that God formed with His people was sealed by Abraham, who cut several animals into two-piece sections and then walked between the sections. In the Hebrew language, to "make a covenant" was to "cut a covenant," reflecting this ancient custom of walking between the two pieces of an animal carcass. By this action they signified that they agreed to the terms of the covenant. This also may have expressed their wish that if the covenant was broken, the offending party would suffer the same fate as the slaughtered animals.

AUGUST 24 | Read Jeremiah 36–38

36:1–10 Jeremiah enlists a scribe named Baruch to write down his prophecies of God's judgment against the nation of Judah. Baruch then reads the prophet's words to the people in the temple.

36:11–26 King Jehoiakim of Judah sends for the scroll after he hears about Jeremiah's written message. To show his contempt for the prophet, he burns the scroll bit by bit as it is read by one of his aides.

36:27–32 Jeremiah reproduces the destroyed scroll by dictating God's message again to Baruch. He also expands the original message of judgment. The Lord declares that King Jehoiakim will be judged severely for destroying the scroll.

37:1–21 Jeremiah is imprisoned on the false charge that he is deserting his own people to seek refuge among the Babylonian army. King Zedekiah asks him if he has any word from the Lord for Judah, since the nation is under attack by the enemy. Jeremiah's reply is not what the king wants to hear: "Thou shalt be delivered into the hand of the king of Babylon" (v. 17).

38:1 13 Jeremiah's enemies throw him into a dungeon or pit—perhaps a cistern with mud in the bottom—and leave him to die. With King Zedekiah's permission, Ebed-melech, a servant of the king, pulls the prophet out of the pit.

38:14–28 King Zedekiah summons Jeremiah in secret and asks him what he should do. Jerusalem is running out of food and water because of the prolonged Babylonian siege. The prophet tells him the only way to save himself and the city is to surrender to the Babylonian army.

....

Baruch The friend and scribe of the prophet Jeremiah. Baruch recorded Jeremiah's messages warning of the impending defeat of the nation of Judah (Jer. 36:4–32). Like Jeremiah, he fled to Egypt after the fall of Jerusalem (Jer. 43:1–7).

....

Baruch's Ink and Paper *Then Baruch answered them, He [Jeremiah] pronounced all these words unto me with his mouth, and I wrote them with ink in the book [scroll, NIV]* (Jer. 36:18).

The ink used by Baruch and other ancient scribes was made by mixing soot, lampblack, or ground charcoal with water and gum. The scroll on which he wrote Jeremiah's prophecies was probably made from the papyrus plant or from animal skins. While this writing was primitive by modern standards, it held up well. The manuscripts in the collection known as the Dead Sea Scrolls, discovered in 1947, were still legible, even though they had been written about 2,000 years before.

AUGUST 25 | Read Jeremiah 39–41

39:1–10 Just as Jeremiah had predicted for many years, the Babylonians conquer Judah. After a long siege, they break down the walls of Jerusalem and burn the city. King Zedekiah and his sons are captured when they try to escape. The proud king of Judah is forced to watch as his sons are executed. Then the Babylonians put out his eyes and carry him away in chains to their capital city. Also forced into exile are the elite members of Jewish society. The peasants are left behind to cultivate the land (2 Kings 25:1–12).

39:11–14 King Nebuchadrezzar (a KJV variant of *Nebuchadnezzar*) of Babylon releases Jeremiah from prison, treats him with kindness, and allows him to remain in Judah.

39:15–18 Jeremiah assures Ebed-melech, who had pulled him out of a cistern (38:1–13), that his life will be spared because of his trust in the Lord.

40:1–6 The Babylonians treat Jeremiah with kindness and allow him to decide whether he wants to go to Babylon or stay in Jerusalem. He decides to stay with the poor of the land who have been left behind.

40:7–41:18 The Babylonians place Gedaliah in charge of affairs in Judah. Ishmael, a Jewish zealot, incites a mob and assassinates Gedaliah, along with several Babylonian citizens who were helping to keep order in the land (2 Kings 25:22–25).

Gedaliah A friend of the prophet Jeremiah (Jer. 39:14; 40:5–6). After the fall of Jerusalem to the Babylonians in 587 BC, Gedaliah was made supervisor of the vinedressers left in the land (2 Kings 25:22–25).

Johanan A supporter of Gedaliah, governor of Judah (2 Kings 25:22–23), who took a remnant of the Jews to Egypt, in spite of the prophet Jeremiah's warning (Jer. 41:16–18; 43:4–6).

AUGUST 26 | Read Jeremiah 42–44

42:1–22 Representatives of the Jewish remnant left in Judah ask Jeremiah what they should do. They are apparently afraid of retaliation from the Babylonians for Gedaliah's assassination; they wonder if they should seek safety in Egypt. Jeremiah predicts they will be destroyed if they flee to Egypt. He advises them to stay in Judah.

43:1–7 Disregarding Jeremiah's advice, the Jewish remnant seeks refuge in Egypt, carrying Jeremiah and Baruch with them.

43:8–44:30 Jeremiah warns the Jewish remnant in Egypt that it is futile to try to hide from God's judgment in a foreign land. The Babylonians will eventually conquer Egypt, and they will be carried into exile to join their Jewish countrymen who have already been settled in Babylon.

Queen of Heaven A fertility goddess worshiped by the citizens of Jerusalem during the idolatrous days before the fall of the nation of Judah (Jer. 7:18; 44:17). This may have been the goddess Ashtaroth, or Asherah.

AUGUST 27 | Jeremiah 45–47

45:1–5 Jeremiah assures his faithful scribe, Baruch, that Baruch's life will be spared in the devastating events that lie ahead.

46:1–47:7 These chapters contain Jeremiah's prophecies against the nations. God's judgment will be poured out against the nations that surround Judah as well as Judah itself. Marked for destruction because of their idolatry are Egypt (chap. 46) and the Philistines (chap. 47).

No A thriving Egyptian city on both sides of the Nile River that served as the capital of upper Egypt (Nah. 3:8). No was destroyed in 81 BC, as predicted by the prophet Jeremiah (Jer. 46:25). *Thebes*: NIV, NLT.

Amon, God of Thebes *I [God] will punish the multitude of No [Amon god of Thebes, NIV], and Pharaoh, and Egypt, with their gods, and their kings* (Jer. 46:25).

This verse is part of Jeremiah's declaration that God would bring down the Egyptians because of their idol worship. "No" refers to Thebes, the thriving capital of Upper Egypt that was clustered on both sides of the Nile River. The Hebrew word translated as "multitude" by the King James Version actually refers to the Egyptian god Amon, the chief deity of the city of Thebes. Little is known about Amon. Some think he was a personification of the sun. The Egyptians did practice sun worship, but the name of their sun god was Ra. One theory is that the qualities of Amon and Ra eventually merged into one supreme Egyptian sun god known as Amon-Ra.

AUGUST 28 | Read Jeremiah 48–49

48:1–47 Moab marked for destruction because of their idolatry.

49:1–39 The Ammonites (49:1–6), Edom (49:7–22), Damascus (49:23–27), Kedar and Hazor (49:28–33), and Elam (49:34–39) marked for destruction because of their idolatry.

Judgment against Moab *Moab. . .hath not been emptied from vessel to vessel. . . therefore his taste remained in him, and his scent is not changed* (Jer. 48:11).

This verse refers to a step in the process of making wine when it was poured from one jar to another to improve its taste. Jeremiah declared that Israel's enemy, Moab, had not yet experienced devastation by an enemy nation—or being "emptied from vessel to vessel."

But this would change in the future when Moab would be judged by the Lord for its sin. God would "empty his [Moab's] vessels, and break their bottles" (Jer. 48:12).

AUGUST 29 | Read Jeremiah 50–51

50:1–51:64 Babylonia (chaps. 50–51) is marked for destruction because of idolatry.

Merodach The pagan Babylonian god of war whose overthrow was predicted by the prophet Jeremiah (Jer. 50:2). *Marduk*: NIV.

AUGUST 30 | Read Jeremiah 52

52:1–34 The book of Jeremiah ends with a review of one of the greatest tragedies in the history of God's people: the fall of Jerusalem to the Babylonian army. This chapter covers the same events as those described in chapter 39 (see also 2 Kings 24–25). Perhaps Jeremiah revisited this national tragedy to remind his readers of the perils of refusing to follow the Lord.

An Eighteen-Month Siege *So the city [Jerusalem] was besieged unto the eleventh year of king Zedekiah* (Jer. 52:5).

Siege warfare was the main tactic used against walled cities of Bible times. This verse and the surrounding verses tell us how long the Babylonian siege of Jerusalem lasted. The siege began "in the ninth year. . .in the tenth month" (v. 4) of King Zedekiah's reign and ended eighteen months later "in the fourth month" (v. 6) of the eleventh year of his reign. In siege warfare, the enemy outside the walls always had the upper hand. The army could post sentries to halt the movement of food and water into the city until its inhabitants were starved into submission. This is what happened with Jerusalem: "The famine was sore in the city, so that there was no bread for the people of the land" (v. 6). About 130 years before Judah (the Southern Kingdom) fell to the Babylonians, the Assyrians overran the city of Samaria and defeated Israel (the Northern Kingdom). Their siege of Samaria lasted three years (2 Kings 17:5).

AUGUST 31 | Read Lamentations 1–2

1:1–22 Jerusalem, capital of the nation of Judah, was once a proud and prosperous city. But now it lies in ruins, devastated and looted by the Babylonian army. Its streets were once filled with people, but now it is almost deserted. The Babylonians have carried the leading citizens of Judah into captivity, leaving behind only a few peasants and farmers (2 Kings 25:1–12). The city is like a destitute widow who mourns for her family.

2:1–22 Why did this happen? The prophet Jeremiah declares that Jerusalem has only itself to blame for its predicament. The Lord had warned Judah for many years that the nation would be defeated by a foreign enemy unless it forsook its worship of false gods and turned back to the one true God. Now God has "thrown down, and hath not pitied: and he hath caused thine enemy to rejoice over thee" (v. 17).

Trampled by God's Judgment *The LORD hath trodden the virgin, the daughter of Judah, as in a winepress* (Lam. 1:15).

Jeremiah referred to the city of Jerusalem as "the virgin, the daughter of Judah." He lamented the destruction of the city by the Babylonian army in 587 BC. Jerusalem had been trodden down like grapes in a winepress. In Bible times the juice was extracted from grapes to make wine by crushing them underfoot in a vat, or winepress, carved out of solid rock. God's judgment is also described as a winepress in Isa. 63:3 and Rev. 14:19–20; 19:15.

SEPTEMBER 1 | Read Lamentations 3–5

3:1–42 Out of his despair over Jerusalem's plight, Jeremiah sees a glimmer of hope. After all, the Babylonians have spared the lives of most of the Jewish people (v. 22). Perhaps through God's mercy and grace they will survive their ordeal of captivity in Babylon and be restored to their homeland at some future time.

3:43–66 Once again, Jeremiah is overwhelmed by the suffering and humiliation of the people of Judah. Their enemies had laughed and cheered when Jerusalem fell. The prophet asks God to pay them back for their cruelty.

4:1–20 These verses contain more stark pictures of the devastation of Jerusalem. Jeremiah condemns the priests and prophets for failing to lead the people back to God. This would have kept divine judgment from falling on the city.

4:21–22 The nation of Edom, an enemy of the Israelites for many years, apparently participated in the capture and destruction of Jerusalem (see the book of Obadiah). Jeremiah predicts that Judah will eventually be restored, but Edom will be permanently wiped out by the Lord.

5:1–22 Jeremiah reviews the numerous sufferings of the people of Judah. Then he prays for God to grant them restoration and forgiveness: "Turn thou us unto thee, O LORD, and we shall be turned; renew our days as of old" (v. 21).

Mercy Compassion for others. God's mercies are abundant (1 Pet. 1:3) and fresh every morning (Lam. 3:22–23). Paul described God as "the father of all mercies" (2 Cor. 1:3). Jesus commended the Samaritan who showed mercy for a wounded traveler (Luke 10:36–37). *Compassion*: NIV.

Offscouring Refuse; something vile or despised (Lam. 3:45). Paul indicated that faithful Christians may be regarded as "the scum of the earth" by the world (1 Cor. 4:13). *Scum*: NIV; *filth*: NRSV.

Foxes in Jerusalem *Because of the mountain of Zion, which is desolate, the foxes walk upon it* (Lam. 5:18).

Jeremiah used this word picture to show the desolation of Jerusalem (referred to as "Zion") after it was captured, plundered, and destroyed by the Babylonians. The city was virtually empty, since the leading citizens of Judah had been carried away to Babylon as captives. Once-thriving Jerusalem was now the haunt of foxes and other wild animals. The Hebrew word for "foxes" is often rendered as "jackals" (see NIV). These animals, similar to wild dogs, were scavengers. Jackals prowling through Jerusalem gives an even more vivid portrait of the plight of the city.

SEPTEMBER 2 | Read Ezekiel 1–3

1:1–28 Ezekiel has a vision of four winged creatures known as cherubim. God's glory appears among these creatures.

2:1–10 The Lord informs Ezekiel that He has called him as His messenger to the Jewish exiles in Babylon.

3:1–27 Ezekiel eats a roll, or scroll, on which God's message to His rebellious people is written. This symbolizes the prophet's acceptance of God's message and mission to the Jewish exiles.

Chebar A river or canal of Babylonia where Jewish captives settled during the Exile. Ezekiel's visions came to him at Chebar (Ezek. 1:3; 10:15, 20).

Almighty A title of God that indicates His absolute power and majesty. God used this term to identify Himself as He talked to Abraham (Gen. 17:1). Ezekiel portrayed God in this light in his vision of God's glory (Ezek. 1:24; 10:5). "Almighty" is also used of Christ (Rev. 1:8; 19:15).

"Son of Man" in Ezekiel *And he said unto me, Son of man, stand upon thy feet, and I will speak unto thee* (Ezek. 2:1).

The title "son of man" was often used for the prophet Ezekiel (Ezek. 2:1; 34:2). It set him apart as a representative member of the human race who was on a special mission for God. Like Ezekiel, Jesus—who often called Himself "Son of Man"—was also a representative sent by God, but His mission was to provide salvation for sinful humanity.

SEPTEMBER 3 | Read Ezekiel 4–7

4:1–17 At God's command, Ezekiel uses a clay tile and an iron pan to enact the Babylonian siege against Jerusalem. He eats tiny amounts of food for several days to show the starvation conditions that existed in Jerusalem before the city fell.

5:1–17 Ezekiel shaves his beard and his head with a sword. Then he burns the hair to show that God has judged His people with the sword of the Babylonians because of their unfaithfulness.

6:1–14 God's destruction has fallen upon the mountains of Judah and those who worshiped false gods upon these high places.

7:1–27 The doom that God has promised against Judah because of the idolatry of the people is now unleashed in full force against the land: "According to their deserts will I judge them; and they shall know that I am the LORD" (v. 27).

A Record in Clay *Son of man [Ezekiel], take thee a tile [clay tablet, NIV], and lay it before thee, and pourtray upon it the city, even Jerusalem* (Ezek. 4:1).

God made a strange request of the prophet Ezekiel. He asked him to draw upon a clay tablet a picture of the city of Jerusalem under siege by the Babylonian army. This was to serve as a warning to the people about the forthcoming judgment of God against Jerusalem and the nation of Judah. In Bible times clay tiles or tablets about six by nine inches in size were often used as writing material, just like paper is used today. Characters were etched into these tablets with a metal pen while the clay was soft. When hardened in a kiln, the writing on these tiles was virtually indestructible. Archaeologists have discovered many of these clay tablets in the ruins of ancient cities. They shed light on the culture and customs of the ancient world.

SEPTEMBER 4 | Read Ezekiel 8–11

8:1–18 Ezekiel is transported in a vision to the temple in Jerusalem. Here God shows him how the temple has been desecrated through the worship of false gods.

9:1–11 God commands that a special mark be placed on every person in Jerusalem who is grieved by the desecration of the temple. They will be saved when Jerusalem falls, but everyone without this mark will be destroyed (Rev. 9:4; 14:1).

10:1–22 Ezekiel has a vision of the same four-winged creatures, or cherubim, that he had in chapter 1. God's glory leaves the temple and rests above these cherubim. This signifies that God's glory will eventually leave the temple because His people have polluted this holy place with their pagan worship practices.

11:1–25 Ezekiel speaks against certain leaders of Jerusalem who are predicting prosperity rather than disaster for the city. He declares that the future of God's people rests with the Jewish exiles in Babylon. God will eventually restore His remnant to their homeland (2 Chron. 36:22–23).

....

Cherubims An order of angelic, winged creatures (Gen. 3:24). Their function was to praise God and glorify His name (Ezek. 10:18–20).

Adonai The Hebrew name for God, translated "Lord" (Ezek. 11:8).

....

Idols in the Temple *So I [Ezekiel] went in and saw; and behold every form of creeping [crawling, NIV] things, and abominable [detestable, NIV] beasts, and all the idols of the house of Israel, portrayed upon the wall round about* (Ezek. 8:10).

In a vision the prophet Ezekiel saw the temple of the Jewish people in Jerusalem. He was shocked to see on its walls paintings or sculptures of unclean animals that God's people were not supposed to eat (Lev. 11:1–19). But even more shocking were the representations of pagan gods that adorned its walls. This was God's way of showing the prophet that His people were guilty of breaking the first of the Ten Commandments: "Thou shalt have no other gods before me" (Exod. 20:3). Pagan temples of the ancient world were decorated with images of false gods. God's people had adopted the pagan worship practices of the surrounding nations. They were marked for God's judgment unless they turned back to Him.

Apocalyptic Language in Ezekiel *Then I looked, and, behold, in the firmament that was above the head of the cherubims there appeared over them as it were a sapphire stone, as the appearance of the likeness of a throne* (Ezek. 10:1).

Ezekiel is one of the few books in the Bible that contains apocalyptic literature. This was a distinctive type of writing that used visions, numbers, strange creatures, angels, and demons to express religious truths (Ezek. 10:1–17). The best-known example of apocalyptic literature in the Bible is the book of Revelation in the NT.

SEPTEMBER 5 | Read Ezekiel 12–15

12:1–28 At God's command, Ezekiel acts out the fall of Jerusalem and the exile of the people to Babylon.

13:1–23 Ezekiel denounces false prophets who are telling the people what they want to hear rather than proclaiming God's message of judgment (Jer. 28). He also condemns false prophetesses who are leading the people astray through witchcraft and the reading of signs to foretell the future.

14:1–23 God will not tolerate the worship of false gods by His people. He demands their exclusive loyalty (Josh. 24:15). He will judge the nation of Judah for their false worship.

15:1–8 God's people were often compared to a vine (Isa. 5:1–7; Hosea 10:1), but their idolatry has turned them into a vine that bears no fruit. They wlll be cut down and burned by the fire of God's judgment (Luke 13:6–9).

Untempered Morter A thin layer of clay used as a protective coating on the exterior walls of buildings. The term is used figuratively of the futile promises of false prophets (Ezek. 13:10–15; 22:28). *Whitewash*: NIV, NRSV.

Useless as a Wild Vine *Shall wood be taken thereof [from a vine] to do any work? or will men take a pin of it to hang any vessel thereon?* (Ezek. 15:3).

Ezekiel compared the nation of Judah to a wild vine. Just as a vine of this type yields no lumber—not even as much as a pin or peg to hang a pot on—so Judah had become useless to the Lord because of the sin and rebellion of the people. Domestic vines such as the grape are useful because of the fruit they produce. Throughout their history the Israelites were often spoken of as a fruitful vine (Gen. 49:22). But even a grapevine is useless if it fails to produce grapes (Jer. 2:21). Ezekiel looked in vain for the fruits of righteousness and holiness among the people of his time.

SEPTEMBER 6 | Read Ezekiel 16–17

16:1–63 This long chapter is a parable about God's relationship with His people Israel. The Lord adopted Israel when she was an orphan, lavishing her with His love and care. But she rejected Him and turned to the worship of pagan gods. While Israel will receive its deserved punishment, God will not give up on His people. He remains faithful to His covenant promises: "I will establish my covenant with thee; and thou shalt know that I am the LORD" (v. 62).

17:1–24 The two eagles in this chapter represent Babylonia and Egypt. The vine represents the nation of Judah, which broke its oath of allegiance to Babylonia and turned to Egypt for help. God will punish Judah for this act of disobedience, but He will eventually rebuild His people through a faithful remnant who follow His commands.

Parable A short story drawn from daily life that is used to convey an important truth; a favorite teaching device used by Jesus (Matt. 13:3). In the OT, Nathan told a parable to convict King David of his sin of adultery (2 Sam. 12:1–7). Jesus used parables to present truth to His receptive hearers and to conceal the lesson from those who were critical or unreceptive (Matt. 13:10–16, 35). Drawn from daily life, His parables revealed lessons about salvation, the kingdom, and the future life (Luke 15).

SEPTEMBER 7 | Read Ezekiel 18–21

18:1–32 The people of Judah were sometimes fatalistic in their attitudes, blaming their ancestors for their current problems. Ezekiel declares that each person is accountable for his or her own sins: "The soul that sinneth, it shall die. The son shall not bear the iniquity of the father, neither shall the father bear the iniquity of the son" (v. 20).

19:1–14 In this mournful poem, Ezekiel laments the kings who ruled Judah during the tragic period just before the nation fell to the Babylonians.

20:1–44 Several leaders of Judah ask Ezekiel if he has a message from the Lord. The prophet responds by giving them a history lesson, showing that the Israelites have tended to be sinful and rebellious from the very beginning of their existence as a nation.

20:45–21:32 Because of their rebellious history, God will send His wrath against His people. His agent of judgment will be the Babylonians, who will destroy Jerusalem as well as the capital of the Ammonites.

A Lion in a Pit *She [Judah] brought up one of her whelps [cubs, NIV]: it became a young lion. . . . The nations also heard of him; he was taken in their pit* (Ezek. 19:3–4).

During the final days of the nation of Judah, King Jehoahaz was captured and taken to Egypt (2 Kings 23:31–34). This is probably the event to which Ezekiel referred in this verse. Although the king seemed ferocious like a "young lion," he was at the mercy of the Egyptians once he stumbled into their trap. In Bible times lions and other large animals were often trapped in pits. The trappers dug a deep hole in the ground and covered it with tree limbs and a layer of dirt. Once the animal fell into the pit, it could be easily captured or killed.

SEPTEMBER 8 | Read Ezekiel 22

22:1–31 Jerusalem was supposed to be the "holy city." Instead, it has become the "bloody city" (v. 2) because of its sin, idolatry, and denial of justice to the poor. Jerusalem will be judged severely by the Lord for its corruption.

Heathen A word for ethnic groups besides the Jews (Ezek. 22:15). It was also used for unbelievers, pagans, or Gentiles (Gal. 1:16). *Nations*: NIV, NRSV. *Gentiles*: NIV, NRSV.

Babylonians Sign-Reading *The king of Babylon stood. . .at the head of the two ways [at the junction of the two roads, NIV], to use divination [seek an omen, NIV]: he made his arrows bright, he consulted with images, he looked in the liver* (Ezek. 21:21).

Ezekiel told the people of Judah that the king of Babylonia was coming into their territory on a mission of conquest. He would stop at a fork in the road and decide whether to take the road toward Jerusalem or to go the other way and attack the capital city of the Ammonites (Ezek. 21:19–20). To decide which road to take, the king would read the signs by using one of three possible methods. He might cast lots by drawing an arrow out of his quiver and throwing it down to see which way it pointed. He could consult his pagan gods. Or he could have one of his priests "read" the liver of a sacrificial animal and advise him on which city to attack. Such superstitious sign-reading was practiced by the pagan nations of Bible times. But God declared black magic and divination off-limits to His people (Deut. 18:10–11).

SEPTEMBER 9 | Read Ezekiel 23–24

23:1–49 In this parable of two adulterous sisters, Ezekiel portrays the nation of Israel (Northern Kingdom) as Aholah and the nation of Judah (Southern Kingdom) as Aholibah. Their lust leads them to pursue their lovers with reckless abandon. Judah saw Israel punished with defeat and exile because of Israel's sins, but in spite of this warning, Judah continued her sinful ways.

24:1–14 Ezekiel portrays Jerusalem as a cooking pot. Its citizens will be stewed like meat in the fire of God's judgment when the Babylonians besiege the city (2 Kings 25:1–12).

24:15–27 God warns Ezekiel that his wife will soon die, but he is not to mourn her death. This is a sign to the Jewish exiles in Babylon that they will soon be cut off from their relatives in Jerusalem when the city is overrun by the Babylonians.

Immorality Behavior that violates established moral principles or laws. This word is used to condemn illicit sexual activity outside of marriage (Prov. 2:16; Rom. 1:26–27) and to describe Israel's worship of pagan gods (Ezek. 23:8, 17).

A Tale of Two Sisters *She [Aholibah] doted upon [lusted after, NIV] the Assyrians her neighbours, captains and rulers clothed most gorgeously, horsemen riding upon horses, all of them desirable young men* (Ezek. 23:12).

One of Ezekiel's most famous prophecies is his portrayal of the nations of Israel (the Northern Kingdom) and Judah (the Southern Kingdom) as two adulterous sisters named Aholah and Aholibah (Ezek. 23). Both sisters lusted after the "desirable young men" of the surrounding nations. Ezekiel meant by this that both Israel and Judah turned away from the Lord and worshiped the pagan gods of their neighbors. God warned both nations that He would punish them for their sin unless they changed their behavior, but they refused. Their sin eventually led to the downfall of both sisters. The Northern Kingdom fell to the Assyrians, and Judah was overrun by the Babylonians. Ironically, these were two of the nations or lovers with whom Aholah and Aholibah had committed adultery.

SEPTEMBER 10 | Read Ezekiel 25–27

25:1–27:36 These chapters contain Ezekiel's prophecies of God's judgment against the nations: Ammon (25:1–7); Moab (25:8–11); Edom (25:12–14); the Philistines (25:15–17); Tyrus, or Tyre (26:1–28:19).

Mount Hermon The highest mountain in Syria, with an elevation of almost 10,000 feet (Josh. 12:1). It was also called *Sirion* and *Shenir* (Deut. 3:9) and *Senir* (Ezek. 27:5).

SEPTEMBER 11 | Read Ezekiel 28–30

28:1–20 Additional prophecies against Tyrus, or Tyre.

28:20–30:26 Ezekiel prophesies judgment against Zidon, or Sidon (28:20–26) and Egypt (chaps. 29–32).

SEPTEMBER 12 | Read Ezekiel 31–32

31:1–32:32 Ezekiel prophesies judgment against Egypt.

Buried with Weapons *They [the Egyptians] have laid their swords under their heads* (Ezek. 32:27).

This verse appears among Ezekiel's prophecy against Egypt. It refers to the Egyptian custom of burying their fallen soldiers with their weapons of war. Many soldiers of the ancient world slept with their weapons by their side, ready for instant action. So it was natural for the Egyptians to think that their warriors should take their weapons with them into the afterlife.

SEPTEMBER 13 | Read Ezekiel 33–34

33:1–20 The Lord tells Ezekiel that the duty of a watchman is to sound a warning in times of danger. This is also the mission of a true prophet of God.

33:21–33 News that the city of Jerusalem has fallen reaches Ezekiel. He passes this on to the other Jewish exiles in Babylon.

34:1–31 The leaders of Judah will be punished because they have exploited and misled the people rather than guiding them in the ways of the Lord. In contrast to such undependable human leaders, God is a true Shepherd. He will eventually bring His people back to their homeland to feed on fertile pastures.

Prophet An inspired messenger called by God to declare His will (Ezra 5:2). Prophets were described as God's servants (Zech. 1:6), watchmen (Ezek. 3:17), and holy men (2 Pet. 1:21). In the NT, the prophets were cited as a noble example of patient suffering (James 5:10). Another word for prophet is *seer.*

SEPTEMBER 14 | Read Ezekiel 35–36

35:1–15 The nation of Edom, referred to as "mount Seir" (v. 2) by Ezekiel, joined in the humiliation of Judah when Jerusalem fell to the Babylonians. God will repay this callous act. The prophet Obadiah also condemned Edom for these acts of treachery (see the book of Obadiah).

36:1–38 This chapter represents a turning point in the book of Ezekiel. Up to now, the prophet has spoken mainly of God's judgment against the nation of Judah. But now that God's judgment has reached its climax with the fall of Jerusalem, Ezekiel will spend the rest of his book giving hope to the Jewish exiles in Babylon. In the future God will restore His people to their homeland. He will give them a new heart and fill them with a new spirit.

Edom The land where the descendants of Esau settled. It was in extreme southern Palestine in the barren territory below the Dead Sea. Mount Seir was located in this territory (Gen. 36:8). Edom was referred to by the Greeks and Romans as *Idumaea* (Mark 3:8).

SEPTEMBER 15 | Read Ezekiel 37–39

37:1–14 Ezekiel has a vision of a valley filled with dry, lifeless bones. God's Spirit enters the bones, and they spring to life. This symbolizes the forthcoming spiritual restoration of the nation of Israel.

37:15–28 At God's command, Ezekiel picks up two sticks. These represent the two separate nations of Israel (Northern Kingdom) and Judah (Southern Kingdom). The prophet declares that God will unite His people into one kingdom under one king—"David my servant" (v. 24). This is a title for the promised Messiah. This prophecy was fulfilled with the coming of Jesus.

38:1–39:29 Ezekiel looks into the future and predicts a great battle between the forces of evil and the people of God. Several evil nations, under the leadership of Gog, attack God's people, but they are defeated when God intervenes. The apostle John, writing in the book of Revelation, uses Gog's evil forces to represent all who oppose God in the final battle in the end times under the leadership of Satan (Rev. 20:8).

Valley of Dry Bones A vision of the prophet Ezekiel. When Ezekiel addressed the bones, representing Israel's exile in a foreign land, they came to life by God's Spirit. This served as God's assurance that His people would return one day to their native land (Ezek. 37:1–14).

Messages on Wood *The sticks whereon thou [Ezekiel] writest shall be in thine hand before their [Israel's and Judah's] eyes* (Ezek. 37:20).

God told Ezekiel to write messages on two separate sticks, representing the nations of Judah (Southern Kingdom) and Israel (Northern Kingdom). Then he was to place the two sticks together. This represented the time when the two nations would become one again and be ruled over by the messianic King. Messages were often written on long, narrow strips of wood in Bible times. The practice is referred to as early as the time of Moses (Num. 17:2–3).

SEPTEMBER 16 | Read Ezekiel 40–42

40:1–42:20 The book of Ezekiel ends with the prophet's glorious vision of a new temple rebuilt on the site of Solomon's temple in Jerusalem. This must have brought hope to the Jewish exiles in Babylon, since Solomon's temple had been destroyed when Jerusalem fell to the Babylonian army.

Cubit The standard unit for measurement of length, equivalent to about eighteen inches (Gen. 6:15–16).

SEPTEMBER 17 | Read Ezekiel 43–44

43:1–44:31 These chapters give a description of the altar and the duties and privileges of the Levites and priests.

Glory Splendor, honor, or perfection. The "glory of the LORD" signifies the supreme perfection of His nature (Exod. 16:7). Jesus also partook of the glory of His Father (John 2:11). He shares His divine glory with all believers (John 17:5–6).

SEPTEMBER 18 | Read Ezekiel 45–46

45:1–46:24 Instruction is given for division of land (with a portion for the temple), using honest scales, the sacrificial system, and daily aspects of worship.

Homer The standard unit of dry measure, equal to about six bushels (Ezek. 45:11).

Bath *Ye shall have just balances [accurate scales, NIV], and a just ephah, and a just bath* (Ezek. 45:10).

The bath was the standard unit by which liquids such as oil and wine were measured in OT times. It was equal to about six gallons. The bath was equivalent in liquid measure to the ephah in dry measure. This command from Ezekiel about honesty in buying and selling affirms the same principle spelled out in the Mosaic law (Deuteronomy 25:13).

SEPTEMBER 19 | Read Ezekiel 47–48

47:1–48:35 These chapters describe the borders of the land and tribal allotments.

Jehovah-shammah The name of a city of the future envisioned by the prophet Ezekiel, indicating that "the LORD is there" (Ezek. 48:35).

SEPTEMBER 20 | Read Daniel 1–2

1:1–7 Daniel and his three friends—Shadrach, Meshach, and Abednego—are carried to Babylon as captives after Judah is defeated by the Babylonians under King Nebuchadnezzar (2 Kings 25:1–12). These four young Jewish men are selected for training in Babylonian customs and culture before being placed in government service in Babylon.

1:8–21 Daniel and his three friends refuse to defile themselves with the rich foods and strong wine they are required to eat while in training for government service. Eating only vegetables ("pulse," v. 12) and water, they grow stronger than all the other young men in the training program.

2:1–11 King Nebuchadnezzar of Babylonia has a dream that he is not able to recall. None of his wise men or magicians can tell him what he dreamed.

2:12–45 Daniel is able to tell Nebuchadnezzar what he dreamed and what it meant. The prophet tells the king that he will continue for a while as a mighty ruler over a broad territory. But his successors will not be able to hold this kingdom together.

2:46–49 King Nebuchadnezzar appoints Daniel to a high position in his administration. Also promoted are Daniel's three friends: Shadrach, Meshach, and Abednego.

....

Daniel A prophet of the OT known for his faithfulness to the God of Israel among the pagan Babylonians and Persians. Refusing to worship King Darius, he was thrown into a den of lions but was miraculously delivered by the Lord (Dan. 6:1–24). *Belteshazzar*: Babylonian form (Dan. 1:7).

Pulse Food made of vegetables, such as peas or beans; the food eaten by Daniel and his friends instead of the king's provisions (Dan. 1:12–16).

....

Looting of the Temple *He [King Nebuchadnezzar] brought the vessels into the treasure house of his god* (Dan. 1:2).
When the Babylonian army captured and plundered the city of Jerusalem, King Nebuchadnezzar seized the golden utensils, spices, jewels, and other valuable items that belonged to the Jewish temple. He carried these valuables to Babylon, where he deposited them in the treasure house of a temple devoted to the worship of a pagan Babylonian god. This fulfilled a prophecy that Isaiah had issued to the people of Judah about 100 years before: "The days come, that all. . .which thy fathers have laid up in store. . .shall be carried to Babylon" (Isa. 39:6).

SEPTEMBER 21 | Read Daniel 3–4

3:1–7 King Nebuchadnezzar fashions a statue of himself from gold and has it set up at a prominent site in Babylonia. He orders all the people in his kingdom to bow down and worship the image at his command.

3:8–18 Enemies of Daniel's three friends inform the king that these young Jewish men will not worship the golden image. When Nebuchadnezzar questions them about this, they reply: "O king. . .we will not serve thy gods, nor worship the golden image which thou hast set up" (v. 18).

3:19–30 Because of their disobedience of the king's order, Shadrach, Meshach, and Abednego are thrown into a hot furnace. But an angel protects them, and they emerge untouched and unharmed by the flames. King Nebuchadnezzar is so impressed by this miracle that he orders everyone in Babylonia to be respectful toward the God whom they worship. He also promotes Shadrach, Meshach, and Abednego to higher positions in his administration.

4:1–37 Daniel interprets another dream of King Nebuchadnezzar—and it happens just as Daniel predicts. Toward the end of his reign, the king is struck by a strange disease—perhaps mental illness. Convinced he is an animal, he forages in the pastures, eating grass with the livestock. But he apparently recovers from this illness long enough to recognize Daniel's God as the one true God (vv. 34–37).

Abed-nego One of Daniel's three friends. Thrown into the fiery furnace by King Nebuchadnezzar of Babylonia (Dan. 3:13–27), he was later promoted by the king after his miraculous deliverance at the hand of God (Dan. 3:28–30). *Azariah*: Hebrew form (Dan. 1:7).

Meshach The Babylonian name for Daniel's friend who was thrown into the fiery furnace for refusing to worship an idol (Dan. 1:7). He was saved through God's miraculous intervention. His Hebrew name was *Mishael* (Dan. 1:6).

Shadrach The Babylonian name of Hananiah, one of Daniel's friends, who was cast into the fiery furnace but miraculously delivered at God's hand (Dan. 3).

Into the Fire *And whoso falleth not down and worshippeth shall the same hour be cast into the midst of a burning fiery furnace* (Dan. 3:6).

This furnace was big enough to hold Daniel's three friends—Shadrach, Meshach, and Abed-nego. It was probably a huge kiln used to cure bricks for the king's ambitious building projects. It was pressed into service as an execution chamber for anyone who refused to bow down and worship King Nebuchadnezzar as a god. The heat from the fire was so intense that the guards who threw the three men into the furnace were burned to death (Daniel 3:22). But God delivered His three servants without so much as "an hair of their head singed" (Daniel 3:27).

SEPTEMBER 22 | Read Daniel 5–6

5:1–12 Belshazzar, successor of Nebuchadnezzar as king of Babylonia, is partying with friends and officials of his administration. In the midst of the merrymaking, a hand appears and writes some words on the wall. None of his wise men or magicians can make sense of the message.

5:13–31 Called to interpret the handwriting, Daniel gives Belshazzar the bad news: The days of the Babylonian kingdom are numbered. God will deliver the nation into the hands of the Medes and Persians. That very night Belshazzar is killed, and the glory days of Babylonia come to an end.

6:1–13 Daniel wins the favor of the new Persian regime and the victorious king, Darius, who names him to a high position in his administration. But Daniel has some political enemies, and they conspire to have him killed. They persuade King Darius to issue a decree making it unlawful for anyone to pray to any god except the king. Daniel continues his practice of praying to God as he has always done.

6:14–28 Because of his disobedience, Daniel is thrown into a den of lions. The next day Darius finds him standing among the lions unharmed because God sent an angel to protect him. The king issues an order for all the people to "tremble and fear before the God of Daniel" (v. 26).

Belshazzar The son or grandson of Nebuchadnezzar and the last king of the Babylonian Empire (Dan. 5:1–2). Daniel interpreted a mysterious handwriting on the wall for Belshazzar as a prediction of doom for the Babylonians (Dan. 5:17). That night, Belshazzar was killed when the Persians captured Babylonia (Dan. 5:30–31).

Unchangeable Persian Laws *O king, establish the decree. . .that it be not changed, according to the law of the Medes and Persians, which altereth not* (Dan. 6:8).

The enemies of Daniel in Persia asked King Darius to issue a law against worshiping any god other than the king himself. They knew this would trap Daniel, since he would refuse to bow down to any god other than the supreme Lord of the universe. The ancient Medes and Persians considered their laws infallible and irreversible. Once a decree was ordered by the king, it could not be changed or wiped off the books. For example, the Persian law authorizing the extermination of the Jews in Esther's time was not canceled. But the king issued another decree warning the Jews about the death warrant and authorizing them to act in self-defense against their enemies (Esther 8:5–11).

SEPTEMBER 23 | Read Daniel 7–9

7:1–28 Daniel has a vision that foretells events of the future. He sees four beasts that represent four future earthly kings. The fourth beast will triumph over all the nations of the earth. A horn on the fourth beast represents a ruler who will oppose God and persecute those who follow the Lord. But eventually God's eternal kingdom will be established.

8:1–27 Daniel has a vision of a ram and a goat. The ram, representing the kingdoms of Media and Persia, is defeated by a goat. This foretells the rise of Alexander the Great and the Greek Empire that he would establish. At Alexander's death, his empire would be divided among his generals: "Four kingdoms shall stand up out of the nation" (v. 22).

9:1–19 Daniel realizes that the seventy-year captivity of the Jewish people by the Babylonians and Persians is almost over (Jer. 29:10). So he prays a beautiful prayer of intercession and deliverance for his people.

9:20–27 These verses contain the famous "seventy weeks" prophecy of Daniel, revealed to him by the angel Gabriel. Most interpreters believe these seventy weeks should be interpreted as seventy times seven years—or a period of 490 years. Thus, this prophecy refers to the coming of the Messiah, Jesus Christ, about 490 years from the time when the Jews were allowed to return to Jerusalem from the exile to resettle their homeland.

Ancient of Days A title for God used by the prophet Daniel to show His ruling authority over the world empires of his day (Dan. 7:9–22). *Ancient One*: NRSV.

Abomination of Desolation The action of Antiochus Epiphanes in sacrificing a pig in the Jewish temple about 165 BC. This despised act of the Syrian ruler is considered fulfillment of Daniel's prophecy (Dan. 9:24–27; Matt. 24:15).

SEPTEMBER 24 | Read Daniel 10–12

10:1–11:45 This vision is revealed to Daniel after a period of fasting and prayer while he stands by the Hiddekel (Tigris) River in Persia. Strengthened by an angel after his period of fasting, Daniel falls into a trance and receives a revelation of events of the future. He foresees a struggle between a "king of the south" and a "king of the north." Many interpreters believe this refers to the battle for supremacy between two generals of Alexander the Great after Alexander's death about 300 years after Daniel's time.

12:1–13 An angel reveals to Daniel that the Jewish people can expect a period of tribulation in the future. But those who persevere will experience joy and a new beginning in the Lord. Even Daniel is not given perfect understanding of events that will happen in the end-time (vv. 8–9). But he is assured of God's eternal presence as he waits for Him to act: "Go thou thy way till the end be: for thou shalt rest, and stand in thy lot at the end of the days" (v. 13).

Michael An archangel who was thought to serve as a prince and guardian over the nation of Israel (Dan.10:21; 12:1).

Alexander the Great Greek ruler and world conqueror. He took the throne in 336 BC and extended his empire from Greece around the Mediterranean Sea to Egypt and then to India. Although he is not mentioned by name in the Bible, Alexander is perhaps the "mighty king" of Dan. 11:3–4. (See also Dan. 7:6; 8:21.)

Ptolemy The title of Greek kings who ruled throughout Egypt and Palestine from about 323 to 30 BC. These kings are possibly referred to in Daniel's visions (see Dan. 11:5–30). Their kingdom eventually fell to the Romans.

BOOKS OF THE MINOR PROPHETS

The last twelve books of the Old Testament are known as the minor prophets. This does not mean they are of minor importance. The title refers to the short length of the books and the fact that they were placed after the major prophets in the compilation of the Old Testament.

If all the minor prophets were compiled into one book, their total length would be about equal to that of the book of Isaiah. Though brief, the books and the prophets who wrote them delivered God's powerful message to several different situations over a period of about 400 years.

Amos and Hosea preached to the Northern Kingdom before that nation fell to the Assyrians in 722 BC. Six of the minor prophets—Obadiah, Joel, Micah, Nahum, Zephaniah, and Habakkuk—ministered in the Southern Kingdom. God sent the prophet Jonah to preach judgment and repentance to the pagan nation of Assyria. Three of these prophets—Haggai, Zechariah, and Malachi—encouraged and challenged the Israelites after they returned to their homeland following the exile among the Babylonians and Persians.

SEPTEMBER 25 | Read Hosea 1–5

1:1–11 God calls Hosea to deliver His message to the wayward nation of Israel (Northern Kingdom). At God's command, Hosea marries a prostitute named Gomer. She bears three children, and they are given symbolic names that represent God's intention to punish Israel.

2:1–13 Just as Gomer had committed adultery before she married Hosea, so has Israel been guilty of spiritual adultery in God's sight (Isa. 3:1–25). The people have worshiped false gods and have been unfaithful to the one true God. He will judge them for these rebellious acts.

2:14–23 After God has punished and disciplined His people, He promises to restore them to His favor. His kindness and mercy will be showered upon them once again.

3:1–5 Hosea's wife, Gomer, apparently returns to her life as a prostitute and is sold as a slave. God directs Hosea to buy her back. This shows God's redemptive love. For a while, the people of Israel will also lose their freedom to an enemy nation as punishment for their sin. But God will eventually redeem them and restore them as His people.

4:1–19 God gives a detailed list of the sins that Israel has committed. These include killing, stealing, lying, and committing adultery. But their greatest sin is worshiping false gods.

5:1–15 Even the priests have turned away from following God and are leading the people astray. Hosea also declares that the nation of Judah is just as guilty as Israel of forsaking the Lord and going its own way (v. 10).

. . . .

Hosea A prophet who delivered God's message of judgment to the Northern Kingdom in the years shortly before this nation fell to the Assyrians in 722 BC. Author of the book of Hosea, he is best known for his marriage to a prostitute in obedience of God's command (Hosea 1:2–9). *Osee*: Rom. 9:25.

Ishi A symbolic name meaning "my husband" to be given to God when the Israelites returned to Him (Hosea 2:16–17). Ishi was to be used instead of Baali because the name Baal was associated with a pagan god.

. . . .

Indulgent Worship *The children of Israel. . .look to other gods, and love flagons of wine [sacred raisin cakes, NIV]* (Hosea 3:1).

The prophet Hosea condemned the people of the Northern Kingdom for their worship of Baal, a pagan fertility god. He described them as indulgent worshippers who loved "flagons of wine." The Hebrew word rendered as "flagons of wine" by the KJV is translated as "sacred raisin cakes" by the NIV. This is probably a more accurate translation, since cakes made of raisins, or dried grapes, were considered a delicacy in Bible times. They may have been eaten in connection with immoral worship ceremonies at the altars of Baal.

SEPTEMBER 26 | Read Hosea 6–10

6:1–7:16 Some of the people of Israel have been convicted of their sin and have turned back to God. But their repentance was a sham, and they have fallen right back into idolatry. Hosea declares that their goodness "is as a morning cloud, and as the early dew it goeth away" (6:4).

8:1–14 The nation of Israel will experience God's law of sowing and reaping. They will reap God's terrible punishment for the sins they have sown: "They have sown the wind, and they shall reap the whirlwind" (v. 7).

9:1–10:15 Hosea announces the specific punishment that God has in store for Israel. Because of their idolatry, the people will be carried away as captives by the Assyrians (10:6; see 2 Kings 18:9–12).

. . . .

Assyria An ancient kingdom between the Tigris and Euphrates rivers that became the dominant power in the ancient world from about 900 to 700 BC. The aggressive and warlike Assyrians were known for their cruelty in warfare, often cutting off their victims' hands or heads and impaling them on stakes. For this cruelty and their pagan worship, they were soundly condemned by the OT prophets (Isa. 10:5; Ezek. 16:28; Hosea 8:9). The region that developed into Assyria was originally settled by the hunter Nimrod, a descendant of Noah (Gen. 10:8–12). An early name for Assyria was *Asshur,* after a son of Shem who was connected with their early history (Gen. 10:11). About 722 BC King Shalmaneser of Assyria overthrew the Northern Kingdom of Israel, enslaved many of its inhabitants, and resettled the region with foreigners (2 Kings 18:10–11). Several years later Sennacherib invaded Judah (2 Kings 18:13) and exacted tribute from King Hezekiah (2 Kings 18:14–16). *Assur:* Ezra 4:2.

. . . .

Sowing and Reaping in Hosea *They have sown the wind, and they shall reap the whirlwind* (Hosea 8:7).

The prophet Hosea's metaphor of sowing the wind and reaping the whirlwind (Hosea 8:7) would have been well understood in the agricultural society of his day. A farmer expects a few planted seeds to grow into an abundant crop. Likewise, sin will yield a crop of wickedness. The apostle Paul may have had this passage from Hosea in mind when he warned the Galatian believers, "Whatsoever a man soweth, that shall he also reap" (Gal. 6:7).

SEPTEMBER 27 | Read Hosea 11–14

11:1–12 This chapter shows God's everlasting love for His people. He compares the nation of Israel to a little child whom He guided and taught as He led them out of slavery in Egypt. Now Assyria will rule over them for a time, but the Lord will eventually restore His people through His grace.

`12:1–13:16` These chapters return to the theme of God's judgment against Israel because of the people's worship of false gods. The prophet declares that Samaria (capital city of Israel) "shall become desolate; for she hath rebelled against her God" (13:16).

`14:1–9` Hosea closes his book with a plea for Israel to repent and return to the Lord before it is too late. The path to forgiveness and restoration is open if the people will turn from their rebellious ways.

`Ephraim` A name often used symbolically for the nation of Israel (Hosea 11:12; 12:1).

`Relief from the Yoke` *I [God] drew them [Israelites] with cords of a man, with bands of love: and I was to them as they that take off the yoke on their jaws* (Hosea 11:4).

In this verse Hosea portrays the love of God for His special people, the Israelites. Although they had rebelled against Him again and again, He kept pulling them back into His fellowship with "bands of love." Hosea also compared the love of God to relief given to oxen when they were wearing heavy wooden yokes while working in the fields. These yokes had to be lifted up by their masters to enable the animals to lower their heads so they could eat or drink. God is the great "yoke lifter" who shows mercy and love to His people.

SEPTEMBER 28 | Read Joel

`1:1–20` The land of Judah is invaded by a huge swarm of locusts. The flying insects, similar to grasshoppers, destroy all the vegetation in their path, even stripping leaves and bark from the trees (Exod. 10:12–15). With their crops destroyed, the people face the prospect of starvation. Joel calls on the priests to proclaim a fast and to gather the people to God's house for prayer and repentance.

`2:1–11` The prophet declares that this locust plague is only a shadow of what the approaching "day of the LORD" (v. 1) will be like. This time of God's judgment and punishment will be "a day of darkness and of gloominess, a day of clouds and of thick darkness" (v. 2; see Jer. 46:10).

`2:12–17` But it is not too late for Judah to repent. Joel calls on the people to forsake their sinful ways and turn to the Lord.

`2:18–27` In response to the repentance of His people, God will withhold His judgment and give them many blessings instead. He will send the rains and give them an abundant harvest, more than enough to replace the crops devastated by the locusts.

`2:28–32` Even more abundant are the spiritual blessings that God will send upon His people if they remain faithful to Him. He promises to send His Spirit "upon all flesh" (v. 28)—not just on prophets and priests but on ordinary people. The apostle

Peter quoted this passage on the day of Pentecost to show that God had fulfilled this promise by sending His Spirit to empower the early Christian believers (Acts 2:16–21).

3:1–21 Joel looks into the future to the day of messianic blessing for the people of God. But this will also be a day of judgment for the pagan nations as well as individuals who have refused to acknowledge Jesus as Savior and Lord: "Multitudes, multitudes in the valley of decision: for the day of the LORD is near in the valley of decision" (v. 14).

....

Joel A prophet of Judah in the days of King Uzziah and author of the OT book that bears his name. He predicted the outpouring of God's Spirit at Pentecost (Joel 2:28–32; Acts 2:16–21), proclaimed salvation through Christ (Joel 2:32), sounded the note of God's universal judgment (Joel 3:1–16), and pictured the eternal age with blessings for God's people (3:17–21).

Former Rain The first rain of the growing season, essential for the germination of seed and the growth of young plants (Joel 2:23). *Autumn rain*: NIV; *early rain*: NRSV.

Valley of Jehoshaphat A place where God will judge the nations in the end-time, according to the prophet Joel (Joel 3:2–14). This site is believed to be part of the Kidron Valley between Jerusalem and the Mount of Olives. The name may refer to a symbolic "valley of decision," where God will judge all nations.

....

Destruction by Locusts *That which the palmerworm hath left hath the locust eaten; and that which the locust hath left hath the cankerworm eaten; and that which the cankerworm hath left hath the caterpiller eaten* (Joel 1:4).

A locust plague, such as the one described by Joel in this verse, was one of the worst disasters that could happen in the agricultural society of Bible times. Millions of these insects, similar to grasshoppers, would descend on the land and devour the crops. Scarcity of food—and even widespread starvation—could follow. The eighth plague that God sent against the Egyptians to convince Pharaoh to release the Hebrew slaves was a swarm of locusts (Exod. 10:12–15). Joel's account of a swarm of locusts in his time details the four stages in the development of this destructive insect: (1) a hatchling emerges from the egg (palmerworm); (2) it develops wings and begins to fly (locust); (3) it becomes strong enough to begin eating vegetation (cankerworm); and (4) as a fully grown adult, it flies in a swarm with millions of others to do its most destructive work (caterpiller).

SEPTEMBER 29 | Read Amos 1–5

1:1–2 Amos is from the village of Tekoa in Judah (Southern Kingdom). But he is sent to proclaim God's judgment against Israel (Northern Kingdom).

1:3–2:5 God's judgment is first pronounced against the cities and nations surrounding Israel: Damascus (1:3–5); Gaza (1:6–8); Tyrus, or Tyre (1:9–10); Edom (1:11–12); Ammon (1:13–15); Moab (2:1–3); and Judah (2:4–5).

2:6–16 God lists the sins for which the nation of Israel will be punished. These include worshiping idols instead of the one true God, cheating the poor, and persecuting the prophets whom God sends as His spokesmen.

3:1–15 The Lord reminds the citizens of Israel that He brought them out of Egypt when they were a slave people and made them into a nation that belongs to Him (Exod. 12:33–42). But He will just as surely punish them unless they turn from their rebellious ways.

4:1–3 Amos refers to the wives of the wealthy Israelites as "kine [cows] of Bashan" (v. 1). They are just as guilty as their husbands because they encourage the men to oppress the poor to support their extravagant lifestyle.

4:4–13 God has punished Israel for its sin and extravagance in many different ways. But these reprimands have failed to turn the people back to Him.

5:1–17 Amos issues a lament against Israel, as if the nation has already fallen to a foreign oppressor and experienced God's judgment. But he also declares that the people can avoid this fate if they will turn to God: "Seek the LORD, and ye shall live" (v. 6).

5:18–27 Commitment to the Lord must go deeper than worship rituals such as bringing offerings to the altar and singing songs of praise. God requires genuine repentance and righteous living from His people: "Let judgment run down as waters, and righteousness as a mighty stream" (v. 24; see Isa. 58).

. . . .

Amos A herdsman from Tekoa in the Southern Kingdom (Judah) who prophesied against the Northern Kingdom (Israel) during the tenure of King Jeroboam II (Amos 1:1; 7:14–15). Known as the great "prophet of righteousness" of the OT, he condemned the rich and indulgent for oppressing the poor (Amos 8:4–6) and foretold Israel's collapse and captivity by Assyria (Amos 7:17). Amos was a contemporary of the prophets Isaiah and Hosea.

Seven Stars A brilliant cluster of stars named for the seven daughters of Atlas and Pleione in Greek mythology (Amos 5:8). *Pleiades*: NIV, NRSV.

. . . .

Bad News for the Wealthy *They [wealthy class of Israel] sold the righteous for silver, and the poor for a pair of shoes* (Amos 2:6).

Two of God's highest expectations for His people, the Israelites, were that they would practice righteousness and show compassion toward the poor. In this verse Amos charged the wealthy class of Israel—the Northern Kingdom—with violating both these commands. They were so calloused toward righteousness that they thought they could buy and sell it like any other commodity. Rather than treating the poor with fairness and justice, they were selling them into slavery because they could not pay their debts. Sometimes these debts were no more than the minor sum required to buy a cheap pair of sandals! Amos declared that God would judge the wealthy for such greed and lack of compassion.

SEPTEMBER 30 | Read Amos 6–9; Obadiah

Amos

6:1–14 Amos makes it clear what will happen to Israel if the people do not turn from their sinful ways. They will be taken away as captives into a foreign land.

7:1–9 Amos sees three visions of judgment promised by the Lord against Israel: grasshoppers (vv. 1–3), fire (vv. 4–6), and a plumb line (vv. 7–9). The plumb line is a dramatic demonstration that Israel does not measure up to God's standards.

7:10–17 Amaziah the priest rejects Amos's message and tells him to go back to Judah. Amos pronounces God's judgment against Amaziah because he refuses to hear the word of the Lord.

8:1–14 Amos sees a vision of a basket of ripe fruit. This shows that Israel is ready for God's judgment, just as ripe fruit is ready to eat.

9:1–15 God's judgment falls on Israel. Although the people try to hide, He hunts them down. But God's grace is also evident in the midst of His judgment. He promises to preserve a faithful remnant of people who will eventually return to their homeland.

Obadiah

1 The Lord gives Obadiah the prophet a message of judgment that he is to speak against the nation of Edom.

2–5 God condemns the pride and vanity of Edom. The Edomites considered themselves invincible in their fortress cities—particularly the capital of Sela. But the Lord makes it clear through Obadiah that He will bring them down (Ezek. 25:12–14).

6–9 References to Esau in these verses show the ancestry of the Edomites. They were descendants of Esau, the twin brother of Jacob (Gen. 25:9–28). The problems between the nations of Israel and Edom had begun with the conflict between these two brothers many centuries before Obadiah's time (Gen. 25:19–28; 27:1–41).

10–16 The Lord will use an enemy nation to defeat Edom. Such punishment is deserved because of Edom's treatment of Judah. The Edomites stood by when foreigners attacked Jerusalem. They even carried away spoils from the city and prevented Jewish fugitives from fleeing to safety.

17–21 In contrast to the humiliation and defeat of Edom, God will bless His people Israel. After the exile in Babylon, they will return and possess the land that God has promised to Abraham and his descendants.

Obadiah A prophet of Judah and author of the OT book that bears his name (Obad. 1). He probably lived after the destruction of Jerusalem in 587 BC. Nothing more is known about him.

....

Amos and Sycomore Figs *I [Amos] was no prophet, neither was I a prophet's son; but I was an herdman, and a gatherer of sycomore fruit* (Amos 7:14).

Amos was a lowly shepherd from the tiny village of Tekoa (Amos 1:1) in Judah (Southern Kingdom). But he was called to declare God's judgment against the rich people of the neighboring nation, Israel (Northern Kingdom). This verse shows that he did not claim to be a learned and sophisticated messenger. His only credential was his call from the Lord. The "sycomore fruit" that Amos mentioned was a type of wild fig that grew in his native Judah. These figs were inferior in quality to the domesticated figs that are mentioned several times in the Bible (Num. 13:23; 1 Sam. 25:18; Mark 11:12–21). Only the poorest people of the land grew and ate sycamore figs.

Brought Low by the Lord *The pride of thine heart hath deceived thee [Edom], thou that dwellest in the clefts of the rock, whose habitation is high; that saith in his heart, Who shall bring me down to the ground?* (Obad. 1:3).

The prophet Obadiah delivered his brief prophecy against the Edomites, ancient enemies of the Israelites. In 587 BC, the people of Edom had joined in the looting of the city of Jerusalem when it was ransacked by the Babylonian army. Edomite cities were built on the high cliffs and crags of the mountains around the Dead Sea. They thought they were invincible in these strongholds. But Obadiah declared that they would be brought low by the Lord because of their mistreatment of His people.

OCTOBER 1 | Read Jonah

1:1–3 God calls Jonah to pronounce judgment against Nineveh, capital city of the Assyrian Empire. But Jonah runs from God and catches a ship bound for Tarshish in the opposite direction from Nineveh.

1:4–16 A violent storm strikes the ship. The superstitious crew casts lots to determine who is responsible for the storm. The lot falls on Jonah, who admits he is running from God's call. He advises the sailors to toss him overboard to appease the Lord's anger.

1:17 God saves Jonah by sending a great fish to swallow him and keeping him alive for three days in the stomach of the fish (Matt. 12:40).

2:1–10 Jonah prays an eloquent prayer for deliverance. The Lord hears his prayer and has him ejected from the fish unharmed and placed on the shore.

3:1–4 The Lord calls on Jonah again to proclaim His message to the city of Nineveh. This time Jonah obeys and delivers God's message of judgment against the Ninevites (Luke 11:32).

3:5–10 The citizens of Nineveh repent of their wicked ways and turn to the Lord in repentance. God withholds the disaster He had threatened against the city.

4:1–3 Jonah gets angry because the Lord extends mercy and forgiveness to the Ninevites. In self-pity, he asks God to take his life.

4:4–8 Jonah builds a hut on the eastern side of Nineveh. Here he waits to see what will happen to the city. God causes a vine to grow up over his head to shelter him from the sun and to cool his anger. Then the Lord causes the vine to die, and Jonah is miserable in the sun and hot wind. He again wallows in self-pity and wishes he were dead.

4:9–11 God condemns Jonah because he is more concerned about a vine than he is about the people of the city of Nineveh. He reminds Jonah that He is a merciful and forgiving God who loves all people, even the pagan Assyrians.

Jonah An OT prophet who was swallowed by a "great fish" while fleeing from God's call to preach to the pagan citizens of Nineveh in Assyria (Jon. 1:17). In predicting His death and resurrection, Jesus referred to Jonah's experience (Luke 11:30; *Jonas*).

Nineveh The capital of Assyria on the Tigris River where the prophet Jonah preached God's message of judgment. Founded by Asshur, a son of Shem, Nineveh reached the height of wealth and splendor during Jonah's time (Jon. 3:3). It was taken by the Medes about 750 BC and destroyed by the Medes and Babylonians about 606 BC. *Nineve*: Luke 11:32.

Superstitious Sailors *Come, and let us [sailors on Jonah's ship] cast lots, that we may know for whose cause this evil is upon us* (Jon. 1:7).

Sailors of ancient times tended to be very superstitious because of their constant exposure to the dangers of the sea. When a storm struck the ship in which Jonah was escaping from the call of the Lord, they assumed the pagan gods were punishing them because of their displeasure with one person on board. To find out who this person was, they cast lots—a custom similar to rolling dice or drawing straws in modern times. These lots may have been round stones or flat sticks of various lengths. Exactly what they looked like is not known. The casting of lots as a method of decision making is mentioned several times in the Bible (Lev. 16:8–10; Num. 33:54; Josh. 14:2; 1 Chron. 25:8–9; Acts 1:26).

OCTOBER 2 | Read Micah

1:1–16 God announces through the prophet Micah that He will judge the cities of Samaria and Jerusalem (v. 1). Jerusalem was the capital city of Judah (Southern Kingdom), while Samaria was the capital of Israel (Northern Kingdom). God plans to punish both nations because they have turned away from Him to worship false gods.

2:1–11 Micah condemns the wealthy people of Judah and Israel because they are cheating the poor. He accuses them of lying awake at night, making plans to strip the poor of their houses and fields. But God is also making plans. He intends to send disaster against the rich and proud.

2:12–13 Judah and Israel will be defeated by a foreign nation. But God will preserve a small group of people—a faithful remnant—who will remain loyal to Him. He will use this minority to rebuild His people.

3:1–4 Many of the problems of Judah and Israel can be traced to their political leaders. They have lost the ability to distinguish between good and evil, so they lead the people astray (Ezek. 11:3).

3:5–7 Even the prophets fail to follow the Lord. They are called to be the moral conscience of the people. But instead they are prophesying that good times will continue and that Judah and Israel have nothing to fear (Jer. 14).

3:8–12 The Lord repeats His promise of judgment against the two nations because of their widespread sin and corruption.

4:1–13 This chapter mixes the themes of judgment and blessing in reverse order. Judah will be defeated and carried into exile by the pagan nation of Babylonia (vv. 9–13; see 2 Kings 25:1–12). But after the exile is over, the Jewish people will return to their homeland (2 Chron. 36:22–23). They will enjoy an era of peace and prosperity. From Jerusalem, God will extend His witness and influence to all the nations (vv. 1–8).

5:1–15 This chapter foretells the defeat of Israel (Northern Kingdom) by the Assyrians. But in the midst of this prophecy is another look into the future that has universal implications. A Deliverer or "ruler in Israel" (v. 2) will be born in Bethlehem. This messianic prophecy was fulfilled with the birth of Jesus about 700 years after Micah's time (Luke 2:1–7).

6:1–16 The Lord rehearses all the mighty deeds He has performed for His people. What does He expect in return? Not burnt offerings, fasting, and empty rituals—but obedience to His commands and commitment to His principles of love and justice: "What doth the LORD require of thee, but to do justly, and to love mercy, and to walk humbly with thy God?" (v. 8).

7:1–20 Micah mourns ("Woe is me!" v. 1) when he reviews the sins of Judah and Israel. He wonders if there is one righteous person left in the land. This drives him to place his trust in the holy and righteous God. He is also a God of justice and forgiveness. After His people receive their deserved punishment, He will shower them with mercy and love: "He will have compassion upon us; he will subdue our iniquities; and thou wilt cast all their sins into the depths of the sea" (v. 19).

Micah A prophet of the OT, a contemporary of Isaiah, whose ministry paralleled the reigns of kings Jotham, Ahaz, and Hezekiah from about 750 to 687 BC (Mic. 1:1). A stern prophet of judgment, he denounced the social injustices of his time (Mic. 2:1–3).

Sitting in the Shade *They shall sit every man under his vine and under his fig tree; and none shall make them afraid* (Mic. 4:4).

Micah used these word pictures to portray the future for God's people. After the coming of the Messiah, they would enjoy peace and prosperity, symbolized by resting in the shade. In the hot, dry climate of Palestine, people often escaped from the sun's oppressive heat by sitting under a grapevine or fig tree. Its thick branches and broad leaves made the fig tree an ideal shade. When Philip found Nathanael and brought him to Jesus, Nathanael was sitting under a fig tree. He was probably resting in its shade and meditating on God's Word (John 1:45–51).

OCTOBER 3 | Read Nahum; Habakkuk

Nahum

1:1 The prophet Nahum receives a message of judgment from God. This message is to be proclaimed against Nineveh, capital of the Assyrian Empire.

1:2–8 Nahum paints a graphic picture of a powerful God who will judge the pagan city of Nineveh. But at the same time, those who serve Him have nothing to fear: "The LORD is good, a strong hold in the day of trouble" (v. 7).

1:9–15 God will destroy the idols and images of the pagan Assyrian religious system. But He will restore the nation of Judah and its system of worship of the one true God.

2:1–13 This chapter describes Nineveh under siege as God's judgment falls upon the city. Once known as "the dwelling of the lions" (v. 11), Nineveh is now weak and helpless as it cowers before its enemies. Just as Assyria had once robbed and looted other nations, now it will be stripped of its treasures.

3:1 Nahum declares, "Woe to the bloody city!" Assyria was known for its violence and cruelty in warfare. They disabled captive enemy soldiers by cutting off their hands. Rival political leaders were often impaled on stakes. Now these acts of cruelty will be carried out against the Assyrians.

3:2–19 Nahum continues his description of the defeat of Nineveh. Its streets will be littered with corpses, and it will be ransacked and burned. Not a single person will mourn the fall of Nineveh, because everyone has felt the effects of its evil and wickedness during its glory days.

Habakkuk

1:1–4 Habakkuk begins his book not with a declaration of the Word of God to others but with a question directed to God Himself. The prophet wants to know why God allows His people, the nation of Judah, to continue committing sin without subjecting them to judgment.

1:5–11 The Lord assures Habakkuk that He does intend to hold His people accountable for their wrongdoing. Even now He is raising up an enemy nation, the Chaldeans (Babylonians), who will serve as His instrument of punishment against the people of Judah. When He does judge His people, it will be harsh and effective. The Babylonians are a "bitter and hasty nation" (v. 6) known to be "terrible and dreadful" (v. 7).

1:12–2:1 The Lord's answer presents Habakkuk with another dilemma. The Babylonians are unrighteous people who worship pagan gods. Are they not more evil and wicked than those whom God will send them against? How can God use them to carry out His will? The prophet climbs upon a tower to wait for God's answer to this question.

2:2–20 God honors Habakkuk's question with a forthright answer. He is using the Babylonians not because of who they are or are not but because He can work His sovereign will as He desires. After He finishes with the Babylonians, He will also judge them for their evil ways. The Lord ends His answer to the prophet with a gentle rebuke that shows He does not have to justify His actions to anyone: "The LORD is in his holy temple: let all the earth keep silence before him" (v. 20; see Job 42:1–6).

3:1–19 In a beautiful prayer of submission, Habakkuk accepts the judgment of God against His people and the method He will use to bring it about. Praising God for His wonderful works, he declares, "I will rejoice in the LORD, I will joy in the God of my salvation" (v. 18).

· ·

Nahum A prophet of Judah from Elkosh who prophesied against Nineveh before 612 BC, probably during the reign of King Hezekiah (Nah. 1:1, 8, 13); author of the book of Nahum.

Hind A female deer. The word is used symbolically to show spiritual resilience (Hab. 3:19; Ps. 18:33).

Habakkuk A prophet of Judah who was probably a contemporary of Jeremiah; the author of the book that bears his name (Hab. 1:1; 3:1).

· ·

Assyrian Terror *The shield of his mighty men is made red, the valiant men are in scarlet: the chariots shall be with flaming torches in the day of his preparation* (Nah. 2:3).

Nahum's description of Assyrian warriors and their battle gear shows why they struck terror in the hearts of those who faced them in battle. The uniforms of Assyrian soldiers were scarlet in color, and they carried shields painted red, or perhaps overlaid with copper. They may have used these colors to make the blood from their wounds hard to see. In hand-to-hand combat, they wanted to give no sign that would infuse the enemy with hope and courage. The "flaming torches" on their war chariots may have been whirling blades on the axles designed to damage and immobilize the wheels of enemy chariots. Or this could refer to the weapons in their chariots that flashed in the sunlight, giving the appearance of burning torches. Assyria was noted for its cruelty in warfare. Their warriors would cut off the feet and hands of captives as a terror tactic to intimidate nations into surrendering to their rule.

OCTOBER 4 | Read Zephaniah; Haggai

Zephaniah

1:1 During the days of King Josiah of Judah, God calls the prophet Zephaniah to deliver His message of judgment.

1:2–18 Judah has turned away from the Lord and is worshiping false gods. Punishment for this serious sin will come upon Judah on the great day of the Lord. This will be "a day of trouble and distress, a day of wasteness and desolation. . .a day of clouds and thick darkness" (v. 15). No one in Judah will escape this time of judgment.

2:1–3 But even while preaching God's coming judgment, Zephaniah holds out hope. He urges the people of Judah to seek the Lord and follow His commands. Those who do so may possibly "be hid in the day of the Lord's anger" (v. 3).

2:4–15 God's wrath will extend beyond the land of Judah to the surrounding pagan nations. He will also punish the Philistines (vv. 4–7), the Moabites (vv. 8–11), the Ethiopians (v. 12), and the Assyrians (vv. 13–15).

3:1–7 As the capital city of Judah, Jerusalem will suffer the same fate as the rest of the nation. Because it has been polluted through worship of false gods, it will fall to foreign oppressors (2 Kings 25:1–12).

3:8–20 Although God is angered by Judah's idolatry, He has not given up on His people. He will preserve a faithful remnant who will remain loyal to Him. God will use them to resettle the land and bear witness of Him to others when they return from their time of captivity in a foreign land.

Haggai

1:1–11 The Lord commands the prophet Haggai to address the people who have returned to Jerusalem after the exile in Babylon (2 Chron. 36:22–23). He is to challenge them to resume the task of rebuilding the temple. Haggai declares that they are suffering hard times because they have not rebuilt God's house as a place of worship.

1:12–15 The people respond to Haggai's challenge by beginning the work. The prophet delivers God's promise that He will be with them during the reconstruction project.

2:1–9 God realizes some of the people will be discouraged because the rebuilt temple will not be as large or as beautiful as the original temple. So Haggai encourages the people not to make such comparisons. What really matters is whether the temple brings glory and honor to God. The Lord promises to fill it with His presence so "the glory of this latter house shall be greater than of the former" (v. 9).

2:10–19 Haggai declares to the priests that a defiled object cannot be made clean through contact with a holy object. In the same way, the completed temple will have no magical qualities. The people should not think they will be made clean through contact with the temple. Holiness comes through devoting oneself to God and following His commands.

2:20–23 Haggai encourages Zerubbabel, a Jewish leader who has been appointed governor of Judah by the Persians (Hag. 1:1). God makes it clear that Zerubbabel has been placed in this important position for a good reason. He will use the governor to bring many blessings to His people.

⋯⋯⋯⋯⋯⋯⋯⋯⋯⋯⋯⋯⋯⋯⋯⋯⋯⋯⋯⋯⋯⋯⋯⋯⋯⋯⋯⋯⋯⋯⋯

Zephaniah A priest and friend of Jeremiah and author of the OT book that bears his name. Zephaniah often served as a messenger between Jeremiah and King Zedekiah of Judah (Jer. 21:1–2). After Jerusalem fell, Zephaniah was killed by the Babylonians (Jer. 52:24–27).

Desire of All Nations A title for the coming Messiah that emphasizes His universal rule and power (Hag. 2:6–7). *Desired of all nations*: NIV; *treasure of all nations*: NRSV.

⋯⋯⋯⋯⋯⋯⋯⋯⋯⋯⋯⋯⋯⋯⋯⋯⋯⋯⋯⋯⋯⋯⋯⋯⋯⋯⋯⋯⋯⋯⋯

Thirty Vessels Short *When one came to the pressfat [wine vat, NIV] for to draw out fifty vessels out of the press, there were but twenty* (Hag. 2:16).

The Hebrew word rendered as "pressfat" by the KJV refers to a winepress or an olive press. These stone presses were used in Bible times to squeeze the oil out of olives for making fuels to burn in lamps or to press the juice out of grapes for making wine. What Haggai is saying is that God will give the people less harvest than they expect unless they get their priorities straight and resume the task of rebuilding the temple. We can't shirk our responsibility to God and expect Him to shower us with blessings.

Zerubbabel as a Signet Ring *In that day. . .will I [God] take thee, O Zerubbabel . . .and will make thee as a signet: for I have chosen thee, saith the LORD of hosts* (Hag. 2:23).

In ancient times a signet ring functioned much like a personal signature does today. A king or other high official would stamp an official document with the symbol on his ring to establish its legality and show that it was issued under his authority. God compared Zerubbabel, the Jewish governor of Jerusalem, to a signet ring. He had invested Zerubbabel with the highest honor and would use him as His representative to bring about His purposes in the city of Jerusalem.

When the pharaoh of Egypt appointed Joseph to a high position in his administration, he gave Joseph his signet ring to show that he had the authority to act in his behalf (Gen. 41:42).

OCTOBER 5 | Read Zechariah 1–4

1:1–6 Zechariah calls upon the people to repent and turn from their sinful ways back to the Lord (James 4:8).

1:7–17 The prophet has a vision of four horsemen, or watchmen, who report that "all the earth. . .is at rest" (v. 11). This is a sign that it is time for the Jewish exiles to return from Persia to their homeland to rebuild the city of Jerusalem (2 Chron. 36:22–23).

1:18–21 The four horns in Zechariah's vision in these verses represent the nations that had defeated Judah. These foreign nations have been defeated, so the return of Jewish exiles to Jerusalem can now proceed with no interference.

2:1–13 In this vision, Zechariah sees a man with a measuring line who is preparing to measure the wall of Jerusalem. But this measurement is not necessary, since God will serve as the protector of the city: "I, saith the LORD, will be unto her a wall of fire" (v. 5).

3:1–10 The high priest Joshua is cleansed and restored to his office in this vision of Zechariah. This prepares the way for the coming of the Messiah, who is referred to as "the Branch" (v. 8; see also 6:9–15).

4:1–14 In this vision, Zechariah sees a golden candlestick, or lampstand, with an olive tree on the left side and another olive tree on the right side. The message of the vision is that God will provide the resources to enable Zerubbabel, the governor of Jerusalem, to complete the rebuilding of the temple (Hag. 2:20–23).

Month of Sebat *Upon the four and twentieth day of the eleventh month, which is the month Sebat [Shebat, NIV], in the second year of Darius* (Zech. 1:7).

Zechariah had eight visions that he recorded in his book. In this verse he tells us the exact month and day on which his first vision occurred. The Jewish month of Sebat closely parallels our month of February. Many scholars believe this vision of the prophet—a man on a red horse among the myrtle trees (1:8)—can be precisely dated at February 24, 519 BC, by using the phrase "the second year of Darius." We know from secular history that King Darius began his reign over Persia about 521 BC.

OCTOBER 6 | Read Zechariah 5–9

5:1–4 Zechariah's vision of the flying scroll ("roll," v. 1) represents God's curse against any person who steals from others or swears falsely.

5:5–11 The basket ("ephah," v. 6) in this vision represents the cleansing of the land of Judah. The sins of the people are in the basket, which is taken away to Babylonia.

6:1–8 Zechariah's vision of the four chariots is similar to his first vision (1:7–17). God is in control, and He exercises His sovereignty over the entire world.

6:9–15 A crown is placed on the head of Joshua the high priest. He symbolizes the promised Branch, or the Messiah (chap. 3).

7:1–8:23 These chapters address the question of fasting among God's people. Since the temple is being rebuilt, should the people continue to fast? God replies that He intends to bless His people and to turn their fasts into occasions of joy.

9:1–8 God declares that He will punish the pagan nations surrounding Judah because of their worship of false gods.

9:9–17 These verses describe the arrival of the long-promised messianic King, riding on a young donkey. This passage was fulfilled by Jesus when He made His triumphant entry into Jerusalem in this fashion (Matt. 21:5).

OCTOBER 7 | Read Zechariah 10–14

10:1–11:17 The earthly leaders of Judah have led the nation astray (Jer. 8). God promises that He will guide His people; they can count on Him to lead them with justice and mercy.

12:1–14 God empowers His people for a great battle against the nations, and victory is assured. The phrase "They shall look upon me whom they have pierced" (v. 10) has been interpreted as a reference to Christ and His suffering (John 19:37).

13:1–14:21 In the final days, the Lord will cleanse and bless Jerusalem and establish His eternal rule throughout the world.

Holiness and Horses *In that day shall there be upon the bells of the horses, HOLINESS UNTO THE LORD* (Zech. 14:20).

In this verse Zechariah foresees a future time when all the nations will acknowledge and worship the one true God. The praise of the Lord will be so widespread that even horses will have "HOLINESS UNTO THE LORD" inscribed on the bells on their harnesses. These are the same words embroidered on the hat worn by the high priest of Israel (Exod. 28:36).

It was customary among the nations of Bible times to hang bells on the harnesses of their warhorses. This gave them a regal, military appearance. The noise produced by the bells also may have conditioned the horses for the noise of battle.

OCTOBER 8 | Read Malachi

1:1–5 Malachi begins his message to the exiles who have returned to Jerusalem by assuring them of God's love. His love for Israel is evident because He allowed the Jewish exiles to return and resettle their land (2 Chron. 36:22–23). God continues to honor the covenant He made centuries ago with Abraham (Gen. 12:1–5). By contrast, the land of Edom has been destroyed and will not be reclaimed by the Edomites.

1:6–14 But God is displeased with the response of the people to His love. They have grown cold and casual in their devotion to Him. They are bringing sick and defective animals to offer as sacrifices rather than presenting the best from their flocks. This is a flagrant violation of His commands (Lev. 22:20).

2:1–9 Even the priests are neglecting their responsibilities. As spiritual leaders, they are supposed to be leading the people in the ways of the Lord. But they are actually leading people astray through their waywardness and neglect.

2:10–16 The spiritual condition of the people is reflected in their family problems. Many Israelite men have married women from the surrounding nations who worship pagan gods (Ezra 10:10–17). And some of the older men are divorcing the wives of their youth to marry younger pagan women. God is displeased with these practices.

2:17–3:5 The Lord declares that He is getting tired of the whining of the people about His apparent lack of judgment against the ungodly. He assures them that He is aware of the actions of the wicked and He will deal with them as they deserve when the time is right.

3:6–10 God declares that the people are guilty of withholding tithes and offerings that belong to Him. This is another example of their lack of commitment and spiritual zeal.

3:11–18 Apparently, some Israelites were complaining that their service to God had not been rewarded. God seemed to bless the unrighteous while bringing suffering upon the righteous. The Lord rebukes this pessimistic attitude. Those who truly belong to Him, He says, will "discern between the righteous and the wicked, between him that serveth God and him that serveth him not" (v. 18).

4:1–3 The coming day of the Lord, when God exercises His judgment, will have two different realities. To the wicked, it will be like a consuming hot oven. But those who belong to God will experience joy when they see "the Sun of righteousness arise with healing in his wings" (v. 2; see Joel 2:1–11).

4:4–6 These verses form a fitting conclusion not only to Malachi but to the entire OT. They look back to God's law that was revealed to Moses many centuries before. But they also look forward to the fulfillment of this law with the coming of Christ. Four hundred years after the end of Malachi, God sent one final prophet known as John the Baptist to prepare the way for the promised Messiah. Jesus identified John as the Elijah who is promised in verse 5 (Matt. 17:10–13).

Malachi An OT prophet and the author of the book that bears his name. His name means "my messenger" (Mal. 1:1). He lived after the Babylonian Exile and was probably a contemporary of the prophet Nehemiah.

Immutability An attribute of God's nature that refers to His unchangeableness (Mal. 3:6). The unchangeable nature of Christ assures us that God's mercy is constant (Heb. 13:8). God, who cannot lie, offers an anchor of hope for all believers, who are the "heirs of promise" (Heb. 6:17–19).

God's Book of Remembrance *A book of remembrance was written before him [God] for them that feared the Lord* (Mal. 3:16).

God promised through the prophet Malachi that He would write in a "book of remembrance" the names of all the people who honored and worshiped Him. This metaphor probably comes from the ancient Persian custom of keeping an official record of those who rendered special service to the king. King Ahasuerus of Persia was looking through such a book when he discovered that Mordecai the Jew had saved him from an assassination plot (Esther 6:1–2).

THE NEW TESTAMENT

The second grand division of the Bible is the New Testament. Unlike the Old Testament, which was written over a period of many centuries, the twenty-seven books of the New Testament were inspired by God and written down by human authors across a period of about sixty years.

The great event that brought the New Testament into being was the life and ministry of Jesus Christ. He fulfilled the promises that God made to His people in the Old Testament by establishing a new covenant (the word *testament* means "covenant") based on the spiritual principles of grace and forgiveness rather than the keeping of the law. This new covenant between God and His people was sealed with the atoning death of His own Son.

The four major divisions of the New Testament are:

1. the four Gospels, accounts of the life and ministry of Jesus
2. the Acts of the Apostles, a book of history that traces the growth of the early church after the death and resurrection of Jesus
3. the thirteen epistles, or letters, of the apostle Paul
4. the eight letters classified as general epistles, written by early church leaders other than Paul to various churches and individuals.

Additional information on each division follows.

THE GOSPELS

Jesus Christ is the cornerstone of the church and the Christian faith, so it is appropriate that the New Testament opens with not one account but four separate records of His life and ministry—the Gospels of Matthew, Mark, Luke, and John. These reports were written either by Jesus' apostles who witnessed His work firsthand (Matthew and John) or by persons who recorded the eyewitness testimony of those who had known Jesus in the flesh (Mark and Luke).

These Gospels are selective accounts rather than complete biographies of the life of Jesus. The Gospel writers focused on the final three years of Jesus' life when He conducted His teaching and healing ministry. Their purpose was to show how God revealed Himself supremely in the life of His Son. Even with their narrow three-year focus, they tell us only a few of the things He did. The apostle John declared in his Gospel: "There are also many other things which Jesus did, the which, if they should be written every one, I suppose that even the world itself could not contain the books that should be written" (John 21:25).

The Gospels of Matthew, Mark, and Luke are known as the Synoptic Gospels. This designation comes from the Greek word *synopsis*, which means "seeing together." There is a great deal of overlap and repetition among these three Gospels. They report many of the same events from the life of Jesus, using a similar chronology and even repeating the information almost word for word in many cases. Of course, each of these Gospels also contains material about Jesus not found in any other account.

In contrast to the Synoptic Gospels, the Gospel of John takes a unique approach to the life of Jesus. The apostle John does more than just tell us about the things that Jesus said and did. He goes beyond the obvious to give us the theological meaning behind His teachings and miracles.

We are fortunate to have four separate Gospel witnesses to the Jesus event. While they overlap and repeat one another at certain points, together they enrich and expand our understanding of who He was and what He did.

Note: Throughout the following summaries of the Gospels, **bold face cross references** indicate that you'll find additional information about particular events in the highlighted summaries.

OCTOBER 9 | Read Matthew 1–4

1:1–17 Matthew begins his Gospel by tracing Jesus' genealogy through forty-two generations from Abraham up to Joseph and Mary. (For a different genealogy of Jesus, see Luke 3:23–38.)

1:18–25 Joseph is disturbed when Mary becomes pregnant while they are betrothed to each other. But an angel assures him that this pregnancy is of divine origin. Joseph marries Mary, and they name their firstborn son Jesus.

2:1–12 Wise men from the east arrive in Jerusalem to worship the newborn "King of the Jews" (v. 2). They are sent to Bethlehem, where the scriptures predicted this King would be born (Mic. 5:2). In Bethlehem, the wise men present gifts of gold, frankincense, and myrrh to the young Jesus.

2:13–18 The jealous and paranoid King Herod of Judah slaughters all the male children under two years of age around Bethlehem in an attempt to kill the young Jesus. But Joseph is warned in a dream to take the boy and His mother to a safe place in the land of Egypt.

2:19–23 After Herod dies, Jesus and His family return to Judah. They settle in the city of Nazareth, the ancestral home of Mary and Joseph (parallel passage: **Luke 2:39–40**).

3:1–12 In the wilderness of Judea, the forerunner of Jesus, John the Baptist, begins preaching his message of repentance and the coming kingdom (parallel passages: **Mark 1:1–8; Luke 3:1–20**).

3:13–17 Jesus is baptized by John the Baptist in the Jordan River. God shows His approval by declaring, "This is my beloved Son, in whom I am well pleased" (v. 17) (parallel passages: **Mark 1:9–11; Luke 3:21–22**).

4:1–11 At the beginning of His public ministry, Jesus faces a series of temptations from Satan (parallel passages: **Mark 1:12–13; Luke 4:1–13**).

4:12–17 Leaving His hometown of Nazareth, Jesus moves to Capernaum in Galilee and launches His public ministry. He continues the message that John the Baptist, His forerunner, had been preaching: "Repent: for the kingdom of heaven is at hand" (v. 17) (parallel passages: **Mark 1:14–15; John 4:45**).

4:18–22 Jesus calls two different pairs of brothers—Peter and Andrew, James and John—away from their fishing nets to become His followers and disciples (parallel passages: **Mark 1:16–20; Luke 5:1–11**).

4:23–25 Jesus travels throughout the region of Galilee, preaching the Gospel of the kingdom of God and healing the sick. As His fame spreads, crowds flock to Him from as far away as Judea and the city of Jerusalem in southern Palestine (parallel passages: **Mark 1:35–39; Luke 4:42–44**).

Herod The name of several Roman rulers in Palestine during NT times: (1) Herod the Great (ruled 37 to 4 BC), in power when Jesus was born, who ordered the slaughter of innocent children (Matt. 2:3–16). Herod reconstructed the temple in Jerusalem and completed other ambitious building projects. (2) Herod Archelaus (ruled 4 BC to AD 6), the son and successor of Herod the Great as Roman ruler in Judea soon after the birth of Jesus (Matt. 2:22). (3) Herod Antipas (ruled 4 BC to AD 39), who granted his wife's request that John the Baptist be executed. This was the Herod who returned Jesus for sentencing by Pilate (Luke 23:6–12). (4) Herod Philip (ruled 4 BC to AD 33), ruler in extreme northern Galilee at the time when Jesus began His public ministry (Luke 3:1, 19–20). (5) Herod Agrippa I (ruled AD 37–44), who persecuted the apostles and executed James, leader of the Jerusalem church (Acts 12:1–23). (6) Herod Agrippa II (ruled AD 50–100), before whom Paul made his defense at Caesarea (Acts 25:13–26:32).

Capernaum A city on the northwestern shore of the Sea of Galilee that served as the headquarters for Jesus during His Galilean ministry (Matt. 9:1; Mark 2:1). Capernaum was the home of His disciples Matthew (Matt. 9:9), Simon Peter, Andrew, James, and John (Mark 1:21–29).

Winnowing The process of separating chaff or straw from the grains of wheat by beating the stalks and throwing them into the air; symbolically, to rid oneself of sin or worldly desire (Matt. 3:12).

Decapolis A Roman province or district with a large Greek population that was situated mostly on the eastern side of the Jordan River in northern Palestine (Matt. 4:25).

Joseph and Mary's Betrothal *When as his mother Mary was espoused [pledged to be married, NIV] to Joseph, before they came together, she was found with child of the Holy Ghost* (Matt. 1:18).

In Bible times a marriage was arranged through a legal agreement between the parents of the groom and the bride. The groom's parents selected a woman for their son to marry, then paid the bride's parents a dowry, or bride price, to compensate them for the loss of her services as a daughter. The period between the time of this legal agreement and the actual marriage of the couple was known as the betrothal. The future groom and bride were espoused or pledged to each other during this time in a formal agreement that was as legally binding as marriage itself. The betrothal could be broken only by a legal proceeding similar to a divorce. It was during the time of her betrothal to Joseph that Mary discovered she was pregnant. This was certainly grounds for Joseph and his family to dissolve their marriage agreement with Mary and her parents. But Joseph was informed by an angel that Mary's pregnancy was due to the miraculous action of the Holy Spirit. This child from her womb would be the Messiah, the Son of God, who would "save his people from their sins" (Matt. 1:21). Joseph believed this message from the Lord, and he went forward with his plans to take Mary as his wife (Matt. 1:24).

OCTOBER 10 | Read Matthew 5–7

`5:1–7:29` Jesus delivers His famous Sermon on the Mount to His followers. It describes the type of behavior expected of those who are true citizens of the kingdom of God. Jesus covers several distinctive themes in these teachings: (1) The Beatitudes (5:3–12). The word *blessed*, meaning "happy," describes the rewards in store for those who live as citizens of God's kingdom. (2) Salt and light (5:13–16). Christian living by citizens of God's kingdom bears a positive witness in the world. (3) Authentic righteousness (5:17–48). We must go beyond rituals and external appearances and live by the deeper meaning of God's laws. (4) The dangers of hypocrisy (6:1–18). Matters of worship such as giving, praying, and fasting must grow out of the right motives. (5) Getting priorities in order (6:19–34). Anxiety over lesser matters will disappear when we put God's kingdom first. (6) Not judging (7:1–6). The citizens of God's kingdom must not judge and condemn people with a harsh, critical attitude. (7) The importance of prayer (7:7–12). We may claim the blessings of prayer that God has promised to those who follow Him. (8) The two ways (7:13–14). Believers must choose the narrow way that leads to life, not the broad and popular way that leads to certain destruction. (9) Fruit-bearing (7:15–20). A genuine follower of the Lord will perform deeds and render service that bring honor and glory to Him. (10) Actions versus words (7:21–23). Obeying God is more important than a long speech about how committed we are to Him. (11) The solid foundation (7:24–29). Jesus' parable about the man who built his house on a rock shows how important it is to plant our lives on the unshakable foundation of the Lord and His Word.

- -

`Righteousness` An attribute of God that signifies His holiness, sinlessness, and justice (Ps. 35:24). Through faith in Christ, God's righteousness is imputed or granted to believers (Titus 3:5). Christians are encouraged to pursue the interests of God's righteous kingdom (Matt. 6:33).

`Sermon on the Mount` Jesus' ethical teachings in Matt. 5–7, delivered to His followers on a hillside near Capernaum. Subjects covered include true happiness (5:3–12); Christian influence (5:13–16); relation of the law and Christian conduct (5:17–48); the practice of charity, prayer, and fasting (6:1–18); God and possessions (6:19–24); freedom from anxiety (6:25–34); judging others (7:1–6); the key to God's blessings (7:7–12); warnings about deception (7:13–23); and building life on a secure foundation (7:24–27).

- -

`Salt of the Earth` *Ye [followers of Jesus] are the salt of the earth: but if the salt have lost his savour [loses its saltiness, NIV], wherewith shall it be salted? it is thenceforth good for nothing* (Matt. 5:13).

Salt added flavor to food, and it was also used to preserve meat in a society in which refrigeration and cold storage did not exist. Jesus used the imagery of salt to describe His followers. If they did not demonstrate their distinctive purity and holiness as His people, they would have no influence in the world. Christians have no higher calling than to serve as the "salt of the earth" in a sinful and decadent culture.

OCTOBER 11 | Read Matthew 8–9

8:1–4 Jesus heals a man with leprosy (parallel passages: **Mark 1:40–45; Luke 5:12–16**).

8:5–13 Jesus expresses His surprise at the faith of a centurion, a Roman military officer. He heals the man's servant at a distance (parallel passage: **Luke 7:1–10**).

8:14–17 Many sick people from Capernaum seek Jesus for healing after He heals Peter's mother-in-law (parallel passages: **Mark 1:29–34; Luke 4:38–41**).

8:18–22 Jesus challenges His followers to be fully committed to Him (parallel passage: **Luke 9:57–62**).

8:23–27 Jesus calms a storm on the Sea of Galilee. The disciples are amazed at His power (parallel passages: **Mark 4:35–41; Luke 8:22–25**).

8:28–34 Jesus casts demons out of two wild men among the tombs (parallel passages: **Mark 5:1–20; Luke 8:26–39**).

9:1–8 Several scribes accuse Jesus of blasphemy after He heals a paralyzed man and forgives his sins (parallel passages: **Mark 2:1–12; Luke 5:17–26**).

9:9–13 Jesus calls Matthew, a tax collector, to leave his tollbooth and follow Him and become His disciple (parallel passages: **Mark 2:13–17; Luke 5:27–32**).

9:14–17 Jesus is asked why He and His disciples do not fast. He replies that fasting is an external law or rite that is being displaced by spiritual principles. The kingdom of God that has arrived in Jesus cannot conform to the rituals of the Pharisees (parallel passages: **Mark 2:18–22; Luke 5:33–39**).

9:18–26 Jesus heals a woman with a hemorrhage and raises the daughter of a synagogue ruler from the dead (parallel passages: **Mark 5:21–43; Luke 8:40–56**).

9:27–31 Jesus heals two blind men and orders them not to tell anyone about this miracle.

9:32–35 Jesus heals a demon-possessed man who is unable to speak. The Pharisees charge Him with performing miracles through the power of Satan.

9:36–38 The spiritual needs of the people move Jesus to compassion. He prays for more workers to minister to these needs.

....

Matthew A tax collector who became a disciple of Jesus (Matt. 9:9) and writer of the Gospel that bears his name. He was also known as *Levi* (Mark 2:13–17; Luke 5:27–32).

....

242 | GEORGE W. KNIGHT

Total Paralysis *Then saith he [Jesus] to the sick of the palsy [the paralytic, NIV], Arise, take up thy bed* (Matt. 9:6).

The word *palsy* is used in the KJV to describe a person who is totally paralyzed. The Gospels use this word only of the man whose friends let him down through the roof of a house on a blanket so he could be healed by Jesus (Matt. 9:1–6; see also Mark 2:1–12; Luke 5:17–26). Matthew's Gospel eliminates the details about this man being let down through the roof. But scholars believe this is the same healing miracle—with these details added—reported by Mark and Luke. The apostle Peter also healed a man who was totally paralyzed (Acts 9:32–34).

OCTOBER 12 | Read Matthew 10–11

10:1–4 From among all His followers, Jesus selects twelve men to serve as His disciples (parallel passages: **Mark 3:13–19; Luke 6:12–16**).

10:5–42 Jesus sends His twelve disciples out to preach the Gospel of the kingdom of God and to heal the sick. He warns them that they will be rejected and persecuted in some places. But they can depend on God's promise of guidance and protection (parallel passages: **Mark 6:7–13; Luke 9:1–6**).

11:1–19 After being imprisoned by King Herod, John the Baptist wonders if Jesus really is the Messiah whom he has announced in his preaching. He sends two of his followers to Jesus to find out. Jesus assures John that He is indeed the spiritual deliverer whom God has sent. He also commends John for his faithfulness to the task of paving the way for His work (parallel passage: **Luke 7:18–35**).

11:20–24 Jesus condemns the cities of Chorazin, Bethsaida, and Capernaum in the region of Galilee for their spiritual stubbornness and lack of belief in Him and His teachings.

11:25–30 Jesus commends the common people ("babes," v. 25), who are open to His teachings, in contrast to the proud Pharisees ("the wise and prudent," v. 25), who are critical of His ministry. He invites all who are burdened down by a religion of legalistic rule-keeping to find relief and rest in Him.

The Twelve The twelve apostles or disciples chosen by Jesus. They were Andrew; Bartholomew (Nathanael); James, son of Alphaeus; James, son of Zebedee; John; Judas; Lebbaeus (Thaddaeus); Matthew; Philip; Simon the Canaanite; Simon Peter; and Thomas (Matt. 10:1–4; Mark 3:13–19; Luke 6:12–16).

OCTOBER 13 | Read Matthew 12–13

12:1–8 The Pharisees criticize Jesus and His disciples for picking grain on the Sabbath to satisfy their hunger. According to their interpretation, this breaks the law that prohibits working on the Sabbath (Exod. 31:14). Jesus replies that human needs must take precedence over ritual laws. Besides, as the Messiah, God's Son, He is "Lord even of the sabbath day" (v. 8) (parallel passages: **Mark 2:23–28; Luke 6:1–5**).

12:9–14 Jesus heals a man's withered hand in the synagogue on the Sabbath. The Pharisees again accuse Him of breaking the Sabbath law and begin to plot His destruction (parallel passages: **Mark 3:1–6; Luke 6:6–11**).

12:15–21 Jesus heals many sick and diseased people among the crowds that follow Him. Matthew the Gospel writer identifies Jesus with the Suffering Servant in the book of Isaiah (vv. 17–21; see Isa. 42:1–4) (parallel passage: **Mark 3:7–12**).

12:22–23 Jesus heals a demon-possessed blind man who cannot speak.

12:24–37 The Pharisees charge that Jesus heals people by the power of Satan. He responds by stating that Satan would not act against himself by casting demons (satanic beings) out of a person. He turns this charge back on the Pharisees by showing that they are committing blasphemy by attributing the work of God to Satan (parallel passage: **Mark 3:20–30)**.

12:38–45 The scribes and Pharisees ask Jesus to show them some spectacular sign to prove that He is the Messiah. He refuses, knowing that no sign will be strong enough to overcome their unbelief. He does tell them that they will be given a continuing sign at some future time—His resurrection from the dead after three days in the grave.

12:46–50 According to Jesus, His true relatives, in a spiritual sense, are those who "do the will of my Father" (v. 50) (parallel passages: **Mark 3:31–35; Luke 8:19–21**).

13:1–9 Jesus delivers the parable of the sower to a crowd beside the Sea of Galilee. The sower threw seed on four different types of soil: wayside soil (v. 4), rocky soil (v. 5), soil where thorns grew (v. 7), and good soil (v. 8) (parallel passages: **Mark 4:1–9; Luke 8:4–8**).

13:10–17 Jesus explains to His disciples why He speaks in parables. These stories drawn from everyday life communicate spiritual truths to people with open minds. But they conceal truth from proud know-it-alls such as the Pharisees who are not open to new revelation from God (parallel passages: **Mark 4:10–12; Luke 8:9–10**).

13:18–23 Jesus tells His disciples that the four types of soil in the parable of the sower represent the different responses that people make to the claims of the kingdom of God (parallel passages: **Mark 4:13–20; Luke 8:11–15**).

13:24–30 The parable of the wheat and the tares (weeds) teaches that good and evil will exist in intermingled fashion until the final judgment. Then they will be separated. Good will be rewarded, and evil will be punished.

13:31–35 These two parables—mustard seed and leaven—teach the same truth: The kingdom of God may seem small and insignificant in the beginning, but it will grow to render an effective influence throughout the world (parallel passage: **Luke 13:18–21**).

13:36–43 Jesus explains the meaning of the parable of the wheat and the tares (weeds) to His disciples.

13:44–46 These two parables—the hidden treasure and the pearl of great price—teach that a person should be willing to pay any price to claim the blessings of God's kingdom.

13:47–50 This parable of the net is similar to the parable of the wheat and the tares (weeds). The kingdom of God, symbolized by the net, will inevitably collect people who are both good and bad. But they will be separated at the final judgment.

13:51–52 This brief parable depicts a householder or landowner mixing both old and new to provide for his family. With His fresh teachings, Jesus brings many new insights to the traditions from the past. Both are essential for those who belong to the kingdom of God.

13:53–58 Jesus returns to His hometown of Nazareth, where He teaches in the local synagogue. But He is rejected because of the "hometown boy" syndrome. He declares that "a prophet is not without honour, save in his own country, and in his own house" (v. 57) (parallel passage: **Mark 6:1–6**).

Pharisees Members of a Jewish sect pledged to uphold the oldest traditions of Israel. In Jesus' time the Pharisees were the most powerful party—political or religious—among the Jews. Jesus exposed the hypocrisy of the Pharisees, who emphasized minute details of the law while neglecting more important issues such as justice, mercy, and love (Matt. 23:1–7). Pharisees in the NT who were known for their generosity and noble spirit were the apostle Paul, Nicodemus, Gamaliel, and Joseph of Arimathea.

Gentile A member of any ethnic group other than the Jewish race. The Jews looked down on other races as barbarous and unclean (Jer. 9:26). Jesus, however, abolished this distinction through His atoning death and His acceptance of all people through repentance and faith (Gal. 3:28).

Eating Grain off the Stalk *His [Jesus'] disciples were an hungered, and began to pluck the ears of corn [heads of grain, NIV], and to eat* (Matt. 12:1).

While passing by a field of wheat or barley on the Sabbath, Jesus' disciples stripped some grain from the stalks. They rubbed it in their hands to remove the outer husks, then popped the grain into their mouths. Wheat or barley was usually ground into flour, then baked into bread. But when bread was not available, eating grain right off the stalk was a quick way to satisfy one's hunger. The OT law permitted hungry travelers to pIck and eat handfuls of grain from fields along the road (Deut. 23:25).

OCTOBER 14 | Read Matthew 14–16

14:1–12 John the Baptist is imprisoned by King Herod because he condemned Herod's adulterous marriage to his brother Philip's wife, Herodias. She succeeds in having John the Baptist executed (parallel passage: **Mark 6:14–29**).

14:13–21 Jesus multiplies a little bread and a few fish to feed more than 5,000 hungry people (parallel passages: **Mark 6:30–44; Luke 9:10–17; John 6:1–14**).

14:22–33 Jesus walks on the water to join His disciples in a boat on the Sea of Galilee. Peter tries his "water legs" but sinks because of a lack of faith. The disciples are amazed and declare that Jesus is "the Son of God" (v. 33) (parallel passages: **Mark 6:45–52; John 6:15–21**).

14:34–36 Jesus heals many sick and diseased people in the land of Gennesaret (parallel passage: **Mark 6:53–56**).

15:1–20 Several scribes and Pharisees criticize Jesus because He and His disciples do not perform a ritual washing of their hands before eating. He replies that externals such as food that go into the body do not defile a person. The impure thoughts and ideas that come from within a person are the real sources of defilement (parallel passage: **Mark 7:1–23**).

15:21–28 Jesus heals the daughter of a Gentile woman and expresses amazement at her great faith (parallel passage: **Mark 7:24–30**).

15:29–39 Jesus feeds a hungry crowd of more than 4,000 people by miraculously multiplying seven loaves of bread and a few fish (parallel passage: Mark 8:1–10). This miracle was performed for non-Jews in Gentile territory. Earlier He had fed more than 5,000 Jews in Jewish territory (see Matt. 14:13–21).

16:1–12 Jesus condemns the hypocrisy of the Pharisees and Sadducees and warns His disciples to avoid their teachings (parallel passage: **Mark 8:11–21**).

16:13–20 In the region of Caesarea-Philippi, Jesus commends the apostle Peter for his faith after he proclaims Jesus as the Messiah and the Son of God (parallel passages: **Mark 8:27–30; Luke 9:18–20**).

16:21–28 Jesus reveals to His disciples that He will be killed by the religious leaders and then resurrected. He condemns Peter for refusing to believe this prediction (parallel passage: **Mark 8:31–9:1**).

Herodias The wife or queen of Herod Antipas, the Roman provincial ruler of Palestine, who had John the Baptist executed. Herodias was angry with John because of his criticism of her immorality and illicit marriage (Matt. 14:1–11).

OCTOBER 15 | Read Matthew 17–19

17:1–13 Jesus demonstrates His future glory by being transfigured before three of His disciples—Peter, James, and John. God speaks from a cloud, "This is my beloved Son, in whom I am well pleased; hear ye him" (v. 5) (parallel passages: **Mark 9:2–13; Luke 9:28–36**).

17:14–21 Jesus casts a stubborn demon out of a boy. He expresses disappointment in His disciples because their lack of faith prevented them from healing the boy (parallel passages: **Mark 9:14–29; Luke 9:37–42**).

17:22–23 Jesus again predicts His death and resurrection (parallel passages: **Mark 9:30–32; Luke 9:43–45**).

17:24–27 Jesus miraculously produces a coin to pay the yearly temple tax for Himself and Peter.

18:1–10 Jesus uses a child as an illustration to teach His disciples about the meaning of humility and service to others (parallel passages: **Mark 9:33–50; Luke 9:46–50**).

18:11–14 Through the parable of the lost sheep, Jesus shows His disciples that His mission is to seek and save lost and hurting people.

18:15–22 Jesus teaches His disciples just how far citizens of the kingdom of God should go to reclaim those who have wronged them. Love and forgiveness have no limit.

18:23–35 Through the parable of the unforgiving servant, Jesus teaches that all who have been forgiven should extend forgiveness to others.

19:1–12 In answer to a question from the Pharisees, Jesus discusses the meaning of marriage and the issue of divorce (parallel passage: **Mark 10:1–12**).

19:13–15 Jesus welcomes and blesses little children (parallel passages: **Mark 10:13–16; Luke 18:15–17**).

19:16–30 The rich young ruler turns away with regret because his wealth is more important to him than becoming a follower of Jesus (parallel passages: **Mark 10:17–31; Luke 18:18–30**).

....

Transfiguration of Jesus A radical transformation in the Savior's appearance through which God was glorified. Accompanied by His disciples Peter, James, and John, Jesus went to a mountain at night to pray. Moses and Elijah appeared and discussed Jesus' death, emphasizing Jesus as the fulfillment of the Law and the Prophets (Matt. 17:1–8). This experience attested Christ's divinity and mission and helped prepare Jesus and His disciples for the events leading to His death.

Shekinah A visible manifestation of God's glory, usually as a bright light, fire, or cloud (Exod. 13:21; Matt. 17:5).

....

A Tax for the Temple *They [temple officials] that received tribute money came to Peter, and said, Doth not your master [Jesus] pay tribute?* (Matt. 17:24)

This verse refers to the annual tax designated for maintenance and support of the temple in Jerusalem. Every Jewish male was required to pay this tax. Perhaps the temple officials who collected this tax approached Peter about paying it because Jesus and His disciples were hard to pin down. Their teaching and healing ministry kept them moving from place to place. The NIV translates the Greek word for "tribute money" in this verse as "two-drachma tax." The standard Greek coin of that time was the drachma. It took two of these coins to pay the tax. The drachma was roughly equivalent to the Roman coin known as the denarius. A common laborer of Bible times would often be paid one denarius for a full day's work.

OCTOBER 16 | Read Matthew 20–21

20:1–16 This parable is known as the workers in the vineyard. The laborers worked for different lengths of time, but all were paid the same. The message is that God relates to citizens of His kingdom with mercy and grace and gives us more than we deserve.

20:17–19 On His way to Jerusalem, Jesus again tells His disciples that He will be executed in that city—but He will be resurrected on the third day after His death (parallel passages: **Mark 10:32–34; Luke 18:31–34**).

20:20–28 The mother of James and John, two of Jesus' disciples, asks Him to give her sons prominent places in His kingdom. He teaches the disciples that His kingdom is spiritual rather than physical in nature (parallel passage: **Mark 10:35–45**).

20:29–34 Jesus heals two blind men at Jericho (parallel passages: **Mark 10:46–52; Luke 18:35–43**).

21:1–11 Jesus is acclaimed by the crowds as the long-expected Messiah when He rides into Jerusalem on a donkey. Riding a lowly donkey fulfills the prophecy of Zech. 9:9 and also shows that Jesus is a spiritual king, not the political deliverer whom the people were expecting (parallel passages: **Mark 11:1–11; Luke 19:28–44; John 12:12–19**).

21:12–22 Jesus drives out merchants who are buying and selling in the temple. He pronounces a curse on a fig tree that is bearing no fruit. The barren fig tree symbolizes the dead traditions of the Pharisees and other religious leaders of the nation (parallel passages: **Mark 11:12–26; Luke 19:45–48**).

21:23–27 Jesus answers the objections of the Pharisees and asserts His divine authority over the temple (parallel passages: **Mark 11:27–33; Luke 20:1–8**).

21:28–32 In this parable of the vineyard workers, a contrast is drawn between the Pharisees and the sinners. The Pharisees were supposed to be doing God's work (they promised to work in the vineyard but did not), but their stubbornness and traditions kept them from entering God's kingdom. But the sinners were open and teachable (they refused to work in the vineyard at first but then did so) and thus able to become citizens of the kingdom.

21:33–46 The wicked husbandmen, or tenant farmers, in this parable represent the religious leaders of Israel. They are rejecting Jesus as God's Son, so God will turn to others—even Gentiles (Acts 13:46)—and offer them the opportunity to become citizens of God's kingdom (parallel passages: **Mark 12:1–12; Luke 20:9–19**).

Commercialism in the Temple *Jesus went into the temple. . .and cast out all them that sold and bought in the temple, and overthrew the tables of the moneychangers, and the seats of them that sold doves* (Matt. 21:12).

These commercial activities that upset Jesus were being conducted in an outer court of the Jewish temple during the observance of the Passover in Jerusalem. All male Jews were expected to attend this festival, even if they lived a long distance from Jerusalem. The moneychangers were probably exchanging foreign coins of these pilgrims for the appropriate coins with which to pay the temple tax. These pilgrims were also expected to provide animals for sacrifice on the altar of the temple during this celebration. Merchants were selling animals for this purpose as a convenience so pilgrims would not have to bring them along on their trip to the holy city. Jesus was angry about the crass commercialism of the scene. Temple officials may have been profiting personally from the buying and selling. He quoted Isa. 56:7 ("Mine house shall be called an house of prayer") and accused the merchants of defiling the temple: "But ye have made it a den of thieves" (Matt. 21:13).

OCTOBER 17 | Read Matthew 22–23

22:1–14 This parable of the marriage feast teaches essentially the same truth as the parable of the wicked husbandmen (Matt. 21:33–46). The Jewish people who have rejected the Messiah will be turned away from the messianic feast, and Gentiles will be brought in to take their place at the table (Rom. 15:16).

22:15–22 The Pharisees and Herodians try to trap Jesus with a question about paying taxes to the Roman government. Jesus silences them by pointing out that people have a dual obligation—to the state or civil government as well as to God, the ultimate authority (parallel passages: **Mark 12:13–17; Luke 20:20–26**).

22:23–33 Jesus also deals skillfully with a question from the Sadducees that is designed to make Him look foolish. Whose wife would a woman be in the afterlife if she had been married to several different men? Jesus tells the Sadducees they are assuming the afterlife will be like life here on earth. But the spiritual realities of the life beyond will be different: "In the resurrection they neither marry, nor are given in marriage, but are as the angels of God in heaven" (v. 30) (parallel passages: **Mark 12:18–27; Luke 20:27–40**).

`22:34–40` Jesus tells a teacher of the law that the command to love your neighbor as yourself (Lev. 19:18) is just as important as the command to love God (Deut. 6:4–9) (parallel passage: **Mark 12:28–34**).

`22:41–46` In a discussion with the Pharisees, Jesus rejects the popular thinking of the day that the Messiah would be a human descendant of King David (2 Sam. 7:8–16). Jesus identifies Himself as the Messiah and the divine Son of God (parallel passages: **Mark 12:35–37; Luke 20:41–44**).

`23:1–36` Jesus condemns the scribes and Pharisees because of their hypocrisy, dishonesty, pride, spiritual blindness, and preoccupation with external matters In religion (parallel passages: **Mark 12:38–40; Luke 20:45–47**).

`23:37–39` Jesus expresses His sorrow over the city of Jerusalem because of its failure to accept Him as the Messiah (parallel passage: **Luke 13:34–35**).

. . . .

Sadducees A priestly aristocratic party of NT times that—in contrast to the Pharisees—rejected the oral traditions of the Jewish faith and accepted only the original teachings of Moses as authoritative. They did not believe in a bodily resurrection (Matt. 22:23) or angels and spirits (Acts 23:8). They often opposed Jesus and His teachings (Matt. 16:6, 12).

Iniquity Sin, wickedness, or evil. Jesus taught that evil or iniquity originates in the heart, or from within (Matt. 23:28). Christ redeems believers from their iniquity, purifies them, and sets them apart for His service (Titus 2:14). *Wickedness*: NIV.

. . . .

Phylacteries and Tassels *They [the Pharisees] make broad their phylacteries, and enlarge the borders [tassels, NIV] of their garments* (Matt. 23:5).

In this verse, as in all of Matthew 23, Jesus denounced the scribes and Pharisees for their hypocrisy and legalism. The Pharisees were noted for their attempts to keep the OT law in every minute detail. Over the centuries they had added their own interpretations of the law that they considered as binding as the original law itself. Phylacteries were little boxes containing strips of parchment on which portions of the law were written. The Pharisees wore these boxes on their foreheads and hands as a literal obedience of the Lord's command, "Thou shalt bind them [God's laws] for a sign upon thine hand, and they shall be as frontlets between thine eyes" (Deut. 6:8). Tassels were decorative fringes that the Pharisees wore on their clothes to remind them of God's laws (Deut. 22:12). The problem with these displays of piety among the Pharisees is that they were done just for show. Jesus declared that they worked hard to observe the externals of religion while omitting "the weightier matters of the law, judgment, mercy, and faith" (Matt. 23:23).

OCTOBER 18 | Read Matthew 24–25

24:1–51 This chapter is known as Jesus' great prophetic discourse. He predicts the destruction of the temple in Jerusalem and discusses events that will take place in the end-time before His second coming (parallel passages: **Mark 13:1–37; Luke 21:5–38**).

25:1–13 Through the parable of the ten virgins, Jesus teaches His followers to be in a state of watchful readiness at all times. His second coming may occur at any time—probably when it is least expected (1 Thess. 5:1–11).

25:14–30 In the parable of the talents, two servants multiplied the money entrusted to them by their master. But one was lazy and earned no interest on his talent. This parable teaches that we are to be good stewards of the gifts and abilities granted to us by the Lord.

25:31–46 Jesus compares the separation of people at the final judgment to the work of shepherds, who would separate the sheep from the goats in their flocks at the end of the day. Jesus identifies so closely with people in extreme need—the lonely, hungry, and imprisoned—that ministry to such people will be counted as service to Christ Himself.

....

False Prophet A person who delivers a false or misleading message under the pretense that it comes from God. Believers are warned to beware of false prophets (Matt. 24:11, 24; 2 Pet. 2:1).

....

Be Prepared *Then shall the kingdom of heaven be likened unto ten virgins, which took their lamps, and went forth to meet the bridegroom. And five of them were wise, and five were foolish. They that were foolish took their lamps, and took no oil with them* (Matt. 25:1–3).

These verses are part of Jesus' parable about the wise and foolish virgins who were invited to a wedding celebration. In Bible times the groom went to the home of his bride and took her to his own home, accompanied by his friends as they celebrated along the way. These virgins were probably friends of the bride who were supposed to join the procession at some point as it passed by. Since the wedding was at night, all ten virgins carried tiny oil-burning lamps to light the path as they walked with the rest of the wedding party. The wise virgins carried an extra supply of oil for their lamps, but the foolish virgins did not. When the wedding procession was delayed, the foolish virgins were unable to join in the celebration of this joyful occasion. Jesus' message in the parable is this: Be prepared. The second coming of Christ can happen at any moment, and we need to be ready at all times.

OCTOBER 19 | Read Matthew 26

26:1-5 Members of the Jewish Sanhedrin meet to plot how they can capture Jesus and have Him executed. They realize they must do this discreetly because of Jesus' popularity among the people (parallel passages: **Mark 14:1-2; Luke 22:1-2**).

26:6-13 A woman (according to the Gospel of John, it was Mary of Bethany) anoints the head of Jesus with an expensive perfume. Jesus interprets this as an anointing in preparation for His death and burial (parallel passages: **Mark 14:3-9; John 12:1-8**).

26:14-16 Judas, a disciple of Jesus, agrees to betray Jesus for thirty pieces of silver and lead the religious leaders to Him at an opportune time (parallel passages: **Mark 14:10-11; Luke 22:3-6**).

26:17-19 Jesus instructs His disciples to make preparations for a meal that they will eat together to observe the Jewish Passover (parallel passages: **Mark 14:12-16; Luke 22:7-13**).

26:20-25 During the Passover meal, Jesus identifies His disciple Judas as His betrayer (parallel passages: **Mark 14:17-21; Luke 22:21-23; John 13:21-30**).

26:26-30 Jesus observes the Last Supper with His disciples (parallel passages: **Mark 14:22-26; Luke 22:14-20**).

26:31-35 Jesus predicts that all His disciples will abandon and deny Him during His arrest and trial (parallel passages: **Mark 14:27-31; Luke 22:31-38; John 13:31-38**).

26:36-46 Jesus agonizes in prayer in the Garden of Gethsemane about His forthcoming suffering and death. His disciples fall asleep and fail to support Him in His hour of need (parallel passages: **Mark 14:32-42; Luke 22:39-46**).

26:47-56 Judas leads a group of temple guards sent by the Sanhedrin to the place where Jesus is praying in the Garden of Gethsemane. He identifies Jesus by greeting Him with a kiss. Jesus is arrested and taken away (parallel passages: **Mark 14:43-52; Luke 22:47-53; John 18:1-12**).

26:57-68 Jesus appears before the high priest Caiaphas and the rest of the Jewish Sanhedrin. Peter follows and waits outside the house of the high priest to see what will happen. The Sanhedrin declares Jesus guilty of blasphemy when He admits He is the Son of God (parallel passages: **Mark 14:53-65; Luke 22:63-71**).

26:69-75 Outside the house of the high priest, Peter denies that He knows Jesus when he is questioned by three different people. The crowing of a rooster makes Peter realize that Jesus' prediction of his denial has come true (parallel passages: **Mark 14:66-72; Luke 22:54-62; John 18:15-27**).

Mount of Olives A hill in eastern Jerusalem where Jesus was betrayed by Judas on the night before His crucifixion (Matt. 26:30, 47). The branches of olive trees from the Mount of Olives were used to make booths for the Feast of Tabernacles (Neh. 8:15). *Mount Olivet*: Acts 1:12.

The Ultimate Sacrificial Lamb *The disciples did as Jesus had appointed them; and they made ready the Passover* (Matt. 26:19).

Jesus and His disciples were in Jerusalem for the observance of the Passover. This was the most significant festival of the Jewish people, celebrated each year to memorialize their deliverance from slavery in Egypt. The central event of this celebration was the eating of a lamb. Before this lamb was roasted, its blood was sprinkled by the priests on the base of the altar in the temple. This symbolized the blood sprinkled on the doorposts of Israelite houses in Egypt to ward off the angel of death whom God sent throughout the land (Exod. 12:1–13). When the disciples "made ready the passover," they probably secured a lamb and had it sacrificed by the priests and prepared it appropriately for eating by Jesus and the other disciples. Little did they know that within a few hours the crucified Jesus would become the ultimate Passover Lamb whose blood would become an everlasting atonement for sin.

Chief Priests *Judas, one of the twelve, came, and with him a great multitude. . . from the chief priests and elders of the people* (Matt. 26:47).

The phrase "chief priests" in this verse probably refers to the leaders or directors of the twenty-four groups of priests into which the priesthood was divided in David's time (1 Chron. 24:1–5). These twenty-four divisions of the priesthood probably presided at the altar in the tabernacle or temple on a rotating basis. In NT times, these "chief priests" may have included the high priest as well as priestly members of his immediate family.

OCTOBER 20 | Read Matthew 27–28

27:1–2 The Sanhedrin finds Jesus guilty of blasphemy under the Jewish law. Determined to have Him executed, they take Him to Pontius Pilate, the Roman provincial governor of Judea. Only the Romans had the authority to pronounce and carry out the death sentence (parallel passages: **Mark 15:1; Luke 23:1**).

27:3–10 Judas has a change of heart when he realizes his actions have condemned an innocent man. He returns the betrayal money and then commits suicide (Acts 1:16–20).

27:11–26 Jesus appears before Pontius Pilate, the Roman governor. Pilate realizes Jesus is an innocent man. But he is also under pressure from the religious leaders, who are determined to have Him executed. He tries to get Jesus released by using the custom of setting one prisoner free at the whim of the people during a major Jewish holiday. But the people call for the release of another prisoner named

Barabbas instead. Finally, Pilate condemns Jesus to death by crucifixion (parallel passages: **Mark 15:2–15; Luke 23:13–25; John 18:28–19:16**).

27:27–31 Jesus is mocked and abused by Roman soldiers before they lead Him away to the crucifixion site (parallel passage: **Mark 15:16–20**).

27:32 A bystander, Simon of Cyrene, is pressed into service to carry the cross of Jesus (parallel passages: **Mark 15:21; Luke 23:26–31**).

27:33–37 Jesus is crucified at a site known as Golgotha ("place of the skull") just outside the walls of Jerusalem (Heb. 13:12). The placard on His cross that specifies His crime reads, "THIS IS JESUS THE KING OF THE JEWS" (v. 37). This indicates that He was probably executed on the false charge that He was a political revolutionary who challenged the power and authority of the Roman government (parallel passages: **Mark 15:22–26; Luke 23:32–38; John 19:17–24**).

27:38–44 Jesus is mocked and ridiculed by people in the crowd as well as two thieves who are being crucified at the same time (parallel passages: **Mark 15:27–32; Luke 23:39–43**).

27:45–54 Jesus' suffering and death are accompanied by several mysterious events, including an earthquake at the moment when He dies (parallel passages: **Mark 15:33–39; Luke 23:44–48**).

27:55–56 Several women from Galilee who are followers of Jesus are among the crowd at the crucifixion site (parallel passages: **Mark 15:40–41; Luke 23:49; John 19:25–27**).

27:57–60 Joseph of Arimathea buries the body of Jesus in his own tomb (parallel passages: **Mark 15:42–46; Luke 23:50–54; John 19:38–42**).

27:61 Mary Magdalene and "the other Mary" (probably the mother of Jesus' disciple James, the son of Alphaeus), followers of Jesus, mourn at the tomb where Jesus is buried (parallel passages: **Mark 15:47; Luke 23:55–56**).

27:62–66 After talking to Pilate, the religious leaders station guards at the tomb where Jesus is buried and seal the entrance with a large stone.

28:1–10 Mary Magdalene and "the other Mary" (see Matt. 27:61) visit the tomb of Jesus on Sunday morning after His death and burial two days before. They are greeted by an angel, who tells them He has been raised from the dead. The angel instructs them to tell His disciples this good news. Then Jesus Himself greets the women to assure them and calm their fears (parallel passages: **Mark 16:1–8; Luke 24:1–8; John 20:1–2**).

28:11–15 The Jewish Sanhedrin bribes the guards who were on duty at Jesus' tomb in an attempt to deny the claims of His resurrection. These guards spread the rumor that Jesus' disciples took His body out of the grave before daybreak on Sunday morning.

28:16–20 Jesus meets with His disciples in Galilee and charges them with His Great Commission (Acts 1:8). They are to continue His mission of bringing people into the kingdom of God (parallel passages: **Mark 16:14–18; Luke 24:44–49**).

Potter's Field A burial place for poor people outside Jerusalem. This field was bought with the betrayal silver returned by Judas to Jewish officials (Matt. 27:6–8).

Scourged Severely beaten with a leather strap containing bits of sharp metal. This punishment was limited to forty lashes (Deut. 25:3). Jesus was scourged before His crucifixion (Matt. 27:26). *Flogged*: NIV, NLT.

Veil A screen or curtain that separated the Holy Place and the Holy of Holies in the tabernacle and temple. This veil was torn at Christ's death to symbolize direct access of all people to God's salvation through Jesus Christ (Matt. 27:51). *Curtain*: NIV, NRSV (Heb. 4:14–16).

A Badge of Honor *They [the Roman soldiers] crucified him [Jesus], and parted [divided up, NIV] his garments, casting lots* (Matt. 27:35).

None of the Gospels (Matthew, Mark, Luke, and John) go into detail about the crucifixion of Jesus. They didn't have to. The people of NT times knew all about this cruel form of capital punishment and the pain and suffering it inflicted. The victim's wrists were nailed to a horizontal crossbeam; then it was raised into position and attached to a stake fixed firmly in the ground. Sometimes the feet were crossed and nailed to the stake. Without any support for the body except the nails through the feet and wrists, the victim slumped forward on the cross. This put pressure on the heart and lungs, making breathing difficult. A slow, painful death usually occurred after two or three days from a combination of shock, fatigue, asphyxiation, and loss of blood. Sometimes the victim's legs were broken with a club as an act of mercy to hasten death. This was not necessary in Jesus' case because He died after only a few hours on the cross (Matt. 27:45–50). The Gospel of John declares that this was a fulfillment of the OT prophecy, "A bone of him shall not be broken" (John 19:36; see Ps. 34:20). To the Jewish people, crucifixion was a despicable and dishonorable way to die (Gal. 3:13). But Jesus turned the cross into a symbol of hope and a badge of honor and self-sacrifice (Philippians 2:5–8).

OCTOBER 21 | Read Mark 1–3

1:1–8 John the Baptist, forerunner of Jesus, begins preaching (parallel passages: **Matt. 3:1–12; Luke 3:1–20**).

1:9–11 Jesus is baptized by John (parallel passages: **Matt. 3:13–17; Luke 3:21–22**).

1:12–13 Jesus is tempted by Satan (parallel passages: **Matt. 4:1–11; Luke 4:1–13**).

1:14–15 Jesus begins preaching in the region of Galilee (parallel passages: **Matt. 4:12–17; John 4:45**).

1:16–20 Jesus beckons Peter and Andrew and James and John to follow Him (parallel passages: **Matt. 4:18–22; Luke 5:1–11**).

1:21–28 Jesus casts demons out of a man in the synagogue at Capernaum on the Sabbath. The people are amazed at His power and authority (parallel passage: **Luke 4:31–37**).

1:29–34 Jesus heals Peter's mother-in-law; many sick people come to Him for healing (parallel passages: **Matt. 8:14–17; Luke 4:38–41**).

1:35–39 Jesus preaches and heals throughout Galilee (parallel passages: **Matt. 4:23–25; Luke 4:42–44**).

1:40–45 Jesus heals a man with leprosy. He ignores Jesus' instructions not to tell anyone about his miraculous healing, and people from a wide area flock to Jesus (parallel passages: **Matt. 8:1–4; Luke 5:12–16**).

2:1–12 Four men lower their paralyzed friend through the roof to Jesus for healing. Jesus also forgives his sins and is accused of blasphemy by a group of scribes (parallel passages: **Matt. 9:1–8; Luke 5:17–26**).

2:13–17 Jesus calls the tax collector Matthew, also known as Levi, to become His disciple (parallel passages: **Matt. 9:9–13; Luke 5:27–32**).

2:18–22 Jesus explains to the Pharisees why He and His disciples do not observe the ritual of fasting (parallel passages: **Matt. 9:14–17; Luke 5:33–39**).

2:23–28 The Pharisees condemn Jesus for violating the law against working on the Sabbath (Exod. 20:8–11) by picking grain to eat (parallel passages: **Matt. 12:1–8; Luke 6:1–5**).

3:1–6 Jesus angers the Pharisees by healing a man's withered hand on the Sabbath (parallel passages: **Matt. 12:9–14; Luke 6:6–11**).

3:7–12 People from many distant cities flock to Jesus because they have heard about His ability to heal (parallel passage: **Matt. 12:15–21**).

3:13–19 Jesus chooses twelve followers to serve as His disciples (parallel passages: **Matt. 10:1–4; Luke 6:12–16**).

3:20–30 Jesus answers the charge of the Pharisees that He is healing people who are possessed by demons through the power of Satan (parallel passage: **Matt. 12:24–37**).

3:31–35 Jesus' mother and brothers come to the place where He is teaching. They send word that they would like to see Him. Jesus affirms that His true relatives are those who do the will of God (parallel passages: **Matt. 12:46–50; Luke 8:19–21**).

. . . .

Herodians An influential Jewish group that favored Greek customs and Roman law in NT times. The Herodians joined forces with the Pharisees against Jesus (Mark 3:6).

Galilee A Roman province in northern Palestine during NT times and the area where Jesus spent most of His earthly ministry (Mark 3:7). Because of its far-north location, Galilee had a mixed population of Jews and Gentiles. The prophet Isaiah referred to it as "Galilee of the nations" (Isa. 9:1). *Galilee of the Gentiles*: NIV.

Boanerges A name meaning "sons of thunder," given by Jesus to James and John, the sons of Zebedee (Mark 3:17). This was a reference to their fiery zeal.

. . . .

Going through the Roof *They [four friends of the paralyzed man] uncovered the roof where he [Jesus] was: and when they had broken it up, they let down the bed wherein the sick of the palsy [paralyzed man, NIV] lay* (Mark 2:4).

This verse shows the determination of the friends of a disabled man to get him to Jesus for healing. They brought their friend in a blanket or pallet to the house where Jesus was teaching. Unable to get into the building because of the crowd, they climbed an exterior stairway to the roof. After ripping a hole in the roof, they lowered him down to Jesus. The roofs of most houses in Bible times were built in three steps. First, beams or logs were laid across the tops of the exterior walls. These beams were then overlaid with thatch, consisting of tree branches and straw. Finally, the thatch was topped with a layer of clay that was hardened in the sun. In a climate in which rainfall was minimal, these roofs would hold up well if the clay was rolled and hardened on a regular basis. Tearing through a roof like this was a simple matter. It was also easy to repair.

OCTOBER 22 | Read Mark 4–6

4:1–9 Jesus delivers the parable of the sower from a fishing boat on the Sea of Galilee (parallel passages: **Matt. 13:1–9; Luke 8:4–8**).

4:10–12 In answer to a question from His disciples, Jesus explains why He teaches through parables (parallel passages: **Matt. 13:10–17; Luke 8:9–10**).

4:13–20 Jesus explains the meaning of the parable of the sower to His disciples (parallel passages: **Matt. 13:18–23; Luke 8:11–15**).

4:21–25 Citizens of the kingdom of God should let their influence penetrate the world, just as a candle or lamp is placed on a stand to light a room (parallel passage: **Luke 8:16–18**).

4:26–29 This parable of the seed growing quietly is found only in the Gospel of Mark. It teaches that the kingdom of God is God's work. He allows us as His followers to sow the seed, but God causes the seed to grow and produce a harvest.

4:30–32 Jesus in this parable compares the kingdom of God to a mustard seed. Although it is a tiny seed, it grows into a large plant. The kingdom of God is also destined to grow from obscurity into an influential force throughout the world.

4:33–34 Jesus continues to speak in parables and to explain their meaning to His disciples.

4:35–41 Jesus calms a storm and rebukes His disciples for their lack of faith (parallel passages: **Matt. 8:23–27; Luke 8:22–25**).

5:1–20 Jesus casts numerous demons out of a wild man who lived among the tombs in the country of the Gadarenes. The demons enter a herd of pigs, and they drown in the Sea of Galilee. Jesus sends the healed man into the cities of that region to tell others what Jesus has done for him (parallel passages: **Matt. 8:28–34; Luke 8:26–39**).

5:21–43 Jesus heals a woman with a hemorrhage who slips through the crowd to touch the edge of His robe. He also raises from the dead the daughter of a synagogue ruler named Jairus (parallel passages: **Matt. 9:18–26; Luke 8:40–56**).

6:1–6 Jesus is rejected by the unbelieving citizens of His hometown of Nazareth (parallel passage: **Matt. 13:53–58**).

6:7–13 Jesus sends His disciples out to preach and heal (parallel passages: **Matt. 10:5–42; Luke 9:1–6**).

6:14–29 Herodias, the wife of King Herod, uses her daughter's influence with the king to have John the Baptist executed. Herodias wanted John killed because he had condemned her adulterous affair with the king (parallel passage: **Matt. 14:1–12**).

6:30–44 A huge crowd follows Jesus to an isolated area when He withdraws to rest and pray. As the day draws to a close, He has compassion on them because they have not eaten all day. He multiplies five loaves of bread and two fish to feed the crowd of more than 5,000 people. So thorough is this miracle that twelve baskets of food are left over (parallel passages: **Matt. 14:13–21; Luke 9:10–17; John 6:1–14**).

6:45–52 Jesus joins His disciples in a boat on the Sea of Galilee by walking on the water (parallel passages: **Matt. 14:22–33; John 6:15–21**).

6:53–56 Jesus and His disciples put ashore at the land of Gennesaret, where He heals many people (parallel passage: **Matt. 14:34–36**).

....

Sea of Galilee A freshwater lake about fourteen miles long and seven miles wide that took its name from the surrounding Roman province. Fed by the Jordan River, it provided the livelihood for many commercial fishermen, including several disciples of Jesus: James, John, Peter, and Andrew (Mark 1:16–20). Jesus calmed the waters of this lake after He and His disciples were caught in a boat in a sudden storm (Mark 4:35–41). *Sea of Chinneroth*: Josh. 12:3; *Lake of Gennesaret*: Luke 5:1; *Sea of Tiberias*: John 21:1.

....

Living among the Dead *There met him [Jesus] out of the tombs a man with an unclean spirit, who had his dwelling among the tombs* (Mark 5:2–3).

This man who met Jesus was possessed by demons. He may have been driven out of the villages of "the country of the Gadarenes" (Mark 5:1) and forced to live a life of isolation in a cemetery because of his violent, unpredictable behavior (Mark 5:5). The "tombs" mentioned in this passage were probably natural caves or burial chambers that had been dug out of solid rock. Tombs like this were commonly used by the upper-class families of Bible times. This poor, deranged man may have been living among the bones of the dead in one of these burial caves. The NIV states specifically that he was living "in the tombs," not "among the tombs."

OCTOBER 23 | Read Mark 7–9

7:1–23 Jesus explains to the scribes and Pharisees why He and His disciples do not perform ritualistic hand-washings before eating (parallel passage: **Matt. 15:1–20**).

7:24–30 Jesus heals a Gentile woman's daughter (parallel passage: **Matt. 15:21–28**).

7:31–37 Jesus heals a deaf man with a speech impediment, and he begins to speak clearly.

8:1–10 Jesus performs a second feeding miracle—this one for Gentiles (parallel passage: **Matt. 15:29–39**).

8:11–21 Jesus warns His disciples to stay away from the Pharisees and their teachings (parallel passage: **Matt. 16:1–12**).

8:22–26 Jesus heals a blind man outside the city of Bethsaida.

8:27–30 Peter confesses Jesus as the Christ, God's Anointed One. Jesus cautions them to tell no one that He is the Messiah (parallel passages: **Matt. 16:13–20; Luke 9:18–20**).

8:31–9:1 Jesus informs His disciples about His future death and resurrection (parallel passage: **Matt. 16:21–28**).

9:2–13 Jesus is transfigured before three of His disciples, and He talks again about His forthcoming death (parallel passages: **Matt. 17:1–13; Luke 9:28–36**).

9:14–29 Jesus encourages the faith of the father of a demon-possessed boy. Then He casts out the stubborn demon and heals his son (parallel passages: **Matt. 17:14–21; Luke 9:37–42**).

9:30–32 Jesus again predicts He will be killed and then resurrected (parallel passages: **Matt. 17:22–23; Luke 9:43–45**).

9:33–50 Jesus teaches His disciples the meaning of true greatness for those who are citizens of God's kingdom (parallel passages: **Matt. 18:1–10; Luke 9:46–50**).

Corban A Hebrew word meaning a sacred gift, or an offering devoted to God. Jesus condemned the Pharisees for encouraging people to make such gifts while neglecting to care for their own parents (Mark 7:11–13).

Jesus and the Scribes *Then came together unto him [Jesus] the Pharisees, and certain of the scribes [teachers of the law, NIV]* (Mark 7:1).

The scribes and Pharisees are often mentioned together as if they were united in their opposition to Jesus (see Matt. 15:1; Luke 5:21; John 8:3). The office of scribe developed in OT times when they were charged with the responsibility of copying the scriptures. Laboriously copying a sacred document by hand was the only way to reproduce and pass on God's commands in written form. By NT times scribes had assumed the task of interpreting and teaching God's law as well as copying it. This is why they are mentioned often with Pharisees as those who were opposed to Jesus. Both were committed to preserving the traditions that had grown up around the original written law. They considered these additions as binding as the law itself. Jesus criticized these "sacred traditions," broke many of them Himself during His teaching and healing ministry, and insisted they were not as authoritative as God's law in its original form (Matt. 15:5–6; Mark 7:5–6; Luke 6:1–5).

OCTOBER 24 | Read Mark 10–11

10:1–12 Jesus discusses with the Pharisees the meaning of marriage and the problem of divorce (parallel passage: **Matt. 19:1–12**).

10:13–16 The disciples try to keep children away from Jesus, but He welcomes and blesses them and declares that a citizen of the kingdom must become "as a little child" (v. 15) (parallel passages: **Matt. 19:13–15; Luke 18:15–17**).

10:17–31 The rich young ruler refuses to follow Jesus (parallel passages: **Matt. 19:16–30; Luke 18:18–30**).

10:32–34 Jesus again speaks with His disciples about His forthcoming death (parallel passages: **Matt. 20:17–19; Luke 18:31–34**).

10:35–45 Jesus' disciples James and John ask for places of prominence and honor in His kingdom (parallel passage: **Matt. 20:20–28**).

10:46–52 On His way to Jerusalem, Jesus heals a blind man named Bartimaeus at Jericho (parallel passages: **Matt. 20:29–34; Luke 18:35–43**).

11:1–11 Jesus makes His triumphal entry into Jerusalem (parallel passages: **Matt. 21:1–11; Luke 19:28–44; John 12:12–19**).

11:12–26 Jesus places a curse on a barren fig tree and drives out merchants who are conducting business in the temple (parallel passages: **Matt. 21:12–22; Luke 19:45–48**).

11:27–33 Jesus assures the Pharisees of His divine authority over the temple (parallel passages: **Matt. 21:23–27; Luke 20:1–8**).

Court of the Gentiles An outer court in the Jewish temple beyond which Gentile worshipers could not go. The splitting of the curtain between this court and the inner court at Jesus' death symbolized the Gentiles' equal access to God (Matt. 27:51; Eph. 2:11–14).

Straight-Up Prayer *When ye [Jesus' followers] stand praying, forgive, if ye have aught against any* (Mark 11:25).

This teaching of Jesus on prayer and forgiveness shows that standing was one common stance while praying in Bible times. The person would address his prayer to God by lifting his hands toward heaven with the palms up. This is the way King Solomon prayed when he dedicated the newly constructed temple in Jerusalem to the Lord (1 Kings 8:22).

OCTOBER 25 | Read Mark 12–13

12:1–12 In this parable, Jesus compares the religious leaders of Israel to wicked husbandmen, or tenant farmers (parallel passages: **Matt. 21:33–46; Luke 20:9–19**).

12:13–17 The Pharisees and Herodians question Jesus about paying taxes to the Roman government (parallel passages: **Matt. 22:15–22; Luke 20:20–26**).

12:18–27 Jesus deals with a question from the Sadducees about the resurrection (parallel passages: **Matt. 22:23–33; Luke 20:27–40**).

12:28–34 Jesus answers a question from a teacher of the law on which is the greatest commandment (parallel passage: **Matt. 22:34–40**).

12:35–37 Jesus challenges the thinking of the Pharisees about the Messiah who would spring from the line of David (parallel passages: **Matt. 22:41–46; Luke 20:41–44**).

12:38–40 Jesus denounces the Pharisees for their pride and hypocrisy (parallel passages: **Matt. 23:1–36; Luke 20:45–47**).

12:41–44 Jesus praises a poor widow for her sacrificial offering (parallel passage: **Luke 21:1–4**).

13:1–37 Jesus predicts the destruction of the temple in Jerusalem and discusses end-time events (parallel passages: **Matt. 24:1–51; Luke 21:5–38**).

New Testament Night Watches *Watch ye therefore: for ye know not when the master of the house cometh, at even [in the evening, NIV], or at midnight, or at* *the cockcrowing [when the rooster crows, NIV], or in the morning [at dawn, NIV]* (Mark 13:35).

During OT times, the Jews divided the night into three "watches" or divisions of time. But after the Romans occupied their territory, they adopted the Roman pattern of the four-watch night. Jesus referred to these four watches in His instructions to His disciples that they should always be ready for His return: the first ("even") at three hours after sunset, the second three hours later at midnight, the third ("cockcrowing") at three hours before sunset, and the fourth ("morning") at dawn with the rising of the sun. These were the same times when the Roman soldiers guarding Peter in prison rotated their shifts (see Acts 12:4).

OCTOBER 26 | Read Mark 14–16

14:1–2 The Jewish Sanhedrin plots to arrest Jesus and have Him executed (parallel passages: **Matt. 26:1–5; Luke 22:1–2**).

14:3–9 A woman anoints Jesus with an expensive perfume (parallel passages: **Matt. 26:6–13; John 12:1–8**).

14:10–11 Judas makes arrangements to betray Jesus (parallel passages: **Matt. 26:14–16; Luke 22:3–6**).

14:12–16 Two of Jesus' disciples select a location where they will partake of a Passover meal with Jesus (parallel passages: **Matt. 26:17–19; Luke 22:7–13**).

14:17–21 Jesus predicts that one of His disciples will betray Him (parallel passages: **Matt. 26:20–25; Luke 22:21–23; John 13:21–30**).

14:22–26 Jesus institutes the memorial meal (1 Cor. 11:23–26), known today as the Lord's Supper (parallel passages: **Matt. 26:26–30; Luke 22:14–20**).

14:27–31 Jesus predicts that all His disciples, including Peter, will deny Him (parallel passages: **Matt. 26:31–35; Luke 22:31–38; John 13:31–38**).

14:32–42 Jesus prays with a heavy heart in the Garden of Gethsemane (parallel passages: **Matt. 26:36–46; Luke 22:39–46**).

14:43–52 Jesus is arrested in the Garden of Gethsemane (parallel passages: **Matt. 26:47–56; Luke 22:47–53; John 18:1–2**).

14:53–65 Jesus is declared guilty of blasphemy when He appears before the Jewish Sanhedrin (parallel passages: **Matt. 26:57–68; Luke 22:63–71**).

14:66–72 Peter denies that he knows Jesus (parallel passages: **Matt. 26:69–75; Luke 22:54–62; John 18:15–27**).

15:1 The Sanhedrin delivers Jesus to the Roman governor in an attempt to have Him sentenced to death (parallel passages: **Matt. 27:1–2; Luke 23:1**).

15:2–15 Pilate, the Roman governor, sentences Jesus to death by crucifixion (parallel passages: **Matt. 27:11–26; Luke 23:13–25; John 18:28–19:16**).

15:16–20 Jesus is mocked by Roman soldiers (parallel passage: **Matt. 27:27–31**).

15:21 Simon of Cyrene, a bystander, carries the cross of Jesus to the crucifixion site (parallel passages: **Matt. 27:32; Luke 23:26–31**).

15:22–26 Jesus is crucified at a site known as Golgotha (parallel passages: **Matt. 27:33–37; Luke 23:32–38; John 19:17–24**).

15:27–32 As He hangs on the cross between two thieves, Jesus is taunted by the crowd (parallel passages: **Matt. 27:38–44; Luke 23:39–43**).

15:33–39 For three hours before Jesus dies, darkness covers the earth. He quotes from Ps. 22:1 and cries out in despair, "My God, my God, why hast thou forsaken me," (v. 34). Upon His death, the huge curtain in the temple is ripped from top to bottom. Shaken by these mysterious happenings, a Roman centurion declares, "Truly this man was the Son of God" (v. 39) (parallel passages: **Matt. 27:45–54; Luke 23:44–48**).

15:40–41 Several women stand watch at the cross as Jesus is crucified (parallel passages: **Matt. 27:55–56; Luke 23:49; John 19:25–27**).

15:42–46 Jesus is buried in the tomb of Joseph of Arimathea (parallel passages: **Matt. 27:57–60; Luke 23:50–54; John 19:38–42**).

15:47 Women mourn at the tomb where Jesus is buried (parallel passages: **Matt. 27:61; Luke 23:55–56**).

16:1–8 Women discover that Jesus is gone when they visit the tomb to anoint His body on Sunday morning (parallel passages: **Matt. 28:1–10; Luke 24:1–8; John 20:1–2**).

16:9–11 The resurrected Jesus appears to Mary Magdalene (parallel passage: **John 20:11–18**).

16:12–13 Jesus appears to two of His followers on their way to Emmaus (parallel passage: **Luke 24:13–35**).

16:14–18 Jesus commissions His disciples (Acts 1:8) to continue His work (parallel passages: **Matt. 28:16–20; Luke 24:44–49**).

16:19–20 Jesus ascends to His Father (Acts 1:9), and His disciples continue His ministry, as they were commanded (parallel passage: **Luke 24:50–53**).

Abba An Aramaic word meaning "father," used by Jesus while praying in Gethsemane (Mark 14:32, 36). It was also used by Paul to express the Christian's sonship with God the Father (Rom. 8:15).

Missions The process of carrying out Jesus' Great Commission to disciple and teach all peoples. Even in the OT, Abraham was called to be a blessing to all nations (Gen. 12:1–3), and Jonah was sent by the Lord to preach to the pagan citizens of Nineveh (Jon. 1:2). Missions is prompted by God's love (John 3:16) and humankind's lost condition (Rom. 3:9–31).

Believers are equipped for the task of missions by the Holy Spirit's presence (Acts 1:8), the Word of God (Rom. 10:14–15), and the power of prayer (Acts 13:1–4). Christ's followers are to evangelize all nations, baptize believers, and teach His commands (Matt. 28:19–20).

....

Bread of Betrayal *He [Jesus] answered. . . It is one of the twelve, that dippeth with me in the dish* (Mark 14:20).

People of Bible times did not use utensils such as forks and spoons to eat their meals. They picked up the food with their hands. But some dishes such as stew or gravy had to be scooped up with a piece of bread. This is the method of eating to which Jesus referred in this verse. In John's Gospel this bread used to pick up liquid food is call a "sop." Jesus handed the bread to Judas, clearly identifying him as the betrayer (John 13:26).

OCTOBER 27 | Read Luke 1

1:1–4 Luke begins his Gospel by addressing his friend Theophilus. He wants Theophilus to hear from him the truth about Jesus and His work. Luke also wrote the book of Acts. He also began this book with a word to Theophilus (Acts 1:1).

1:5–7 An elderly priest named Zacharias and his wife, Elisabeth, are godly, righteous people. But they have not been able to have children.

1:8–17 The angel Gabriel appears to Zacharias while he is burning incense in the temple. He informs the elderly priest that he and Elisabeth will be blessed with a son whom they are to name John. He will grow up to become a great prophet who will prepare the way for the coming of the long-expected Messiah.

1:18–25 Zacharias expresses doubt that this will happen. The angel informs him that he will be punished for his disbelief by not being able to speak until the child is born.

1:26–33 The angel Gabriel also visits Mary, a young woman who lives in the city of Nazareth in the region of Galilee. Gabriel informs Mary that she will become pregnant and give birth to the long-expected Messiah. She is to give Him the name Jesus, which means "Savior."

1:34–38 Mary wonders how this birth can happen, since she is a virgin. The angel assures her that her pregnancy will occur supernaturally through the power of the Holy Spirit. The angel also informs Mary of the pregnancy of her cousin Elisabeth in the region of Judea.

1:39–56 Mary visits her cousin Elisabeth. They rejoice together about God's actions in their lives. Mary sings a beautiful song of thanksgiving known as the Magnificat (vv. 46–55). It expresses her joy that God will fulfill His promise of a Messiah for Israel through this child who will come from her womb.

1:57–66 The child of their old age is born to Zacharias and Elisabeth. Following the orders of the angel Gabriel, they name him John. The punishment for Zacharias's doubt is lifted, and he is able to speak again.

1:67–80 In this prophetic song known as the Benedictus, Zacharias expresses his thanks to God for the coming of the Messiah and the role his son, John, will play in preparing the way for His mission.

First Advent of Christ The birth of Jesus Christ in human form to the virgin Mary. His coming was foretold in the OT (Isa. 7:14; 9:6). Joseph was reassured by an angel that Mary's pregnancy was supernatural (Matt. 1:20–21). The angel Gabriel announced His coming birth to Mary (Luke 1:26–35).

Jesus was born to Mary in Bethlehem (Matt. 1:25; 2:1). His birth was revealed to shepherds (Luke 2:8–16). Wise men from the East brought gifts to the Christ child (Matt. 2:1–11). His birth was defined as a redemptive mission (Matt. 1:21–23; Luke 2:10–11). It nullified the OT ceremonial system (Heb. 9) and introduced the Gospel age (Acts 3:20–26).

Magnificat The poem or song of the Virgin Mary upon learning she would give birth to the Messiah (Luke 1:46–55). Mary praised God for remembering "the lowliness of his servant" (NRSV) and for keeping His promise to bless Abraham and his descendants.

Zacharias and Elisabeth *There was. . .a certain priest named Zacharias, of the course of Abia: and his wife was of the daughters of Aaron* (Luke 1:5).

Zacharias was the father of John the Baptist, forerunner of Jesus. In this verse Luke shows us that Zacharias was a priest of impeccable credentials. When the priesthood was established in the days of Moses and Aaron, God made it clear that He expected His priests to be physically and morally qualified for the office. They could not have any physical disability or defect (Lev. 21:16–21). They were to be holy, respecting the Lord and obeying His commands (Lev. 21:6). Even their wives were to be persons of high moral character (Lev. 21:7). Zacharias apparently met all these qualifications. His wife, Elisabeth, was even a descendant of Aaron, the first high priest of the Israelites (Exod. 28:1, 29–30).

OCTOBER 28 | Read Luke 2–3

2:1–5 Mary and Joseph, the man to whom Mary is engaged, travel from Nazareth to the city of Bethlehem, Joseph's ancestral home, to register in a census. This registration for taxation purposes had been ordered for all residents throughout the Roman Empire by the emperor, Augustus Caesar.

2:6–7 While Mary and Joseph are in Bethlehem, Jesus is born in a stable. Their accommodations are crude because all the inns are filled with people in town for the census. Jesus' first crib is a feeding trough for livestock.

2:8–14 Angels announce the birth of Jesus to a group of shepherds who are watching over their sheep in the fields outside Bethlehem.

2:15–20 The shepherds hurry into Bethlehem, where they find Mary and Joseph and the baby Jesus. These humble shepherds become the first to announce the birth of "a Saviour, which is Christ the Lord" (Luke 2:11) to others.

2:21–24 When Jesus is eight days old, His parents take Him to the temple in Jerusalem for circumcision and dedication to the Lord, in accordance with Jewish custom (Gen. 17:12; Lev. 12:3).

2:25–35 When Jesus is brought into the temple, an aged man named Simeon recognizes Him as the long-expected Messiah. He prophesies that Jesus will be a light for Gentiles as well as the Jewish people (Eph. 2:11–22). He also declares that His mother's heart will be broken by the suffering He is destined to endure.

2:36–38 An aged prophetess named Anna overhears Simeon's prophecy. She joins in with thanksgiving to God for sending redemption to Israel through this newborn Messiah.

2:39–40 Jesus grows up under the nurture of His earthly parents, Mary and Joseph, in the village of Nazareth in the region of Galilee (parallel passage: **Matt. 2:19–23**).

2:41–52 These verses in Luke give us the only information we have about Jesus' childhood years. When He is twelve years old, He accompanies His parents to Jerusalem to observe the Passover festival (Josh. 5:10–12). On their way back to Nazareth, Mary and Joseph discover that Jesus is missing. Returning to Jerusalem, they find Him sitting among the learned interpreters of the scriptures, both learning from them and contributing His own ideas. It is obvious to everyone that this is no ordinary twelve-year-old boy.

3:1–20 John the Baptist, forerunner of Jesus, launches his preaching ministry (parallel passages: Matt. 3:1–12; Mark 1:1–8). He challenges the people to repent of their sins and get ready for the coming of God's kingdom. Many of his hearers think John is the Messiah, but he makes it clear that he is preparing the way for "one mightier than I" (v. 16) who is the deliverer sent from God.

3:21–22 Jesus is baptized by John (parallel passages: **Matt. 3:13–17; Mark 1:9–11**).

3:23–38 Luke's genealogy of Jesus begins with Joseph and goes all the way back to Adam. (For a different genealogy of Jesus, see Matt. 1:1–17.)

Bethlehem A town in southern Palestine near Jerusalem, also called *Bethlehem-judah* (Judg. 19:18), where Jesus was born in fulfillment of prophecy (Mic. 5:2; Luke 2:4–7). It was called the "City of David" because King David grew up there centuries before (1 Sam. 16:1–13). David's ancestor Ruth gleaned grain in the fields of Boaz nearby (Ruth 2:4–8). Bethlehem was known in OT times as *Ephrath* (Gen. 35:19) and *Ephratah* (Ruth 4:11).

John the Baptist The prophet of righteousness and preacher of repentance who prepared the way for Christ. John's birth, Nazarite lifestyle, and unique role as the Messiah's forerunner were revealed to his father, Zechariah (Luke 1:13–17), and his mother, Elizabeth, a cousin of Mary—the mother of Jesus (Luke 1:5–7, 39–41). John preached repentance and baptized converts in the Jordan River (Matt. 3:1–6), reluctantly agreeing to baptize Jesus after proclaiming Him as the "Lamb of God" (Matt. 3:13–17; John 1:29). John also denounced the hypocrisy of the Pharisees and the immorality and adultery of Herod Antipas, a Roman ruler in Palestine (Matt. 3:7–8; 14:4). He was executed by Herod at the request of his wife, Herodias's, dancing daughter (Matt. 14:3–12). John always magnified Jesus rather than himself (John 3:30), and Jesus commended him highly for his faithfulness (Luke 7:24–28).

Wrapped and Laid in a Manger *She [Mary] brought forth her firstborn son, and wrapped him in swaddling clothes, and laid him in a manger* (Luke 2:7).

After His birth in a stable in Bethlehem, the baby Jesus was placed in a manger, a feeding trough for livestock. This manger may have been hewed out of rock. Stone mangers about three feet long have been discovered in the ruins of King Ahab's stables at the ancient city of Megiddo. The "swaddling clothes" in which Jesus was wrapped after His birth were strips of cloth that were wound tightly around a newborn's body to restrict movement. This custom is also mentioned in Ezekiel 16:4.

OCTOBER 29 | Read Luke 4–5

4:1–13 Beginning in the wilderness, Satan presents a series of temptations to Jesus at the beginning of His public ministry. Jesus rises above these temptations through the power of prayer and the scriptures (parallel passages: **Matt. 4:1–11; Mark 1:12–13**).

4:14–15 Jesus begins His preaching ministry in the region of Galilee.

4:16–30 Jesus preaches in the synagogue in His hometown of Nazareth. He identifies Himself as God's Suffering Servant depicted in the book of Isaiah (Isa. 61:1–2). The townspeople are enraged because they consider this blasphemous, so they try to kill Jesus. But He slips away and leaves the town.

4:31–37 Jesus makes Capernaum in the region of Galilee His headquarters city. He heals a demon-possessed man in the synagogue on the Sabbath. His reputation grows as people express amazement at His power and authority (parallel passage: **Mark 1:21–28**).

4:38–41 Jesus heals Peter's mother-in-law in Capernaum (parallel passages: **Matt. 8:14–17; Mark 1:29–34**).

4:42–44 Jesus preaches and heals in other cities throughout the region of Galilee (parallel passages: **Matt. 4:23–25; Mark 1:35–39**).

5:1–11 Jesus astonishes Peter by producing a miraculous catch of fish after Peter and his partners had worked all night without catching anything. Then Jesus calls Peter and his partners, the brothers James and John, to leave their fishing nets and become His followers (parallel passages: **Matt. 4:18–22; Mark 1:16–20**).

5:12–16 Jesus heals a man with leprosy (parallel passages: **Matt. 8:1–4; Mark 1:40–45**).

5:17–26 Jesus heals a paralyzed man and forgives his sins (parallel passages: **Matt. 9:1–8; Mark 2:1–12**).

5:27–32 Jesus calls Matthew (also known as Levi), a tax collector, to become His disciple. Scribes and Pharisees criticize Him for associating with tax collectors and sinners. Jesus explains that His mission is "not to call the righteous, but sinners to repentance" (v. 32) (parallel passages: **Matt. 9:9–13; Mark 2:13–17**).

5:33–39 Jesus tells why He and His disciples do not fast (parallel passages: **Matt. 9:14–17; Mark 2:18–22**).

. . . .

Publican A Jewish citizen who purchased the right to collect taxes in a specific area of his country for the Roman government. Publicans were hated and looked upon as traitors by their fellow citizens (Matt. 5:46). Matthew (Matt. 9:9–11) and Zacchaeus (Luke 19:1–10) were prominent publicans who followed Jesus. *Tax collector:* NIV, NRSV.

. . . .

Reading in a Synagogue *He [Jesus] went into the synagogue on the sabbath day, and stood up for to read* (Luke 4:16).

This synagogue in which Jesus read the OT scriptures was in Nazareth, his hometown in the province of Galilee. Synagogues were built in towns and cities throughout Palestine. Their purpose was not to replace the temple in Jerusalem that served as the central place of worship and sacrifice for all Israel. Synagogues existed to teach the law to local people. A community synagogue was presided over by a leader who had been elected by its members. Priests had no official role in synagogues, although they often attended and were honored by being asked to read the scriptures during the service. Jesus was not a priest or a member of the religious establishment. His reading in the Nazareth synagogue shows that common, everyday "laypeople" who were known in the community were often asked to participate in the service. In addition, His ministry as a teacher and healer had begun to attract attention throughout Galilee (Luke 4:14–15). Jesus read from the book of Isaiah and identified Himself as the Servant of the Lord whom the prophet had written about (Luke 4:17–21).

OCTOBER 30 | Read Luke 6–7

6:1–5 Jesus answers the charge that He is desecrating the Sabbath; He claims to be "Lord also of the sabbath" (v. 5) (parallel passages: **Matt. 12:1–8; Mark 2:23–28**).

6:6–11 The Pharisees are enraged because Jesus heals a man's withered hand on the Sabbath (parallel passages: **Matt. 12:9–14; Mark 3:1–6**).

6:12–16 After spending all night in prayer, Jesus selects twelve men from among His followers to serve as His disciples, or apostles. He will train them to continue His work after His ministry on earth has ended (parallel passages: **Matt. 10:1–4; Mark 3:13–19**). See Acts 1:13.

6:17–49 These verses contain Luke's version of Jesus' teachings known as the Sermon on the Mount. A longer and more complete record of these teachings appears in Matthew 5:1–7:29.

7:1–10 Jesus heals the servant of a centurion, a Roman military officer (parallel passage: **Matt. 8:5–13**).

7:11–17 Jesus has compassion on a widow in the city of Nain. He raises her only son from the dead.

7:18–35 Jesus answers a question from John the Baptist about whether He really is the Messiah (parallel passage: **Matt. 11:1–19**).

7:36–50 A sinful woman anoints Jesus with an expensive perfume while He is a dinner guest in the home of Simon the Pharisee. Jesus uses her actions to teach Simon a lesson in forgiveness and gratitude.

....

Apostle A person personally commissioned by Christ to represent Him (Matt. 10:1–4). The original twelve apostles or disciples were chosen by Jesus after He had prayed all night (Luke 6:12–16). Apostles are persons sent with a special message or commission (John 15:16). Jesus empowered His apostles to cast out evil spirits and to heal (Matt. 10:1). Paul regarded himself as an apostle because of his encounter with Christ on the Damascus Road and his personal call by Jesus to missionary work (1 Cor. 15:8–10). In Paul's letters, persons who saw the risen Christ and who were specially called by Him are regarded as apostles (1 Cor. 15:5–8).

Zelotes A member of a political-religious party of zealous Jews in NT times whose aim was to overthrow Roman rule and establish a Jewish theocracy. Jesus' disciple known as Simon the Canaanite may have been a member of this party or sympathetic with its views (Luke 6:15). *Zealot*: NIV, NRSV.

OCTOBER 31 | Read Luke 8–9

8:1–3 Jesus conducts another teaching and healing tour throughout the region of Galilee. Accompanying Him and His disciples are several women followers, including Mary Magdalene, whom He had healed of demon possession.

8:4–8 Jesus teaches the crowds with the parable of the sower (parallel passages: **Matt. 13:1–9; Mark 4:1–9**).

8:9–10 Jesus explains why He teaches in parables (parallel passages: **Matt. 13:10–17; Mark 4:10–12**).

8:11–15 Jesus reveals the meaning of the parable of the sower to His disciples (parallel passages: **Matt. 13:18–23; Mark 4:13–20**).

8:16–18 Jesus delivers the parable of the candle, or lampstand (parallel passage: **Mark 4:21–25**).

8:19–21 Jesus identifies His true relatives as those who follow God (parallel passages: **Matt. 12:46–50; Mark 3:31–35**).

8:22–25 Jesus calms a storm on the Sea of Galilee (parallel passages: **Matt. 8:23–27; Mark 4:35–41**).

8:26–39 Jesus heals a demon-possessed man who lives in a cemetery (parallel passages: **Matt. 8:28–34; Mark 5:1–20**).

8:40–56 Jesus heals a woman with a hemorrhage and raises the daughter of Jairus from the dead (parallel passages: **Matt. 9:18–26; Mark 5:21–43**).

9:1–6 Jesus gives His disciples power and authority and sends them out to teach and heal (parallel passages: **Matt. 10:5–42; Mark 6:7–13**).

9:7–9 Herod, the Roman ruler of Galilee, hears about Jesus and His miracles. He wonders if He could be John the Baptist returned from the dead.

9:10–17 Jesus performs a feeding miracle for more than 5,000 hungry people (parallel passages: **Matt. 14:13–21; Mark 6:30–44; John 6:1–14**).

9:18–20 Peter confesses Jesus as the Christ, the Anointed One sent from God (parallel passages: **Matt. 16:13–20; Mark 8:27–30**).

9:21–27 Jesus predicts that He will be killed by the religious leaders and then resurrected. He teaches His disciples about the high cost and rewards involved in following Him.

9:28–36 Jesus is transfigured before three of His disciples (parallel passages: **Matt. 17:1–13; Mark 9:2–13**).

9:37–42 Jesus heals a demon-possessed boy (parallel passages: **Matt. 17:14–21; Mark 9:14–29**).

9:43–45 Jesus again predicts His death and resurrection (parallel passages: **Matt. 17:22–23; Mark 9:30–32**).

`9:46–50` Jesus teaches His disciples that true greatness consists of rendering service to others (parallel passages: **Matt. 18:1–10; Mark 9:33–50**).

`9:51–56` Jesus is rejected by the citizens of a Samaritan village. He rebukes His disciples James and John because they want to destroy the village.

`9:57–62` Jesus declares that people must count the cost of full commitment before they agree to become His followers (parallel passage: **Matt. 8:18–22**).

....

`Mary Magdalene` A woman who witnessed the crucifixion and visited the tomb of Jesus (Matt. 27:55–61). She told the apostles of Jesus about the empty tomb (John 20:1–2) and was one of the first persons to see the risen Lord (Mark 16:9).

`Joanna` A woman who was a faithful follower of Jesus (Luke 8:1–3). She prepared spices for His burial and proclaimed His resurrection (Luke 23:55–56; 24:1–10).

`Demon Possession` Invasion and control of a person by evil spirits. In NT times, these demons often caused disability (Mark 9:17–25), mental anguish (Matt. 8:28), and antisocial behavior (Luke 8:27–39). Jesus cast demons out of several people—an act that showed His power over the demonic forces of Satan (Mark 1:25; 9:29).

NOVEMBER 1 | Read Luke 10–11

`10:1–24` Jesus sends seventy of His followers out after empowering them to teach and heal. They return with reports of great success among the people.

`10:25–37` Jesus uses the parable of the good Samaritan to teach an expert in the law what it means to be a compassionate neighbor to others.

`10:38–42` Jesus visits the sisters Mary and Martha. He teaches Martha that she should be more concerned about learning from Him than she is about getting the housework done.

`11:1–13` In response to a question from His disciples, Jesus teaches them how to pray. Verses 2–4, which parallel Matthew 6:9–13, are known as the Lord's Prayer, or the Model Prayer.

`11:14–28` Jesus answers those who are accusing Him of casting demons out of people through the power of Beelzebub, the chief of demons. Jesus shows that the charge is ridiculous. To cast out evil spirits through the power of Satan would mean that Satan is divided against himself.

`11:29–36` The scribes and Pharisees ask Jesus to show them some spectacular sign to prove that He is who He claims to be. He responds that the only sign they will be shown is the sign of the prophet Jonah. Just as Jonah was delivered by the Lord from the stomach of a great fish after three days (Jon. 1:17; 2:10), so Jesus will be killed and raised from the dead after three days.

11:37–54 Jesus criticizes the Pharisees because of their hypocrisy, legalism, and emphasis on external matters in religion.

Bethany A village near the Mount of Olives outside Jerusalem (Mark 11:1) and home of Lazarus, Mary, and Martha—friends of Jesus (John 11:1). Jesus ascended to heaven from Bethany (Luke 24:50).

Martha The sister of Mary and Lazarus (John 11:1–2). Jesus rebuked Martha because of her unnecessary worry after she welcomed Him into her home (Luke 10:38–42). She grieved at the death of her brother, Lazarus, and sought Jesus' help (John 11:20–22).

Lazarus A brother of Mary and Martha whom Jesus raised from the dead. This event impressed the common people (John 11:41–45) but provoked the Jewish leaders to seek the death of both Jesus and Lazarus (John 11:47–57; 12:10–11).

Don't Waste Time *Salute [greet, NIV] no man by the way [on the road, NIV]* (Luke 10:4).

Jesus gave these instructions to seventy of His followers when He sent them out on a teaching and witnessing mission. It seems strange that He would forbid them from greeting the very people whom they were sent to reach. But Jesus did not restrict them from greeting strangers with a friendly "hello." He was referring to the elaborate and drawn-out salutations with which the Jewish people sometimes greeted one another. They would bow again and again, ask about the health and welfare of all the members of their respective families, and repeat their wishes for the peace and prosperity of the other several times. This type of greeting took a lot of time. "Greet people quickly, and be on your way," is what Jesus was saying. "Let's use every precious minute we have to bring people into God's kingdom."

NOVEMBER 2 | Read Luke 12–13

12:1–12 Jesus warns His disciples to beware of the teachings and traditions of the Pharisees. He also warns that anyone who denies the works of God is guilty of the unforgivable sin of blasphemy against the Holy Spirit.

12:13–21 Through the parable of the rich fool, Jesus warns against misplaced priorities—considering possessions and material wealth more important than commitment to God.

12:22–34 Jesus teaches His disciples not to be overly concerned about their physical needs but to seek first "the kingdom of God; and all these things shall be added unto you" (v. 31).

12:35–48 Through the parable of the unfaithful servant, Jesus teaches His followers to be watchful and ready for His second coming (1 Thess. 5:1–11).

12:49–59 Jesus makes it clear that the time of His death is drawing near. People should be aware of this critical moment and turn to God in repentance and faith.

13:1–9 Jesus' parable of the barren fig tree teaches that the Jewish people have failed in their mission as God's special people. But He is giving them one last chance to show their obedience by accepting His Son Jesus and becoming citizens of His kingdom.

13:10–17 A synagogue ruler criticizes Jesus after He heals a woman with a crooked back on the Sabbath. Jesus points out that the Jewish law allowed livestock to be led to water on the Sabbath. Wasn't this woman more important than an ox or a donkey?

13:18–21 The parables of the mustard seed and the leaven show that the kingdom of God will eventually become a strong force in the world (parallel passage: **Matt. 13:31–35**).

13:22–30 The Jewish people thought they had an exclusive claim on God's love and generosity and that all non-Jews were excluded. But Jesus declares that the kingdom of God belongs to those who turn to Him in repentance and faith.

13:31–33 Jesus ignores a warning from the Pharisees to leave Galilee because of a supposed threat from Herod, the Roman ruler in the region.

13:34–35 Jesus predicts that the city of Jerusalem will be punished by the Lord because it has refused to accept Him as the Messiah (parallel passage: **Matt. 23:37–39**).

- -

Kingdom of God The spiritual reign of God in the hearts of believers (Luke 17:20–21). Partially attained in this life for those who seek God's will, God's kingdom will be fully established in the world to come (John 18:36). Jesus preached the "gospel of the kingdom" (Mark 1:14) and taught His disciples to seek His kingdom (Matt. 6:33) and to pray for its arrival on earth (Matt. 6:10). Unrepentant sinners cannot inherit this kingdom (Eph. 5:5). It is reserved for those who repent (Matt. 3:2) and experience spiritual rebirth (John 3:3–5). Other phrases for this kingdom are "kingdom of heaven" (Matt. 4:17) and "kingdom of Christ" (Col. 1:13).

NOVEMBER 3 | Read Luke 14–15

14:1–6 Jesus defends His healing of a man with the dropsy (a condition that causes a buildup of fluid in the body) on the Sabbath.

14:7–14 Citizens of the kingdom of God should not seek positions of glory and honor for themselves. Humble service to others should be their main concern.

14:15–24 This parable of the great supper shows that the nation of Israel has refused God's glorious invitation to enter His kingdom. Now God is establishing a covenant relationship with the Gentiles—those once considered outsiders and sinners. Any person who accepts God's invitation and turns to Him in repentance and faith is included in God's kingdom, no matter what his or her race or ethnic background (Acts 15:19).

14:25–35 Following Jesus involves sacrifice. A person should consider the cost before making a commitment to discipleship.

15:1–32 Two of the three parables in this chapter about something lost—a lost coin and a lost son—are unique to the Gospel of Luke. The parable of the lost sheep also appears in Matthew's Gospel (Matt. 18:11–14). These parables show that God's love has no limits. He is relentless in His efforts to seek and restore to His favor those who are lost.

Dining with a Pharisee *He [Jesus] went into the house of one of the chief Pharisees to eat bread on the sabbath day* (Luke 14:1).

Jesus' clash with the Pharisees throughout the Gospels may lead us to believe that all Pharisees were bad or that Jesus condemned them all. But this verse shows us otherwise. A leader among the Pharisees apparently invited Jesus to dine in his home on the Sabbath, and He accepted the invitation. Jesus used the occasion to teach this man and several other Pharisees about His healing mission and His superiority over the Sabbath (Luke 14:3–6). Two other Pharisees in the Gospels are also worthy of commendation. Nicodemus was a Pharisee who was known for his inquiring mind and search for truth (John 3:1–12). Joseph of Arimathea was probably a Pharisee since he was a member of the Sanhedrin. He claimed the body of Jesus and buried it in his own new tomb (Mark 15:43–46; Luke 23:53; John 19:38).

NOVEMBER 4 | Read Luke 16–17

16:1–18 The dishonest manager in this parable is shrewd enough to look ahead and prepare for his future security. Believers should show the same foresight in their preparation for eternal life in fellowship with God.

16:19–31 The parable of the rich man and Lazarus shows the tragedy of a life devoted to earthly pleasures with no concern for spiritual values. The rich man's lifestyle of indulgence shuts him off from fellowship with God—an eternal separation that continues in the afterlife.

17:1–10 Jesus teaches that the lives of those who are citizens of God's kingdom should be characterized by forgiveness and service (Eph. 6:7). We serve others not for reward or commendation but because service is what God has called us and equipped us to do.

17:11–19 Jesus heals ten men with leprosy while on His way to Jerusalem. He commends the one man among the ten—a Samaritan—who seeks Jesus out to express His gratitude.

17:20–37 Jesus tells the Pharisees that the kingdom of God is already present. He stands among them as God's Son, the Messiah, the personification of the kingdom that God is building in the hearts of those who believe in Him. He also discusses the final consummation of this kingdom in the future, when He will return as the victorious King over all creation in His second coming (1 Thess. 4:13–17).

Abraham's Bosom A symbolic expression for the blissful state after death (Luke 16:22). The Jews believed they joined their forefathers, particularly "father Abraham," upon their death (Gen. 15:15).

Second Coming Christ's return to earth to punish the wicked and unbelieving and to receive glory from believers (2 Thess. 1:7–10). This event will happen suddenly, and Jesus will be "revealed from heaven with his mighty angels" (2 Thess. 1:7). He will raise the dead (1 Thess. 4:13–17), destroy death (1 Cor. 15:25–26), gather the redeemed (Matt. 24:31), judge the world (Matt. 25:32), and reward God's people (Matt. 16:27). Christians should be prepared for the Lord's coming (Matt. 24:42) and remain faithful in Christian service (1 Cor. 15:58).

NOVEMBER 5 | Read Luke 18–19

18:1–8 This parable of the persistent widow teaches an important lesson about prayer: We should be consistent and persistent in the prayer requests we present to God.

18:9–14 Through this parable of the Pharisee and the publican (tax collector), Jesus teaches about humility in prayer. God rejects the self-righteous prayer of the proud Pharisee, but He accepts the prayer of the publican because he admits his sin and unworthiness.

18:15–17 Jesus welcomes little children (parallel passages: **Matt. 19:13–15; Mark 10:13–16**).

18:18–30 Jesus challenges the rich young ruler to sell all his possessions and follow Him (parallel passages: **Matt. 19:16–30; Mark 10:17–31**).

18:31–34 Jesus again tells His disciples that He will be executed in Jerusalem, then resurrected (parallel passages: **Matt. 20:17–19; Mark 10:32–34**).

18:35–43 Jesus heals a blind man near Jericho (parallel passages: **Matt. 20:29–34; Mark 10:46–52**).

19:1–10 A tax collector named Zacchaeus climbs a tree to get a better look at Jesus as He passes through Jericho. Confronted by Jesus, he vows to give half of his possessions to the poor and to repay fourfold any excess taxes he has collected "by false accusation" (v. 8).

19:11–27 This passage is known as the parable of the pounds. Ten servants are given one pound (a sum of money) each to manage for their master while he is gone. The servant who plays it safe and fails to increase his pound is criticized by his master. This parable teaches that we are held accountable for our management of God's resources.

19:28–44 Jesus is greeted and praised by the crowds as He rides into Jerusalem (Zech. 9:9). He weeps over the city because of its unbelief (parallel passages: **Matt. 21:1–11; Mark 11:1–11; John 12:12–19**).

19:45–48 Jesus drives out the merchants who are buying and selling in the temple (parallel passages: **Matt. 21:12–22; Mark 11:12–26**).

Zacchaeus A wealthy tax collector who, after a conversation with Jesus at Jericho, vowed to give half of his wealth to the poor and make fourfold restitution to those whom he had cheated. Jesus declared that salvation had come to Zacchaeus (Luke 19:1–10).

Twice-a-Week Fasting *I [self-righteous Pharisee] fast twice in the week, I give tithes of all that I possess* (Luke 18:12).

These are the words of the self-righteous Pharisee in Jesus' parable about the Pharisee and the tax collector. The Pharisee tried to justify himself in God's sight by claiming he had kept the letter of the law. But the tax collector realized he was a sinner and cast himself on God's mercy (Luke 18:9–14). Fasting twice a week, as the Pharisee claimed to do, was not commanded in the Law of Moses. This was probably a custom instituted by the Pharisees as an addition to the law that they practiced scrupulously. The message of this verse is that we can't buy our way into heaven by observing certain rituals. We are justified in God's sight only through faith in Jesus Christ and His atoning death on our behalf.

NOVEMBER 6 | Read Luke 20–22:38

20:1–8 Jesus responds to the charge of the Pharisees by claiming that He has authority over the temple (parallel passages: **Matt. 21:23–27; Mark 11:27–33**).

20:9–19 Jesus condemns the religious leaders of Israel by comparing them to wicked husbandmen, or tenant farmers (parallel passages: **Matt. 21:33–46; Mark 12:1–12**).

20:20–26 Jesus is questioned by His enemies about paying taxes to the Roman government (parallel passages: **Matt. 22:15–22; Mark 12:13–17**).

20:27–40 Jesus avoids a trick question from the Sadducees about the resurrection (parallel passages: **Matt. 22:23–33; Mark 12:18–27**).

20:41–44 Jesus uses scripture to show the scribes that the Messiah from the line of David is more than an earthly king (parallel passages: **Matt. 22:41–46; Mark 12:35–37**).

20:45–47 Jesus condemns the Pharisees for their pride and dishonesty (parallel passages: **Matt. 23:1–36; Mark 12:38–40**).

21:1–4 A sacrificial offering in the temple by a poor widow draws Jesus' praise (parallel passage: **Mark 12:41–44**).

21:5–38 Jesus discusses events that will occur in the end-time before His second coming (parallel passages: **Matt. 24:1–51; Mark 13:1–37**).

22:1–2 The Jewish Sanhedrin plots the death of Jesus (parallel passages: **Matt. 26:1–5; Mark 14:1–2**).

22:3–6 Judas makes a deal with the Sanhedrin to betray Jesus (parallel passages: **Matt. 26:14–16; Mark 14:10–11**).

22:7–13 Jesus sends Peter and John to find a room where He and His disciples can partake of the Passover meal together (parallel passages: **Matt. 26:17–19; Mark 14:12–16**).

22:14–20 Jesus turns the Passover meal with His disciples into a supper that memorializes His forthcoming sacrificial death (1 Cor. 11:23–26). He institutes the new covenant with all believers by declaring that the bread represents His broken body and the wine represents His blood, "which is shed for you" (v. 20) (parallel passages: **Matt. 26:26–30; Mark 14:22–26**).

22:21–23 Jesus reveals to His disciples that one of them will betray Him (parallel passages: **Matt. 26:20–25; Mark 14:17–21; John 13:21–30**).

22:24–30 Jesus' disciples begin to argue over which of them is the most important. Jesus teaches them that the greatest citizen in the kingdom of God is the one who is self-giving in service to others.

22:31–38 Jesus tells Peter that he will face great temptation from Satan during the next several hours. He predicts that Peter will deny Him three times before the rooster crows at daybreak (parallel passages: **Matt. 26:31–35; Mark 14:27–31; John 13:31–38**).

. . . .

New Covenant God's final covenant with His people through which His grace is expressed to all believers. Prophesied by the prophet Jeremiah (Jer. 31:31–34), the new covenant was symbolized by Jesus at the Passover meal with His disciples. He called the cup the "new covenant in my blood" (Luke 22:20 NIV, NRSV). Christ, mediator of a new and better covenant, assures our eternal inheritance (Heb. 8:6–8, 13; 9:11–15; 12:24).

Simon Simon Peter, one of the twelve apostles or disciples of Christ and the leader of the church in Jerusalem after the resurrection and ascension of Jesus. A fisherman from Galilee, Peter followed Jesus after he was encouraged to do so by his brother Andrew (John 1:40–41). He was called *Cephas* by Jesus, a name meaning "stone" (John 1:42), perhaps indicating the promise that Jesus saw in him in spite of his reckless temperament and impetuous personality.

Peter swore he would never forsake Christ, but he denied Him three times on the night before His crucifixion (Matt. 26:69–75). He went on to become a bold spokesman for Christ in the early years of the Christian movement (Acts 2:14–40). Peter's surname was *Bar-jona* (Matt. 16:17). *Son of Jonah*: NIV, NRSV

Herod's Temple in Jerusalem *Some spake of the temple, how it was adorned with goodly [beautiful, NIV] stones and gifts* (Luke 21:5).

When Jesus entered Jerusalem for the Passover celebration, His disciples were impressed with the Jewish temple that was being remodeled and expanded by Herod the Great, Roman ruler over Palestine. According to the Jewish historian Josephus, its white marble and gold-accented trim were dazzling to the eyes. Herod began this building project about 15 BC in order to curry the favor of the Jews. It was still under construction about forty-five years later when Jesus and His disciples came to the holy city to observe the Passover. Finally completed in AD 64, the temple was destroyed—as Jesus predicted (Luke 21:6)—when the Roman army put down a rebellion by the Jewish people in AD 70. The temple in Jerusalem has never been rebuilt. Today a Moslem mosque known as the Dome of the Rock occupies the site.

NOVEMBER 7 | Read Luke 22:39–24:53

22:39–46 Jesus pours out His heart to God in agonizing prayer in the Garden of Gethsemane (parallel passages: **Matt. 26:36–46; Mark 14:32–42**).

22:47–53 Jesus is betrayed by Judas and arrested by the Jewish Sanhedrin (parallel passages: **Matt. 26:47–56; Mark 14:43–52; John 18:1–12**).

22:54–62 Peter follows Jesus when He is led away to the house of the Jewish high priest for interrogation by the Sanhedrin. Questioned outside the house by three different people, he denies that he knows Jesus (parallel passages: **Matt. 26:69–75; Mark 14:66–72; John 18:15–27**).

22:63–71 Jesus is found guilty of blasphemy by the Jewish Sanhedrin when He admits He is the Son of God (parallel passages: **Matt. 26:57–68; Mark 14:53–65**).

23:1 Determined to have Jesus executed, the Sanhedrin delivers Him to Pontius Pilate, the Roman governor of Judea (parallel passages: **Matt. 27:1–2; Mark 15:1**).

23:2–12 After questioning Jesus, Pilate is convinced He is innocent. Trying to shift responsibility for a ruling in His case, Pilate sends Jesus to Herod, the Roman governor of Galilee, who is visiting Jerusalem during the Passover celebration. Herod refuses to get involved and sends Jesus back to Pilate.

23:13–25 Pilate finally gives in to the cries of the crowd and sentences Jesus to death by crucifixion (parallel passages: **Matt. 27:11–26; Mark 15:2–15; John 18:28–19:16**).

23:26–31 A citizen of Cyrene named Simon carries Jesus' cross to the crucifixion site. Addressing a group of women in the crowd, Jesus prophesies that great calamity will fall upon the nation of Israel in the future. He may have been referring to the destruction of Jerusalem by the Roman army in AD 70 (parallel passages: **Matt. 27:32; Mark 15:21**).

23:32–38 Jesus is crucified at a site known as Calvary (Latin for "Golgotha") (parallel passages: **Matt. 27:33–37; Mark 15:22–26; John 19:17–24**).

23:39–43 Jesus is crucified between two criminals. One of these men ridicules Jesus, but the other turns to Him in repentance and faith and is assured that he will be with Jesus in paradise (parallel passages: **Matt. 27:38–44; Mark 15:27–32**).

23:44–48 Jesus' suffering and death are accompanied by several supernatural events that can only be explained as acts of God (parallel passages: **Matt. 27:45–54; Mark 15:33–39**).

23:49 Several women from Galilee watch from a distance as Jesus is crucified (parallel passages: **Matt. 27:55–56; Mark 15:40–41; John 19:25–27**).

23:50–54 A wealthy man from Arimathea named Joseph claims the body of Jesus and buries it in his own tomb (parallel passages: **Matt. 27:57–60; Mark 15:42–46; John 19:38–42**).

23:55–56 Women followers from Galilee note the tomb where Jesus is buried so they can anoint His body with spices after the Sabbath is over (parallel passages: **Matt. 27:61; Mark 15:47**).

24:1–8 Several women visit the tomb on Sunday morning to anoint Jesus' body. Two angels inform them that Jesus has been raised from the dead (parallel passages: **Matt. 28:1–10; Mark 16:1–8; John 20:1–2**).

24:9–12 The disciples are skeptical when informed by these women that Jesus has been resurrected. Peter runs to the tomb to check out their story. But he is not certain what to believe when he finds the tomb empty (parallel passage: **John 20:3–10**).

24:13–35 The risen Christ talks with two of His followers as they walk along the road to the village of Emmaus. He vanishes as they prepare to have a meal together, and they realize this was the resurrected Lord. They report this appearance of Jesus to His disciples in Jerusalem (parallel passage: **Mark 16:12–13**).

24:36–43 Jesus appears among His disciples. He convinces them they are not seeing a vision or a ghost by showing them His hands and feet and eating a meal in their presence.

24:44–49 Jesus charges His disciples to continue His mission by preaching "repentance and remission of sins. . .among all nations" (v. 47) (parallel passages: **Matt. 28:16–20; Mark 16:14–18**).

24:50–53 Jesus blesses His disciples and ascends to His Father (parallel passage: **Mark 16:19–20**).

Council The highest court of the Jewish nation in NT times, composed of seventy-one priests, scribes, and elders and presided over by the high priest. The Council accused Jesus of blasphemy against God, but it didn't have the power to put Jesus to death. It brought Him before Pilate, the Roman procurator, for sentencing (Matt. 26:65–66; John 18:31; 19:12). The Council also brought charges against Peter and John and the other apostles (Acts 4:1–23; 5:17–41) and Paul (Acts 22–24). *Sanhedrin*: NIV.

Seven Sayings from the Cross The seven separate utterances that Jesus made as He suffered on the cross: (1) "Father, forgive them" (Luke 23:34); (2) "To day shalt thou be with me in paradise" (Luke 23:43); (3) "Woman, behold thy son!" (John 19:26); (4) "My God, my God, why hast thou forsaken me?" (Matt. 27:46); (5) "I thirst" (John 19:28); (6) "It is finished" (John 19:30); and (7) "Father, into thy hands I commend my spirit" (Luke 23:46).

The Jewish Scriptures *All things must be fulfilled, which were written in the law of Moses, and in the prophets, and in the psalms, concerning me [Jesus]* (Luke 24:44).

Jesus spoke these words to His disciples when He appeared among them in Jerusalem after His resurrection. He declared that He had fulfilled all the things foretold about the Messiah in the Jewish scriptures. The scriptures used by the Jews in Jesus' time Included the books in our present OT, but they were arranged differently than in our modern Bibles. Jesus mentioned the three major divisions of the Jewish scriptures: (1) the Law of Moses. This is what we refer to today as the Pentateuch—Genesis, Exodus, Leviticus, Numbers, and Deuteronomy. (2) The Prophets. This section included Joshua, Judges, 1 and 2 Samuel, 1 and 2 Kings, and all the prophets except Daniel. (3) The Psalms. Included in this section were the Psalms, the book for which the entire section was named, as well as Proverbs, Job, Song of Solomon, Ruth, Lamentations, Ecclesiastes, Esther, Daniel, Ezra, Nehemiah, and 1 and 2 Chronicles.

NOVEMBER 8 | Read John 1–3

1:1–5 John begins his Gospel with the creation, affirming that Christ, God's Son ("the Word," v. 1), participated with the Father in the creation of the world (Gen. 1:1, 26).

1:6–8 John the Baptist was sent to prepare the way for Jesus and to announce His coming into the world (Mark 1:1–8).

1:9–18 Christ left His place of honor with the Father and was born into the world in the form of a man in order to bring people to God (Phil. 2:5–8).

1:19–34 Jesus meets John the Baptist at the place where he is preaching and baptizing. John identifies Him clearly as the long-expected Messiah.

1:35–42 Andrew, a disciple of John the Baptist, follows Jesus. Andrew brings his brother Simon Peter and introduces him to Jesus.

1:43–51 Jesus calls Philip and his friend Nathanael to become His disciples.

2:1–11 Jesus performs His first miracle by turning water into wine at a wedding celebration in the town of Cana in the region of Galilee.

2:12 Accompanied by His mother and His brothers, Jesus visits the city of Capernaum in the region of Galilee.

2:13–25 Jesus drives out merchants who are conducting business in the temple during the Passover celebration. He charges them with desecrating the house of His Father.

3:1–21 Jesus explains the meaning of the new birth to Nicodemus, a ruler of the Pharisees.

3:22–24 Jesus and His disciples minister in the region of Judea, not far from the place where John the Baptist is preaching and baptizing.

3:25–36 John the Baptist points people to Jesus as the Messiah, the Son of God, who holds the keys to eternal life.

. . . .

John the Apostle A fisherman from Galilee, the son of Zebedee and brother of James, who became one of the twelve apostles of Jesus (Matt. 4:21–22). He was described as the disciple "whom Jesus loved" and a member of Christ's inner circle of disciples, which included his brother James and Simon Peter (Mark 5:37; 9:2; 14:33). John was ambitious for position and prestige in Christ's kingdom (Mark 10:35–37), but he showed a willingness to die for Jesus (Mark 10:38–39). Associated with Peter in bold evangelism in Jerusalem after Jesus' ascension (Acts 4:13; 8:14–15), John left Jerusalem about AD 65 for Ephesus, where he wrote the Fourth Gospel and the three epistles of John. He wrote the book of Revelation while exiled as a political prisoner on the island of Patmos (Rev. 1:9–11).

Incarnation of Christ The birth and existence of Christ in human form. This was foretold by the OT prophets (Isa. 7:14). When Jesus was born into the world, He was described as "the Word. . .made flesh" (John 1:14). Belief in the incarnation of Christ is a mark of the Christian (1 John 4:2–3).

Lamb of God A title of Christ that emphasizes the sacrificial nature of His life and His atoning death. This aspect of His ministry was foretold by the prophet Isaiah (Isa. 53:7). John the Baptist greeted Jesus with this title (John 1:29, 36). As the Lamb of God, Jesus is worthy of eternal honor and praise (Rev. 5:12–13).

Bethsaida A fishing village on the Sea of Galilee; the home of Andrew, Peter, and Philip—apostles of Jesus (John 1:44). Some scholars believe the Bethsaida where the 5,000 were fed (Luke 9:10–17) was a different city with the same name.

. . . .

Humility of John the Baptist *He [Jesus] it is. . .whose shoe's latchet [thongs, NIV] I [John the Baptist] am not worthy to unloose* (John 1:27).

Although John the Baptist was divinely selected to serve as the forerunner of Jesus (Luke 1:76), he was aware of his unworthiness of such an honor. He declared in this verse that he was not even worthy to bend down and untie the leather thongs that held Jesus' sandals on His feet. But Jesus recognized John's greatness and commended him for his faithfulness: "Among them that are born of women there hath not risen a greater than John the Baptist" (Matt. 11:11).

NOVEMBER 9 | Read John 4–5

4:1–4 Jesus leaves the region of Judea in the south to travel to the region of Galilee in the north. During this journey He chooses deliberately to pass through the territory of the Samaritans.

4:5–44 Jesus stops at a well outside a Samaritan village and asks a woman for a drink of water. He talks with her about her life of sin and reveals to her that He is the long-expected Messiah. She brings many people from her village to meet Jesus, and they also become believers.

4:45 Jesus finds a receptive audience when He begins preaching in the region of Galilee (parallel passages: **Matt. 4:12–17; Mark 1:14–15**).

4:46–54 A nobleman, or royal official, from Capernaum seeks out Jesus in the town of Cana about twenty miles away. He begs Jesus to heal his sick son. Jesus heals the boy at a distance while his father is traveling back to Capernaum.

5:1–15 Jesus is criticized for healing a lame man on the Sabbath at the pool of Bethesda in Jerusalem.

5:16–47 Jesus defends His healing on the Sabbath by declaring that He has been given all authority as God's Son. Furthermore, He is doing the work that His Father has sent Him to do.

. . . .

Samaritan An inhabitant of the district of Samaria between Judea and Galilee. These people were considered inferior by the Jews because of their mixed-blood ancestry going back to their intermarriage with foreign colonists placed there by the Assyrians (2 Kings 17:3–24). Jesus, however, associated with Samaritans (Luke 9:51–52; John 4:4–30) and even used a kindhearted Samaritan as an example of a good neighbor (Luke 10:29–37).

Bethesda A pool in Jerusalem believed to have miraculous healing powers. Jesus healed a lame man at this pool (John 5:2–8). *Beth-zatha*: NRSV.

NOVEMBER 10 | Read John 6–7

`6:1–14` Jesus multiplies a boy's lunch of five pieces of bread and two fish to feed more than 5,000 hungry people (parallel passages: **Matt. 14:13–21; Mark 6:30–44; Luke 9:10–17**).

`6:15–21` Jesus walks on the water to join His disciples in a boat on the Sea of Galilee (parallel passages: **Matt. 14:22–33; Mark 6:45–52**).

`6:22–65` Many people look for Jesus, expecting a handout because they hear He has fed more than 5,000 hungry people. He teaches them that He is God's Son, the true "bread of life" who offers eternal life to all who place their faith in Him.

`6:66–71` Many of Jesus' followers turn away when He does not live up to their expectations of the Messiah. Peter, speaking for the other disciples, declares that they will continue to be His faithful followers. Jesus predicts that one of the Twelve will betray Him.

`7:1–9` The brothers of Jesus do not believe that Jesus is the Messiah. In a mocking and skeptical tone, they urge Him to attend the Feast of Tabernacles in Jerusalem where He can declare openly that He is the Messiah.

`7:10–52` Jesus decides to attend the celebration in Jerusalem without revealing that He is the Messiah. But His teachings and His reputation as a healer and miracle worker cause a division among the people. Some believe He is the Messiah, while others deny this possibility. Nicodemus, a Pharisees who had talked with Jesus earlier (John 3:1–21), urges his fellow Pharisees not to condemn Jesus for blasphemy until they have more solid evidence against Him.

`7:53–8:11` Jesus forgives a woman who is accused of adultery and condemns the self-righteousness of her accusers: "He that is without sin among you, let him first cast a stone at her" (8:7).

....

`Sudden Storms on Lake Galilee` *The sea arose by reason of a great wind that blew* (John 6:18).

Jesus' disciples were crossing the Sea of Galilee in a small fishing boat when they were caught in a sudden storm. This freshwater lake, about thirteen miles long by eight miles wide, is fed by the Jordan River. It sits about seven hundred feet below sea level in an area surrounded by high mountains. Cool winds frequently rush down from these mountains and mix with the warm air on the surface of the lake. The result is a sudden, violent storm such as that which overwhelmed the disciples.

NOVEMBER 11 | Read John 8–9

`8:12–30` Jesus angers the Pharisees by claiming to be the Son of God and the light that God has sent to deliver the world from darkness (1 John 1:7).

`8:31–59` Jesus further angers the Pharisees by questioning their claim that they are "children of Abraham." If they were truly Abraham's descendants, He declares, they would be doing the works of Abraham rather than plotting to have Him killed. As the eternal, preexistent Son of God, He is superior to Abraham: "Before Abraham was, I am" (v. 58).

`9:1–41` Jesus heals a man who had been blind all his life. The Pharisees question Jesus' credentials, since He had sinned, according to their legalistic laws, by performing this healing on the Sabbath. They question the man about this healing, and he stands his ground in defense of Jesus. After this healed man becomes a believer, Jesus declares that the Pharisees are the real blind people in this situation; they fail to see the truth because of their sin and prejudice.

`Siloam` A reservoir in Jerusalem supplied with water through King Hezekiah's underground tunnel from a spring outside the city (2 Kings 20:20). Jesus commanded a blind man to wash in the Pool of Siloam for healing (John 9:6–7).

NOVEMBER 12 | Read John 10–11

`10:1–21` This is one of Jesus' "I am" statements in the Gospel of John. He compares Himself with a shepherd who watches over his sheep. As the Good Shepherd, Jesus will make the ultimate sacrifice for those who follow Him: "The good shepherd giveth his life for the sheep" (v. 11).

`10:22–42` Jesus declares to the religious leaders of Israel that He is the Christ, the Son of God. They accuse Him of blasphemy and try to execute Him by stoning. But He slips away to an isolated spot in the wilderness of Judea to rest and pray.

`11:1–44` Jesus is informed that His friend Lazarus of Bethany has died. After two days He goes to Bethany, where He is met by Lazarus's sister Martha. He declares to Martha, "I am the resurrection, and the life" (v. 25), then raises Lazarus from the dead.

`11:45–57` Jesus' raising of Lazarus and His claim to be God's Son drive the Pharisees and the Jewish Sanhedrin into a frenzy. They begin to plot how they can arrest Him and have Him executed.

`Feast of Dedication` An eight-day festival commemorating the Jewish victories that restored the temple during the era of the Maccabees about 160 BC. Jesus attended one of these festivals in Jerusalem (John 10:22–23). This feast was also known as the *Feast of Lights* or *Hanukkah*.

NOVEMBER 13 | Read John 12–13

12:1–8 Mary of Bethany, sister of Lazarus and Martha, anoints Jesus with an expensive perfume (parallel passages: **Matt. 26:6–13; Mark 14:3–9**).

12:9–11 The religious leaders continue their plot against Jesus, even including Lazarus in their accusations because he is responsible for causing many people to believe in Jesus.

12:12–19 Jesus makes His triumphal entry into Jerusalem on a young donkey (parallel passages: **Matt. 21:1–11; Mark 11:1–11; Luke 19:28–44**).

12:20–50 A group of Greeks (Gentiles or non-Jews) ask to see Jesus. They had probably heard about His miracles and unique teachings in regions beyond the Jewish nation. Jesus takes this as a sign that the time of His death is drawing near. He declares that He is the light sent by God to provide salvation for Gentiles as well as Jews—that is, the entire world (Rom. 3:29).

13:1–20 Jesus and His disciples observe the Passover by eating a meal together. He teaches them the meaning of humble service by washing their feet. This was a menial chore that only the lowliest slave would perform for household guests.

13:21–30 During the Passover meal, Jesus predicts that one of His disciples will betray Him. He identifies this disciple by dipping a piece of bread in a bowl of food and giving the bread to Judas (parallel passages: **Matt. 26:20–25; Mark 14:17–21; Luke 22:21–23**).

13:31–38 Jesus gives His disciples a new commandment: "As I have loved you. . .ye also love one another" (v. 34). He also predicts that Peter will deny Him three times (parallel passages: **Matt. 26:31–35; Mark 14:27–31; Luke 22:31–38**).

. . . .

Mary The sister of Martha and Lazarus. She was an eager listener at Jesus' feet while Martha performed household duties (Luke 10:38–41). She anointed the feet of Jesus and wiped them with her hair (John 12:1–3). Jesus defended her contemplative temperament (Luke 10:42).

Spikenard An expensive and highly prized perfume or ointment (Song 4:13–14) that was used to anoint Jesus' hands and feet (John 12:3). *Nard*: NIV, NRSV.

Judas Iscariot The disciple who betrayed Jesus (John 13:2, 26; 18:1–8). The word *Iscariot* identifies Judas as a citizen of Kerioth, a city in southern Judah (Josh. 15:25), to distinguish him from Judas (or Jude), brother of James, who was also one of the Twelve (Luke 6:16). Judas Iscariot apparently served as the treasurer for Jesus and His disciples (John 13:29). After realizing the gravity of his act of betrayal, Judas committed suicide (Matt. 27:3–5).

. . . .

Reclining while Eating *There was leaning on Jesus' bosom [breast] one of his disciples, whom Jesus loved* (John 13:23).

This verse describes the time when Jesus was eating the Last Supper with His disciples on the night before He was crucified. They were not seated at a high table, as some popular paintings show, but they were reclining around a low table, in accordance with the custom of that time. Each person thrust his legs out to the side and leaned on his elbow while taking food from the table. This is how it was possible for John, the "disciple whom Jesus loved," to be leaning back against the bosom, or breast, of Jesus, who was immediately behind him.

NOVEMBER 14 | Read John 14–16

14:1–16:33 Jesus delivers an extended farewell to His disciples. He tells them He is going to prepare a place for them (14:3–4), promises to send the Holy Spirit to guide them after He is gone (14:16–18, 26; 16:7–13), encourages them to abide in Him as the true vine (15:1–8), and assures them that the persecution they will experience in the world will be bearable since He has overcome the world (16:32–33).

Holy Spirit The third person of the Trinity. The OT contains glimpses and promises of the Holy Spirit (Gen. 1:2, 6:3; Zech. 4:6), and the Spirit rested on Jesus from His birth (Luke 1:35), but the full manifestation of the Spirit's power occurred at Pentecost after Jesus' resurrection and ascension to the Father (Acts 2:1–21). Jesus promised He would send the Holy Spirit as a comforter and advocate in His absence (John 14:16; 1 John 2:1). The Spirit would glorify the Son (John 15:16), empower believers (John 14:12–27), and convict unbelievers of sin and coming judgment (John 16:8–11). Another function of the Holy Spirit is to inspire the scriptures, thus providing guidance and direction to believers.

NOVEMBER 15 | Read John 17:1–19:16

17:1–26 These verses are known as Jesus' High Priestly Prayer. He prays for Himself, that He will glorify the Father in His suffering and death that are now just a few hours away (vv. 1–5), for His disciples (vv. 6–19), and for all future believers (vv. 20–26).

18:1–12 Jesus is arrested by officers from the Jewish Sanhedrin after Judas leads them to the spot where He can be found—probably the Garden of Gethsemane (parallel passages: **Matt. 26:47–56; Mark 14:43–52; Luke 22:47–53**).

18:13–14 Jesus appears first before Annas, father-in-law of Caiaphas the high priest.

18:15–27 Jesus next appears before Caiaphas the high priest and the rest of the Jewish Sanhedrin (v. 24). Standing outside the house of the high priest, Peter denies that he knows Jesus (parallel passages: **Matt. 26:69–75; Mark 14:66–72; Luke 22:54–62**).

18:28–19:16 Jesus appears before the Roman governor Pontius Pilate, who sentences Him to death by crucifixion (parallel passages: **Matt. 27:11–26; Mark 15:2–15; Luke 23:13–25**).

Caiaphas The Jewish high priest who presided at the trial of Jesus and advised that He be put to death (Matt. 26:57–66; John 18:12–14). After Jesus' resurrection, the apostles John and Peter also appeared before Caiaphas (Acts 4:6).

Pilate The procurator or Roman governor of Judea (ruled about AD 26–36) who presided at Jesus' trial. An opportunist, Pilate was unwilling to condemn Jesus as a criminal (John 18:28–38), so he sought to have him tried by Herod at the next judicial level (Luke 23:11). Then he proposed that Jesus be the prisoner customarily dismissed at Passover, but this move also failed (John 18:39–40). Finally he released Jesus to be crucified but tried to dodge responsibility for the decision (Matt. 27:24–25).

NOVEMBER 16 | Read John 19:17–21:25

19:17–24 Jesus is crucified at a site known as Golgotha (parallel passages: **Matt. 27:33–37; Mark 15:22–26; Luke 23:32–38**).

19:25–27 Jesus' mother and two other women—Mary the wife of Cleophas and Mary Magdalene—look on as Jesus is crucified. Jesus commends His mother to the care of His disciple John ("the disciple standing by, whom he loved," v. 26) (parallel passages: **Matt. 27:55–56; Mark 15:40–41; Luke 23:49**).

19:28–30 Jesus dies on the cross after the soldiers give Him vinegar to drink as a painkiller.

19:31–37 After Jesus dies, soldiers pierce His side with a sword to make sure He is dead. Jesus had died quickly, so it was not necessary for the soldiers to break His legs to hasten His death. This fulfills the scripture that no bones of the sacrificial lamb offered during Passover were to be broken (Exod. 12:46; Num. 9:12).

19:38–42 Joseph of Arimathea, a secret follower of Jesus, claims His body to give it an appropriate burial. Joseph is assisted by Nicodemus (John 3:1–21), who brings perfume and spices to anoint the body. They bury Jesus in a new tomb that has never been used (parallel passages: **Matt. 27:57–60; Mark 15:42–46; Luke 23:50–54**).

20:1–2 Mary Magdalene discovers the body of Jesus is missing when she visits the tomb on Sunday morning. She reports this to His disciples Peter and John (parallel passages: **Matt. 28:1–10; Mark 16:1–8; Luke 24:1–8**).

20:3–10 Peter and John rush to the tomb to check out Mary's report that Jesus' body has been taken away (parallel passage: **Luke 24:9–12**).

20:11–18 Mary Magdalene remains outside the tomb after Peter and John leave. Two angels tell her that Jesus has been resurrected from the dead. Then Jesus appears before Mary and reveals Himself clearly as the risen Christ. She reports this to His disciples (parallel passage: **Mark 16:9–11**).

20:19–25 The resurrected Jesus appears to His disciples in a place where they are hiding because of their fear of the Jewish religious leaders. He convinces them He is the risen Christ by showing them the wounds on His hands and side. Jesus' disciple Thomas is not present during this appearance. He refuses to believe that Jesus is alive until he can see Him with his own eyes.

20:26–31 Jesus appears among His disciples again—this time when Thomas is present. He deals with Thomas's skepticism by inviting Him to touch the wounds in His hands and side. Believing, Thomas declares, "My Lord and my God" (v. 28).

21:1–14 Jesus appears to seven of His disciples at the Sea of Galilee. He prepares and eats a meal with them to prove they are not seeing a ghost or a vision.

21:15–19 Jesus forgives Peter for his denials and reinstates him to full service as His disciple, charging him to "feed my sheep" (v. 17). He predicts that Peter will suffer persecution and death because of his faithfulness to the risen Lord.

21:20–23 Jesus deals with Peter's question about how long His disciple John ("the disciple whom Jesus loved," v. 20) will live.

21:24–25 Jesus' disciple John, the author of this Gospel, vows that the things he has written about Jesus are authentic eyewitness accounts. He also declares that Jesus did many things he has not included in this Gospel. If he had written about all these events, John says, "the world itself could not contain the books that should be written" (v. 25).

Calvary A hill just outside the city walls of Jerusalem where Jesus was crucified (Luke 23:33). The word comes from a Latin word meaning "skull," thus "place of the skull." The Aramaic form of this word is *Golgotha* (Mark 15:22). *The Skull*: NIV, NRSV.

Nicodemus An influential Pharisee who talked with Jesus about the new birth. Jesus impressed upon him the necessity of being born of the Spirit (John 3:1–7). Later, Nicodemus cautioned the Jewish officials not to prejudge Jesus (John 7:50–51). He helped prepare Jesus' body for burial (John 19:39).

Carrying the Cross *And he [Jesus] bearing his cross went forth* (John 19:17).
A cross strong enough to hold the weight of a man and long enough to be placed in the ground and have the victim elevated at the same time would probably be too heavy for a person to carry. Thus, Jesus probably carried only the horizontal beam to the crucifixion site. Here he was stripped naked, laid on the ground, and nailed to the beam, which was then raised and attached to the upright post. This form of execution was so cruel and degrading that it was never imposed by the Roman government against its own citizens.

Supernatural Peace *The same day at evening. . .came Jesus and stood in the midst, and saith unto them [His disciples], Peace be unto you* (John 20:19).

According to John's Gospel, this was Jesus' first appearance to His disciples after His resurrection. His first word to them was the common greeting used by the Jewish people of that day—a wish for their peace, wholeness, and well-being. When Jesus greeted them with these words, perhaps the disciples remembered a promise of His supernatural peace and presence that He had made to them while training them for the task of carrying on His work: "Peace I leave with you, my peace I give unto you: not as the world giveth, give I unto you. Let not your heart be troubled, neither let it be afraid" (John 14:27).

ACTS, A HISTORY OF THE EARLY CHURCH

Acts is a one-of-a-kind book in the New Testament. It is not a Gospel, since it contains only a few verses about the life and ministry of Jesus (Acts 1:1–10). Neither is Acts an epistle, or letter, to early Christians or churches, like the rest of the books in the New Testament canon. Acts is in a class by itself, and that is why it is treated here as a major section of God's Word.

The full title of Acts in the King James Version is "The Acts of the Apostles." But it could also be called "The Acts of the Holy Spirit," since it reports on the actions of the Spirit in the birth and development of the church. Jesus promised His followers that they would be empowered by His Spirit to carry on His work (Acts 1:8). This is exactly what happened as believers lived out their faith and shared the Gospel in the pagan culture of their time.

NOVEMBER 17 | Read Acts 1–2

1:1–5 Luke, the author of Acts, reminds his friend Theophilus (v. 1) of the things he wrote about Jesus in his other book, the Gospel of Luke. Theophilus is also mentioned by Luke in the opening verses of his Gospel (Luke 1:3).

1:6–9 Jesus ascends to His Father after assuring His followers that they will receive power throughout the world (Mark 16:19–20).

1:10–11 Two angels tell His followers that Jesus will return to earth again someday.

1:12–15 About 120 followers of Jesus, including His disciples and several women, meet together in Jerusalem.

1:16–26 Under the leadership of the apostle Peter, also known as Simon (Mark 1:16–18), this group of followers selects Matthias to replace Judas as one of the twelve apostles.

2:1–13 While celebrating the festival of Pentecost (Lev. 23:15–21) in Jerusalem, Jesus' apostles are filled with the Holy Spirit. Their normal spoken language is either Aramaic or Greek. But these followers of Jesus begin to speak in several different languages that are recognized by Jews from different parts of the world who are gathered at Jerusalem for the Pentecost celebration. Some of these Jews are amazed at this display, but others accuse the apostles of being drunk with "new wine" (Acts 2:13).

2:14–42 In a great speech known as his "Pentecost Sermon," the apostle Peter assures the crowd that their strange speech is a fulfillment of the ancient prophecy of Joel 2:28–32. He turns their attention to Jesus, who has empowered the apostles with the Holy Spirit. Then he declares, "Repent, and be baptized every one of you in the name of Jesus Christ for the remission of sins, and ye shall receive the gift of the Holy Ghost" (v. 38). Three thousand people turn to Jesus in repentance and are baptized.

2:43–47 The apostles perform wonders and signs among the people in Jerusalem. The followers of Jesus pool their resources to care for the needy among their fellowship.

. . . .

Aceldama A field near Jerusalem purchased with the money that Judas was paid to betray Jesus. The name means "field of blood" (Acts 1:15–19). *Akeldama*: NIV; *Hakeldama*: NRSV.

Libya The Greek name for the continent of Africa west of Egypt (Acts 2:10). Persons from Libya were in Jerusalem on the day of Pentecost (Acts 2:10). The man who carried Jesus' cross was from Cyrene, Libya's chief city (Matt. 27:32). In the OT, Libya was also called *Phut* (Ezek. 27:10) and *Lubim* (Nah. 3:9).

. . . .

Sabbath Day's Journey *Then returned they [early Christian believers] unto Jerusalem from the mount called Olivet, which is from Jerusalem a sabbath day's journey* (Acts 1:12).

Jesus ascended to heaven from the Mount of Olives after delivering a farewell message to these believers (Acts 1:6–9). This hill east of Jerusalem is just a few minutes' walk from the city. This tells us that a "sabbath day's journey" was probably less than a mile. The prohibition against working on the Sabbath (Exod. 20:8–11) led to this regulation about a Sabbath day's journey. Walking farther than this short distance permitted on the day of worship was considered work, and thus a violation of the Sabbath law. Jesus may have had this regulation in mind when He told His followers they might have to flee to escape persecution in the end-time: "Pray ye that your flight be not. . .on the sabbath day" (Matt. 24:20).

NOVEMBER 18 | Read Acts 3–5

3:1–11 Peter and John heal a lame man outside the temple in the name of Jesus.

3:12–26 Peter preaches another strong sermon to the people of Jerusalem. He urges them to repent and be baptized in the name of Jesus—the one whom they have rejected but whom God has raised and designated as the Prince of Life.

4:1–22 Peter and John are arrested and questioned by the Jewish Sanhedrin about their healing of the lame man outside the temple. They are released after they declare boldly that the man was healed through the power of Jesus. But the Sanhedrin warns them not to continue to speak or teach in the name of Jesus.

4:23–31 Peter and John meet with other believers. Together, they pray for strength and boldness to continue to preach about Jesus, in spite of the threats from the Jewish Sanhedrin. God honors their prayers by strengthening them again with the Holy Spirit (John 14:16–18; Acts 2:1–13).

4:32–37 These early believers continue their practice of pooling their resources in order to care for the needy among their fellowship (Acts 2:43–47). Barnabas sells his land and places the proceeds in the common treasury.

5:1–11 Ananias and his wife, Sapphira, sell a field and pretend to place all the proceeds in the common treasury of the church. But they actually keep part of the money for themselves. They pay with their lives for lying to God.

5:12–16 The apostles perform signs and wonders, including healing the sick, among the people of Jerusalem. The church continues to grow with the addition of many believers (Acts 2:41).

5:17–32 The apostles are imprisoned by the Sanhedrin for continuing to preach about Jesus. Released by an angel, they go right back to bearing witness about Jesus and His resurrection. They are dragged before the Sanhedrin again, only to declare, "We ought to obey God rather than men" (v. 29).

5:33–42 Gamaliel advises the other members of the Sanhedrin to release the apostles, with the observation that their work will come to an end if it is not in God's will. After a beating, the apostles return to their preaching, "rejoicing that they were counted worthy to suffer shame for his name" (v. 41).

Barnabas A Jewish Christian who befriended Paul after Paul's conversion, introduced the apostle to the Jerusalem church (Acts 9:27), and traveled with Paul during the first missionary journey (Acts 11:22–26). *Joses*: Acts 4:36.

Immediate Burial *The young men arose, wound him [Ananias] up [wrapped up his body, NIV], and carried him out, and buried him* (Acts 5:6).

Ananias, an early Christian believer, was struck dead when he lied about his contribution to the church's common treasury. He was buried immediately by his fellow believers. Burial on the day of death was the customary practice in Palestine in NT times. Embalming was not practiced by the Jews, and a body would deteriorate quickly in the sweltering climate. Bodies were often prepared for burial by being wrapped with strips of cloth. This procedure is suggested by the NIV translation of this verse. Spices were sometimes placed among these layers of cloth. This is how Joseph of Arimathea and Nicodemus prepared the body of Jesus for burial (John 19:38–40).

NOVEMBER 19 | Read Acts 6–7

6:1–7 Greek-speaking members of the early church complain that their widows are not receiving their fair share in the church's food-distribution efforts. The church selects seven men of Greek-speaking background to coordinate this ministry.

6:8–15 Stephen, one of the seven men selected to coordinate food distribution for the church, speaks boldly for Jesus in a debate with a group of Jewish zealots. They accuse him of blasphemy and drag him before the Jewish Sanhedrin for trial.

7:1–53 In a long speech before the Sanhedrin, Stephen reviews the history of the Jewish people. He accuses the religious leaders of rejecting God's messengers and disobeying His commands at every turn. This includes their rejection of Jesus as the Messiah.

7:54–60 Enraged by these accusations, the Jewish leaders execute Stephen by stoning him to death.

Proselyte A Gentile who converted to Judaism. Some of these converts renounced their pagan lifestyle but refused to accept such Jewish practices as circumcision. Well-known proselytes of the Bible include Cornelius, Lydia, and Nicolas of Antioch (Acts 6:5). *Convert*: NIV.

Alexandria A city of Egypt founded by Alexander the Great that was a cultural center and capital city of Egypt in NT times. Citizens of Alexandria opposed Stephen (Acts 6:9). Apollos was a native of this city (Acts 18:24). Paul left Malta for Rome on a ship from Alexandria (Acts 28:11). Seventy Jewish scholars were commissioned in this city to translate the OT from Hebrew to Greek—the famed version of the Bible known as the Septuagint.

Stephen A zealous believer who became the first martyr of the Christian cause. A Jewish believer of Greek background, Stephen was among the seven "deacons" selected by the early church to provide relief for other Greek-speaking Christians (Acts 6:5–8). His criticism of OT laws and traditions brought him into conflict with Jewish leaders, and he was stoned to death on a charge of blasphemy (Acts 7:55–60).

NOVEMBER 20 | Read Acts 8–9

8:1–4 A Pharisee named Saul (later known as the apostle Paul) is a consenting bystander when Stephen is killed. Stephen's death stirs open persecution from the Jewish religious leaders against the church in Jerusalem. Saul is one of the ringleaders in these efforts to stamp out the church. Many believers flee Jerusalem and carry the message of Jesus wherever they go.

8:5–17 Philip, one of the seven men selected to distribute food to the needy, preaches the Gospel in the region of Samaria. Many Samaritans believe on Jesus Christ and are baptized. Peter and John come to Samaria from Jerusalem to help Philip in this evangelism effort.

8:18–25 Peter condemns Simon the magician for trying to buy the power of the Holy Spirit with money.

8:26–40 Philip witnesses in the desert to a eunuch from Ethiopia, an official under Candace the queen. The eunuch is baptized by Philip on his testimony of faith that "Jesus Christ is the Son of God" (v. 37).

9:1–7 Saul the persecutor is converted to Christianity in a dramatic encounter with the risen Christ on the road to Damascus, Syria (Acts 22:4–10).

9:8–18 Saul is struck with blindness for three days following his conversion experience. God sends a believer named Ananias to find Saul in Damascus and to restore his sight. The Lord makes it clear that Saul is a part of His plan to reach the Gentiles with the Gospel (Acts 13:44–50).

9:19–25 Saul angers the Jews in Damascus by preaching about Jesus in the synagogue. They attempt to kill him, but Saul escapes when his fellow believers let him down in a basket over the city wall.

9:26–31 Returning to Jerusalem, Saul attempts to join the Christian fellowship. But he is met with suspicion and distrust because of his previous persecution of the church. Barnabas speaks up for Saul and convinces them he is a genuine believer. Saul eventually returns to Tarsus, his hometown, because of threats against his life from the unbelieving Jews in Jerusalem.

9:32–35 In Lydda Peter heals a man named Aeneas of the palsy.

9:36–43 Peter raises Dorcas, a female believer who "was full of good works" (v. 36), from the dead, in Joppa.

. . . .

Paul the Apostle The great apostle to the Gentiles; defender and advocate of the Christian faith in its early years through his thirteen NT letters. A complex personality, Paul demonstrated both toughness and tenderness in his devotion to Christ. His teachings are both profound and practical (Phil. 3:7–10). Paul's Hebrew name as a Jew of Benjamite ancestry was Saul, but his Roman name was Paul (Acts 13:9). A Roman citizen born at Tarsus in Cilicia (Acts 22:3), he was a tentmaker by trade—a vocation by which he often supported himself as a minister to the churches that he established (Acts 18:3). A strict Pharisee and member of the Jewish Sanhedrin, Paul opposed Christianity in its early years in Jerusalem. He consented to the death of Stephen, the first martyr of the church (Acts 7:58–8:1). He was on his way to persecute Christians at Damascus when he was converted to Christianity in his famous "Damascus road" experience (Acts 9:1–19). From that point on, Paul was zealous for the cause of Christ.

Under the sponsorship of the church at Antioch in Syria, Paul undertook three great missionary journeys to the Roman world, extending westward through Cyprus and Asia Minor into Europe (Acts 13–21). His traveling companions on these tours included Barnabas, John Mark, Timothy, Silas, Titus, and Luke. Along with his successes in making disciples, healing, and planting churches, he suffered a "thorn in the flesh" (2 Cor. 12:7), was frequently arrested, was stoned, and was imprisoned (Acts 16:22–23). Falsely accused by his enemies, he appealed to the Roman emperor for justice (Acts 25:10–12). After an arduous voyage by ship, he spent two years in Rome under house arrest. While guarded by Roman soldiers, he received friends and preached the Gospel (Acts 28:16–31; Phil. 1:12–14). Four of Paul's epistles—Ephesians, Colossians, Philippians, and Philemon—were written from Rome. Most scholars believe he was beheaded in Rome about AD 67 during Nero's reign (Phil. 2:17; 2 Tim. 4:6–8).

Damascus The capital city of Syria, located north of Mount Hermon in northern Palestine. Paul was traveling to Damascus to persecute Christians when he met the risen Lord in a life-transforming vision (Acts 9:1–8). Damascus is considered the oldest continually inhabited city in the world. *Syria-damascus*: 1 Chron. 18:6.

NOVEMBER 21 | Read Acts 10–12

10:1–8 Cornelius, a Roman centurion and thus a Gentile, is a godly man who worships the one true God. In a vision, God instructs Cornelius to send for the apostle

Peter, who will tell him what he should do. Cornelius obeys and sends three servants to Joppa to find Peter at the house of Simon the tanner.

10:9–16 As Cornelius's servants draw near the city of Joppa, Peter is praying in the outdoor space on top of Simon's house. In a vision, Peter sees a group of unclean animals that are forbidden as food for the Jews (Lev. 11:1–47). But God instructs Peter to kill and eat these animals. When Peter protests, God declares, "What God hath cleansed, that call not thou common" (v. 15). This is God's way of telling Peter that Gentiles are included in God's plan of salvation. No one is to be excluded from His love and grace.

10:17–23 Just then, Cornelius's three servants arrive. Peter learns they want him to go to Caesarea to talk with Cornelius. Then he invites them in to spend the night.

10:24–48 The next day Peter travels to the home of Cornelius and preaches the Gospel to him and his entire household. They repent, turn to Jesus, receive the Holy Spirit, and are baptized. This is dramatic evidence of God's inclusion of the Gentiles in His redemptive plan (John 12:20–50).

11:1–18 Leaders of the church in Jerusalem question Peter about the conversion of Cornelius and other Gentiles. One faction in the church is upset that Peter associated with uncircumcised Gentiles. But when Peter explains what happened, most of the church leaders are pleased. They declare, "Then hath God also to the Gentiles granted repentance unto life" (v. 18).

11:19–24 God blesses the work of a new church that has been planted among the people of Greek-speaking background in the city of Antioch in Syria. The Jerusalem church sends Barnabas to guide this new work, and it grows dramatically under his leadership.

11:25–26 Barnabas travels to Tarsus (Acts 9:27–30) and enlists Saul/Paul to help him in the church at Antioch.

11:27–30 A severe famine strikes the Mediterranean area, as foretold by the prophet Agabus. Barnabas and Saul/Paul deliver a relief offering from their area to the suffering Christians in Judea around Jerusalem.

12:1–5 Herod Agrippa I, Roman ruler over Palestine, executes the apostle James (Mark 1:19–20) and imprisons the apostle Peter.

12:6–19 Peter is miraculously delivered from prison by an angel and reunited with believers who are praying for his release.

12:20–25 Herod is struck dead by the Lord for allowing himself to be elevated to the status of a god in the eyes of the people.

Cornelius A Roman soldier from Caesarea who sought out the apostle Peter at Joppa and became the first Gentile convert to Christianity (Acts 10). This event showed clearly that the Christian faith was meant for Gentiles as well as Jews (Acts 15:7–11).

Baptism A rite signifying a believer's cleansing from sin through Christ's atoning death. John the Baptist baptized converts to signify their repentance (Matt. 3:6–8). Jesus was baptized by John in the Jordan River to fulfill all righteousness and to set an example for us (Matt. 3:15).

In the NT church, Gentiles who received the Holy Spirit were promptly baptized (Acts 10:44–48). Christian baptism memorializes the death, burial, and resurrection of Christ (Rom. 6:3–5). For the believer, baptism is a testimony of faith and a pledge to "walk in newness of life" with Jesus Christ (Rom. 6:4).

Praying on the Housetop *Peter went up upon the housetop to pray about the sixth hour [about noon, NIV]* (Acts 10:9).

This may seem to us like a strange place to pray, but it made perfect sense to Peter. The roofs of houses in Bible times might be compared to our modern patios. They were flat and easily accessible by an exterior stairway. People often went to the roof for rest and relaxation, particularly at night to catch a cooling breeze. Peter probably went to the roof so he could be alone in prayer, since he was a visitor in the house of Simon the tanner (Acts 10:5–6).

NOVEMBER 22 | Read Acts 13–14

13:1–3 The Holy Spirit selects Barnabas and Saul/Paul for missionary work. The church at Antioch obeys the Spirit's leading by sending them out after praying and fasting and commissioning them to this task through the laying on of hands. The work of Barnabas and Paul described in Acts 13:4–14:28 is known as the apostle Paul's first missionary journey.

13:4–12 On the island of Cyprus, Paul and Barnabas witness to the governor of the region, and he becomes a believer. Paul rebukes a magician or sorcerer named Bar-jesus when he tries to hinder their work.

13:13 Leaving Cyprus, Paul and Barnabas stop at the city of Perga in the province of Pamphylia. John Mark, who has been accompanying them on the trip, decides to return to Jerusalem.

13:14–43 Paul preaches about Jesus in the Jewish synagogue in the city of Antioch in the province of Pisidia. The staunch Jews are skeptical of his message, but it is well received by Gentiles (Acts 10:45) and religious proselytes.

13:44–50 On the next Sabbath a crowd gathers in the city to hear Paul speak again. This time the Jews openly condemn Paul and accuse him of blasphemy. They expel Paul and Barnabas from the city. The two missionaries declare: "It was necessary that the word of God should first have been spoken to you [Jews]: but seeing ye put it from you, and judge yourselves unworthy of everlasting life, lo, we turn to the Gentiles" (v. 46; see Rom. 3:29). This represents a turning point in the ministry of Paul. From now on he will direct most of his evangelistic efforts to the Gentiles because of their openness to the Gospel message.

13:51–14:5 Many Gentiles and Jews of Greek-speaking background turn to the Lord in Iconium. But Paul and Barnabas are eventually forced to leave the city because of strong opposition from the Jews.

14:6–20 In the province of Lycaonia, Paul and Barnabas preach in the cities of Lystra and Derbe. When Paul heals a lame man, the superstitious citizens of Lystra think the missionaries are gods. At Lystra Paul is also delivered miraculously by the Lord from a mob of Jewish zealots who try to stone him to death.

14:21–28 Paul and Barnabas return to their sending church at Antioch of Syria. This brings Paul's first missionary journey to a close. On the return trip the missionaries stop at the places they had visited, "confirming the souls of the disciples, and exhorting them to continue in the faith" (v. 22). They also appoint elders (Acts 20:17) to lead the churches they had founded. The church at Antioch rejoices when they learn that God has "opened the door of faith unto the Gentiles" (v. 27) through the ministry of Paul and Barnabas.

....

Elder In the NT, a local church leader who served as a pastor and teacher (1 Tim. 5:17).

....

The Synagogue Leader *The rulers of the synagogue sent unto them [Paul and Barnabas], saying. . .if ye have any word of exhortation. . .say on* (Acts 13:15).

During Paul's first missionary journey, he and his associate, Barnabas, attended worship services at the local synagogue in Antioch of Pisidia. They were invited to speak to the other worshipers by the rulers or presiding officers of the synagogue. A synagogue ruler was elected to his position by other members of the congregation. His responsibility was to plan the services, enlist readers and speakers, and preside at the worship proceedings. Most mentions of this synagogue officer in the NT refer to only one ruler (Mark 5:36–38; Luke 13:14). But this passage in Acts mentions more than one ruler. Perhaps a division of responsibilities was required in larger synagogues.

NOVEMBER 23 | Read Acts 15–17

15:1–6 A faction within the church insists that Gentiles must convert to Judaism and be circumcised in accordance with the Law of Moses before they can be saved. Leaders of the church meet at Jerusalem to consider the matter.

15:7–35 The apostle Peter, followed by Paul and Barnabas, speaks against circumcision as a requirement for Gentile believers. James, the half brother of Jesus and a leader in the church, issues the church's opinion that all persons, Jews and Gentiles alike, are saved through faith alone (Rom. 3:21–31). Paul and Barnabas deliver this good news to the church at Antioch.

15:36–41 Paul and Barnabas prepare to set out on a second missionary journey. But they disagree on whether to take John Mark, who had left them and returned home on their first trip (Acts 13:13). Finally, the two missionaries agree to go their separate ways. Barnabas takes John Mark and sails for the island of Cyprus. Paul travels north through the provinces of Syria and Cilicia, accompanied by Silas, a believer in the church at Antioch.

16:1–3 Paul and Silas strengthen believers in Derbe and Lystra, two cities where Paul had preached during his first missionary tour (Acts 14:6–20). This stop begins Paul's second missionary journey, which continues through Acts 18:22. At Lystra Paul meets a young believer named Timothy, whom he enlists as a helper in his missionary work (1 Tim. 1:1–2).

16:4–10 After traveling through several provinces, Paul and Silas are persuaded by the Holy Spirit not to enter the regions of Asia and Bithynia. Through a vision they are beckoned instead into the province of Macedonia.

16:11–15 In the city of Philippi (Phil. 1:1) in Macedonia, a businesswoman named Lydia and her entire household become believers.

16:16–24 Paul and Silas heal a demented slave girl. They are thrown into prison on charges from her master, who was profiting from her fortune-telling abilities.

16:25–40 As they sing praises to God, Paul and Silas are freed miraculously from prison by an earthquake. The jail keeper and his entire household are baptized by Paul after they turn to the Lord.

17:1–9 Unbelieving Jews create an uproar in the city of Thessalonica after Paul preaches in the Jewish synagogue. But several Gentiles become believers.

17:10–14 Paul finds an open and eager audience in the city of Berea: "They received the word with all readiness. . .and searched the scriptures daily, whether those things were so" (v. 11). But enraged Jews who have followed Paul and Silas from Thessalonica drive them out of the city.

17:15–34 While waiting for Silas and Timothy to join him in Athens, Paul preaches to the philosophers and intellectuals in this cultured Greek city. Most are skeptical, especially about the resurrection of Jesus (1 Cor. 15:1–11). But a few are receptive and turn to the Lord.

....

Judaizers An early Christian sect that advocated that Gentiles must be circumcised before they could become Christians (Acts 15:1). They were denounced by Paul, who insisted that believers are justified by faith alone (Acts 15:12; Gal. 6:15). The Judaizers were also opposed by Peter and James at the Jerusalem Council (Acts 15:8–19).

Jerusalem Council A conference held during the early days of the Christian movement to determine how Gentile believers would be received into the church. Participants representing the church at Antioch and the church in Jerusalem included Peter, Paul, Barnabas, and James. The issue was whether Gentile converts first had to identify with Judaism by being circumcised before they could be baptized and received as full members of the church (Acts 15:6). The council concluded that since Gentile and Jewish believers are saved by grace alone, circumcision was unnecessary (Acts 15:6–19). This solution averted a conflict that would have hampered missionary efforts and could have made Christianity a sect of Judaism.

A Desperate Jailer *He [the jailer at Philippi] drew out his sword, and would have killed himself, supposing that the prisoners had been fled* (Acts 16:27).

God sent an earthquake to release Paul and Silas from their prison cell in the city of Philippi. Along with these missionaries, all of the other prisoners were also set free. Under Roman law, prison keepers were held strictly accountable for the prisoners under their guard. If one escaped, the keeper assumed his punishment. It is likely that some of these prisoners were being tortured or would face such treatment in the future or were being held for capital crimes. Since all of the prisoners in this situation were set free, the jailer considered committing suicide a better fate than undergoing these punishments

NOVEMBER 24 | Read Acts 18–19

18:1–18 Paul travels from Athens to Corinth, where he joins forces with a Christian couple, Aquila and Priscilla. They support themselves as tentmakers for eighteen months while witnessing for Christ and establishing a church in this pagan city (1 Cor. 1:1–9).

18:19–22 After preaching for a while in the city of Ephesus, Paul returns to his home base—the church at Antioch. This brings to an end his second missionary journey.

18:23 Paul begins his third and final missionary journey by traveling through the provinces of Galatia and Phyrgia, encouraging new believers and strengthening their churches. This journey will end with his return to Jerusalem in Acts 21.

18:24–28 Apollos, a zealous new believer from Alexandria, Egypt, preaches in the church at Ephesus. After instructions in the faith from Aquila and Priscilla, he moves on to the province of Achaia to minister in the church at Corinth.

19:1–7 Paul arrives in Ephesus, where he finds several believers who were followers of John the Baptist (John 4:1). He instructs them about Jesus and baptizes them in His name.

19:8–23 Paul continues his work in Ephesus and the surrounding province of Asia. In addition to preaching and teaching, he performs miraculous healings among the people. Black magic and superstition yield to the power of the Word of God.

19:24–41 Believers in Ephesus are threatened by a mob under the leadership of Demetrius, a silversmith. The Gospel was cutting into the profits of those who made and sold miniature replicas of the pagan goddess Diana. But the crowd disperses quietly when calmed down by the town clerk.

. . . .

Apollos A Jewish believer from Alexandria in Egypt who worked with the church at Ephesus after it was founded by Paul. Eloquent and learned, Apollos was a disciple of John the Baptist (Acts 18:24–25). Aquila and Priscilla instructed him in the true doctrines of the faith, and he became an effective church leader, preaching also in Achaia and Corinth with great success (1 Cor. 3:4–6, 22). Paul mentioned Apollos as one whom a faction of the Corinthian church favored (1 Cor. 1:12).

Aquila A Christian believer who, with his wife, Priscilla, worked with Paul at Corinth (Acts 18:2) and continued Paul's work at Ephesus (Acts 18:24–26). They were also associated with the church at Rome (Rom. 16:3).

. . . .

Pagan Charms *A certain man [of Ephesus] named Demetrius, a silversmith, which made silver shrines for Diana [Artemis, NIV], brought no small gain unto the craftsmen* (Acts 19:24).

Paul worked in the city of Ephesus for almost three years—longer than he stayed at any other one place. A city of about 300,000 people, it was a strategic center for the planting of the Gospel in the Gentile world. The pride of Ephesus was a large, ornate temple devoted to the worship of Diana, or Artemis, a pagan goddess. Demetrius and other craftsmen of the city made their living by making and selling miniature replicas of this pagan goddess. These were probably worn as charms on necklaces or bracelets by worshipers of this goddess. When the citizens of Ephesus began turning to the Lord and quit buying these pagan charms, Demetrius incited a riot against Paul (Acts 19:24–29). Religious tolerance was out of the question when pagan profits were at stake.

NOVEMBER 25 | Read Acts 20:1–23:10

20:1–5 Paul takes several believers on a preaching and witnessing tour through the provinces of Macedonia, Greece (Achaia), and Asia.

20:6–12 In the city of Troas, Paul preaches late into the night in an upstairs room. A young man named Eutychus goes to sleep and falls from the window. Paul revives him and stays with him until he regains his strength.

20:13–16 Paul decides to go to Jerusalem in time to celebrate the feast of Pentecost. He catches a ship headed for Miletus, a seaport city not far from Ephesus.

20:17–38 Paul sends word for the elders of the church at Ephesus to meet him at Miletus. He delivers a tearful farewell address and predicts that this is the last time they will see one another. He encourages them to remain true to the Gospel that he has planted in their midst. Paul also tells the church elders about his feeling that trouble awaits him in Jerusalem: "I go. . .not knowing the things that shall befall me there" (v. 22).

21:1–9 After sailing across the Mediterranean Sea, Paul's ship docks at the coastal city of Tyre, about 100 miles north of Jerusalem. At Tyre he meets and encourages other believers, then travels south to the city of Caesarea, the home of Philip the evangelist (Acts 8:5–17, 26–40).

21:10–15 At Tyre Paul is warned by a prophet named Agabus that he will be arrested by the Jews if he goes to Jerusalem. But Paul pushes on and finally arrives in the city. This brings to an end Paul's third missionary journey.

21:16–26 Paul greets the leaders of the church at Jerusalem. They rejoice over the acceptance of the Gospel by the Gentiles under his ministry. At their suggestion, Paul agrees to serve as sponsor for several men who are undergoing purification rituals in the Jewish temple.

21:27–36 Paul is grabbed by an angry mob of Jews. They jump to the conclusion that he has taken a Gentile into an area of the temple reserved only for Jews—and thus polluted the holy sanctuary. A quick-acting detachment of Roman soldiers rescues Paul from the angry crowd.

21:37–22:22 Paul addresses the crowd, telling them he was a zealous Jew just like them until he was converted in a dramatic encounter with Jesus Christ (Acts 9:1–7). But the crowd renews their cry that he deserves to die for his blasphemous actions.

22:23–29 The Roman soldiers take Paul away to one of their own prisons where he will be safe from the Jewish mob. They prepare to force him to talk by giving him a scourging (beating), but Paul reveals that he is a Roman citizen. This guarantees that he will be treated with respect and fairness while in Roman custody.

22:30–23:10 Paul appears before the Jewish Sanhedrin. He causes dissension among the members of this body when he declares that Jesus was resurrected from the dead. The Roman soldiers return Paul to their own prison for his protection.

Agabus A Christian prophet who warned Paul in Antioch of Syria of a worldwide famine (Acts 11:28). At Caesarea, Agabus used a symbolic demonstration to predict Paul's impending arrest (Acts 21:10–11).

NOVEMBER 26 | Read Acts 23:11–25:27

23:11 The Lord appears to Paul and informs the apostle that he will bear witness of Him in Rome, capital city of the Roman Empire (Acts 28:17–31).

23:12–22 Paul's nephew warns the Roman commander of a plot by Jewish zealots to kill the apostle.

23:23–35 The Roman commander, Claudius Lysias, sends Paul to the seat of the Roman provincial government at Caesarea. Here Paul is to stand trial before Felix, governor of the province.

24:1–21 The Jews from Jerusalem present their charges of blasphemy against Paul before Felix. Speaking eloquently in his own defense, Paul shows the charges to be false.

24:22–27 Felix holds Paul in prison at Caesarea for two years, hoping the apostle will buy his freedom with a bribe.

25:1–12 Festus succeeds Felix as the Roman provincial governor over Judea. He asks Paul if he is willing to have his case heard before the Jewish Sanhedrin in Jerusalem. The apostle realizes he cannot receive a fair trial in such an arrangement, so he appeals his case to Rome—the right of every Roman citizen.

25:13–27 While Paul is waiting to go to Rome, Festus discusses Paul's case with Herod Agrippa II, another Roman ruler over the Jewish territories. Agrippa asks for Paul to be brought before him so he can hear his story firsthand. Festus is glad to comply. He hopes this appearance by Paul will give him some specific charge against the apostle that he can send with him to Rome.

Paul's Right of Appeal *Festus. . .answered, Hast thou [Paul] appealed unto Caesar? unto Caesar shalt thou go (Acts 25:12).*

Festus was the Roman governor of Judea who agreed to hear the charges against Paul brought by the Jewish leaders. When Festus suggested that the apostle be sent back to the Jewish court, Paul invoked his rights as a Roman citizen. He appealed his case to Rome, the capital city, where he would be assured of a fair trial (Acts 25:10–11). In Paul's time, a person could become a Roman citizen by birth or by buying this special status. Roman officials often granted these rights to non-Romans who had rendered special service to the empire. Although Paul was a Jew, he had been born a Roman citizen (Acts 22:28). How his parents had obtained their citizenship rights is unknown.

NOVEMBER 27 | Read Acts 26–28

26:1–32 Paul makes a passionate defense speech before Festus and Agrippa. He recounts his conversion experience and tells how he was called by the Lord to serve as an apostle to the Gentiles (Acts 9:1–7). Agrippa is so moved by Paul's remarks that he declares, "Almost thou persuadest me to be a Christian" (v. 28). Both Festus and Agrippa agree that Paul is innocent of the charges against him. But since he had appealed his case to Caesar, to Rome he must go.

27:1–13 Paul sails for Rome as a prisoner of the Roman Empire. The first part of their journey takes them several hundred miles to an area near the island of Crete in the Mediterranean Sea. The captain of the ship plans to land at a port known as Phoenix to wait out the approaching winter storms.

27:14–20 But the ship never reaches Crete. Struck by a violent winter storm, it drifts off course as it is buffeted by the crashing waves. The crew throws part of the ship's tackle overboard to give it more stability in the rough seas.

27:21–26 Paul assures the crew and the other passengers that no lives will be lost in this storm. This has been revealed to him in a vision by a messenger from the Lord. But the ship will be wrecked and they will be "cast upon a certain island" (v. 26).

27:27–38 As the ship drifts into shallow water, Paul urges everyone to eat so they will have strength to escape when they run aground.

27:39–44 The ship is torn apart by the violent waves when it hits land. But everyone on board escapes to the shore, as Paul had predicted.

28:1–6 The passengers and crew find themselves on the island of Melita (now know as Malta). Paul impresses the native islanders by surviving a bite from a poisonous snake.

28:7–11 Paul conducts a healing ministry during his three months on the island.

28:12–16 Paul sets sail again, making several stops along the way before finally arriving at Rome, capital city of the Roman Empire.

28:17–29 Paul takes the initiative to meet with a group of Jews in Rome. His message about Jesus is received by some but rejected by others.

28:30–31 For two years, while under house arrest in Rome, Paul preaches the message of Christ to many people (Phil. 1:12–13). He witnesses "with all confidence, no man forbidding him" (v. 31).

. . . .

Melita An island south of Sicily in the Mediterranean Sea where Paul was shipwrecked while sailing to Rome (Acts 28:1–8). *Malta*: NIV, NRSV.

. . . .

Perils of the Sea *Fearing lest we [Paul and shipmates] should have fallen upon rocks, they [sailors] cast four anchors out of the stern, and wished for the day* (Acts 27:29).

Acts 27 reports on the voyage of Paul to Rome and the wreck of his ship in a ferocious storm. Ancient sailing ships were at the mercy of the winds. This verse reports that the crew tossed out four anchors from the rear of the ship to keep it from being broken to pieces on the rocky shore. This chapter of Acts also tells us that the captain of this ship was pushing his luck by sailing to Rome so late in the year. Most ships that sailed the Mediterranean Sea apparently docked in a protected bay or inlet until the storms of winter were over (Acts 27:7–12). Several actions were taken to save the ship when the storm struck with its full fury. The crew pulled ropes or cables tightly around the hull to keep it from breaking apart (Acts 27:17). They also lightened the ship by throwing the cargo and even its pulleys and ropes for hoisting the sails into the sea (Acts 27:19, 38).

LETTERS OF THE APOSTLE PAUL

As a proud Pharisee, the apostle Paul (also known as Saul) was a zealous persecutor of the Christian movement during its early years (Acts 7:58). But he was converted to Christianity in a dramatic encounter with the living Lord on the road to the city of Damascus about AD 35 (Acts 9:1–8). From then until his death about thirty years later, he preached the Gospel and founded churches with a holy passion. His travels in the service of Christ took him hundreds of miles throughout the ancient world. Toward the end of his ministry, he even traveled by ship to the city of Rome, capital of the Roman Empire (Acts 28:14–16).

Because Paul's ministry covered such a large area, he used epistles, or letters, to communicate with the churches he founded as well as with the members of these new congregations. In these epistles he dealt with problems in the churches, instructed new believers in the essentials of the Christian faith, and encouraged local church leaders to remain faithful to their calling.

Thirteen of these Pauline letters are included in the New Testament. Nine were written to churches: Romans, 1 and 2 Corinthians, Galatians, Ephesians, Philippians, Colossians, and 1 and 2 Thessalonians. Four were written to individuals: 1 and 2 Timothy, Titus, and Philemon.

NOVEMBER 28 | Read Romans 1–3

1:1–7 Paul identifies himself as an apostle and servant of Christ and extends greetings to believers in the city of Rome, capital of the Roman Empire.

1:8–13 Paul had never visited Rome, but he assures the Roman Christians that he has heard from others about their stalwart faith. He expresses his desire to visit them in the future.

1:14–16 The apostle feels he has a responsibility to present the Gospel to people of all backgrounds and circumstances—the uncultured as well as the cultured and the foolish as well as the wise (Gal. 3:26–29). The Gospel of Jesus Christ is a powerful force that brings salvation to all who believe.

1:17 Paul introduces the concept of the righteousness of God, a key idea in the book of Romans. Because God is righteous, He condemns sin and judges sinners. But He has provided a way by which people can fulfill the righteousness that He demands. All who believe in Christ are justified before God, and they receive power for victorious living as His disciples (Eph. 2:1–10).

1:18–32 These verses portray the plight of Gentiles, or non-Jews. God has revealed Himself to them through His creation. But they have ignored His message and worshiped false gods, pursuing their own evil desires. Apart from God and His righteousness, they stand condemned and hopeless because of their immoral and depraved behavior.

2:1–16 God is a righteous judge. He will not judge some people because of their sin and overlook others. All who sin can expect to reap the consequences of their sin when God calls them to account. He will judge them in accordance with their deeds, not on the basis of their knowledge or ethnic background.

2:17–29 The Jewish people thought of themselves as superior to others in a moral sense because they had received God's special revelation through the Law of Moses. But they had failed to obey the law. Therefore, Paul declares, being a Jew and having God's law do not make a person righteous in God's sight.

3:1–8 Paul admits that the Jewish people do have one significant difference that sets them apart from the Gentiles. Through the Jews God has revealed and preserved His written Word, the scriptures. This is the standard by which all people—Jews as well as Gentiles—will be judged by the Lord.

3:9–20 Quoting from several OT passages, the apostle shows that righteousness before God is not something that a person attains by his or her own moral goodness, by observing the law, or by being born a Jew. The truth is that "there is none righteous, no, not one" (v. 10; see Ps. 14:1–3).

3:21–31 How, then, are people made righteous before God? Through throwing themselves in faith upon the atoning death of Jesus Christ. Jew and Gentile alike are justified not by their works but by their reliance on Jesus and His saving grace (Eph. 2:1–10).

Saint A NT word for a Christian believer set apart for God's service (Rom. 1:7; Heb. 6:10). In the OT, the word refers to a pious Jew (Ps. 16:3). Spiritual blessings are reserved for the saints of God's kingdom (Col. 1:12).

Enmity Deep animosity toward another (Gen. 3:15). This sin is characteristic of unredeemed persons (Rom. 1:29–30; 8:7).

Greeks and Barbarians *I [Paul] am debtor both to the Greeks, and to the Barbarians; both to the wise, and to the unwise* (Rom. 1:14).

Paul meant by these words that he was under obligation—by virtue of his call from God—to share the Gospel with all types of people. This included the Greeks, a highly civilized and cultured people, as well as the barbarians—a general term for the unlearned and unsophisticated. The Greeks referred to any person who was not a citizen of Greece as a "barbarian," just as the Jews thought of all non-Jewish people—no matter what their ethnic background—as "Gentiles."

NOVEMBER 29 | Read Romans 4–7

4:1–25 In this chapter, Paul uses the example of Abraham from the OT to show that God has always justified people on the basis of their faith. Abraham was childless, but he had faith that his descendants would become God's special people. The Lord declared Abraham righteous on the basis of his faith in this divine promise (James 2:23).

5:1–11 The fruits of justification by faith before God are many. The believer enjoys "peace with God" (v. 1) and is able to overcome trials and tribulations (v. 3).

5:12–21 All members of the human race are infected by Adam's sin of rebellion against God in the Garden of Eden (Gen. 3). The punishment for these sins is death. But we have been delivered from this death sentence by Jesus Christ, who laid down His life on our behalf. Just as Adam was the first member of a lost race, Jesus is the first member of a saved race, or the Second Adam. He brings release from the judgment that our sins deserve.

6:1–14 Receiving God's forgiveness through faith in Christ does not mean that we are set free to sin at will. Believers are united to Christ in such a way through their conversion experience that they want to please their Lord through holy and righteous living. The "old self" is no longer in control. We are set free from slavery to sin to service in God's kingdom.

6:15–23 Paul challenges his readers to reject the way of sin and death and to choose the path that leads to abundant living in the Lord: "For the wages of sin is death; but the gift of God is eternal life through Jesus Christ our Lord" (v. 23).

7:1–13 Keeping God's law was the criterion by which righteousness was measured in OT times (Deut. 6:1–3). But the law had only succeeded in stimulating people to greater sin. Humanity's sinful nature has not been changed by the law.

7:14–25 Paul gives his own personal testimony to illustrate the stubbornness of man's sinful nature. In his own strength, he was unable to overcome the sins of the flesh. The harder he tried to keep the law, the lower his tendency to sin dragged him down.

Justification The act or event when God both declares and makes a person just or right with Him (Rom. 4:25; 5:9). Justification is not accomplished by personal merit or good works (Gal. 2:16) but by God's grace through personal faith in Christ (Rom. 5:18; Eph. 2:8–9). To be justified is to have peace with God and hope for eternity (Titus 3:5–7).

Sin Rebellion against God. Adam and Eve's disobedience in the Garden of Eden resulted in the introduction of sin into the human race (Rom. 5:12–14). Sin is committed against three parties: ourselves (Prov. 8:36), others (Rom. 5:12), and God (Ps. 51:4; 1 Cor. 8:12). Sin is described as transgression (Matt. 15:3), perversion of the right (1 John 5:17), disobedience (Rom. 5:19), rebellion (Isa. 1:2), and lawlessness (1 John 3:4). The consequence of unforgiven sin is spiritual death, but God's gift to the believer is eternal life through Jesus Christ (Rom. 6:23).

Antinomianism The concept that grace exempts a person from the moral law. According to Paul, this idea is based on an erroneous view of grace (Rom. 6:1–2). Inconsistent with life in the spirit, antinomianism may cause a weak brother to stumble (1 Cor. 8:9). Abuse of Christian liberty violates the spirit of brotherly love (Gal. 5:13–16).

NOVEMBER 30 | Read Romans 8–11

8:1–27 But believers who have found new life in Christ have a different story to tell. Energized by the power of the Holy Spirit, they are not victimized by sin and death. God's indwelling presence strengthens Christians and enables them to walk in the path of holiness and righteousness.

8:28–39 Reflecting on God's goodness and the redemption provided in His Son causes Paul to break out in a glorious song of praise. In spite of all the testings and troubles that confront God's people, they can rest assured that they are "more than conquerors" (v. 37) through Christ who loves them.

9:1–11:36 In these three chapters, Paul addresses the question of why the Jews, his own people, have rejected the Gospel. His conclusion is that they missed the mark by stubbornly seeking justification with God by keeping the law. But some among the Jews have seen the light and have accepted Jesus by faith as the only way to salvation. This remnant of the saved gives Paul hope for the future of the Jewish people.

Divine Election The doctrine that deals with God's choice of persons who will be redeemed. Conflicts between God's electing grace and Christ's invitation that "whosoever will" may come to Him are not easily resolved. God's intentional will is for all to "come to repentance" and be saved (2 Pet. 3:9), but those who reject His Son will be lost (John 5:40). God's grace is unmerited (Rom. 9:11–16), but it will be lavished on those who are committed to His truth and His will for their lives (2 Thess. 2:13). The elect are characterized by Christlikeness (Rom. 8:29), holiness (Eph. 1:4), good works (Eph. 2:10), and eternal hope (1 Pet. 1:2–5).

Adoption and Salvation *Ye [believers in Christ] have received the Spirit of adoption [sonship, NIV], whereby we cry, Abba, Father* (Rom. 8:15).

Paul compared the process by which believers are justified to the process of adoption in Roman culture. If a Roman man had no son by biological birth, he could adopt one. One of his slaves might even be adopted as a son. The adopted son took the name of the father and had all the rights that would have been extended to a biological child.

Paul also made this comparison between adoption and salvation in his letter to the Galatians. After being delivered from bondage to sin and adopted into God's family, the believer is "no more a servant, but a son; and if a son, then an heir of God through Christ" (Gal. 4:7).

DECEMBER 1 | Read Romans 12–13

12:1–2 Total commitment to the Lord leads believers to have a new outlook on life. Resisting the temptations of the world, we make doing God's will our main concern.

12:3–8 God has given different spiritual gifts to the members of His body, the church. We should use these gifts not to bring honor to ourselves but to glorify the Lord and to enrich and build up the congregation (1 Cor. 14).

12:9–21 Love toward others, particularly fellow church members, gives evidence of our new life in Christ. Christian love is such a powerful force that it enables us to "overcome evil with good" (v. 21; see 1 Cor. 13).

13:1–7 Paul encourages his readers to respect the civil authorities, to pay their taxes (Matt. 22:15–22), and to live as good citizens of their nation (Luke 20:20–26). He believes human government is used by the Lord as a restraining influence on sin and disorder.

13:8–14 All the commandments, Paul declares, are summed up in this: "Thou shalt love thy neighbour as thyself" (v. 9; see Matt. 22:35–40). He also encourages the Roman Christians to be on the watch for Christ's return.

Spiritual Gifts Gifts bestowed freely by the Holy Spirit upon believers (James 1:17) for the edification of fellow believers and the church (Rom. 1:11; 1 Cor. 12:28). Gifts listed in Romans are preaching, serving, teaching, encouraging, giving, leading, and helping others (Rom. 12:6–8). Gifts listed in 1 Corinthians are wisdom, knowledge, faith, healing, miracles, prophecy, discernment of spirits, tongues, and interpretation of tongues (1 Cor. 12:8–11). Love is the supreme spiritual gift (1 Cor. 12:31; 13:13).

Self-denial Voluntary limitation of one's desires, a requirement of Jesus for His followers (Matt. 16:24). Paul also urged Christians to make an offering of themselves to God (Rom. 12:1). Sacrifices for Christ's sake will be rewarded (Luke 18:29–30).

DECEMBER 2 | Read Romans 14–16

14:1–23 Believers should live in harmony with one another. Apparently, some of the Roman Christians were critical of their fellow believers for eating certain food. Paul urges them not to judge one another on such trivial issues. "For the kingdom of God is not meat and drink," he declares, "but righteousness, and peace, and joy in the Holy Ghost" (v. 17).

15:1–13 The foundation of Christian unity consists of mutual respect and acceptance among all believers. Paul holds up Christ as an example because He "received us to the glory of God" (v. 7).

15:14–33 Paul is confident that his readers will continue to serve as faithful witnesses in the capital city of the Roman Empire, just as he has shared the Gospel as a traveling missionary. He intends to make a missionary trip to Spain, and he will visit them in Rome when he passes through.

16:1–2 Paul commends Phebe to the church at Rome. She may have carried this letter from him to the Roman believers.

16:3–16 Paul extends personal greetings to several believers in the Roman church, including Priscilla and Aquila (v. 3; see Acts 18:1–3).

16:17–20 Some problem had caused divisions in the church at Rome. Paul urges the believers to deal decisively with the troublemakers.

16:21–27 Paul extends personal greetings to the church from several of his missionary associates. He concludes with a beautiful doxology of praise to God for His faithful love.

Accountability The biblical principle that each person is answerable to God and responsible for his or her actions (Rom. 14:12). Accountability also involves the obligation to act with love toward fellow believers (Rom. 14:15–19).

Abstinence To refrain from eating or drinking harmful substances or participating in sinful acts. Priests and Nazirites abstained from strong drink (Num. 6:1–4). Gentile Christians were advised to abstain from fornication and idolatry (Acts 15:20). All believers are counseled by Paul to refrain from any practices that might offend a weak brother (Rom. 14:21).

Goodness Purity and righteousness; a fruit of the Spirit that should characterize followers of Christ (Gal. 5:22). True goodness comes from God, who is holy, righteous, merciful, and loving (Ps. 31:19; Rom. 15:14).

Phebe A believer at Cenchrae near Corinth who was commended by Paul for her support of him and others (Rom. 16:1–2). *Phoebe*: NIV, NRSV.

DECEMBER 3 | Read 1 Corinthians 1–6

1:1–9 Paul opens his letter with traditional greetings to believers in the church at Corinth (Acts 18:1–11), wishing them grace and peace.

1:10–17 Strife and division marred the Corinthian church. Some claimed to be following Apollos, while others were loyal to Cephas (Peter) and Paul. Perhaps those of the "Christ" party (v. 12) were claiming to be "super Christians."

1:18–31 Paul declares that people who follow their own drives and desires will always end up at odds with one another. The Corinthians should seek God's wisdom to help them achieve unity and peace, because "the foolishness of God is wiser than men" (v. 25).

2:1–5 Paul declares that he preached the Gospel with simplicity when he ministered among the Corinthians. The results prove that God's power energized his message.

2:6–16 Human beings cannot discover God's wisdom on their own. But God has given us His written Word that tells us about Him and His nature. The Holy Spirit enables us to interpret His written Word. These two gifts from God lead us to understand "the mind of Christ" (v. 16).

3:1–9 The quarreling of the Corinthians over human leadership shows they are immature in their spiritual development. God, not human leaders, is the source of wisdom and spiritual growth.

3:10–15 Jesus is the foundation on which every believer's life should be built. Anything less than Him and His divine purpose will not stand the test of time (Matt. 7:24–27).

3:16–23 Each believer is a temple of the Holy Spirit, a place where God dwells. Jesus should be the focus of our lives. In Him alone—not human leaders—should we place our trust.

4:1–7 Human leaders in the church should find their joy in serving as "ministers of Christ" (v. 1). The standard by which He will judge their work is whether they are faithful to Him. God has given us different gifts to be used in His service (Rom. 12:3–8). We should exercise these gifts to His glory.

4:8–13 Spiritual leaders should not build little empires for themselves. It is their duty to accept suffering, if necessary, in the service of God and His people (1 Pet. 2:18–25).

4:14–21 Paul makes a personal appeal for unity in the church at Corinth. He was a spiritual father to many of them because they had been converted under his ministry. He urges them to follow his example as a faithful disciple of Christ.

5:1–8 In these verses Paul deals with the problem of sexual sin. A believer in the church at Corinth was involved in a sexual relationship with his "father's wife" (v. 1)—probably his stepmother. The apostle criticizes the Corinthian Christians for ignoring the problem and allowing it to continue. He advises the church to exercise discipline by expelling the unrepentant sinner.

5:9–13 Paul makes a distinction between relating to nonbelievers and associating with fellow believers. We are not to judge nonbelievers and isolate ourselves from them. Rather, we are to bear our witness for Jesus before them. But we are called to withdraw from fellow believers who continue in willful sin. Church discipline is designed to reclaim and restore those who have wandered away from the Lord (Matt. 18:15–22).

6:1–11 The apostle expresses disappointment that some of the believers at Corinth are taking one another to civil courts, perhaps to settle financial claims. He urges them to settle their differences through committees of their fellow believers.

6:12–20 Paul declares that sexual relationships outside the bonds of marriage are a perversion of God's plan. Sexual immorality is actually a sin against one's own body because of the Bible's teaching on the one-flesh relationship (Gen. 2:24). Believers should view their bodies as a temple, or residence, for the Holy Spirit of the Lord.

- -

Gladiator Apostles *I [Paul] think that God hath set forth us the apostles last, as it were appointed to death: for we are made a spectacle unto the world, and to angels, and to men* (1 Cor. 4:9).

In this verse Paul compares himself and the other apostles of the NT to the gladiators who were "set forth. . .last" in the Roman arena. These were slaves or criminals who were forced to fight experienced gladiators or wild animals without weapons and who were quickly "appointed to death." Paul was saying that he and the other apostles of NT times had made sacrifices to advance the Gospel—and the Corinthian believers had been blessed by their witnessing efforts. Paul's words were prophetic. Most of the apostles of the early church, including this great missionary to the Gentiles, were eventually martyred for their faith.

DECEMBER 4 | Read 1 Corinthians 7–10

7:1–40 In this chapter Paul answers questions from the Corinthians on the nature and meaning of marriage. The married state is the best option for most people, he declares, but singlehood also has advantages for those who can control their sexual passions. Believers who are married to unbelievers should remain married. But if the unbeliever should leave the relationship, the Christian is released from the bonds of marriage and is free to get married again (vv. 12–16). All believers should live with happiness and contentment in the lifestyle in which God has placed them (vv. 17–24).

8:1–13 In this chapter Paul addresses the problem of meat sacrificed to pagan gods in the city of Corinth. Some believers felt that eating this meat after it had been sacrificed was no problem for worshipers of Christ. But others thought this practice was an act of idolatry. The apostle agreed, in principle, that it was acceptable to eat this meat because all creation belongs to God (v. 6). But he urged believers to abstain from eating such meat if the practice offended weaker Christians (vv. 9–11).

9:1–27 This chapter consists of Paul's testimony about his motivation for ministry. He was not just preaching about the principles of making personal sacrifices and living as an example for the Corinthians. He had given up his freedom to do as he pleased and had accommodated himself to the needs of others in order to bring them to the Lord: "I am made all things to all men, that I might by all means save some" (v. 22).

10:1–22 Paul warns the Corinthian believers to stay away from idol worship. He uses the example of the Israelites during the wilderness wandering years to show how easy it is to give in to the temptation to worship pagan gods (Num. 25:1–18).

10:23–11:1 Paul returns to the issue of meat sacrificed to idols (see 1 Cor. 8:1–13). Such meat is neither good nor bad in itself. But our freedom in the Lord should not blind us to the fact that we must avoid certain activities that hinder our Christian witness before others. We bring glory to God when we seek the good of others, not our individual rights.

. . . .

Discipline and Training *Every man that striveth for the mastery is temperate in all things* (1 Cor. 9:25).

This is one of many references in Paul's writings to the Greek games that were similar to our modern Olympics. An athlete who expected to win at these games had to be "temperate in all things," or undergo a strict regimen of discipline and training. Paul was comparing the Christian life to the discipline required of these Greek athletes. Believers are saved to a life of service in the cause of Christ. Every day should bring us closer to the goal of total commitment to Christ and His work: "That the man of God may be perfect, thoroughly furnished unto all good works" (2 Tim. 3:17).

DECEMBER 5 | Read 1 Corinthians 11–13

11:2–16 According to Paul, female believers in Corinth were to cover their heads during public worship and men were to worship with their heads uncovered. This was apparently the accepted custom in Corinthian society. He saw no need for believers to reject these customs if they did not hinder the worship of Christ.

11:17–34 The Corinthians were desecrating the Lord's Supper by turning It Into a feast. The rich were eating like gluttons while the poor were getting shoved aside because they had no food to bring. This added to the problem of factions in the church (see 1 Cor. 1:10–17). Paul exhorted the church to stop this feasting and to make the Lord's Supper an occasion for remembering the sacrificial death of Jesus Christ on their behalf (Luke 22:14–20).

12:1–31 In this chapter Paul addresses the issue of spiritual gifts. The more spectacular gifts—such as speaking in tongues, prophecy, and teaching—are not more important than the other, more subdued gifts. All work together to edify and build up the body of Christ. The apostle compares the church to a human body, pointing out that all parts of the body contribute to the healthy operation of the whole.

13:1–13 This is known as the "love chapter" of the Bible. No matter how gifted or talented a person may be, he is nothing but "sounding brass" or "a tinkling cymbal" (v. 1) if he does not exercise these gifts in the spirit of love (Rom. 12:9–21).

· ·

Agape A Greek word for selfless love, the type of love that characterizes God (John 15:13; 1 John 3:16). Agape is primarily an act of the will rather than the emotions (John 3:16; Rom. 5:8). Agape love for others is a badge of discipleship (John 13:34–35). This love is the greatest and most enduring of all Christian virtues (1 Cor. 13).

· ·

Speech Based on Love *Though I [Paul] speak with the tongues of men and of angels, and have not charity [love, NIV], I am become as sounding brass [a resounding gong, NIV], or a tinkling [clanging, NIV] cymbal* (1 Cor. 13:1).

The Greek word translated as "charity" or "love" in this verse is *agape*—self-giving love that asks for nothing in return. No matter how eloquent in speech a person may be—even if he speaks several languages—this amounts to nothing if his words are not spoken in love. Pagan worship in Paul's time was often accompanied by strange noises, the clang of gongs and cymbals, and loud blasts on trumpets. Paul declared that the speech of the Corinthian believers was no better than these meaningless rituals unless spoken in love.

DECEMBER 6 | Read 1 Corinthians 14–16

14:1–40 Some believers in the Corinthian church were elevating the gift of speaking in tongues above all other gifts. Paul declares that prophecy is actually the most important gift because it builds up and edifies the church. Speaking in tongues should be practiced only if an interpreter is present to clarify the meaning of the message to others. Paul's concern was that everything should be done "decently and in order" (v. 40) in a public worship service.

15:1–11 Some Corinthian Christians had doubts about the bodily resurrection. Paul insists on the reality of the resurrection of Jesus because He was seen alive by several different groups after He was raised from the dead (Mark 16:9–11; Luke 24:13–43; John 20:19–29). To Paul, Jesus' resurrection—and its promise of the future resurrection of all believers—is one of the cornerstones of the Christian faith.

15:12–34 The offering of firstfruits was presented by worshipers to the Lord on the first day of the week following Passover. This offering guaranteed the coming harvest (Lev. 23:9–11). This was true of Christ's resurrection as well. His bodily resurrection guaranteed the resurrection of all believers.

15:35–58 Paul insists that believers will experience resurrection with a body that is suitable for its new spiritual environment in the world beyond (1 Thess. 4:13–18). The hope of a future resurrection gives believers the courage to bear up under hardship and suffering for the sake of Christ. In Him we experience victory over sin and death.

16:1–4 Paul encourages the Corinthian Christians to give to an offering he is receiving for the impoverished believers in Jerusalem.

16:5–20 The apostle tells about his plans for a future visit to Corinth. He instructs them to receive Timothy when he visits, and he commends Stephanas and his fellow workers. Paul also sends personal greetings from Aquila and Priscilla (Acts 18:1–3).

16:21–24 Paul closes the letter with a benediction of grace and love to the Corinthian believers.

. . . .

Speaking in Tongues Glossolalia or ecstatic utterances; a spiritual gift exercised by some believers in the NT church. This gift apparently first occurred on the day of Pentecost with the outpouring of God's Spirit on believers (Acts 2:1–13). Paul also mentioned this gift in 1 Cor. 14:2–28, although it is unclear whether this is the same as the phenomenon described in Acts.

Eternal Life Life without end, or everlasting existence. Eternal life was promised to believers at their conversion by Christ (John 11:25–26) and affirmed by the appearance of Moses and Elijah to Jesus and the three disciples (Matt. 17:1–9). Through His resurrection, Christ became the "firstfruits" of eternal life for all believers (1 Cor. 15:12–23). Life everlasting represents God's final victory over sin and death (Rev. 21:4).

Spiritual Body The glorified or redeemed body of believers. Our hope of a glorified body is based on Christ's victory over the grave (Rom. 6:6). Believers will receive a glorified body, free of sin and death, at the return of Christ (1 Cor. 15:50–57). The redeemed body of a believer will be like that of Christ's glorified body (Phil.

3:21), immortal and incorruptible (1 Cor. 15:53–54). Christians need not fear death, because we are provided a new spiritual body "eternal in the heavens" (2 Cor. 5).

Maranatha An Aramaic phrase meaning "come, O Lord" that expresses hope for the second coming of Jesus (1 Cor. 16:22).

DECEMBER 7 | Read 2 Corinthians 1–5

1:1–2 Paul begins his letter with greetings of grace and peace to the Corinthian church (Acts 18:1–13).

1:3–11 The apostle uses his experience of suffering to comfort the Corinthian believers. He had also experienced God as the source of comfort in his afflictions. He assures them that God will comfort them in their sufferings for the sake of the Gospel.

1:12–24 Paul had promised to make a personal visit to the Corinthian church (1 Cor. 16:3–6). In these verses he explains why he has not yet fulfilled his promise: "To spare you I came not as yet unto Corinth" (v. 23). He apparently wanted to give them time to respond to the instructions he had given them in his previous letter—1 Corinthians.

2:1–4 Paul's love for the Corinthian believers was another factor in his delay of his visit. He hopes the church will respond positively to his previous letter so they can rejoice together when he finally visits them at Corinth.

2:5–11 In his previous letter, the apostle had instructed the church to deal with a man who was living in an immoral sexual relationship (1 Cor. 5). The church had apparently done so, and the man had repented. Now Paul encourages the church to forgive the man and restore him to full Christian fellowship.

2:12–17 To Paul, the favorable response of the Corinthians to his instructions was like a sweet fragrance. He expresses thanks to God for the victorious ministry that He gives to His servants.

3:1–3 Paul's credentials as a minister were apparently being questioned by some people in the Corinthian church. He insists that changed lives as a result of his work were all the endorsement his ministry required.

3:4–18 Paul claims to be a minister of the new covenant of grace, which is far superior to the old covenant of law (Heb. 8:1–10:18). Anyone who questions the apostle's ministry must take its superior nature into account.

4:1–18 Paul compares himself as a human minister to an earthen vessel (v. 7), or a clay pot. But God had filled this common, unworthy container with His treasure, or the glory of the Gospel. The sufferings Paul faced in living out his calling were light when compared with the glory God was storing up for him as an eternal reward.

5:1–21 God sent His Son Jesus Christ to reconcile sinners to Himself through His atoning death on the cross. Paul sees his ministry as a part of this divine plan. He serves as an ambassador for Christ, imploring others, "Be ye reconciled to God" (v. 20).

- -

Intermediate State The condition of believers between death and the resurrection. Paul characterized this state as being "absent from the body" (2 Cor. 5:8) while awaiting the resurrection (1 Thess. 4:13–18) and anticipating a glorified body like that of Jesus (Phil. 3:20–21). This condition is also characterized as a sleeplike state (John 11:11) that is enjoyable (Ps. 17:15) and unchangeable (2 Cor. 5:1).

- -

Triumphant in Christ *Thanks be unto God, which always causeth us to triumph [leads us in triumphal procession, NIV] in Christ* (2 Cor. 2:14).

In this verse Paul compares the victory of Christ over death to a Roman military procession. A victorious general and his army would return from a battle with captives and spoils of war in tow. The entire city of Rome would turn out to welcome the warriors with loud shouts and joyful music. To Paul, Christ's victory over the grave was more impressive than Roman military triumphs that led to such lavish displays. And more significantly, all believers share in this victory procession of Christ.

DECEMBER 8 | Read 2 Corinthians 6–9

6:1–13 Paul reminds the Corinthians of the suffering he has endured as a minister of the Gospel. He wants them to understand that troubles and tribulations are a natural result of serving Christ (1 Pet. 4:12–17).

6:14–18 The apostle makes an eloquent plea for the Corinthian believers to throw off evil and unbelief and to follow the commands of Christ. They are not to be "unequally yoked together with unbelievers" (v. 14).

7:1–16 Titus apparently brought a report to Paul that the Corinthians had responded favorably to his words of rebuke and instruction in his previous letter— 1 Corinthians. Paul expresses his joy at the news of their repentance.

8:1–9:15 In these two chapters, Paul discusses in detail the offering he had mentioned in his previous letter (1 Cor. 16:1–4). This was an offering he was taking among the churches of the province of Macedonia to assist the Christians in Jerusalem who were suffering from a famine. To motivate the Corinthian believers to give to this fund, Paul reminds them of Jesus' example of giving His life unselfishly on their behalf (Phil. 2:1–11). He also set before them the method by which they should give: "Every man according as he purposeth in his heart, so let him give; not grudgingly, or of necessity: for God loveth a cheerful giver" (9:7).

- -

Spirit A word that denotes our reason, conscience, and nobler affections (2 Cor. 7:1; Eph. 4:23)—in contrast to the soul—our appetites, passions, and sensations. The root meaning of the word is "wind" (John 3:8).

. . . .

Unequally Yoked *Be ye [Corinthian believers] not unequally yoked together with unbelievers* (2 Cor. 6:14).

Paul was probably alluding in this verse to a familiar prohibition in the Mosaic Law: "Thou shalt not plow with an ox and an ass [donkey] together" (Deut. 22:10). The reason for this law was that a donkey was an unclean animal, while the ox was among the clean animals that Jews were permitted to eat. What's more, they would have been out of step with each other in their pull against the plow. Paul's point is that the believers of Corinth should leave the patterns and habits of their old life of unbelief behind. They should live in accordance with their new status as members of God's family.

DECEMBER 9 | Read 2 Corinthians 10–13

10:1–11 Apparently, a rebellious element in the Corinthian church was critical of Paul and resistant to his authority. In these verses Paul answers their charge that he is a weak and timid leader. He assures them that his leadership approach is consistent, whether addressing them by letter or speaking to them face-to-face.

10:12–18 Paul refuses to buy into the game of his opponents in Corinth. They were claiming to be superior to Paul in their leadership ability. Rather than arguing the point, Paul declares that God's assessment is the only thing that matters.

11:1–6 Paul warns against deceitful teachers who would lead the Corinthian believers to follow them rather than point the church to Christ.

11:7–15 Paul had supported himself while preaching the Gospel in the Corinthian church (Acts 18:1–3). He expresses his frustration that his enemies have criticized him even for this. He charges these critics with trying to undermine his leadership by using false and deceitful tactics.

11:16–33 In these verses the apostle lists the various troubles he has suffered as a minister of the Gospel. This litany of tribulations proves that he is a true follower of Christ. The same cannot be said of those who are questioning his leadership.

12:1–10 This passage contains Paul's famous "thorn in the flesh" statement (v. 7). This disability, possibly an eye disease, helped the apostle to come to the realization that God's power is made perfect in human weakness. In their human frailties, servants of the Lord must depend on His never-failing strength.

12:11–21 Paul has spoken boldly to the Corinthians to build them up in their faith. He assures them that he is not interested in their money or possessions. He has poured himself out gladly on their behalf.

13:1–10 The apostle promises the Corinthian Christians that he will visit them soon. He warns them that he will deal forthrightly with any who are in willful rebellion against the Lord.

13:11–14 Paul closes his letter with a beautiful benediction, praying that God's love and grace will abide with the Corinthian believers.

Thorn in the Flesh An unknown affliction from which the apostle Paul prayed to be delivered (2 Cor. 12:7–8). Some scholars believe it was an eye ailment, since he normally dictated his epistles and apologized for his own large handwriting (Gal. 6:11).

Paul's Escape in a Basket *Through a window in a basket was I [Paul] let down by the wall* (2 Cor. 11:33).

The event to which Paul refers in this verse is reported in the book of Acts (9:22–25). Paul traveled to the city of Damascus to persecute Christians. But after his dramatic conversion, he witnessed for Christ among the Jews of the city. Other believers had to help him escape over the city wall when the Jews determined to kill him. The window out of which Paul escaped may have been in a house that was built into or on top of the defensive wall of Damascus. Such "wall houses" were common in some cities. This was the type of house in which Rahab the prostitute lived. She helped several Israelite spies escape over the city wall from the window in her house in Jericho (Josh. 2:15).

DECEMBER 10 | Read Galatians 1–6

1:1–5 Paul opens his letter to the Galatian Christians with wishes for grace and peace in the name of Jesus Christ.

1:6–10 The apostle expresses his disappointment that the Galatians have turned away from the true Gospel he has preached to them; they are now following a false gospel.

1:11–24 Apparently the Judaizers at Galatia were claiming that Paul had no authority to preach the Gospel among them. In response to this charge, Paul reviews the facts about his conversion and call from God to serve as an apostle (Acts 9:1–20).

2:1–10 At first, early leaders of the church, such as Peter, James, and John, were hesitant to accept Paul because he had been a persecutor of the church. But they eventually recognized his call from God and his apostleship (Acts 9:26–30).

2:11–14 Paul tells the Galatians how he rebuked Peter and Barnabas because they were led astray by a group of zealous Jews in the church at Antioch. Apparently Peter and Barnabas gave in to their demands that Gentiles had to be circumcised and keep the Jewish law before they could become Christians. On this issue, Paul declares, he "withstood him [Peter] to the face" (v. 11).

2:15–21 Paul declares that repentance and faith alone justify a person in God's sight. Nothing else is to be added to these basic requirements for salvation (Rom. 3:28).

3:1–4:31 In these two chapters, Paul contrasts the freedom that believers experience in Christ with the restrictions of the Jewish law. Anyone who would exchange the grace of Jesus Christ for keeping the Jewish law, as the Galatians were tempted to do, was foolish indeed. The Judaizers have been insisting on making Gentiles sons of Abraham through the rite of circumcision. But Paul declares that Gentile Christians are already Abraham's sons because they share the faith that he demonstrated (3:7, 29).

5:1–15 Freedom in Christ is not a license to live as one pleases. We are saved to a life of love and service toward others. Believers are compelled by God's grace to follow only one law—the royal law of love: "All the law is fulfilled in one word. . . Thou shalt love thy neighbour as thyself" (v. 14).

5:16–6:10 In these verses Paul gives some specific examples of behavior that should characterize the believer: "love, joy, peace, long-suffering, gentleness, goodness, faith, meekness, temperance" (5:22–23). These attitudes and characteristics are "the fruit of the Spirit" (5:22) in the believer's life—a natural result of God's grace and love in the human heart. Following a list of do's and don'ts in the law is a poor substitute for such a radiant pattern of life.

6:11–18 Paul closes his letter to the Galatians by reminding them that Jesus and His death on the cross are the central focus of the salvation story—not whether a person should be circumcised: "For in Christ Jesus neither circumcision availeth any thing, nor uncircumcision, but a new creature" (v. 15).

Benevolence Generosity toward others. Paul commended generosity toward the needy (Gal. 2:10). Christian benevolence should be shown toward God's servants (Phil. 4:14–17) and even our enemies (Prov. 25:21).

"Up" to Jerusalem *After three years I [Paul] went up to Jerusalem to see Peter* (Gal. 1:18).

Paul indicates in the previous verse that he was in Damascus, Syria (Gal. 1:17), when he traveled to Jerusalem to see Peter. Damascus was north of Jerusalem. Why didn't Paul say that he went "down" to the city to see Peter? To most people today, "up" refers to northern locations and "down" to southern sites. Jerusalem was built on high hills in a mountainous territory about 2,500 feet above sea level. To the Jews, whatever the direction from which they approached Jerusalem, it was always "up" (Luke 2:42).

Marks of Persecution *I [Paul] bear in my body the marks of the Lord Jesus* (Gal. 6:17).

In Paul's time slaves were branded with distinctive marks to show that they belonged to their masters, much as cattle are branded in modern times. Paul declared that his body bore marks from the persecution he had endured in Christ's service. These showed that he belonged to the Lord Jesus. The apostle named some of these marks of persecution in 2 Corinthians 11:24–25: "Five times received I forty stripes save one. Thrice was I beaten with rods, once was I stoned."

DECEMBER 11 | Read Ephesians 1–6

1:1–2 Paul opens his letter by referring to the Ephesian Christians as "saints" (v. 1). This word as used in the NT means those who have been set aside for God's exclusive use (Rom. 1:7; Phil. 1:1).

1:3–14 God's redemptive plan for humankind from the beginning involved sending His Son to die for our sins. Paul marvels at such love and grace expressed in the life and sacrificial death of Jesus Christ.

1:15–23 The apostle expresses his thanks for these Ephesian Christians. He wants them to grow in their understanding of the riches of Christ's grace.

2:1–10 Paul reminds the Ephesian believers of the wonder of their salvation in Christ. They were dead in their "trespasses and sins" (v. 1), but God redeemed them and filled their lives with joy. This came about solely through God's grace, not because of any goodness or good works on their part: "By grace are ye saved through faith; and that not of yourselves: it is the gift of God: not of works, lest any man should boast" (vv. 8–9; see Rom. 3:21–31).

2:11–22 Jesus is the great equalizer who has broken down the barriers between different classes and ethnic groups in society (Rom. 1:14–16). All who belong to Him are bound together as one in His love and in His church.

3:1–13 Paul declares that in times past, God's promises have been interpreted as applying mainly to the Jewish people. But this changed with the coming of Christ and His offer of salvation to the Gentiles, as well (Rom. 3:28–29). Paul is pleased that he was selected to help inaugurate this new phase of world redemption: "Unto me. . .is this grace given, that I should preach among the Gentiles the unsearchable riches of Christ" (v. 8).

3:14–21 Again, Paul prays for the Ephesian Christians—this time that they might be strengthened in their faith and in their commitment to Christ.

4:1–6 Paul encourages the Ephesian believers to express through their actions the underlying unity that exists in the body of Christ (1 Cor. 1:10). This calls for patience and humility on the part of all members of the body.

4:7–16 God in His wisdom has given many different gifts to the people in His church. They exercise their gifts as apostles, prophets, evangelists, pastors, and teachers. All these gifts are needed if the church is to function properly (Rom. 12:3–8).

4:17–5:20 This passage is known as the practical section of Ephesians because it deals with the way believers should live. Paul calls on the Ephesians to "put on the new man" (4:24) and to copy the character of God in their daily behavior.

5:21–6:9 Relationships should also reflect the lordship of Christ. Paul has advice on godly living for wives (5:22–24), husbands (5:25–33), children (6:1–3), fathers (6:4), servants (6:5–8), and masters (6:9).

6:10–20 Paul recognizes that living a godly life in a godless world is not an easy task. He urges the Ephesians to put on their spiritual battle gear and to get ready to "stand against the wiles of the devil" (v. 11).

6:21–24 Paul closes his letter with wishes of grace and peace for the Ephesian believers.

. . . .

Atonement Reconciliation of God and man through sacrifice (Rom. 5:11). In OT times such reconciliation was accomplished through animal sacrifices symbolic of the people's repentance. But true reconciliation is made possible by Christ's atoning death and resurrection (Rom. 5:1; Eph. 1:7). Man's justification in God's sight is made possible by repentance and faith (Eph. 2:8). God's righteousness is imparted through Christ's sacrifice (2 Cor. 5:21). His atonement is the foundation for genuine peace (Eph. 2:13–16). All who are redeemed through their acceptance by faith of the sacrifice of Christ are called as ministers of reconciliation (2 Cor. 5:18–21).

Middle Wall of Partition The curtain or barrier in the Jewish temple at Jerusalem that separated Jews and Gentiles. Christ's atonement removed this partition and brought reconciliation and peace to people of all races and nationalities (Eph. 2:14–18). *Barrier*: NIV; *Dividing wall*: NRSV.

. . . .

Sealed by the Spirit *After that ye [Ephesian Christians] believed, ye were sealed with that holy Spirit of promise* (Eph. 1:13).

Paul refers in this verse to the distinct mark of identification that was placed on a letter, contract, or other legal document in Bible times. This seal proved the document's authenticity. Likewise, believers are sealed or authenticated by the Holy Spirit after their conversion. His mark in our lives results in holy and righteous living. God also gives us His spirit as His pledge of our future inheritance of eternal life (2 Cor. 1:22).

Spiritual Battle Gear *Take unto you [Christian believers] the whole armour of God, that ye may be able to withstand in the evil day* (Eph. 6:15).

Paul told the Ephesian believers they needed to equip themselves for spiritual battle, just as the Roman soldiers of his day put on their battle gear to get ready for war. The apostle compared the breastplate of righteousness to the armor that protected a soldier's upper body. The hobnail shoes that soldiers wore symbolized the believer's sure footing in the Gospel. Believers should also carry with them into battle the "shield of faith," the "helmet of salvation," and the "sword of the Spirit, which is the word of God" (Eph. 6:16–17). These items will assure victory in the spiritual battles that believers face in the world.

DECEMBER 12 | Read Philippians 1–4

1:1–2 Paul begins his letter with greetings from himself and his helper, Timothy (Acts 16:1–3), to the church at Philippi (Acts 16:12–40).

1:3–11 Paul prays a beautiful prayer of thanksgiving for the Philippian believers. He remembers them with joy because of their kindness to him and their faithful support of the Gospel.

1:12–26 Although Paul is in prison, he wants the Philippian Christians to realize that God has brought something good out of this experience (Rom. 8:28). It has actually brought greater opportunity for the proclamation of the Gospel and the growth of new believers. The apostle is content in this situation, whether he lives or dies: "To me to live is Christ, and to die is gain" (v. 21).

1:27–30 Paul encourages the believers at Philippi to remain loyal to Christ, even if they should be persecuted for their faith.

2:1–11 Paul uses the example of Christ to motivate the Philippians to live holy and righteous lives in the midst of a selfish world. Verses 6–11 are probably a hymn or confession of faith on the nature of Jesus used in worship services by early believers. Christ was God's Son—fully divine—but He came to earth in the form of a man—fully human—to bring salvation and eternal life to all who believe.

2:12–30 The Philippian believers are encouraged to continue the good work they have started. To help them, Paul promises to send two of his coworkers—Timothy and Epaphroditus.

3:1–11 Paul warns against the corrupting influence of the Judaizers. This group was teaching that Gentile converts must be circumcised and keep the Jewish law before they could become Christians. Paul declares that he was once a strict observer of all Jewish traditions, but he has learned that true righteousness comes only through faith in Jesus Christ.

3:12–4:1 Paul urges his fellow Christians at Philippi to "stand fast in the Lord" (4:1). He points to himself as the example they should follow, since he continues to "press toward the mark for the prize of the high calling of God in Christ Jesus" (3:14).

4:2–9 Apparently there was some problem with divisions in the church at Philippi (1 Cor. 1:11–13). Paul makes a personal appeal for unity to those who are causing trouble and urges the entire church to seek the guidance and counsel of the Lord.

4:10–23 Paul concludes by thanking his Christian brothers and sisters at Philippi for their generous support of him and his ministry. Their gifts had apparently been sent through Epaphroditus while the apostle was in prison (v. 18).

Conversation   A word for behavior or lifestyle. Paul urged Christians to live in accordance with the Gospel of Christ (Phil. 1:27).

Poured Out for the Lord   *If I [Paul] be offered upon the sacrifice and service of your [Philippian believers'] faith, I joy, and rejoice with you all* (Phil. 2:17).

The NIV translates this verse, "Even if I am being poured out like a drink offering on the sacrifice and service coming from your faith." Paul was comparing himself and his life to a sacrifice known as the drink offering. In this ceremony the worshiper poured wine on top of the animal that had been sacrificed as a burnt offering. The wine was vaporized as steam when it hit the hot carcass. This symbolized the rising of the offering to God (Exod. 29:38–41; Hosea 9:4). Paul viewed his life as a drink offering. He rejoiced that it was being poured out in sacrificial service on behalf of the Philippians and other early believers.

DECEMBER 13 | Read Colossians 1–4

1:1–14   Paul opens his letter to the believers at Colosse with a prayer of thanksgiving for the faith and love of these brothers and sisters in the Lord. Paul had never visited this church, but he apparently knew about them through his missionary associate Epaphras (Philem. 23), who had ministered among them (v. 7).

1:15–23   The Colossian believers were being led astray by false teachers, who were challenging the divinity and supremacy of Jesus Christ. The apostle corrects this error by declaring that Jesus is the divine Son of God, the head of the church, and the one in whom God the Father is fully revealed.

1:24–29   Through the church as His body, Jesus is still at work in the world. Paul is pleased to be a minister who labors among the churches as a representative of the living Christ (2 Cor. 5:20).

2:1–23   Paul reminds the Colossian believers of the new life they have experienced as a result of their acceptance of Christ. He encourages them to continue their daily walk in obedience to His commands and to stay anchored to the truth in their doctrinal beliefs. They didn't need some mystical experience to perfect their salvation, as the false teachers were claiming. Their deliverance from sin was "complete in him [Christ]" (v. 10).

3:1–4:6   In these verses Paul contrasts the old way of life with the new patterns of behavior that should characterize a person who has come to know Christ as Lord and Savior. The apostle has practical advice on Christian living for wives (3:18), husbands (3:19), children (3:20), fathers (3:21), servants (3:22), and masters (4:1).

4:7–9   Paul mentions his coworker Tychicus (v. 7), who may have delivered this letter to the Colossian Christians. Tychicus may have been accompanied by the runaway slave Onesimus (v. 9; see Philem. 10).

4:10–18   Paul closes his letter by sending greetings from several of his missionary associates and coworkers.

Colosse A city about 100 miles east of Ephesus and the site of a church to which Paul wrote one of his epistles (Col. 1:2). Whether Paul visited this city is uncertain. *Colossae*: NRSV.

Salvation and Circumcision *In whom [Jesus] also ye [Colossian believers] are circumcised with the circumcision made without hands* (Col. 2:11).

Circumcision—the removal of the foreskin from the male sex organ—was a mark of the covenant between God and His people, the Israelites (Rom. 4:11). In this verse Paul compares the death of Christ on the cross to this ritual. This "circumcision" of Jesus was the event that provided for the salvation of believers. We are also "circumcised" when we die to our sins by committing ourselves to Him as our Lord and Savior.

DECEMBER 14 | Read 1 Thessalonians; 2 Thessalonians

1 Thessalonians

1:1–10 Paul commends the believers at Thessalonica (Acts 17:1, 11–13) for their faith and love, as well as their testimony to the power of the Gospel. Because of Paul's work among them, they had "turned to God from idols to serve the living and true God" (v. 9).

2:1–16 Paul reminds these fellow believers of the time he had spent among them proclaiming the Gospel. He had spoken the truth about Christ with all sincerity, not appealing to their pride or trying to win their favor with flattering words.

2:17–20 Paul has not forgotten these new believers, although he has not seen them for a while. He considers them his "glory and joy" (v. 20).

3:1–13 On a previous occasion while visiting Athens (Acts 17:13–15), Paul had sent his coworker Timothy to check on the new converts at Thessalonica. Timothy brought the apostle a good report about their growth in the Lord. Paul is grateful for this good news, and he offers a prayer of thanksgiving for the Thessalonian Christians.

4:1–12 The apostle reminds his fellow believers of the behavior expected of those who belong to Christ. They are to stay sexually pure, to practice justice, to love one another, and to bear their witness for Christ in a quiet and humble way.

4:13–18 In these verses Paul addresses a question that had been raised by some of the Thessalonian Christians. Apparently some of them expected Jesus to return during their lifetime. What would happen to those believers who had not lived to experience this great event? The apostle assured them that "the dead in Christ shall rise first: Then we which are alive and remain shall be caught up together with them in the clouds, to meet the Lord in the air" (vv. 16–17).

5:1–11 Paul goes on to address the question of when the Lord will return. No one knows. But we can be sure He will return suddenly—and when we least expect it. We should be ready (Matt. 24:42–51).

5:12–24 With a series of short exhortations, Paul tells the Thessalonian believers how they should be living while waiting for the Lord's return.

5:25–28 Paul closes his letter by asking for the grace of the Lord to fill their lives and requesting that they continue to pray for him and his coworkers.

2 Thessalonians

1:1–2 Paul opens his second letter to the Christians at Thessalonica (Acts 17:1, 11–13) with greetings from himself as well as Silas ("Silvanus," v. 1) and Timothy.

1:3–12 Paul thanks God that the Thessalonian Christians are continuing to grow and mature in their faith. This growth is helping them to endure the persecution they are experiencing. He reminds them that the roles of persecutor and perse-cuted will one day be reversed. In the final judgment, believers who have been persecuted in this life will be rewarded by the Lord with eternal life. But persecuting unbelievers will be punished "with everlasting destruction from the presence of the Lord" (v. 9).

2:1–2 Apparently the Thessalonians had been told by false teachers that the day of the Lord or the second coming of Christ had already occurred.

2:3–12 Paul corrects this falsehood. He assures the believers at Thessalonica that the second coming of Christ has not yet happened. This will not occur until after the appearance of "that man of sin. . .the son of perdition" (v. 3). Paul was referring to the Antichrist.

2:13–15 Paul exhorts the Thessalonians to "stand fast" (v. 15) and not be led astray by false teachings about the end times and their eternal inheritance. Their salvation has been purchased by Jesus Christ and sealed by the Holy Spirit because of their belief of the truth.

2:16–17 In a beautiful benediction, Paul prays that these believers will be strength-ened in their faith and belief.

3:1–5 Paul urges the Thessalonian believers to pray for him in his work of planting and nurturing the Gospel.

3:6–15 Some of the Thessalonian Christians had apparently quit working to wait for the second coming of Christ. They may have been expecting others to support them as they waited for the Lord's return. Paul criticized such idleness and exhorted these people to get back to work. Christians are to share the Gospel message with diligence until Jesus returns (Acts 1:8–11).

3:16–18 Paul closes with wishes of grace and peace for the believers at Thessalonica.

Thessalonica A city on the Macedonian coast where Paul preached and founded a church. It was also the scene of a riot incited by Jews who opposed the preaching of Paul and Silas (Acts 17:1–9).

Rapture A doctrine held by some that deals with the transformation of the redeemed into a glorified state at Christ's return (Phil. 3:20–21). The dead in Christ will be raised at Christ's return and given an incorruptible body (1 Cor. 15:51–53). They will be caught up into the air, along with living saints, to meet the Lord (1 Thess. 4:16–17).

Protected by Faith and Love *Let us. . .be sober [self-controlled, NIV], putting on the breastplate of faith and love* (1 Thess. 5:8).

In his letter to the Ephesian Christians, Paul instructed them to put on the "breastplate of righteousness." Here he exhorts the Thessalonian believers to put on the "breastplate of faith and love." The breastplate, or body armor, of a Roman soldier protected the vital organs of the upper body. Likewise, believers are protected from giving in to temptation when we focus on His love for us and exercise faith in His promises.

Paul's Own Handwriting *The salutation of Paul with mine own hand, which is the token in every epistle: so I write* (2 Thess. 3:17).

In Bible times many people wrote letters by dictating them to a secretary—a professional amanuensis, or scribe. This apparently was done occasionally by Paul, the most prolific letter writer of the NT. To prove to the recipients of 2 Thessalonians that this letter was from him—even though it had been written by someone else—Paul wrote the final words in his own handwriting. He also closed 1 Corinthians (16:21) and Colossians (4:18) in the same way. In Paul's letter to the Romans, his secretary identified himself and included his own greeting to the Roman Christians: "I Tertius, who wrote this epistle, salute you in the Lord" (Rom. 16:22).

DECEMBER 15 | Read 1 Timothy 1–6

1:1–2 Paul opens this letter to Timothy (1 Cor. 4:17) by addressing him as his "own son in the faith" (v. 2).

1:3–11 Paul had left Timothy in the church at Ephesus while he moved on to preach the Gospel at other places. The apostle urges Timothy to stay at Ephesus so he can oppose false teachings that are beginning to appear in the church.

1:12–20 Paul had once been a persecutor of the church (Acts 9:1–2). He expresses his amazement to Timothy that God is now using him to spread the Gospel.

2:1–8 Prayer is one of the most important functions of the church. Prayers should be offered for kings and others in authority as well as a church's own members.

2:9–15 Paul reminds Timothy that a specific code of conduct is expected of female believers in the church.

3:1–7 Those believers who serve as bishops or elders in the church must meet certain qualifications (Titus 1:5–9).

3:8–13 High standards are also established for those who would serve as deacons.

3:14–16 Paul expresses his hope that he will soon be able to visit Timothy at Ephesus.

4:1–16 With strong words, Paul condemns those in the church at Ephesus who are teaching false doctrine. He urges Timothy to stand firmly against these false teachings and to exercise discipline against the troublemakers. Although Timothy is young and inexperienced, he should exercise the authority that has been delegated to him by the Lord and officials of the church.

5:1–16 The early church offered financial support to widows, many of whom were destitute (Acts 6:1–7). Paul instructs Timothy on how to conduct this ministry in the church at Ephesus. Older widows are more likely to need this assistance. The families of some widows can help their own. The church should make sure its resources go to those in dire need.

5:17–25 Elders, or pastors, should be selected by the church with great care. Once placed in positions of leadership, they should be treated with respect and compensated for their work.

6:1–10 Paul offers advice for masters and slaves and the rich and the poor. He warns against the blind pursuit of riches (Eccles. 2:8–11) and encourages believers to be content with what they have: "Godliness with contentment is great gain" (v. 6).

6:11–21 Paul closes this letter to Timothy with a charge to be faithful to his calling and to continue to oppose false teachings in the church.

. . . .

Timothy A young missionary friend of Paul, also called *Timotheus* (see Rom. 16:21), who accompanied the apostle on some of his travels and briefly shared his imprisonment at Rome (Heb. 13:23). Born to a Greek father and a Jewish mother (Acts 16:1), Timothy was reared by his mother, Eunice, and grandmother, Lois, in a godly home (2 Tim. 1:5). He was converted during Paul's first visit to Lystra (Acts 16:1) and served for a time as leader of the church at Ephesus (1 Tim. 1:3; 4:12). Paul addressed two of his pastoral epistles to Timothy.

Infidel An unbeliever (1 Tim. 5:8). Infidelity is caused by an unregenerate heart (Rom. 2:5) and hatred of the light (John 3:20). An infidel will be punished by eternal separation from God (2 Thess. 1:8–9). *Unbeliever*: NIV, NRSV.

. . . .

Above-and-Beyond Hospitality *If she [a widow] have lodged strangers, if she have washed the saints' feet* (1 Tim. 5:10).

In this verse Paul gave Timothy some criteria by which he could determine if a widow in the church was a sacrificial servant of the Lord who should receive financial assistance from her fellow believers. One mark of her character was that she had shown hospitality to strangers. Throughout the NT the grace of welcoming strangers into one's home is commended (Rom. 12:13; 1 Pet. 4:9). Another thing that Timothy should look for is whether a widow had gone beyond what was expected In the hosting of strangers. Washing a guest's feet was considered the job of a lowly slave.

DECEMBER 16 | Read 2 Timothy

1:1–7 Paul opens this letter by expressing deep love for Timothy, whom he calls "my dearly beloved son" (v. 2; see 1 Cor. 4:17). The apostle also remembers Timothy in his prayers and has a great desire to see his young coworker.

1:8–18 Although Paul is imprisoned in Rome, he has no regrets about the course his life has taken. He reflects on his years as a witness for Christ and rejoices in the assurance of His presence in all of life's circumstances: "I know whom I have believed, and am persuaded that he is able to keep that which I have committed unto him against that day" (v. 12).

2:1–26 Paul knew better than anyone that staying the course as a Christian minister requires determination, prayer, and commitment to holiness and righteousness in one's daily walk. He counsels Timothy to "flee. . .youthful lusts" and to "follow righteousness, faith, charity, peace" (v. 22).

3:1–13 According to Paul, perilous times are ahead for the church. As the time for Jesus' return draws near, evil will grow stronger, even within the fellowship of the church.

3:14–17 In the midst of such challenging times, Timothy is to stick to the truths revealed in God's written Word. It is a trustworthy and reliable guide for believers (Ps. 119:105).

4:1–8 Paul expects to be executed in Rome at any time. But he can look back over his life with the assurance that he has been faithful to his divine calling: "I have fought a good fight, I have finished my course, I have kept the faith" (v. 7).

4:9–22 Paul closes his second letter to Timothy by mentioning several coworkers who have supported him to the very end, as well as some who have let him down. He sends greetings to "Prisca [Priscilla] and Aquila, and the household of Onesiphorus" (v. 19).

. . . .

Stewardship Wise and responsible use of one's God-given resources. Christian stewardship is based on God's ownership of all things (Gen. 1:1; Ps. 24:1–2) and man's assigned dominion of God's creation (Gen. 1:26; 2:15). Good stewardship involves faithfulness in use of one's time (Eph. 5:16), talents (2 Tim. 1:6; 2:15), and money (Mal. 3:10).

Inspiration Divine influence. God's inspiration is the source of human understanding (Job 32:8). Scripture is inspired by God for our correction and instruction (2 Tim. 3:16). The Holy Spirit moved holy men to prophesy and record God's message (2 Pet. 1:20–21). God has communicated with humans in various ways, including by spoken words (Rev. 1:10–11), dreams (Dan. 7:1), and visions (Ezek. 11:24–25).

Hardship and Sacrifice *Thou [Timothy] therefore endure hardness [hardship, NIV], as a good soldier of Jesus Christ. No man that warreth entangleth himself with the affairs of this life; that he may please him who hath chosen him to be a soldier [his commanding officer, NIV]* (2 Tim. 2:3–4).

Paul continues his imagery from the Roman military by referring to the discipline and singleness of purpose required of a Roman soldier. The ordinary foot soldier in the Roman military was loaded down with his armor and weapons, tools, and rations that would last him for several days. He was sworn through strict discipline and training to obey the orders of his commanding officer without question. Paul was telling Timothy that the Christian life—while it has its rewards—is not an easy path. It requires discipline and sacrifice.

DECEMBER 17 | Read Titus; Philemon

Titus

1:1–4 Paul greets Titus (Gal. 2:1–3) as "mine own son after the common faith" (v. 4) and wishes for him God's "grace, mercy, and peace" (v. 4).

1:5–9 Paul reminds Titus that he has given him the responsibility of appointing elders or pastors to serve the church on the island of Crete. Church leaders such as elders and bishops must be mature people of high moral character who are devoted to the Lord (1 Tim. 3:1–7).

1:10–16 Paul has harsh words for false teachers who are hindering the work of the Lord. His advice to Titus is to "rebuke them sharply" (v. 13) so they will be turned back to the truth.

2:1–10 Titus should overlook no segment of the church in his instructions on how to live the Christian life. Godly behavior is expected of aged men (v. 2), aged women (v. 3), young women (vv. 4–5), young men (vv. 6–8), and servants (vv. 9–10).

2:11–15 All believers are to live "soberly, righteously, and godly" (v. 12) in the world because of the example set for believers by Jesus Christ (Phil. 2:5–8).

3:1–8 What a difference Christ makes in the lives of believers, Paul declares. We who were "foolish, disobedient, deceived" (v. 3) have been delivered from our sin and filled with the "kindness and love of God" (v. 4). Good works are the outgrowth of this new life in Christ.

3:9–11 Paul warns Titus to shun those people who deal in foolish questions and argue about the merits of the OT law. They condemn themselves by such vain and senseless behavior.

3:12–15 Paul plans to send someone to Crete as Titus's replacement. Then he wants Titus to join him.

Philemon

Verses 1–7 Paul, writing from prison in Rome (Acts 28:16, 30–31), greets his fellow believer Philemon in the church at Colosse. Philemon's home may have been the meeting place for the Colossian church, since Paul mentions "the church in thy house" (v. 2).

Verses 8–11 Paul begins his appeal on behalf of Philemon's runaway slave Onesimus by referring to Onesimus as "my son" (v. 10). Apparently Paul had led Onesimus to Christ, and he considered him a Christian brother who was as close to him as a son.

Verses 12–17 Although he preferred to keep Onesimus with him in Rome, Paul was sending him back to Philemon in Colosse. The apostle uses his influence and reputation to persuade Philemon to receive Onesimus back not as a slave but as a brother in Christ: "If thou count me therefore a partner, receive him as myself" (v. 17).

Verses 18–21 Paul even offers to repay Philemon for anything Onesimus might have taken from his master when he ran away. But the apostle also appeals to his spirit of forgiveness and generosity, confident that Philemon will "do more than I say" (v. 21).

Verses 22–25 Paul closes by sending greetings to Philemon from believers who had served as his helpers in the ministry. He also expresses hope that he might be released from prison and come to Colosse for a visit.

Onesimus A slave who was converted under Paul. Onesimus escaped and fled to Rome, where he came under Paul's influence. After his conversion, he returned to his master Philemon with an epistle from Paul, who appealed for Onesimus to be treated with mercy (Col. 4:9; Philem. 10).

Philemon's House Church *To the church in thy [Philemon's] house: Grace to you, and peace* (Philem. 2–3).

Paul sent greetings in this verse to the believers who met in Philemon's house. Groups of believers in NT times did not have church buildings, so they usually met in private homes. Priscilla and Aquila apparently made their home available as a meeting place in both Rome (Rom. 16:5) and Ephesus (1 Cor. 16:19). Early believers also met in the home of Nymphas (Col. 4:15–16).

GENERAL EPISTLES

The last nine books of the New Testament are known as the "general epistles" because they were addressed to broad, general audiences rather than to specific churches or individuals. The exceptions to this categorization are the letters of 2 and 3 John, which were addressed to specific people.

Most of these letters were written during the final years of the first Christian century, about AD 65–95. By this time false teachings had begun to creep into the Christian movement. Many of these epistles were written to correct or condemn these heretical doctrines.

These nine general letters—Hebrews; James; 1 and 2 Peter; 1, 2, and 3 John; Jude; and Revelation—are often called the "catholic (universal) epistles." They portray a Savior whose strength can sustain us in the midst of life's problems.

DECEMBER 18 | Read Hebrews 1–6

1:1–4 The epistle begins by affirming that God has spoken in the past, during OT times, through the prophets. But He has revealed Himself supremely through the life and ministry of His Son, Jesus Christ.

1:5–14 Several OT passages are quoted to show that Jesus is superior to all previous ways in which God has revealed Himself. He is especially superior to angels, messengers who often spoke for God in OT times (Gen. 18:9–10; Exod. 14:19–20).

2:1–4 This is the first of four warning messages in the epistle to the Hebrews (see Heb. 5:11–6:12; 10:19–39; 12:12–29). This message warns believers to pay attention to the salvation offered by Jesus Christ.

2:5–18 Although Christ was God's Son, He was human and thus subject to all the temptations that people face. He is a Savior with whom we can identify: "In that he himself hath suffered being tempted, he is able to succour them that are tempted" (v. 18).

3:1–6 Moses was the great hero of the Jewish people. They considered him greater than the angels, since he had passed on God's law to His people. But Jesus is greater even than Moses. He is like the builder and owner of a house, while Moses is just a butler or servant in the house.

3:7–19 When the Jewish people were wandering in the wilderness, they rebelled against Moses and committed idolatry (Num. 14:1–35). This shows the danger of unbelief. It is an even more serious matter to reject Jesus, since He is superior to Moses.

4:1–13 The writer of Hebrews probably had Joshua in mind when he referred to the Israelites as failing to find rest in the land of promise (v. 1). The implication is that Jesus is superior to Joshua, because He provides rest for all who place their faith in Him.

4:14–16 Jesus Christ is the great High Priest for all believers. Although He was tempted just like we are, He never gave in to sin (Luke 4:1–13). He identifies with us in our temptations because He has experienced all the human emotions that we feel. When we commit ourselves to Him, we will be received with grace and mercy.

5:1–10 Jesus' comparison to Melchisedec (Gen. 14:17–20) is explained more fully in Hebrews 7. As our great High Priest, Jesus suffered on our behalf and became "the author of eternal salvation unto all them that obey him" (v. 9).

5:11–6:12 These verses contain the second warning to the readers of Hebrews (see also Heb. 2:1–4; 10:19–39; 12:12–29). This message cautions those who had professed faith in Christ to press on to maturity in their commitment. As new Christians, they were in the elementary stages of their faith. But they should continue growing in their faith. A mature faith results in works of mercy and righteousness.

6:13–20 Abraham is an example of a person to whom God "made promise" (v. 13; Gen. 12:1–3). But Abraham had the responsibility to obey God in order to bring this promise to fruition. Human obedience is still a vital ingredient in God's plan for His people.

....

Perfection A state of completion or fulfillment. Believers are urged to advance to mature teachings and "perfection" or fulfillment in good works (Heb. 6:1). While disclaiming perfection, Paul urged believers to keep striving for perfection by being like Christ (Phil. 3:12–15). *Maturity*: NIV.

....

Bold Access to the King *Let us therefore come boldly unto the throne of grace, that we may obtain mercy, and find grace to help in time of need* (Heb. 4:16).

As a person becomes famous or rises to a high position, he limits his accessibility to others for his own protection. Many kings of Bible times, for example, could not be approached by anyone but their most trusted advisors. The Persians had a law that anyone who came into their king's presence without his permission could pay with their lives. This verse from Hebrews, when seen against the background of these "unapproachable" kings, makes us realize what a revolutionary Savior Jesus is. Although He is exalted to the highest position as God's Son, He is still as approachable to us as a member of the family or a close friend. We can bring our needs boldly to Jesus and expect to be received joyfully into His presence.

DECEMBER 19 | Read Hebrews 7–13

7:1–28 This entire chapter picks up on the topic of Melchisedec, first mentioned in Hebrews 5:6–10. Melchisedec was the mysterious priest and "king of Salem" who received tithes from Abraham (Gen. 14:17–20). The Bible gives no information about the genealogy or death of Melchisedec. He simply appears out of nowhere, and this implies that his priesthood was eternal. But the priesthood of Christ is greater even than that of Melchisedec. With His atoning death, the OT sacrificial system was abolished. Human priests were no longer needed to offer animal sacrifices to atone for sin. Jesus took care of this "when he offered up himself" (v. 27).

8:1–10:18 This long passage describes the new covenant that was established by Christ. The old covenant between God and His people required them to offer animal sacrifices and to follow prescribed rituals to take away the stain of sin (Lev. 4:1–35). These rituals had to be repeated again and again. But under the new covenant, Jesus offered His own life as a permanent, once-for-all sacrifice for sin.

10:19–39 This is the third warning to the readers of Hebrews (see also Heb. 2:1–4; 5:11–6:12; 12:12–29). This message cautions them to persevere in the commitment they had made to follow Jesus Christ. The author of Hebrews also exhorts them to meet together for regular worship in order to encourage and strengthen one another in the faith. He uses the certainty of Jesus' second coming to motivate them to stand firm in their faith.

11:1–40 This is known as the great "faith chapter" of the Bible. Several heroes of the faith from the OT are mentioned to encourage the readers of Hebrews to remain strong in their own faith. Personalities singled out for their faith include Noah (v. 7), Abraham (vv. 8–10, 17), Jacob (v. 21), Joseph (v. 22), and Moses (vv. 23–29).

12:1–2 Endurance and faithfulness are exemplified by Jesus, who followed the path of obedience all the way to the cross (Phil. 2:8). We as believers should also overcome every obstacle in our path in order to remain faithful to the Lord's call.

12:3–11 Chastening, or God's discipline, is something to be expected by all believers (1 Pet. 4:12–17). Trials and troubles teach us that we are not self-sufficient and that we should look to God for strength and guidance.

12:12–29 These verses contain the fourth and final warning to the readers of the book of Hebrews (see also Heb. 2:1–4; 5:11–6:12; 10:19–39). This message cautions them against developing a stubborn attitude and disobeying the commands of Jesus. God has dealt forcefully with such sin and rebellion in the past, and He will do so again.

13:1–17 Believers are to demonstrate the character of Christ in their lives by loving one another, keeping themselves sexually pure, serving others, and praising and giving thanks to God.

13:18–25 The author of Hebrews closes with a benediction of God's grace and peace for his readers.

. . . .

Intercession Prayer offered on behalf of others. Christ made intercession for those who were crucifying Him (Luke 23:34) and for His disciples (John 17:6–26). Elders of the early church were instructed to pray for the sick (James 5:14–16). Paul prayed for Israel to be saved (Rom. 10:1) and for the Colossians to grow spiritually (Col. 1:9–12). Christ, our high priest, lives to make intercession for us (Rom. 8:34; Heb. 7:25–26). The Holy Spirit helps us intercede for others (Rom. 8:26; 1 Tim. 2:1).

Heavenly City The future city built by God as a dwelling place for those who belong to Him (Heb. 11:13–16). It will be known as "New Jerusalem," the place where God dwells eternally among the redeemed (Rev. 21:2–10).

. . . .

Execution by Sawing *They were stoned, they were sawn asunder [sawed in two, NIV], were tempted, were slain with the sword* (Heb. 11:37).

This verse appears in the famous "roll call of the faithful" chapter in Hebrews. The writer pays tribute to the people of past generations who remained faithful to God in spite of great persecution. Execution by being sawed in two is cruel and inhumane by modern standards, but this form of capital punishment was apparently practiced in the ancient world. It was not out of character for the cruel Assyrians, who were known to cut off the ears and hands of their victims just for sport. But even King David of Judah may have practiced this form of torture and execution against the Ammonites. After capturing their capital city, Rabbah, he "brought out the people that were in it, and cut them with saws, and with harrows of iron, and with axes" (1 Chron. 20:3).

A Lifetime Race *Let us [Christian believers] lay aside every weight, and the sin which doth so easily beset us, and let us run with patience [perseverance, NIV] the race that is set before us* (Heb. 12:1).

In this verse Paul compares the Christian life to the foot race in which Christians competed in the Greek games. The foot race was one of the most popular of the Greek games that were held every year in Athens. To prepare themselves for these races, runners underwent rigorous training, trimming down their bodies to eliminate every ounce of excess fat. On race day they wore light clothing—perhaps no clothes at all—to give themselves every possible advantage in the competition against other runners. These races covered various distances—from short sprints where speed was called for, to longer runs where stamina and endurance were more important. In Paul's thinking the Christian life is like a marathon. It's important for us to remain faithful to Christ during a lifetime of service so we can say with him at the end of the race, "I have finished my course, I have kept the faith" (2 Tim. 4:7).

DECEMBER 20 | Read James

1:1 The "twelve tribes. . .scattered abroad" to which James wrote this letter were probably Jewish Christians who were living outside Palestine.

1.2–18 James encourages these Christians of Jewish background who are being persecuted for their faith. He also cautions them to remain faithful to God, even when they are tempted to do wrong.

1:19–27 The best way to stay true to God and to hold up under persecution is to live out one's faith: "Be ye doers of the word, and not hearers only" (v. 22).

2:1–13 The way of the world is to cater to rich people and to discriminate against the poor. But this is not how believers should relate to people. Everyone should be treated with equal respect, regardless of economic means, social status, or race (Rom. 1:14–16).

2:14–26 In these verses James is not teaching that a person is saved by his or her works. His point is that genuine faith will result in good works. If a person claims to be a believer but does not live righteously or perform acts of service toward others, we have to question whether he or she has really experienced saving faith.

3:1–12 The greatest challenge any person faces is controlling the tongue (Prov. 21:23). Although it is one of the smallest organs of the body, it has the potential to build up as well as to destroy. Only God can give us the self-discipline it takes to tame the tongue.

3:13–4:10 Being wise in the ways of the Lord is different from being wise in the ways of the world. Worldly wisdom leads to strife, conflict, and ungodly lust. But seeking the Lord and His wisdom results in righteousness and treating others with justice and mercy (Zech. 7:9).

4:11–17 James warns his readers about the sin of presumption—making plans with no regard for God and assuming that we have unlimited time in this life. He reminds us that life is only a vapor or a cloud "that appeareth for a little time, and then vanisheth away" (v. 14).

5:1–6 Those who grow rich by cheating the poor will be judged harshly by the Lord. The accumulated riches that they thought would bring them pleasure will actually bring them misery and unhappiness.

5:7–12 James encourages his readers to display persistent devotion to the Lord in the midst of their persecution and suffering.

5:13–18 One key to bearing up under persecution is persistent prayer (Luke 18:1–8). This is one of the most eloquent passages in the Bible on the power of prayer: "The effectual fervent prayer of a righteous man availeth much" (v. 16).

5:19–20 James closes his letter with a plea to his readers to try to reclaim their fellow believers who have strayed from the truth.

⋯⋯⋯⋯⋯⋯⋯⋯⋯⋯⋯⋯⋯⋯⋯⋯⋯⋯⋯⋯⋯⋯⋯⋯⋯⋯⋯⋯⋯⋯⋯⋯⋯⋯⋯

Brothers of Christ The four earthly brothers, or half brothers, of Jesus—James, Joses (Joseph), Simon, and Juda (Jude)—who were born by natural conception to Joseph and Mary after the virgin birth of Christ (Mark 6:3). James was leader of the church in Jerusalem (Acts 15:13–21) and likely the author of the epistle of James (James 1:1). Jude wrote the NT epistle that bears his name (Jude).

⋯⋯⋯⋯⋯⋯⋯⋯⋯⋯⋯⋯⋯⋯⋯⋯⋯⋯⋯⋯⋯⋯⋯⋯⋯⋯⋯⋯⋯⋯⋯⋯⋯⋯⋯

An Eternal Crown *Blessed is the man that endureth temptation: for. . .he shall receive the crown of life, which the Lord hath promised to them that love him* (James 1:12).

Crowns were worn by kings as symbols of authority and power (2 Sam. 1:10). James compared the believer's inheritance of eternal life through the atoning death of Jesus Christ to a crown. This crown, unlike earthly and physical status symbols, will never grow tarnished or lose its luster because of changing cultural standards. It has an "eternal lifetime" warranty from the King of kings and Lord of lords (Rev. 21:5–7).

Patient Waiting *The husbandman [farmer, NIV]. . .hath long patience for it [the harvest], until he receive the early and latter rain* (James 5:7).

The land of Palestine, known for its dry climate, had limited rainfall. Moisture for crop production was supplemented by heavy dews (Deut. 33:13). But every farmer knew that at least two major rainfalls during the year were essential for crops to grow. The early rain in October and November softened the soil for planting. The latter rain of March and April brought a needed boost for the crops before they ripened fully for the harvest. James declared that just as farmers waited patiently from the early rain to the latter rain for their crops to mature, so believers must wait patiently for the second coming of Jesus (2 Tim. 4:8).

DECEMBER 21 | Read 1 Peter

1:1–2 Peter addresses this letter to believers scattered throughout five distant regions of the Roman Empire.

1:3–25 The basis of the believer's hope is Jesus Christ and His resurrection from the dead. He alone provides salvation and the promise of eternal life.

2:1–17 Jesus is the living stone who serves as the foundation for the faith of believers. Although He was rejected by His own people, God made Him the cornerstone of salvation for the world (Eph. 2:20). Those who place their faith in Him are delivered from their sins. They become part of God's "royal priesthood, an holy nation" (v. 9) that bears witness of Him and His kingdom to others.

2:18–25 Peter uses the example of Jesus and His suffering to motivate believers. Just as He suffered to purchase salvation for them, they should endure persecution for His sake with a willing and joyous spirit.

3:1–7 Husbands and wives have a special responsibility to live in obedience to the commands of Christ. Husbands should love and honor their wives, and wives should "be in subjection to your own husbands" (v. 1; see Eph. 5:22–28). Such respectful and humble behavior by wives might lead their unbelieving husbands to the Lord.

3:8–17 Peter appeals to his readers to be united in the Lord, to practice humility and love, and to resist the temptation to seek revenge against those who are causing them pain and suffering.

3:18–22 Jesus was the ultimate sufferer—a case of the just suffering for the unjust "that he might bring us to God" (v. 18). After purchasing our salvation, He is now exalted at God's right hand. All earthly powers and authorities are subject to Him (Rev. 19:1–6).

4:1–11 Again, the example of Christ provides a demonstration of the way believers should live. Peter appeals to his readers to practice love and hospitality toward others, thus serving as "good stewards of the manifold grace of God" (v. 10).

4:12–19 It should not surprise Christians that they are called to suffer persecution for their faith. According to Peter, suffering is actually a badge of honor (Heb. 12:3–11). Just as Christ's suffering was the prelude to His glorification with the Father, so it will be for all believers.

5:1–4 Peter has a special word for the leaders ("elders," v. 1) of the churches to whom he is writing. The elders must have a loving, shepherd spirit and not a dominating attitude toward those whom they serve.

`5:5–9` All the members of the churches are to respect their leaders and to show a kind and humble spirit. They should be on guard against the temptations of Satan (James 4:7).

`5:10–14` Peter closes with a benediction, commending his readers to the grace of God. He also sends greetings from his coworkers Silvanus ("Silas," v. 12; see also Acts 15:40) and Marcus (v. 13; probably John Mark; see also Acts 13:13; 2 Tim. 4:11).

. . . .

`Adversary` An active opponent; a term descriptive of Satan (1 Pet. 5:8). God's wisdom is promised to believers when they face the adversary (Luke 21:15). God's judgment will ultimately fall on His enemies (Heb. 10:27).

. . . .

`Clear Thinking` *Gird up the loins of your mind, be sober* (1 Pet. 1:13).

Both men and women of Bible times wore full-body outer robes that extended almost to the feet. If a person needed to run or do strenuous work, he would tuck the bottom part of his robe into the belt or sash around his waist. This gave him greater freedom of movement. This practice is described by the KJV as "girding up the loins." In this verse, Peter described the need for believers to do constructive thinking as girding up the "loins of your mind." The NIV translates it, "Prepare your minds for action." Peter means that believers should think clearly and reject the hindrances and temptations of the world by focusing on God and His grace. Tucking the robe into the belt is sometimes referred to in the Bible in a figurative sense to denote strength and determination (Job 40:7; Pss. 65:6; 93:1).

`Jesus the Chief Shepherd` *When the chief Shepherd [Jesus] shall appear, ye shall receive a crown of glory that fadeth not away* (1 Pet. 5:4).

In Bible times wealth was often measured by the size of one's flocks and herds of livestock. Some wealthy people had hundreds of sheep, and this required the services of several shepherds. These shepherds would be supervised by a chief shepherd or master shepherd (1 Sam. 21:7). Peter compared Jesus Christ to a chief shepherd. This title is similar to His designation as "that great shepherd of the sheep" in Heb. 13:20. All ministers who lead God's people should remember that they are under-shepherds who work under the supervision of the Great Shepherd or Chief Shepherd—Jesus Christ. He enables then to take care of God's people with wisdom and kindness.

DECEMBER 22 | Read 2 Peter

`1:1–2` Peter opens his letter with wishes for grace and peace to his readers.

`1:3–11` These are some of the greatest verses in the NT on the need for growth in the Christian life. Growing more like Christ involves faith, temperance, patience, godliness, kindness, and love.

1:12–21 The Christian faith does not grow out of hearsay and myth. It is grounded in historical facts and the testimony of eyewitnesses who were with Jesus in the flesh (1 John 1:1–7). We can also trust God's revelation of truth through His written Word.

2:1–22 Peter warns that false teachers from within the church will rise up in the future to lead believers astray. The church should be on guard against such heresies. God will punish such false prophets, just as he has done in the past. They will "utterly perish in their own corruption" (v. 12).

3:1–10 These verses declare the certainty of the second coming of Jesus and the final judgment (1 Thess. 4:13–17). These will happen in God's own time. The fact that they haven't yet happened doesn't mean that God is slow or apathetic. Rather, He is loving and patient, waiting for others to respond to His offer of salvation. He is "not willing that any should perish, but that all should come to repentance" (v. 9).

3:11–18 While waiting for the Lord to return, how should believers conduct themselves? Peter declares that they should live as holy and godly people, continuing to "grow in grace, and in the knowledge of our Lord and Saviour Jesus Christ" (v. 18; see 2 Thess. 3:6–15).

Backsliding The act of turning from God after conversion. The causes of backsliding are spiritual blindness (2 Pet. 1:9), persecution (Matt. 13:20–21), or love of material things (1 Tim. 6:10). This sin separates the backslider from God's blessings (Isa. 59:2). But confession and repentance will bring God's forgiveness (1 John 1:9) and restoration (Ps. 51).

Heresy False teachings that deny essential doctrines of the Christian faith—a serious problem condemned by Paul (1 Cor. 11:19).

Jesus the Light *We [believers] have also a more sure word of prophecy; whereunto ye do well that ye take heed, as unto a light that shineth in a dark place, until the day dawn, and the day star [morning star, NIV] arise in your hearts* (2 Pet. 1:19).

The apostle Peter declared in this verse that Jesus the Messiah had been foretold in the OT. These prophecies were like "a light that shineth in a dark place." But when He arrived on earth, the full light of His glory burst forth, like the dawning of a new day. Jesus as the light is a central theme of the NT. He Himself declared, "I am the light of the world" (John 8:12). Believers are known as "children of light" (Ephesians 5:8).

DECEMBER 23 | Read 1 John

1:1–7 John declares that he was an eyewitness of the earthly ministry of Jesus. As one of the Twelve, he saw Jesus' miracles with his own eyes and listened to His teachings with his own ears. Thus, John is qualified to bear witness about Christ to others (2 Pet. 1:12–21).

1:8–10 Even believers will fall into sin. Rather than denying our wrongdoings, we should confess them and bring them to Jesus for forgiveness.

2:1–6 True believers abide in Christ and keep His commandments.

2:7–17 Another characteristic of believers is love for others (1 Cor. 13). A person who harbors hate toward others is walking in darkness rather than in the light of God's salvation.

2:18–29 John declares that the Antichrist—the embodiment of evil and the archenemy of Christ—will appear during the last days when the return of Jesus draws near. Many false teachers ("many antichrists," v. 18) were denying that Jesus was the Messiah. John interprets this as a sign that the final judgment is close at hand.

3:1–10 John declares that true believers will not continue in a habitual state of sin. God's love guides believers to recognize their sins as soon as they are committed and to seek His forgiveness day by day.

3:11–24 John again encourages believers to love one another. This is the great lesson that Jesus taught His followers (John 13:34).

4:1–6 These verses refute the claim of some false teachers that Jesus did not come to earth in human form. They taught that Jesus was a spirit and that He only seemed to have a physical body. John declares, "Every spirit that confesseth not that Jesus Christ is come in the flesh is not of God" (v. 3).

4:7–21 These verses declare that God's essential character is love and that He is the author of all love (John 3:16). It is logical to John that if God loved us enough to grant us salvation and eternal life, then "we ought also to love one another" (v. 11).

5:1–12 The foundation of the Christian's hope for eternal life is faith in Jesus as God's Son. John boils it down to one simple statement: "He that hath the Son hath life; and he that hath not the Son of God hath not life" (v. 12).

5:13–21 John closes his letter by assuring his readers that they can know with assurance that Jesus is who He claimed to be. They can also pray to Him with full confidence that He will hear and answer in accordance with their needs (James 5:16).

- - - - - - - - - -

Antichrist The archenemy of Christ and all Christians who will be defeated in the end-time. Rooted in the prophecies of Daniel (Dan. 7:7–8), the Antichrist receives his authority and power from Satan (Rev. 13:4). He is lawless and deceitful (2 Thess. 2:3–12; 2 John 7). Characterized as a "beast," the Antichrist will appear before the return of Christ to wage war against Christ and His people (Rev. 13:6–8). However, he will be defeated by Christ and cast into a lake of fire (Rev. 19:20; 20:10).

- - - - - - - - - -

Bowels of Compassion *Whoso. . .seeth his brother have need, and shutteth up his bowels of compassion from him, how dwelleth the love of God in him?* (1 John 3:17).

In Bible times the bowels were considered the seat of emotions and feelings. According to the apostle John in this passage, a person who shuts his "bowels of compassion" has no pity or empathy toward those in need. In our modern figure of speech, we would probably say that a person like this does not have a compassionate heart. The apostle John makes it clear throughout this epistle that love and compassion toward others is one of the marks of an authentic Christian believer: "This commandment have we from him, That he who loveth God love his brother also" (1 John 4:21).

DECEMBER 24 | Read 2 John; 3 John; Jude

2 John

1–3 The author of this letter refers to himself as "the elder" (v. 1). This was probably a title of authority or respect for the apostle John, one of the twelve disciples of Jesus. Nothing is known about the "elect lady" (v. 1) to whom this epistle is addressed. Was John referring to a church or a person? No one knows.

4–6 John is delighted to learn that the elect lady and her children are walking in love (1 Cor. 13). He repeats the commandment that he learned from Jesus: "Love one another" (v. 5; see John 13:34).

7–11 John warns the elect lady to shun false teachers who deny that Jesus Christ came in the flesh (1 John 4:1–6). These were probably members of a heretical sect known as the Gnostics. They taught that Jesus came to earth in spirit form and that He only seemed to suffer and die on the cross.

12–13 John extends closing greetings, with the hope that he will soon be able to make a personal visit.

3 John

1–8 John writes to a fellow believer named Gaius, who was probably a leader in one of the churches of Asia Minor. John commends Gaius for standing for the truth and for showing hospitality to evangelists who traveled from church to church preaching the Gospel.

9–10 John has harsh words for Diotrephes, a believer who apparently had taken control of a local church and refused to receive the apostles and other traveling ministers.

11–12 John endorses a believer named Demetrius and assures Gaius that Demetrius can be trusted to follow the Lord and walk in the truth.

13–14 John extends personal greetings to other believers associated with Gaius and promises to visit him soon.

Jude

1–2 Jude identifies himself as "the servant of Jesus Christ, and brother of James" (v. 1). His brother James, at first a skeptic like Jude, eventually became a believer and assumed a prominent leadership role in the early church at Jerusalem (Acts 15:13).

3–16 Jude urges his fellow believers to "earnestly contend for the faith" in opposition to certain people who were hindering the work of the church. These people were particularly dangerous because they were working from within the fellowship of the church (2 Pet. 2:1–3). Jude describes them as "murmurers, complainers" who were "walking after their own lusts" (v. 16). Apparently they were using the grace of God as a cover for their lifestyles of sin and wickedness.

17–23 Jude contrasts the ungodly behavior of these people with the characteristics of true believers. Those who truly know God reflect the love of Christ (1 John 3:11–24). They are strengthened for godly living through the power of prayer.

24–25 Jude closes with a beautiful benediction that should comfort and strengthen all believers. Jesus is able to keep us from falling and to present us justified before God.

....

The Elder and the Lady *The elder unto the elect [chosen, NIV] lady and her children* (2 John 1:1).

The apostle John identified himself as "the elder," a term that means "pastor" or "bishop." He was an important leader in the early church. Many believe he was associated with the church at Ephesus. The phrase "elect (or chosen) lady," referring to the letter's recipient, is puzzling. Some interpreters think it was a code name for a specific congregation, while others believe John addressed an unnamed female believer. If John did have a specific person in mind, 2 John is the only NT letter addressed to a woman.

The Love Feast *These are spots in your feasts of charity, when they feast with you, feeding themselves without fear* (Jude 12).

The "feasts of charity" to which Jude refers in this verse was probably the love feast, a meal that early Christians ate together as part of their observance of the Lord's Supper. The purpose of this meal was to remember the sacrifice of Christ, since He was eating the Passover meal with His disciples when He turned it into a memorial of His sacrificial death (Luke 22:14–20). In its early years, the love feast was also known as the agape meal. It became a charity meal for the poor in some Christian traditions. Most Christian groups today have dropped this communal meal from their observance of the Lord's Supper.

DECEMBER 25 | Read Revelation 1–3

1:1–3 These verses indicate that the book of Revelation was revealed to the apostle John (Mark 1:17–20) through an angel. But it came directly from the Father through His Son, Jesus Christ. John chose to write this revelation down in the form of a letter. It was probably intended to be read publicly in local congregations.

1:4–8 John addresses this letter to the churches in seven cities that represent the major centers of Christianity in the region of Asia (modern-day Turkey). The theme of his letter is "victory in Jesus." God has guaranteed that His Son, Jesus Christ— "Alpha and Omega, the beginning and the ending" (v. 8)—will reign ultimately over the entire earth (Phil. 2:11).

1:9–20 While in exile on the island of Patmos, John had a vision of the risen Lord. He was told to write down what he saw and to send his message to the seven churches, represented by seven candlesticks. Jesus appeared among these candlesticks; this represented His presence with these congregations. In His hands Jesus held seven stars. These represented "the angels of the seven churches" (v. 20), perhaps angels with responsibility for and authority over these churches.

2:1–7 John writes a specific message to the believers in the church at Ephesus (Acts 19:1–40). Their initial love and enthusiasm for the Lord had cooled, and they needed to rekindle their zeal.

2:8–11 John encourages the church at Smyrna, which was undergoing great persecution. Their faithfulness would be richly rewarded by the Lord.

2:12–17 The church at Pergamos was accused of indulging in idol worship. Unless they repented immediately of their evil, the Lord promised to confront them and to fight against them with the sword of His mouth.

2:18–29 Tolerating immorality and false teaching was the problem of the church at Thyatira. This congregation was exhorted to return to the truth.

3:1–6 The believers in the church at Sardis had lost their spiritual zeal. They needed to wake up and "strengthen the things. . .that are ready to die" (v. 2) so they could bring honor and glory to the Lord.

3:7–13 The church at Philadelphia is the only one of the seven churches that receives no rebuke. In spite of great persecution, this congregation remained faithful to the Lord.

3:14–22 The church at Laodicea is condemned more severely than all the other churches. The problem of these believers was spiritual apathy. They were "neither cold nor hot" (v. 16) about spiritual matters. God promised to deal with this church severely unless they repented of their waywardness.

Apocalypse A Greek word translated "revelation" that refers to an unveiling of the hidden things known only to God (Gal. 1:12). The book of Revelation depicts the end of the present age and the coming of God's future kingdom through symbols, visions, and numbers. This imagery was probably used to hide the message in a time of persecution. Other examples of apocalyptic writing in the Bible are Dan. 7–12, Isa. 24–27, Ezek. 37–41, Zech. 9–12, Matt. 24, and Mark 13.

Seven Churches The seven churches in Asia Minor addressed by John in Revelation. The messages to these churches ranged from warnings and rebukes to commendations for their faithfulness (see Rev. 2–3).

Book of Life God's record of the names of the saved and deeds of the righteous (Mal. 3:16–18). This book will be used as the basis for God's final judgment (Rev. 3:5; 20:12–15). Inclusion in the book of life by virtue of one's salvation by God's grace provides reason for joy (Luke 10:20; Phil. 4:3) and hope of heaven (Rev. 21:27).

A Stone for the Winner *To him that overcometh will I give. . .a white stone* (Rev. 2:17).

This imagery of a white stone has been explained in various ways by interpreters: as a badge of acquittal in a legal case, as an expression of welcome by a host to his guests, or as a voting token used by a voter to indicate his choice of a candidate. Perhaps the most believable explanation is that the apostle John, the author of Revelation, was referring to a white stone given to the winner of an athletic contest. This stone was an admission ticket to the winner's celebration at a later time. This may refer to the time when the faithful, persevering Christian believer will receive his ticket to eternal life and the Lord's great victory celebration in heaven.

DECEMBER 26 | Read Revelation 4–6

4:1–11 This chapter describes a vision in which John saw the Lord in heaven, seated on a throne. Seated around the throne were twenty-four elders, representing angels who administered God's rule throughout the universe. The four creatures described as "beasts" (v. 6) were actually seraphim (Isa. 6:1–3), winged beings, or another order of angels who helped to administer the rule of God in the universe. God's unquestioned rule and authority are clear when these twenty-four elders and four seraphim fall down in worship before Him.

5:1–14 This chapter continues John's vision of God seated on a throne. In His hand God holds a book, or scroll, that is sealed with seven wax seals. One of the elders around the throne declares that only the risen Christ—represented by a Lamb—is worthy to remove the seven seals and open the scroll. God hands the scroll to Jesus. This symbolizes that He has delegated to His crucified and risen Son all authority in heaven and earth. The elders and angels who had previously bowed down to God now fall down in adoration and worship at the feet of Jesus.

`6:1–8:1` This section of Revelation describes the events of God's judgment represented by the seven seals when Jesus removed them from the scroll. Seals 1 through 4 (6:2–8) show the horrors of war, including famine, devastation, and death. Seal 5 (6:9–11) represents the reward of believers who are martyred for their faith. Seal 6 (6:12–17) shows the earthshaking events that will happen before the second coming of Christ. The opening of the seventh seal (8:1) causes an eerie silence in heaven, as all the earth awaits the coming judgment of the Lord.

`Seraphim` Six-winged creatures that sang God's praises and also purified Isaiah's lips in his vision in the temple (Isa. 6:1–7). *Seraphs*: NIV, NRSV.

DECEMBER 27 | Read Revelation 7:1–11:19

`Chapter 7` of Revelation is inserted between the opening of seal 6 and seal 7. This chapter describes a great multitude of people who fall down before God and the Lamb in reverence and worship. These people have been redeemed by the Lamb, and they are in God's presence in heaven.

`8:2–11:19` This section describes the seven trumpet judgments, or God's judgment against the earth and those who have rejected Him. These trumpets are sounded by seven angels.

Trumpet 1 (8:7) brings hail and fire on the earth. Trumpet 2 (8:8–9) brings the destruction of sea life and ships. At the sound of trumpet 3 (8:10–11), a meteorite poisons earth's rivers and streams. Many of the heavenly bodies are darkened with the sounding of trumpet 4 (8:12). Trumpet 5 (9:1–12) brings torment and misery on earth's inhabitants. With trumpet 6 (9:13–21), widespread death occurs. The sounding of the seventh and final trumpet (11:15–19) indicates that the kingdoms of this world will become the kingdoms over which Christ will rule.

`10:1–11:14` is inserted between the sounding of trumpets 6 and 7. Chapter 10 reaffirms the call of the apostle John. He is told to eat a book, or scroll. This recalls the experience of the prophet Ezekiel (Ezek. 2:1–3:11).

In Revelation 11:1–14, the apostle John sees the city of Jerusalem trampled for forty-two months. Two unnamed witnesses are raised up by the Lord to prophesy in His name. After their persecution and death, they are resurrected and called up to heaven. Faithfulness in God's service will be rewarded (Matt. 25:14–29).

`Great Tribulation` A time of great suffering and affliction in the end-time, sent upon the earth by the Lord to accomplish His purposes (Dan. 12:1; Rev. 7:14). Students of the Bible disagree on whether this event will precede or follow Christ's millennial reign or come before the ushering in of the new heavens and new earth.

`Abyss` A word translated literally as "bottomless pit" in the book of Revelation, indicating the place where Satan dwells (Rev. 9:1–2, 11).

Abaddon A Hebrew word meaning "destruction," used to characterize the angel of the bottomless pit (Rev. 9:11). *Apollyon*: Greek form.

. . . .

Symbols of Victory and Joy *A great multitude. . .stood before. . .the Lamb, clothed with white robes, and palms in their hands* (Rev. 7:9).

The "palms" held by this great multitude of believers were palm branches. These were considered symbols of victory and joy (Lev. 23:40; Neh. 8:15). Jesus was welcomed on His triumphant entry into Jerusalem by the crowds waving palm branches (John 12:13). In the New Jerusalem, or heaven, believers will acclaim Jesus as the triumphant Lamb or Savior by waving these same symbols of victory and gladness.

DECEMBER 28 | Read Revelation 12–13

12:1–17 John sees a vision of a woman who gives birth to a male child. Satan, represented by a red dragon, tries to kill the child. But the child is protected and delivered from harm by the Lord. The message of this chapter is that God will protect His church from Satan's threats.

13:1–18 The vision in this chapter shows that Satan continues his efforts to destroy the church. John sees a beast emerge from the sea. He is the Antichrist, the archenemy of Christ, who is determined to destroy the church and all who follow the risen Lord. John also sees a second beast emerge from the earth. As a servant of the first beast, he uses miraculous signs and economic threats to try to turn believers away from loyalty to Christ and to convince them to worship the Antichrist. The symbol for this second beast is the number 666. Six was the number for evil, so triple sixes shows that this beast was thoroughly evil in his personality and intentions.

. . . .

Red Dragon A name for Satan. After being cast out of heaven, Satan turned his fury on God's people (Rev. 12:3–17).

DECEMBER 29 | Read Revelation 14–16

14:1–20 Several short visions of John are recorded in this chapter. He sees the Lamb, Jesus Christ (John 1:36), who has returned to earth and is standing with a multitude of the redeemed on Mount Zion. John also sees several angels, who deliver messages of encouragement to God's people in the midst of persecution and assure them that doom is coming for those who worship the beast.

15:1–16:21 Different aspects of God's judgment have already been revealed through the seven seals (6:1–8:1) and the seven trumpets (8:2–11:19). In this section, another dimension of His judgment is communicated through John's vision of the seven vials (cups or bowls) of God's wrath poured out on the earth by seven angels. These events happen when the contents of the bowls are poured out:

Sores break out on the followers of the beast (bowl 1; 16:2); all sea creatures die (bowl 2; 16:3); fresh waters of the earth turn to blood (bowl 3; 16:4–7); the sun scorches the earth (bowl 4; 16:8–9); darkness and suffering strike the earth (bowl 5; 16:10–11); the Euphrates River dries up (bowl 6; 16:12); and storms and a great earthquake devastate the land (bowl 7; 16:17–18). These bowl judgments give a graphic picture of the wrath of God poured out against unbelievers and an evil world.

Sickle A tool for cutting or harvesting grain (Deut. 16:9). The word is also used as a symbol of God's coming judgment (Rev. 14:14–19).

Megiddo A fortified city west of the Jordan River in the plain of Jezreel associated with the great battle in the end-time. This city was the site of Barak's victory over Sisera (Judg. 4:14–16) and King Josiah's death in a battle with Pharaoh Necho of Egypt (2 Chron. 35:22–24). In this area the final battle between God and the forces of evil will occur (Zech. 12:11; Rev. 16:16). *Megiddon*: Zech. 12:11.

Armageddon A Greek word for the valley between Mount Carmel and the city of Jezreel. This valley was the site of many battles in Bible times due to its strategic location on two major trade routes. Because of its bloody history, this region became a symbol of the final conflict between God and the forces of evil, and of God's ultimate victory (Rev. 16:16).

The Number Seven *And I [John the apostle] saw another sign in heaven. . .seven angels having the seven last plagues* (Rev. 15:1).

The Jewish people thought of seven as a sacred number. It is used often in the Bible to show fullness, completion, and perfection (Gen. 2:2–3; Dan. 9:25). The apostle John uses the number seven throughout the book of Revelation: seven churches (1:4), seven stars (2:1), seven lamps (4:5), seven seals (5:1), seven angels with seven trumpets (8:2), seven thunders (10:4), a beast with seven heads (13:1), seven vials, or bowls (17:1), and seven kings (17:10). By using this number, John declared that God will bring about His perfect judgment in the end-time. All believers will participate in the full and complete victory of Christ over the forces of evil.

DECEMBER 30 | Read Revelation 17–19

17:1–18 In this vision John sees a despicable prostitute seated on a scarlet beast. Her name is Babylon, probably a code name symbolizing the forces of evil that are arrayed against God and the forces of righteousness. She was responsible for the continuing persecution of God's people. An angel explains to John that the beast on which she is seated is the Antichrist.

18:1–24 This vision is a continuation of John's vision in chapter 17. An angel appears and shouts, "Babylon the great is fallen" (v. 2). To John the term *Babylon* symbolized all the evil forces of the world that were allied against God. The Lord has won the victory over Babylon, but pride, idolatry, and immorality have also contributed to its downfall.

19:1–5 The twenty-four elders and the four seraphim around God's throne (see Rev. 4:1–11) fall down and worship God. Thanksgiving is offered for the destruction of Babylon.

19:6–10 John portrays the relationship with Christ that believers would soon begin to experience in terms of a marriage. Christ is the Lamb (Acts 8:32), and the church is His bride (Eph. 5:25–33), and "blessed are they which are called unto the marriage supper of the Lamb" (v. 9).

19:11–21 As "KING OF KINGS, AND LORD OF LORDS" (v. 16), Jesus will return to earth in victory. In a final battle against the forces of evil, He will defeat the Antichrist and the beast that worships him (see Rev. 13:1–18). Then He will cast them alive into "a lake of fire burning with brimstone" (v. 20).

- -

Omnipotence The unlimited and infinite power that belongs to God. This characteristic of God's nature is expressed by His names *almighty* (Gen. 17:1) and *omnipotent* (Rev. 19:6). God controls nature (Amos 4:13) and the destiny of nations (Amos 1–2). God's omnipotence is also expressed by the Holy Spirit's power to convict and save (Rom. 15:19).

- -

A King with Many Crowns *His [the reigning Christ's] eyes were as a flame of fire, and on his head were many crowns* (Rev. 19:12).

John borrowed this imagery from the custom of kings who ruled over more than one country. They would wear several crowns to represent all the nations under their control. For example, the kings of Egypt wore a two-in-one crown to represent the unification of Upper and Lower Egypt under their rule. To the apostle John in this verse, the many crowns worn by Jesus show His universal reign as Savior and Lord throughout the world. The hymn writer expressed it like this:

Crown Him with many crowns,
The Lamb upon His throne;
Hark! how the heav'nly anthem drowns
All music but its own!
Awake, my soul, and sing
Of Him who died for thee,
And hail Him as thy matchless King
Thro' all eternity.

Matthew Bridges,
"Crown Him with Many Crowns"

DECEMBER 31 | Read Revelation 20–22

20:1–15 Looking into the future, John predicts the events of the final days. Satan will be bound and sealed up in the bottomless pit for a period of one thousand years. Then he will be released to work his deception among the nations for a time. Finally, he will be defeated and cast into the lake of fire and brimstone to suffer eternally, along with the Antichrist and the beast. After this the great white throne judgment will occur. The unredeemed—those people whose names do not appear in the Book of Life—will also be cast into the lake of fire.

21:1–8 John foresees that believers will enter a final state of blessedness characterized by a new heaven and a new earth. Grief and pain will be no more. God will live among His people, and they will enjoy continuous fellowship with Him.

21:9–22:5 John's final vision is of the heavenly Jerusalem, where believers will live in the eternal state with God and His Son. No temple exists in this city, "for the Lord God Almighty and the Lamb are the temple of it" (21:22). Its gates are never shut at night as a security measure, because night and darkness do not exist. A river of pure water, representing the water of life (John 7:38), issues from God's throne. Along this river grows the tree of life. John is describing spiritual realities with physical metaphors that his readers could understand.

22:6–21 John concludes Revelation by stating that he has reported accurately the prophecies that God has revealed to him in a series of visions. He urges his readers to remain faithful to the One who is "Alpha and Omega, the beginning and the end, the first and the last" (v. 13; see Rev. 1:8). Thus, the Bible comes to a close with an affirmation of the supremacy of the Lord Jesus Christ.

....

Hell The place of eternal torment reserved for unbelievers. *Sheol,* a Hebrew word rendered as "hell" in the OT, corresponds to the Greek word *Hades,* which means "unseen underworld" or "place of the dead." In the NT both *Hades* and *Gehenna* are rendered as "hell." *Gehenna* is derived from the Valley of Hinnom, a site for pagan worship that became a dumping ground near Jerusalem where filth and dead animals were burned; hence hell's association with the final state of lost souls in a place of eternal fire (Mark 9:47–48). Hell is described as a "lake of fire" (Rev. 19:20), "everlasting destruction" (2 Thess. 1:9), and the "second death" (Rev. 20:14).

Millennium A term for the period of 1,000 years described in Rev. 20:1–8. Opinions vary on how to interpret this period. Premillennialists expect a literal reign of 1,000 years by Christ on earth after His return. Postmillennialists believe that 1,000 years of peace will precede Christ's second coming, during which time much of the world will be converted. While believing in the Lord's return, amillennialists view Christ's millennial reign in a spiritual sense.

Death The end of physical existence. Death is the price humans pay for their sin and rebellion against God, but God provides salvation and eternal life for believers through the atoning death of Jesus Christ (Rom. 6:23). "Second death" is eternal separation from God—the fate of unbelievers (Rev. 20:6).

Gog, Prince of Magog The leader of a tribal people, enemies of the Israelites, who was condemned by the prophet Ezekiel (Ezek. 38:2; 39:1). In the book of Revelation, Gog and Magog represent the forces of evil that oppose God and His people (Rev. 20:8).

Alpha and Omega The first and last letters of the Greek alphabet. Symbolic of the eternity of Christ, this title is applied to God the Father and God the Son (Rev. 1:8; 21:6). The risen Christ described Himself in this fashion, indicating He is the Creator, Redeemer, and Final Judge of all humankind (Rev. 22:13).